ENDANGERED SPLENDOR

Intramuros
Binondo
San Nicolas
Tondo

MANILA'S
ARCHITECTURAL
HERITAGE
1571–1960

Fernando N. Zialcita *and* **Erik Akpedonu**
with **Victor S. Venida**
Additional photographs by **Andrew Chester Ong**

ENDANGERED SPLENDOR

Intramuros
Binondo
San Nicolas
Tondo

1

ATENEO DE MANILA UNIVERSITY PRESS

Ateneo de Manila University Press
Bellarmine Hall, ADMU Campus
Loyola Heights, Katipunan Avenue
Quezon City, Philippines
Tel.: (632) 8426-59-84 / Fax (632) 8426-59-09
E-mail: unipress@ateneo.edu
Website: www.ateneopress.org

© 2021 by Ateneo de Manila University, Erik Akpedonu, and Fernando N. Zialcita

Victor S. Venida retains republication rights for the following essays: "General Issues: Revitalization of Historic Districts in Manila," "Economic Uses for Intramuros," "Reimagining the Former Wall Street of the Philippines," and "Economic Uses for Binondo and San Nicolas," and "Notes on Tondo"

Cover design, book design, and layout by Ali Figueroa
Artistic direction and cover photograph by Erik Akpedonu
Inside cover from Ortigas Foundation Library
Image on back cover (wood carving) donated by Justin Joseph Basco
Cover images for volumes 2 and 3 by Erik Akpedonu
Author photo of Erik Akpedonu by Noel B. San Andres
Book layout assistance by Faith Aldaba, Billie Andrada, and Paolo Tiausas

Copyright for all images and photographs remain with their respective copyright-holders, especially those under Creative Commons or belonging to the public domain. A complete list of the sources for all illustrations can be found on pp. 393–394. Specific source information is also provided in individual captions as necessary.

All rights reserved. No part of this publication may be reproduced, stored in a retrieval system, or transmitted in any form or by any means, electronic, mechanical, photocopying, recording, or otherwise, without the written permission of the Publisher.

The authors wish to acknowledge the valuable support of Narzalina Z. Lim, Regina Sy Co Seteng, and Phyllis Zaballero in funding the field research for this book, and the Institute of Philippine Culture, for partially funding the book's publication.

The National Library of the Philippines CIP Data

Recommended entry:

    Zialcita, Fernando.
        Endangered splendor : Manila's architectural heritage
    1571 - 1960 : Intramuros, Binondo, San Nicolas, Tondo /
    Fernando N. Zialcita and Erik Akpedonu with Victor S. Venida;
    additional photographs by Chester Ong. — Quezon City :
    ATENEO DE MANILA UNIVERSITY PRESS,[2020],©2020.
        xiv, 402 pages ; 25.4 cm

        ISBN 978-621-448-121-7 (HB)
        ISBN 978-971-550-952-7 (SB)
        ISBN 978-971-550-984-8 (PDF)

        1. Historical buildings — Philippines — Manila — Research.
    2. Architecture, Domestic — Philippines — Manila — History —
    Research. I.Akpedonu, Erik. II. Venida, Victor S. III. Ong,
    Chester. I. Title.

Manila has around 100,000 inhabitants. Spaniards, mestizos, native-born Filipinos, Chinese, Armenians, English, French and other nationalities, for there hardly is any type of people in the world which would not have some individual representatives in Manila.

—Joaquin Martinez de Zuñiga,
Estadísmo de las Islas Filipinas o mis viajes por este país (1803)

Contents

xi	On Names of Houses	
xii	Preface	
1	Heritage in a Varied, Changing World	F. Zialcita
29	General Issues:	
	Revitalization of Historic Districts in Manila	V. Venida
45	Endangered Splendor:	
	Manila's Disappearing Heritage	E. Akpedonu

INTRAMUROS

59	Intramuros: Mother City	F. Zialcita
141	Economic Uses for Intramuros	V. Venida
147	Whose Heritage? The Ideological Dimension of Postwar Reconstruction	E. Akpedonu

BINONDO

159	Binondo: Pivot of the Pacific	F. Zialcita
218	Reimagining our Former Wall Street	V. Venida
223	New Meets Old – Contemporary Buildings in Historical Context	E. Akpedonu

SAN NICOLAS

239	San Nicolás: Trade and Revolution	F. Zialcita
303	More Economic Uses for the Two Sister Districts	V. Venida
309	Curse or Blessing?—Moving Immovable Heritage	E. Akpedonu

TONDO

325	Tondo: Warrior Haven	F. Zialcita
375	Toward a Worker-Friendly District	V. Venida
379	Cool Design – Building for a Tropical Climate	E. Akpedonu

389	Acknowledgments
393	Illustration Sources
395	Index

On Names of Houses
NOTE FROM THE AUTHORS

A dilemma faced us while doing the fieldwork for this book. While some house owners did not want to have their names identified as the owners, others were insistent that their names be identified. Unlike in the province, in Manila, we were doing research in a highly diverse, urban society where neighbors do not necessarily know each other. We decided on a middle path.

For some houses, if the original owner was known, it was that name that we appended rather than the name of the current owner, to protect the latter's privacy. In the case of other houses, if the house was well-known in the neighborhood, the district, or even the media as the former house of so-and-so, then that was the name we used. In other cases, many house owners were adamant that we should identify their houses along with their names. Such was their love for their houses. Then there were houses about whose history, we could get no information. Hence only the street address is included. In some districts like Sta. Ana, a prior inventory of houses, along with the names of original builders, had already been taken. This facilitated our naming names.

As Filipinos become more conscious of their architectural legacy, more inventories like what we have done will become common. Indeed there are now architectural inventories being undertaken by some national and municipal bodies. This inventory is our contribution to building pride in our unique legacy as a people.

FIG. 1. Inside San Luis Complex, Intramuros

Preface

GUILLAUME MARCHAND (TRANS. FERNANDO N. ZIALCITA)

This work is neither a monograph of a city nor the portrait of a city but rather an urban novel (*roman de ville*). The authors propose a journey—truly an original idea—and invite the reader to reflect while journeying within the city.

This book is neither a critique of institutions nor a history lesson, but a simple reminder that human beings, city-dwellers and citizens ought not to reinvent history but rather to continue it. Its question centers on the blurred boundary between heritage and modernity: What is the process by which something becomes heritage? This book perfectly validates the notion of "a useable past" proposed by Lewis Mumford and borrowed from the celebrated literary critic Van Wyck Brooks.

The authors invite us to an initiation course (*parcours initiatique*) rather than to a trip on foot around the metropolis of Manila—which a tourist guidebook would offer. The authors want to initiate the reader, treat him like an explorer–traveler and entrust to him the keys for deciphering the urban zone that is Metro Manila.

The reader finds himself in the same shoes as those of the archaeologist Henri Mouhot who, in the nineteenth century, uncovered Angkor's setting which had been invaded by luxuriant *Tetrameles nudiflora* trees and whose splendid ruins had been overwhelmed by them. This image may be somewhat exaggerated. But overall, it is relevant to the metropolis' look which may have kept its architectural treasures but which is now strangled by multiplying electric lines and tangles of all sort, and by an intrusive overhead train network which keeps the visitor from deciphering this magnificent city.

Rightly, the authors remind us that the city of Manila has undergone several earthquakes. We find ourselves back in 1880 beside Alfred Marche, famed explorer and auxiliary naturalist at the Paris' Museum of Natural History, during his photo-taking reportage.

Or we can even imagine ourselves in the eighteenth century with Guillaume Le Gentil de la Galaisière, famous French astronomer who stayed for a period of time in Manila to observe the transit of Venus and who tells us of the mores and customs of this Spanish colony.

Manila is not wanting in unexpected sites. What truly called my attention was the old Bilibid Prison which one cannot appreciate other than from an elevation. Yet this well-known central prison remains a taboo place, no doubt because of suspicious activities which happen nearby. We can easily conclude that commercial activities in it were already in full swing under American rule because, right within the prison, the prisoners sold artisanal objects to tourists. However, the successive growth of informal settlements which formed following the bombing of Manila during World War II, eats away at the enclosure, and has become like a second skin of invasive vegetation. This legendary prison is therefore no longer visible from outside save from two small towers at the main entry that now act as decoration to some haphazard dwellings.

This carceral structure is located at the boundary between the nineteenth and twentieth centuries in the evolution of the city. Hence Claro Recto Avenue has itself become a symbol of the transition from Spanish city to one guided by a master plan under the Americans.

This wonderful opportunity to evoke this city draws from several historical accounts. Yet it enables the anthropologist Dr. Zialcita to challenge the novice reader–traveler to see things as they are and to get out of the hollowed yet aseptic touristic heart of Manila which extends from the Ermita mall, the business district of Makati to the airports of Pasay by inviting him to cross the Pasig River and discover the true Manila.

This city novel follows a subtle framework by basing itself on a variety of field researches and on expertise of all sorts. Seeking to educate is what inspires the authors. They urge the reader to appreciate the living environment for its true worth, they dissuade him from making quick judgments all the while persuading him that taste is not imposed but rather cultivated. This novel's guiding thread is its sensibility. It allows us to awaken our senses fallen asleep because of hyper-globalization, among others, and it allows us to take note to what extent we have forgotten the taste of things, the taste of sharing, the taste of respect . . .

What makes Manila unique is its hybrid character, from which comes its urban form. This is the product of the administrative plan of the Spanish period, of Daniel Burnham's master plan, and of the political organization it has inherited. In its political organization, a powerful local administrative system shaped by the Spanish period co-exists with a nation based administrative system inherited from the Americans. Finally it has an ancestral architecture that metamorphosed into a colonial architecture and then reconfigured into a modern one.

It has been twenty years since I set foot for the first time in Manila. What astounded me the most was the ease of orientation, thanks to this the Manileño could move about and locate himself in this metropolis. And this question of how something becomes heritage—a question that has never left me during all these two decades, has finally been answered in this book by "rousing the senses."

G. Marchand, born in 1968, works at present as an architect in charge of a project for a public agency of the French Ministry of Culture. He enrolled at the National Higher School of Architecture in Paris within a course granting a degree in architectural specialization—under the module "Metropolises of Southeast Asia, and was a prizewinner in the 2003 program "Towards cities," a program organized by the French Association of Artistic Initiatives, an agency under the French Ministry of Foreign Affairs. Thanks to this program, he lived in Manila for three months in the district of Sta. Cruz.

DE STADT MANILHA.

Heritage in a Varied, Changing World

FERNANDO N. ZIALCITA

LONG BEFORE US, OTHER PEOPLE TOO LIVED IN OUR CITIES. SOME of them opened new and important spaces that we continue to use. Like us, they were thoughtful, caring, and practical beings who had to deal with challenges posed by the natural environment and by the city itself as an environment different from a rural village. Through their creations, let us listen to their voices, for there may be lessons we can learn from them that are applicable to our own lives today.

PERSISTING CHALLENGES

There are several challenges facing us. One is constant. Some are traditional, but have become more difficult today. Others are new.

As in the past, the geology of our islands poses threats to our buildings and lives. The Philippines is along the "Ring of Fire" encircling the Pacific Ocean, where tectonic plates rub against each other, causing volcanoes to arise and erupt and generating severe earthquakes, like those that struck Manila in 1645, 1863, and 1880. The Marikina Fault, which runs from north to south on the western side of the Marikina Valley, is tensing up for a major quake, according to experts.

The challenges that persist in more intensified forms are partly environmental, partly social. We live in the tropical zone, which is inherently warm, but our planet as a whole is heating up. Air-conditioning units—traditional palliatives during the last half of the twentieth-century—consume a lot of energy. Energy generation pollutes the environment with exhaust fumes, thus compounding the problem.

Traditionally, alienation has been associated with the city, more than with the rural village. In the latter, the farmer's neighbors are often his relatives. In the former, the urbanite lives surrounded by strangers. As our cities increase in size (particularly in the Philippines with its high birth rate), alienation intensifies dramatically. Neighbors in a district, subdivision, and even in a condominium, attend to their own affairs and ignore each other. Each one lives in isolation with his family, some seeking to be con-

FIG. 2-3. View of Manila and Cavite, c. 1665 (By Johannes Vingboons licensed under Creative Commons Public Domain Dedication/cc-zero, see p. 394); Aerial view of Central Manila today, image courtesy of Paulo Alcazaren (adjacent page: top and bottom)

vivial with their neighbors, but held back by social inhibitions and the lack of shared spaces.

Symbolic constants are needed in everyone's life, no matter how we deem them less important than material gain. The rate of change has accelerated in today's world. Technologies, cityscapes, fashions, customs, and ideas change quickly within less than a generation. While this can stimulate fresh beginnings, it can also lead to a sense of insecurity as familiar, well-loved landmarks disappear, often for purely commercial reasons. Neighborhoods are unnecessarily ravaged just so a clutch of developers can make a profit.

The aesthetic, defined as a sense of order experienced in sensuous form, be this in dressing, painting, music, poetry, or buildings, continues to be important, even if developers think this is of minor importance when commissioning mass housing. For how else to explain the almost instinctive urge among many to improve the appearance of their house, once they have saved some money? Or the hanging of paintings that really have no practical purpose? Unfortunately, most of our cities seem to be getting uglier every day. Garish buildings blight the landscape like fungi; thick black tangles of wires snake above the streets; sidewalks are virtually absent, as are parks, playgrounds, trees, or any kind of greenery for that matter. The list continues indefinitely.

At the same time, new challenges are appearing. On the one hand, a homogeneous culture is spreading globally. Alternatively called "McDonaldization" or "Coca Colonization," this is wiping out the specific virtues of local cultural practices. On the other hand, in response precisely to this bland homogenization, concerned citizenry in progressive cities now realize that a strong sense of place is an important asset in the highly competitive Global Village. It attracts middle-class people, like the well-travelled and well-educated, who want to experience a place in its particularity. Here, natural location plus heritage in all its forms work together to communicate a unique experience felt nowhere else.

Ravaged during the twentieth century by battles with French soldiers and by American carpet bombing, Hanoi has today become a magnet for foreign investments and tourism, mostly for the French and Americans themselves. Why is this so? One reason would be Hanoi's visual configuration. Seated at the confluence of three rivers, Hanoi has lakes of which the most important, Hoan Kiem, opens at its heart and has mythical significance. Tradition says that the national hero Le Loi obtained his magic sword from a Golden Turtle on the eve of his war against the Ming invaders (1418–1427). After his victory, he returned the sword to the Turtle who disappeared into the depths of the lake. Around it are a temple and a theatre where Vietnamese water-puppets reenact scenes from Vietnamese culture and history, like the story of the golden turtle. Close to Hoan Kiem are pagodas and temples, built in the Vietnamese style, and graceful ochre-colored French-style theatres, administrative centers, and villas. There is also the Old Quarter, also called the "36 Streets," whose traditional houses are narrow in front but long and tubular in extension, resulting in sequences of alternating shadowy spaces and abruptly open enclosures. Hanoi offers experiences that are found nowhere else in the Global Village, and that educated tourists are willing to pay for. So, too, would foreign investors for, as they aver, reasons for investing in a foreign city are multiple and complex. At times, what entices them is a city's rich, cultural life. To be fair, however, we should note that Hanoi is not the financial and commercial capital, unlike Saigon (now known as Ho Chi Minh City). Yet the latter preserves wide, walkable tree-lined avenues at its center, French-era villas, and landmarks such as the Opera House.

RESPONSES AND POSSIBILITIES

Our vintage structures emerged as responses to various challenges. At the same time, if we study them carefully, they may offer us clues in resolving current problems.

Bending Houses. The French anthropologist Alfred Marche experienced the severe earthquake of 1880. He writes that during the quake on 20 August, he saw the wooden upper stories of two adjacent houses leaning towards each other as though about to touch. All of a sudden, the tremors ceased. The wooden walls returned to their former position.[1] Brian Villareal, a resident of Quiapo, recounted to me a similar scene during an earthquake some time in 1990. He lives in an *accesoria* (a row house) whose two rows of apartment units are separated from each other by a narrow courtyard. During the quake, the two rows bent towards each other. "Would they fall over?" he wondered. When the tremors ceased, the wooden walls stood straight once again. Though some of the nails on the walls had lifted slightly, the entire structure was intact.

Over the course of centuries, Manileños developed a house style that responded to the unstable ground. Efforts by the early Spanish settlers to build tall houses entirely of stone, as they were used to doing back in the peninsula, failed in the several earthquakes that shook the city, notably that of 1645. They discovered the native wisdom of supporting heavy wooden roofwork on wooden pillars that swayed with the heaving earth. However, stone walls were needed too to minimize the possibility of fire breaking out. The result was a fusion between two building styles—the native and the Spanish. In the so-called *arquitectura mestiza* (literally the "architecture of mixed origins") that appeared by the turn of the seventeenth century, wooden pillars (*haligi*) supported the roof.[2] Wooden walls in the upper story were only screens that carried no weight. Mere enclosures likewise were the stone or brick walls that made up the ground story.

During the severe earthquakes of 1863 and 1880 that devastated Manila, these houses of wood and stone generally held up well—certainly better than those that followed the European ideal of being all in stone. This feat was duly recognized by the Spanish authorities. Engineers, brought over from Spain to help in the reconstruction of Manila, were instructed to pay special attention to the local mixed style of construction (*arquitectura mestiza*) because this had proven more resilient during earthquakes than the all-stone European style (*a la europea*).[3] While the engineers' preferred reinforcing medium was steel, whose popularity had spread in Europe and the US, they recommended continuing the local practice of using walls of stone with wooden frameworks. Guidelines laid down by the *Junta Consultiva de Obras Públicas* (Consultative Board for Public Works), following the earthquake of 1880, stated, "The wooden frameworks, both horizontal and vertical, offer the best guarantee against the tremors' movement."[4] However, they insisted on the use of molave wood because it had shown resistance to rot and termites. If it was not available in large quantities, they recommended, "carbonizing the wood, coating it with tar or covering with lead or a molave sheet that part which is sunken."[5]

Lest we be misunderstood, we do not advocate that all new construction follow the traditional wooden frame with curtain walls. Not at all! What we say rather is that it is important to keep samples of traditional alternative technology alongside present-day practices. Older traditional examples of technology have proven their worth. Why destroy them? We should not be so arrogant as to think that our ancestors were incompetents. It may well happen that future architects and engineers who study them may be inspired to develop new construction styles that will perform better during earthquakes in ways that we cannot imagine today. But first it is important to preserve existing examples of anti-earthquake technology. There is another reason why we should not be too quick in discarding traditional forms of building technology. In one of his several trips to Vigan in the 1990s, the conservation architect David Michelmore reminded us that reinforced concrete has its own limitations. Should a hairline crack appear in the concrete skin, rain can seep in to attack the metal framework deep within. Thus, reinforced concrete, the hallmark of modernity against which previous building technologies are compared and discarded, is itself not invulnerable.

An often-ignored significant aspect of Manila today is its treasury of different anti-earthquake technologies. Most primordial, of course, is the indigenous house of wood and thatch, or of bamboo and thatch, that stands on stilts. An excellent example of this, complete with thatch roof is the Mabini Shrine, the former house of Apolinario Mabini, now located in Sampaloc. Then there is the San Agustin Church where the walls in between the side chapels are actually hidden buttresses that shore up the nave on which rests a huge stone barrel vault. Built in 1891, San Sebastian Church represents an era in the nineteenth-century when all-steel structures became fashionable. Examples are churches in earthquake-prone Costa Rica and Chile, train stations in Europe and the US, and, above all, the Eiffel Tower in France. During the 1920s, the Administration Building of the University of Santo Tomas arose as separate modules that sway independently of each other in case of earthquakes. Finally there is the house of Wood-and-Stone, whose popularity began in the late seventeenth-century and lasted to the 1940s. Structurally, this is the same as the Wood-and-Thatch house mentioned above.

The Wood-and-Stone house may well have influenced the invention of reinforced concrete by William Le Barron Jenney (1832–1907). According to his biographer Carl Condit, in the 1860s he visited Manila on his father's whaling ship.[6] Condit says that his combination of a flexible framework (steel) with a protective and dense material (concrete) may have been influenced by the native house of bamboo. I think rather that it was the combination of a wooden framework and stone in Manila houses that inspired him when building the multi-story Second Leiter Building (1891) in Chicago.

Still Cool. By now everyone has heard the bad news: Earth is getting warmer because of human intervention. We dread to think what temperatures will be like in our part of the tropics decades from now. Unfortunately, modern building practices, popular since the 1950s, exacerbate global warming while adding to our discomfort.

Traditional town and city houses of solid materials, like the Wood-and-Stone house, developed various ways of ventilating their exteriors through careful observation of the environment and skillful innovations. The most basic were roofs with a steep slope (*agua*) on either two or all four sides, coupled with high ceilings. Together they allowed the hot air within the rooms to float upwards. The roof had a wide eave (*alero*) to protect the exterior from both the slashing rain and the strong tropical sun. Vents in the eaves encouraged air to circulate in and out of the roof. Sometimes the vents would be intricately traceried so as to be both ornamental and functional. In addition to the wide eave, a canopy (*media agua*) extended over the windows, again for protection. This metal awning created another opportunity for indulging the urge to decorate. Canopy edges were traceried with various motifs. Thus, while tolerably cool, these houses satisfied the Filipino's love for ornamentation. This balance between practicality and aesthetics also characterized the *accesorias* (row apartments) built before World War II.

Today, however, most buildings that are either single houses or apartment units tend to pay little attention to passive ventilation. Often, ceilings have dropped to as low as 2.5 meters high from the floor. It is not enough that the ventanillas fell out of fashion in the 1940s; windows today are smaller and have lost those sliding panels that open the space fully to the wind. The preference today is for push-out panels. The emphasis is on reducing building costs and passing the burden of cooling the interior to the customer. Let the buyer beware! Given the low ceilings and small window openings, the logical outcome is a heavy reliance on air-conditioning units. But because of the erratic nature of power supply in the city, such dwellings become virtual saunas during a blackout. The air-conditioning unit, aside from being an expensive option, compounds the problem through the exhaust caused by the burning of scarce fossil fuels to generate more electricity. And to cap it all, there is a psychological cost to living in rooms that are narrow, with small windows and low-hanging ceilings.

Again, we are not proposing that the traditional way of cooling interiors is the only option, particularly for commercial, office, and institutional establishments. What we are saying, rather, is that since such a way continues to be relevant for residential units and probably will be much more relevant in the near future again, it does not make sense to destroy remaining examples, replace them with building styles that pollute the environment, add to the expenses of the occupants, and make the occupants feel psychologically confined. Traditional buildings that are environmentally relevant should be maintained and reused.

Convivial Cities. The traditional Latin city emphasizes the courtyard, the street, and the plaza as open spaces that encourage urban residents to mix with each other, to develop new friendships, and to feel a sense of belonging to the city. Open spaces that are either semipublic or public play an important role in the Latin vision of the city as a locale where the individual learns to live with people who are not one's kin.

Prior to the twentieth century, houses in major Filipino towns and cities often had no gardens. Instead they stood cheek to jowl with other houses along a street.

The upper story projected about a meter beyond the ground story over the sidewalk. The large windows opened directly onto the street. The small windows below, the ventanillas, also opened onto the street, though with a difference—they were protected with either grills or balusters. From both types of windows, adults and children alike watched the street's various events take place. Like townhouses in Mediterranean Europe and Manhattan tenements, the traditional Filipino house was a theatre balcony with a front-row view of events in the street spectacle. From this permanent seat, residents could chat with neighbors in the next house on the row, or wave to those across. The climax of street-watching took place during the fiestas when the district, town, or city turned out en masse to join the procession of holy images. Residents in Quiapo and Tondo told me how they feel honored that the annual procession passes right in front of their windows. For during the sacred evening, the holy image of Christ, the Mother, or the saints, travels on a dark sea of candles followed by a cloud of incense, to the beat of drums and horns. Often the image is unconsciously seen as a symbol not only of the divine but also of the local community. For a few uncanny minutes, as the residents pause to join the multitude passing by in prayer, the open *sala* reveals another world.

Traditional *accesorias* share these magical moments that awaken solidarity and more. An inner courtyard may traverse the accesoria, dividing it in half while paradoxically uniting it. This open space becomes a communal space where residents exchange pleasantries in the morning while taking coffee or cooling off in the evening, after coming from school or work. As Brian Villareal says, "This patio is like an extension of our sala." But it is an extension not fenced off but shared with others. At certain times of the year, this inner space becomes a venue where the residents enjoy parties together.

Blocks in the districts of Sta. Cruz and Sampaloc are like accesorias, though built larger. They are entirely surrounded by main streets running at right angles to each other. However, there is a secondary street that divides the block neatly in half, like the two sides of a leaf. In Sta. Cruz, there are even smaller streets that traverse the block, this time running at right angles to the secondary street thus connecting this in another manner to the main streets. Within the secondary street, we see children flocking to an itinerant ice cream vendor, or residents sunning themselves out on lounging chairs, or significantly an occasional party. The secondary street (*kalye* in Sta. Cruz, *eskinita* in Sampaloc) has become a patio where the neighborhood naturally congregates.

Logically the urban milieu inspires the individual to reach out to a community broader than his kin. But the format of his neighborhood may hinder this. An example would be the walls surrounding the gardens and villas of the middle-to-upper-income households. Arch. Ramon Zaragoza recalls that as an adolescent he disliked moving from Quiapo to Quezon City. While their ancestral house in Quiapo formed part of a row of houses along Hidalgo Street, their villa in Quezon City had a large garden surrounded by protective high walls. Come fiesta time, however, in their part of Quezon City, there was no Open House. Neighbors celebrated only with their families. There was little incentive to open their tables to the rest of the neighbors. There is another disadvantage to living in subdivisions in the suburbs, according to various Manila residents who have tried doing so. Peace and quiet do reign but the streets have no life. This may be because subdivisions are strictly residential. There is no mixing of commercial and residential uses. Thus, during the daytime, when most are at work, the streets become desolate. No pedestrians scurrying about, pausing from time to time to peer into a shop. No street vendors advertising their wares. "How boring it is to live in the subdivision," say these various Manila residents. "You count the minutes." In addition, these gated subdivisions shield their residents from the "real world," a world where rich and poor, progressive and conservative, young and old mix and interact, and thus learn to tolerate and live with each other as citizens in a confined space. Essentially, the gated subdivision is deeply un-democratic.

Alienation intensifies in high-rise housing units. This, of course, is not a necessary consequence. Such units need not be alienating if designed sensitively, as in the case of the Syquia Apartments in Malate where each unit has high ceilings and large windows protected by permanent canopies. But the complaint is that the prevailing format of current high-rises consists of apartment units that open out into small corridors. The apartment units are like hotel rooms, each tightly locked against each other. There are no spaces that invite neighbors to acquaint themselves with each other. "How dreary it is to live in such high rises," exclaims Josette, a resident of Sta. Cruz and a psychologist trained at a famous university. "I don't want to live in a box."

Signposts. The sociologist Anthony Giddens has rightly pointed out that we should not have to choose between Marx and Heidegger, between acknowledging the subtle impact of material needs upon our choices and highlighting the perennial quest for meaning. While all human beings must satisfy their material needs in order to continue existing, they also need to make sense of their lives.

The quest for meaning is more alive than ever today. Change has accelerated. Ideas and products that have been barely launched and appreciated are quickly discarded to be replaced with new ones that can sell even better. While fashions in dress changed gradually every year during much of the twentieth century, fashions now change twice or thrice within a year. Such is the case with other products today. Buildings are raised with much fanfare, only to be razed within a few decades. Globalized capitalism must continually destroy in order to sell.

No doubt constant change can spur creativity. But it can also induce exhaustion, anxiety, and disorientation.[7] We humans are the one species that can think back to the past while moving to the future. We look for signposts that connect the different phases of our lives. The loss of an ancestral house can be traumatic, for suddenly, a signpost in one's life vanishes, making it harder to retrieve memorable events. This is not to say that ancestral houses should never be sold or dismantled. Circumstances do appear that make it necessary to dispose of one or the other. The point rather is that we should be cautious in treating such houses as mere commodities and in dismissing people's attachment to their parental property or the neighborhood they grew up in as mere sentimentalism.

What transpires on the individual level is replicated on the social level. Here, too, there is need for landmarks that span generations, even centuries if need be. To elicit the loyalty of its citizens, a town or city should make them aware of its existence as a corporate unity. A public school, a town hall, a light house, or a parish church from centuries past helps make the citizenry realize that their town or city has an existence that transcends their present lives, for it goes back centuries in time and will most likely persist into the future. Moreover, that the town or city exists right now as an institution that demands respect, for it manages an infrastructure (whether material, social, economic, or political) that enables each individual to pursue particular goals. The result should be awe, and possibly pride, in being a citizen of such a place. Landmarks also make citizens realize that their lives, and the lives of their own ancestors, are intertwined with the life of the town or the city. Hence, the need to help it in any way they can.

Some of our city councillors downplay the importance of history and heritage as sentimentalism that will not bring in money. If they had their way they would raze everything old, no matter how beautiful or memory-laden. And yet they expect the citizenry to love their city, and to pay their increasing taxes. But love for a city has many sources. For one, the realization that particular landmarks connect family memories together is one example, as when Ambassador Virgilio Reyes visits Malate Church; he remembers four generations of women in his family who were married at its altar. For this reason, after several transfers, he decided to transfer from Quezon City to Malate. Sometimes the connection with family memory is even physical. The Aranetas no longer live on Calle Hidalgo in Quiapo, but they still visit San Sebastian Church, for some of their ancestors are buried behind the church. Another is the feeling that the community of residence is like a Mother, an *Inang Lungsod* born centuries ago yet still alive, a Mother with thousands of offsprings who are somehow related to each other because of residence. Thus, when I meet someone who tells me that she or he grew up in Quiapo, where I also grew up, I feel an instant connection. But what is it that facilitates this connection? One is the unconscious realization that he, she, and I must have visited similar landmarks like Quiapo Church or San Sebastian, and therefore shared a common physical space. Finally, there is a sense of place generated by a landmark. For Ray Pastrana, a former barangay councillor, the mansions along Hidalgo with their sidewalk arcades mattered to him because it reminded him that he was back in *his* neighborhood. He was home. He regrets their decline because "I want to show to my children that I did not grow up in just any neighborhood."

A Vanishing Sense of Proportion. In a lecture in Madrid that I attended, the Spanish architectural historian Santiago Porras once did a mathematical analysis of the façades of selected Filipino churches from the Spanish era.[8] He wanted to find out if the Golden Mean was present. It was indeed present; the builders were aware of it and used it. But there were then no schools giving formal training in architecture and aesthetics. How could the average artisan have learned to calculate proportions? Jorge Loyzaga, a Mexican architect who visits the Philippines regularly and who is an expert in conservation, says that we should not discount the excellence of training in the guilds. Prior to the triumph of capitalism in the nineteenth century, guilds controlled the transmission of skills and attitudes in the different crafts. The apprentice worked closely with the master artisan for many years; in turn the latter gradually transmitted all that he knew. The apprentice graduated to being a novice, until finally he became a master in his own right. In the process he learned very practical skills, for art, as the philosopher Jacques Maritain reminds us, is practical knowledge. Classroom learning is of no use to the artist if his intelligence and his body do not cooperate to produce a pleasing product. Maritain credits the high standards of European architecture prior to Industrialism to the practical training in the guilds, a training that nonetheless had a solid mathematical grounding.[9]

But were there guilds in the Philippines? This has yet to be studied. What is certain is that there were maestros who were master artisans; they had assistants in their projects. Most likely their assistants learned from their masters by observing and doing.

Many buildings in the Philippines from the seventeenth to the early twentieth centuries manifest a mastery of proportion that seems to be absent in those built within the past three decades. This is ironic given the many architectural schools in the country today, in contrast to their paucity and newness a century ago and earlier. The lack of scale is seen in an important building like the Centennial Hall of Justice, which was named after the Centennial of the Declaration of Philippine Independence. Using the visitor's own body as reference, the Neoclassical columns seem too large and too tall. In contrast, the Neoclassical columns of the older surrounding buildings—the Old Supreme Court, the New Supreme Court, the University of the Philippines in Manila—have just the right height and width vis-à-vis the body of the average visitor. While these older colonnades invite the visitor to come in, the colonnade of the Centennial Hall intimidates. A similar problem is evident in the mural paintings in Binondo Church. Some time in the recent decades, an artist was asked to paint religious scenes on the ceiling. The aim was to have another San Agustin with trompe l'oeil paintings, or even another San Beda Chapel with painted ceilings. But the figures in the Binondo paintings are too large for a ceiling that is relatively low. The decorated ceiling seems ready to fall on the churchgoer because it looks heavy. In contrast, human figures in the San Beda ceiling murals are smaller. Moreover, because twilight skies frame these figures, the murals seem to expand and to open up the ceiling to the world beyond. A disregard for proportion haunts contemporary designs. Sometimes the lobby of an office building has too high an entrance, and thus makes the visitor feel overpowered. At other times, the entrance lobby, as at the new Rizal Library of the Ateneo de Manila University in Quezon City, is too low with doors so narrow that the visitor feels unwelcome. In fact, it feels like a servant's entry! Could it be that the sense of proportion is vanishing because it is not taken seriously in some architectural schools—or in any school for that matter?

And yet it is from correct proportions that Beauty emerges. We regard a man or a woman as attractive because of the seemingly harmonious relationship of the various parts of the body to each other and to the whole. Too large a head or too prominent a nose is viewed as disfiguring and cannot be concealed by wearing expensive clothes and jewels. Similarly in a building, expensive materials and lavish ornamentation cannot make up for poor visual relationships.

Another attractive feature of earlier Filipino architecture is the quality of the details and the workmanship. When decoration is used, as in corbels, friezes, and grills, the forms come out zestful and full-bodied. In contrast to postwar architectural décor, the traditional carved curves are not stiff, awkward, and timid. On the contrary, they were exuberant. The late Irma Estrella, a Quiapo resident, shared this observation with me about carpenters today:

> The carpenters before the War (1941-1945) took their calling seriously. An example was my grandfather, a Master Carpenter. Upset that his instructions to use dowels, rather than nails, were not followed by the carpenters who were hired, he wanted the floor redone. But my mother protested about it being too late to make changes. Carpenters then were proud of their calling, which is not true of carpenters today who see it merely as a job.

To what can we attribute this lack of pride? Is it because living standards have declined? Or because expectations by customers have lowered?

Antonio Bonet Correa is an internationally recognized expert on the baroque, particularly as expressed in Spanish-influenced countries. Since 2008, he has been the Director of the prestigious Real Academia de Bellas Artes de San Fernando of Madrid where several of our best painters studied.[10] He came to Manila as the keynote speaker at a conference organized by Arch. Javier Galván Guijo on Filipino-Hispanic architecture. Together with friends, I had the opportunity to bring him on a tour of churches along Laguna de Bay. He remarked on how original our interpretation of the Baroque was. Admiring the bas-relief of urns and flowers on the façade of Paete church, he said that "*Vuestro barroco es carnoso*" (Your Baroque is fleshy). This sensuous quality is alive in the carved corbels and capitals, in the cut-out roof eaves and canopies that give houses from the 1900s to the 1920s in Manila and the suburbs a festive air. The artist's joy expresses itself in the energy of his works.

A Sense of Place. In this age of globalization, a new challenge confronts us. Our major cities have to compete in the international market for trade and investments. As pointed out above, some of our neighbors do well in projecting the uniqueness of their sense of place. We have yet to capitalize on the unique history and location of our cities. Somehow planning efforts often seem disembodied from geography.

After the US seized control of the Philippines, they sent the well-known urban planner and architect Daniel Burnham to make Manila a worthy capital of their new colony. Burnham had a grand vision of what Manila could be. He recommended saving the Walled City and building a new city instead outside the walls. He was clearly influenced by European models where the historic core is preserved while new urban developments take place outside. Outside the Walls of Intramuros, Manila would, like Washington D.C. and Paris, enjoy broad tree-lined promenades radiating from large plazas. At the same time Manila would maximize its three blessings, "the bay of Naples, the winding river of Paris and the canals of Venice."[11] He wanted a boulevard built along the bay as in Naples, quays along the river as in Paris and streets along the canals as in Venice. Should Manila take full advantage of its location, it would become "equal to the greatest [cities] of the Western world, with [the] unparalleled priceless addition of a tropical setting."[12] Taft Avenue was opened as an artery linking the Pasig River to the southern districts and the towns beyond. Dewey (renamed Roxas) Boulevard was built along the bay and was another artery that connected Manila to Pasay and beyond.

Unfortunately, many Filipino leaders have not shared this admiration for Manila's location. No promenade was built along the Pasig. While the seaside boulevard was built and extended southward, commercial interests are now moving to have the bay reclaimed. Many esteros either disappeared or became dumpsites. The aim is to continue the rehabilitation of the Pasig River, an initiative started under the administration of President Fidel Ramos (1992–1998). Recently, under the leadership of Gina Lopez of the Pasig River Rehabilitation Commission, an attached agency of the Department of Environment and Natural Resources (DENR), pleasant promenades lined with mini-gardens have been opened along cleaned-up esteros, starting with those in Paco.

The terrain outside Manila varies widely and could be an asset too. Malabon stretches along a long enclosed bay; Quezon City is on a flat tableland that spreads east until it ends abruptly as a long cliff over Marikina Valley; San Juan is located on a series of rolling hills; Makati is on another tableland, but this time overlooking the Pasig River.

Over the course of centuries, a unique architectural tradition sprang up in the metropolitan region that, as mentioned above, Spanish engineers brought over by the Crown respected for its resilience and that world traveller Daniel Burnham recognized as both beautiful and practical. Burnham recommended to his disciple William Parsons and other American architects that they examine houses built in the islands during the Spanish period and incorporate some of their features in the new buildings to be constructed. Thus, in Ermita, we have the Manila Hotel, the Museo Pambata (formerly the Elks Club), the Philippine General Hospital, and the Philippine Normal University, that articulate their slanting roofs, display protective roof eaves and canopies over windows, and offer arched galleries that make the visitor feel at home. Despite this concession to local architectural tradition, Thomas Hines says that Parsons "produced buildings of an architectural quality that rivaled the best modern work in Europe and the United States."[13] Our architects today should remember that respect for heritage and innovativeness do not contradict each other. Some are so enthused with California and New York models that they remove those protective sunbreakers and canopies over windows to make their buildings "slick and up-to-date in order to reflect the American look." But we are not, of course, in the US!

Our churches too developed an interesting silhouette, unique in the whole world. Beginning in the eighteenth century, the towers became eight-sided rather than four-sided. Was this the influence of Chinese mestizo artisans who were familiar with the *ba gua*? Taoist cosmology uses eight diagrams enclosed in an octagon to represent the basic constituents of reality. The visual consequence in Manila's Sta. Ana and Binondo (churches) or in the suburban churches of Polo (now Valenzuela), Taguig, and Parañaque are towers that look almost rounded, rather than angular.

Finally, a factor that gives Manila a strong sense of place is the diversity among its districts. Though devastated by the Battle of 1945, Intramuros preserves its seventeenth to eighteenth century fortifications that today are said to be the most extensive of any Hispanic city outside Spain. Intramuros' ambience contrasts vividly with the monumental scale in which American-period Ermita was conceived: a National Civic Center with a solemn procession of public buildings marching from the river to the bay. North of the Pasig, San Nicolas tries to preserve its trove of houses from the 1850s to 1900s arranged on a grid. In contrast, Sta. Cruz north of Recto has houses from the later 1900s to the 1940s, but also arranged on a grid. But here the elongated grid is different. Secondary and tertiary streets subdivide each large block to produce within it convivial spaces for the neighbors.

Adaptation to environmental challenges, conviviality, a sense of proportion, and meaningful signposts all contribute to a sense of place. These constitute various reasons why many countries today, including our Asian neighbors, preserve their architectural heritage. But a question continues to haunt us: How can preserving structures that date from the colonial past foster nationalism or even just patriotism? Should we not obliterate them?

OUR SOURCES OF PRIDE

Paradoxically the need to preserve and promote "heritage" is a concept that gained ground with the invention of the concept of "modernity" itself in the West. Even as societies looked forward to a better future via technological and social innovations, they also looked back to their past to retain what was of value. Outstanding creations by past generations began to be seen as potential sources of communal pride.

Creative Nationalism. Thus "nationalism," itself invented at the same period as modernity, transformed royal palaces with their splendid collections of art into symbols of the creativity of the thousands of anonymous artisans who labored on them often at great cost to their own wellbeing. The Russian Communists launched their Revolution precisely against the oppressiveness of the Empire. However, upon assuming power in 1917 in impoverished Russia, they allocated precious resources to conserving palaces such as Tsarskoye Selo (literally, "Village of the Czars") or pastimes such as the renowned Kirov Ballet. During the Nazi siege of Leningrad (originally St. Petersburg) in 1941–1944, Czarkoeselo was devastated. As in the case of Intramuros' churches and houses, only the shell remained. The victorious Soviets eventually restored the palace to its gilded glory, even though post-1945 Russia was poor and in ruins.

Nearer home, the Chinese Communist Party is zealously pursuing the restoration and adaptive reuse of 1900s to 1930s Beaux Arts and Art Deco office buildings along the Bund in Shanghai. There could be no greater irony. True, these buildings reflect the period when Shanghai was East Asia's financial center. During that same time, however, the Western imperialist powers had managed to carve up China and Shanghai in particular, into virtual colonies called "concessions" where they could avail of cheap Chinese labor. One privileged enclave had an infamous sign, "Dogs and Chinese not allowed." Hence, the Communist Revolution against imperialism, capitalism, and feudalism. So why are the Communists bent on restoring the Bund? Because this is a visible reminder that Shanghai was once a major international financial center. And it can be such again.

Why preserve Intramuros, churches, and houses from the seventeenth to the nineteenth centuries? As indicated earlier in this essay, they can contribute to the development of a strong pride of place. There are dimensions to these structures and to our various districts that, when articulated, enable a people to be proud of city and nation.

Assets in a Global Industry. Will tourism be the biggest industry of the twenty-first century? Our present century opened with such a prediction. With the escalating cost of fossil fuels and their non-renewable nature, we are no longer so sure. Still tourism is indeed a major global industry today and the preservation of heritage is a basic asset. Countries that constitute the top tourist destinations—France, Spain, China—offer a variety of attractions. One of these is definitely cultural heritage. To state the obvious, tourists visit Beijing, Madrid, and Paris in droves not because of the natural scenery or their malls, but because of the artistic wonders.

In the early 1970s, I worked as a guide for almost two years with a tour operator. At that time, the architectural heritage of San Miguel, Quiapo, Escolta, Sta. Cruz, and San Nicolas was still relatively intact. This could have been preserved and highlighted as an important draw. Unfortunately, although we did offer tours of Manila and its environs, my company and the companies I knew thought that sex tourism was really what would attract foreigners, especially the Japanese. Typically our packages emphasized organized visits to brothels. For its part, the City of Manila then as now had no program to preserve its varied heritage and to use this to induce tourists to stay longer than a sex-filled day. Because the City has been slow in understanding that cultural assets can be economic assets as well, Manila has lost many outstanding buildings. It will continue to do so.

There are many reasons why the tourism industry in the Philippines, after growing to around two million visitors under President Marcos, has yet to reach the respectable benchmark of at least five million. One of them is surely the failure of our officials to use the history-and-arts card.

Threats. Manila and its suburbs are now at a crossroads. There are grave threats to their architectural heritage. These are a) fires and demolitions, b) misunderstandings about modernity, c) no comprehensive roadmap either for the city or for a district, and d) good intentions but insensitivity to previous technology.

Since this inventory began in 2008, many beautiful structures we listed in San Nicolas and Quiapo have gone up in flames. Others were simply demolished. One reason is that many of these structures became slum colonies where no one seemed to assume responsibility for checking the electricals. Moreover, property owners are primarily concerned with the value of their lot in the market, not with the potential value of their antique structure. In Manila, antique buildings are not yet regarded by the market as possessing value. This is in contrast to what is happening in particular cities abroad or even in some cities in our country. When in 1991, friends and I in two non-governmental organizations (Save Vigan Ancestral Houses Association Inc. and KaiVigan) launched a campaign to save Vigan's houses, an all-brick nineteenth century house could be had for PHP 200,000. Today because of the efforts of these two NGOs, the enthusiasm of the local government, and a thriving tourism industry, such a house would cost twenty million pesos.[14]

Although there is more respect now for past architecture than in the 1970s, many laymen and even some architects still pooh-pooh achievements of the past and instead value only that which is current and new. In connection with this, some city officials openly say that they want Manila "to look like New York"—with its towers of forty stories or more. They long to be "modern." But international cities more modern than ours, like Shanghai or precisely New York, do leave space for their past achievements. The City of New York protects Greenwich Village, a neighborhood of low-rise buildings centering around a green square, despite the astronomical cost of land in Manhattan. For Greenwich Village (like San Nicolas) has superb stone structures from the nineteenth-century and has been (like Ermita and Malate) the home of great authors, painters, thinkers, and celebrities. Moreover, if Manila wants to be like New York, it should first pay attention to basics, particularly on the street level: sanitation, sewerage, potable water, affordable electricity, broadband connection, a genuine public transport system (rather than a tangle of warring jeepneys and buses), and plenty of green open spaces that the public can enjoy. Otherwise, tower residents quickly realize they are still in the Third World.

A problem facing our cities is that key officials do not seem to have a strategy that will arrest the deterioration of neighborhoods and even districts, induce the middle- and upper income classes to stay instead of migrate to the suburbs, attract quality jobs, develop a unified citywide public transportation, or make housing more affordable for the poor majority. Even if such comprehensive plans have been drawn up by the planning office, they are not discussed in public using current media, nor do they seem to be implemented. In comparison, some of our neighbours, notably Singapore, are systematic about how to address these problems. Indeed, they do planning *per street*, taking into account some of its unique features. Several years ago, I saw such a detailed plan for neighborhoods in a Pakistani city.

Finally, technical knowledge and respect for rigorously gathered data are insufficient.[15] More are interested now in preserving vintage structures. Unfortunately, misconceptions abound as to how antique buildings should be cared for and should look. A widespread error is that "they should look old," meaning dark and unpainted. Or that "they should look textured," thus the stripping off of the protective lime coating. Adobe or volcanic tuff is not as tough as it looks. It is porous; moreover, exposed to the air, it slowly turns to powder. Beginning in the 1970s, churches in Manila and eventually all over the country began to shed off the protective lime covering "to reveal the texture." But the stones in churches in Metro Manila now look sick and are flaking off. The alternative, that of coating them with cement, is just as bad according to the Mexican conservation architect Jorge Loyzaga who visits the Philippines regularly. Cement is a very dense material that seals in the volcanic tuff and keeps it from breathing. Trapped between two layers of cement, the adobe slowly decomposes. It is better to apply a lime coat to the adobe and the brick to protect the stones from weathering while allowing them to breathe. Recently, Christian Alcuaz, a specialist in the conservation of materials, told me that sections of church walls combining adobe and cement now have a hollow sound. How will such walls fare during a major earthquake? Our neighbors in Southeast Asia carefully follow traditional artisanal procedures, for instance, in protecting stone with lime. We too should do so.

Will the public, including developers and government officials, finally wake up and discover the unique assets within the metropolitan region that are not found in neighboring countries? This inventory of Manila's architectural heritage, followed by one on Metro Manila's architectural heritage, was written in hope.

AN INSTRUMENT: THE CULTURAL INVENTORY

A vital instrument for preserving memory is the Cultural Inventory. Although doing a Cultural Inventory has been a standard practice in many countries for generations, it seems to be relatively new in our islands. However, it has become increasingly popular over the past fifteen years. For instance, recently the Provincial Committee on Heritage Sites, Relics and Structures of Cebu's Provincial Government commissioned a Cebu Provincial Heritage Project to train local government units in participatory cultural mapping, conservation management planning, and museum development.[16] The project has documented the entire province's varied patrimony and has published the findings in a book of several volumes. The project is a joint venture between the provincial government and Ramon Aboitiz Foundation. In the team are reputable scholars such as Drs. Resil Mojares, Erlinda Alburo, and Jobers Bersales. In Luzon, the Asian Institute of Tourism has done an inventory of the multi-faceted heritage of Sariaya, Quezon together with various departments of the University of the Philippines. The aim is to develop a more solid base for tourism. I had the pleasure of attending a whole-day reportage by the team to the townspeople on Palm Sunday 2008 and was impressed by its scope and quality. From 2006 to 2007 Dr. Czarina Saloma and Erik Akpedonu scanned the entire province of Bohol for vintage houses, and found more than five hundred, which were inventoried and documented in their book *Casa Boholana*: *Vintage Houses of Bohol* (2011). In April to May 2009, Ateneo de Manila's Cultural Laboratory mapped the heritage of nearby Tayabas (springs, rice terraces, churches, houses, rituals, food, music). This was funded by Fundación Santiago which sees the positive contribution of heritage tourism to job creation at the grassroots level. Though we submitted the documentation in a massive book to the Mayor's Office in December 2009, the latter has yet to release it to the general public. Other Cultural Laboratories by the Ateneo were conducted in 2010 in Intramuros, and 2011 in San Juan, Metro Manila.

Turning to Manila: in 1996, Arch. Maria Theresa Quimpo and I took part in a consulting team, Sarmiento and Associates, hired by the Department of Tourism to develop a Master Plan that, if implemented, would hopefully generate more and better-quality tourism in Manila. For this I did a list of structures for each of the nine "Special Design Areas" that we chose as nuclei. Since the list was short, I suggested to Arch. Quimpo that after the plan was done, together with her team, she should do an Inventory of Manila's Heritage Structures. To be exact, I suggested a survey for speed: photos and addresses only but no description of significance. This she did street by street, district by district, with Ms. Virginia Salomon and hired researchers. The photographer was Sergio Dewey. The survey was funded by the National Commission for Culture and the Arts and was submitted in 2005.

Our Inventory. What we have done in this present project is to take the 2000–2001 survey several steps further:

1. Expand on the initial list of Arch. Mia Quimpo in Manila.

2. Scan all constituent cities and municipalities of the National Capital Region for significant vintage structures.

3. Interview and photo-document each structure on the expanded and new lists, and highlight its architectural, historical, and social significance.

4. State the characteristics of each district and at times the street. The total number of entries to our inventory is around 3,400.

This book is the product of a research project by the Ateneo de Manila University's Institute of Philippine Culture. Funding and support were given by the Society for the Preservation of Philippine Culture under the presidency of Ms Narzalina Lim who was actively supported by Ms Regina Co Seteng and Ms Phyllis Zaballero. The research project began in June 2008 with Dr. Czarina Saloma, a sociologist, and myself as the Project Directors. The Project Manager was research associate Mr. Erik Akpedonu, a German-Ghanian who studied architecture in Germany and has developed a deep love for Philippine heritage architecture. Earlier, in fact, he and his wife, Dr. Saloma, did the island-wide inventory of Bohol's vintage houses, mentioned above. Erik managed the day-to-day operations of the project, researched, processed, and compiled the data. He also trained the young researchers and controlled the quality of the output. Finally, he meticulously reviewed, corrected, and added to the manuscript illustrations and images, and contributed chapters to this book.

The research team represented a wide variety of skills and backgrounds. Many came from fields other than architecture: political science, sociology, anthropology, law, chemistry, art history. Many were graduates of some of the top universities in Manila such as University of Sto. Tomás, University of the Philippines-Diliman, Ateneo de Manila, De La Salle, and San Beda. A common thread was a sincere interest in Philippine heritage architecture. They are: Stephen Pamorada, James Kagahastian, John Arcilla, Cecile Atienza-Sunico, Conrado Bugayong, Diana Moraleda, James Alcantara, Bernardo Arellano, Amaris Cabason, Paolo Camacho, Jan Cayme, Maya Manocsoc, Teresa Marfil, Romeo Galang Jr., Michael Pante, Vanessa Sorongon, Jeffrey Yap, Joven Ramirez, Jose Guerrero, Maria Barriga, Adrian Tumang, Jeffrey Flores, Carlo Montano, Katrina Kwan; and the students of the San Juan Cultural Laboratory 2011: Francis Panuncialman, Ana Tamula, Jan Ong, Mona Yap, Dana Davide, and Harold See. James Kagahastian and Reamur David were our IT-specialists, the former also doing graphic photo editing, as did Erik Akpedonu and Aesha Cruz.

Architects also joined us. Some had just finished their studies, others were experienced practitioners. They were: Richard Tuason Bautista, Justin Basco, Michelle Ting, Ramil Tibayan, Mar Ticao, Michael Bulosan, Janeil Arlegui, Peter Bontuyan, Adrian Tumang, Melinda Laudico, and Charles and Aileen Tobias.

In addition, there were a number of short-term team members who also contributed to the research and documentation effort such as Ivan Man Dy, or who toured us around, like Jose Panlilio. It should be noted that the actual number of researchers at any one given period was much fewer than this complete list. Field researchers worked with us when their own schedule permitted or in between other commitments. The members of the field team thus changed over time.

Archival research was needed to disclose the significance of particular sites and structures. This was done by Ms. Kara Garilao, who holds a Master's in History, for some of Binondo's 1900s to 1940s office structures. Later on we were joined by the late Mr. Pio Andrade Jr. Though his training is in chemistry, he developed a passion for Philippine history. The scientist in him decried the inaccuracies that abound in some of our books; at the same time he knows quite well which crucial books in the Filipiniana Section and the American Historical Collection of the Ateneo de Manila Rizal Library we might need. He played a key role in reviewing some of the earlier statements made in this book. Finally, extensive archival research was done by Erik Akpedonu in archives and libraries in the Philippines and abroad to find and select historic images for this book.

A commonly missing component in heritage inventories is the economic dimension: What economic activities can be initiated in a locality that will generate more quality jobs while at the same time protect heritage? Dr. Victor Venida, an economist with a profound interest in cultural issues, highlighted both actual and potential economic activities that are relevant for each district. These are meant as discussion points for effective long-term urban management. The experience of the major urban centers was that heritage was more successfully preserved when in the context of an urban plan. And effective urban plans from the level of the metropolitan region to the street require regular and constant dialogue among the constituents.

The inventory that we did was very extensive and took a while to fill in. Aside from researching its history, if available, and describing in detail the structure and its various significances, it assessed the current condition of the building, its changes, and future plans for it, among others. For this book, I have focused largely on highlighting the artistic and, when available, historic significance of particular structures.

What were our criteria for choosing particular structures? Significance is multi-layered. For example, a structure like the Main Building of the University of Sto. Tomás is obviously important because of: 1) its artistic design, 2) its history as the seat of the oldest university in the country, 3) its technology as a consciously-designed earthquake-proof building, and 4) its contribution to Philippine society via its thousands of outstanding graduates. It was relatively easy to unearth multi-layered significances for institutional buildings, but not for private houses. Understandably, many house residents either hesitated to state or did not know who the original owners were or when the structures were built. Our criteria for many of the houses were thus a mix of various and varying considerations: historical significance and/or connection to a prominent historic personality, presumed age (the older the better), location (the closer to the core area, the more inclusive), and aesthetic. It was either that the house as a whole had an attractive design and proportion, or it had details that were unique and intricate, or it complemented the streetscape of which it was a part or formed an ensemble with similar vintage structures. Rarity was another criterion. Thus, nineteenth-century houses were all included.

The period covered was 1571–1961. Why the cut-off at 1961? For one, it is easier to judge the significance of a structure that is several decades removed than that of a still-new structure. Another is that there was a respectable standard of excellence that pre-1960s buildings manifested, ordinary though they were, which seemed increasingly scarce in ordinary post-1960s buildings. Garishness, awkward proportions, and lack of functionality have become common since. Finally, by the new definition of heritage structures in the National Cultural Heritage Act of 2009 (RA 10066), any building older than fifty years is *potentially* a heritage structure, unless declared otherwise.

In articulating the aesthetic dimension of each building, I drew on my own background as a student who studied painting in the 1950s under masters such as Mr. Diosdado Lorenzo, my readings in the 1960s on the history of architecture in the library of my uncle-in-law and godfather Arch. Carlos Santos-Viola, my long sessions as a student volunteer in the Ateneo Art Gallery, after it opened in 1960, under the curatorship of Emmanuel Torres and under the special watch of its principal donor, the painter and critic Fernando Zobel de Ayala, and my explorations with friends of the then-still-intact architectural treasures of San Nicolas and Quiapo in the 1960s and 1970s. I also consulted with particular members of the team who had done their own studies on traditional architecture in particular localities: Erik Akpedonu, Romeo Galang Jr., and Arch. Richard Tuason Bautista. These consultations were always fruitful as this book will show. However, I went beyond the purely aesthetic.

For instance, I drew on my interest in social history and on cultural identity to point out the significance of structures and sites for the Philippines, and even for the rest of the world. Being an anthropologist, *culture*—in its broad sense as a system of interpretations of the world, values, customs, and practices—is of paramount interest to me. I realize, however, that cultures differ not only across space, but also across time, even in a single society like the Philippines. We live in a market-oriented society where democratic values are esteemed and where the binding vision of the entire state is supposed to be the *nation* rather than loyalty to a ruler. But our current institutions and values would have seemed strange abstractions to many of the educated in Europe and in non-colonized Siam, China, and Japan back in the 1840s. Indeed, all throughout the nineteenth century, revolutions were fought in Western Europe to establish such institutions and values. Obvious as this difference might be, it seems to be ignored by a number of authors in our country who judge the Spanish period only in terms of values and institutions that we take for granted today. This is like condemning the pre-1840s world for not having the intelligence to make airplanes and computers. Because of these blinders, many are not able to appreciate the significance of the architectural creations of that period.

Three Influential Transitions. The mid-nineteenth century was a period of transition not only for the Philippines but also for the world as a whole. Three transitions took place, whose consequences are still with us:

1. *The transition to a capitalist economy.* While the use of money was already important centuries before, from the 1850s onward it began to rule almost all spheres of

everyday conduct. Barter and the payment of debts and taxes to the state either in kind (eggs, meat, etc.) or in labor services (several weeks of unpaid labor on public roads and buildings) became irrelevant. Instead, all such transactions were to be paid in money, which now became more available as the merchant class marginalized the clergy and the nobility and made business enterprises the prime movers of the state. Henceforth, bank buildings, railroad stations, factories became as important as palaces and churches.

2. *The transition to liberal democracy.* Simple societies, such as hunters-and-gatherers and swidden cultivators elicited the participation of all the male heads in decision-making. It was easy to do so given the smallness of the community and the dominance of kin ties. It was otherwise in state societies where decisions about state affairs were reserved only for the monarch. Even in the Greek city-state, the right to participate in elections was limited only to the male and the freeborn. During the 1850s, the visions of the American Revolution (1772) and French Revolution (1789) became increasingly entrenched in various societies all over the world: all adult citizens had the right to freely choose their leaders. But this was only possible with mass education. Hence, public schools and trade schools became important.

3. *The transition to nationalism.* Pre-nineteenth century monarchies had laws for each locality and for each ethnic group. All were integrated together by an unquestioning loyalty to the monarch who supposedly had semi-divine powers. Instead, it was proposed that the binding force of a state society was nationalism—pride in forming a distinct "nation" with a distinct history, tradition, customs, and achievement. Legal differences between different ethnic groups were replaced by a single national code. In 1889, a single Civil Code was introduced into the islands eliminating the distinction between Spaniards, Chinese, Chinese mestizos, and indios. At the same time José Rizal and Isabelo de los Reyes called attention to the achievements of ordinary, unlettered Filipinos. Hence the upsurge of interest in vernacular art, such as popular architecture, during the century that followed. Vernacular architecture forms the bulk of the entries in this inventory, for in it the spirit of ordinary Filipinos shines through.

Having said all these, I would like to point out that this inventory is but one perspective, albeit one that has been done with care.[17] Ideally this inventory should be complemented with one that has more data on the non-aesthetic significance of particular buildings. Participation by various members of the community would be needed. Because such an inventory would highlight the importance of particular buildings within the consciousness of such members, it can generate stronger support for their preservation.

NOTES

1. Alfred Marche, *Luçon et Palaouan: Six années de voyages aux Philippines* (Paris: Hachette et Cie, 1887), 135.

2. Francisco Ignacio Alcina in 1668 describes it thus: *"Obra que por acá llaman mestiza, por ser parte de piedra y parte de madera."* (A product that is locally called mestizo, for being partly of stone, partly of wood.) Luis Merino OSA, *Arquitectura y urbanismo en el Siglo XIX: Introducción general y monografía* (Manila: Centro Cultural de España with the collaboration of the Intramuros Administration, 1987), 67.

3. Merino, *Arquitectura y urbanismo en el Siglo XIX*, 68.

4. *"Los entramados de madera, tanto horizontales como verticales, ofrecen las mayores garantías contra la acción de los temblores,"* Ibid., 172.

5. *"Debe carbonizar, embrearse y forrarse con plomo ó tablilla de molave la parte empotrada,"* Ibid., 173.

6. Carl W. Condit, *The Chicago School of Architecture: A History of Commercial and Public Building in the Chicago Area, 1875-1925* (Chicago: The University of Chicago Press, 1973). It was Dom Bernardo Perez (Rodrigo Perez III) who brought this to my attention. Unfortunately, I cannot locate the photocopy he sent me in order to give the exact year of Le Baron Jenney's visit to Manila. Meanwhile, Perez's copy was donated to an architectural library.

7. Zygmunt Bauman, "Postmodernity, or Living with Ambivalence," *A Postmodern Reader*, eds. Joseph Natoli and Linda Hutcheon (Albany: State University of New York Press, 1993), 1-24.

8. Porras's landmark study seems not to have been published yet.

9. Jacques Maritain, *Art and Scholasticism, with Other Essays*, trans. J. F. Scanlon (New York: Scribner, 1947).

10. "Antonio Bonet Correa, nuevo director de la Real Academia de Bellas Artes," *Elmundo.es: Cultura y Ocio*, ‹http://www.elmundo.es/elmundo/2008/12/15/cultura/1229372070.html›, Accessed on 24 June 2010.

11. Daniel H. Burnham, *Proposed Improvements at Manila* (Washington DC: Government Printing Office, 1906), 635.

12. Ibid.

13. Thomas S. Hines, *Burnham of Chicago: Architect and Planner* (Chicago: University of Chicago Press, second edition, 2008), 202.

14. The estimate was given to me in 2011 by Mrs. Marjo Villanueva Gasser, one of the founding members of SVAHAI and a pioneer in efforts to save Vigan's heritage. That she is a successful businesswoman gives this datum more weight.

15. These and other related issues are discussed by Arch. Rene Mata in a book that we co-wrote with others, *Balangkas: A Resource Book on the Care of Built Heritage in the Philippines* (Manila: National Commission for Culture and the Arts, 2007). Pertinent too are the articles of Dr. Victor Venida and Dr. Jaime Laya on the economics and financing of heritage preservation.

16. Jobers Bersales, "Past Forward: eGwen surfaces Cebu heritage models," Cebu Daily News/Opinion, Inquirer.net, accessed 23 June 2011, http://services.inquirer.net/print/print.php?article_id=20090820-221179 (20 August 2009).

17. The postmodernists remind us that the Singular Voice (namely myself or even our small group) should be wary of assuming it embodies the Universal. Thus, the importance of listening to a wide variety of voices. See François Lyotard, *The Differend: Phrases in Dispute* (Minneapolis: University of Minnesota Press, 1991).

FIG. 4-5. 19th century esteros were busy waterways; revitalized estero in San Miguel, 2015 (adjacent page: top and bottom)

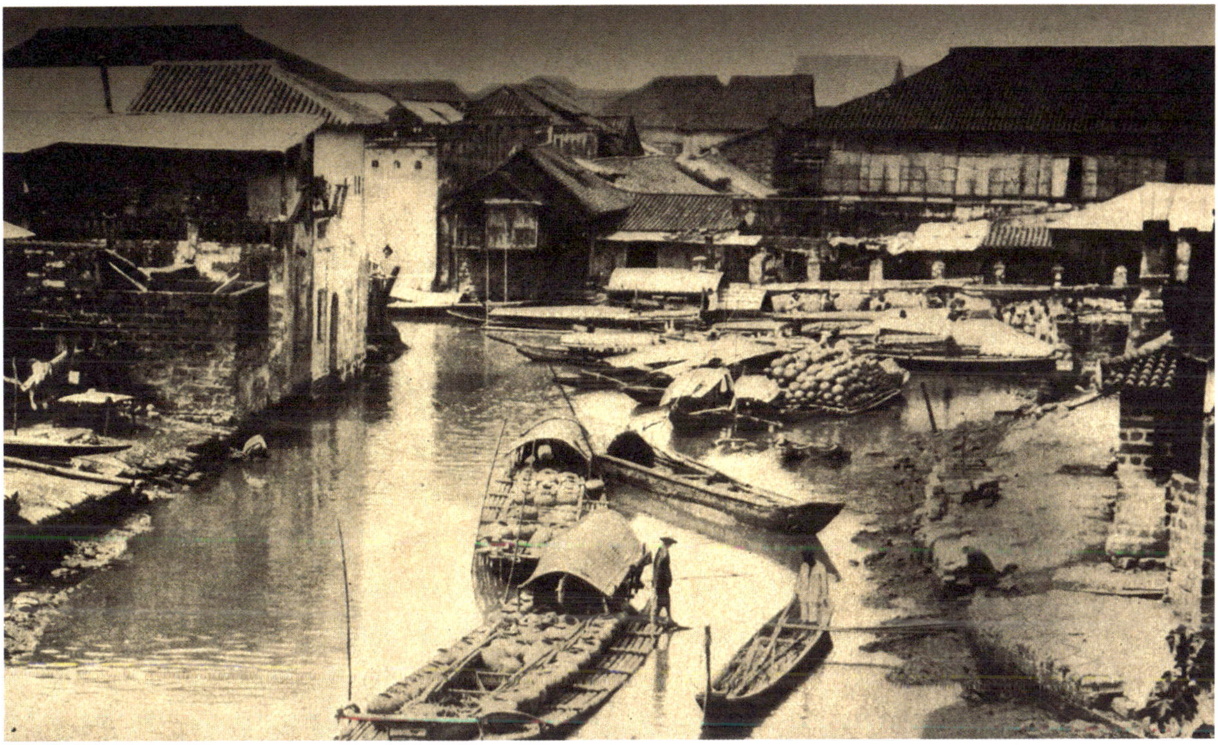

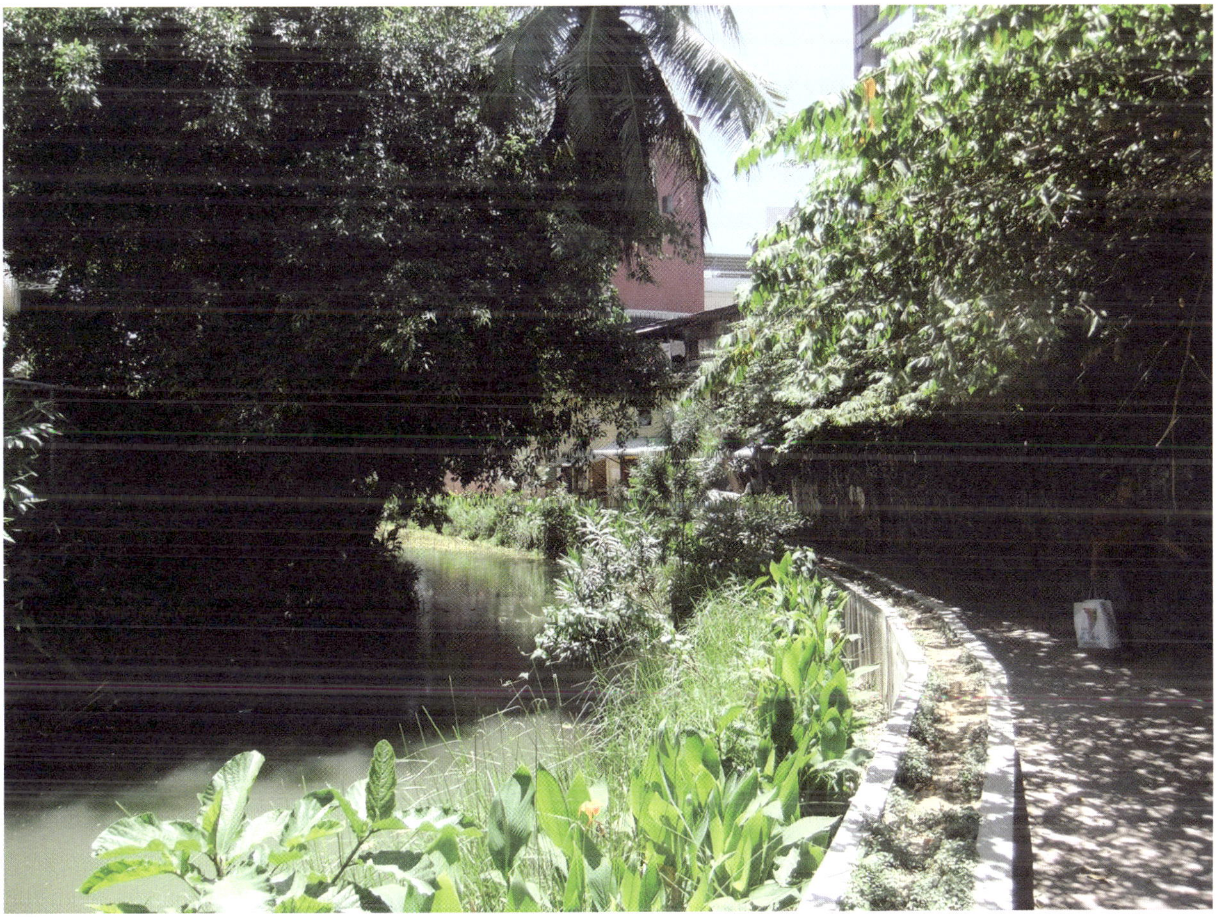

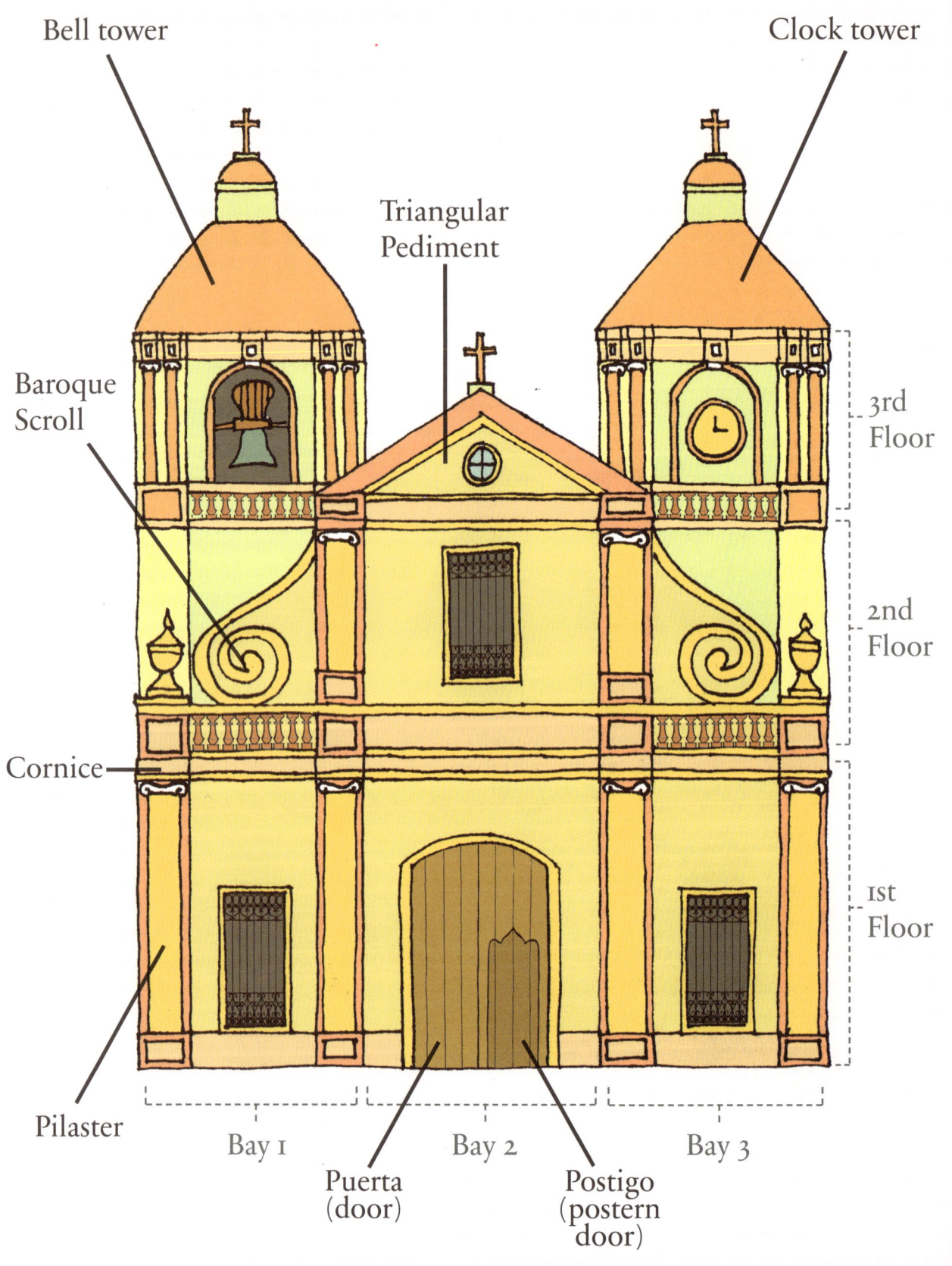

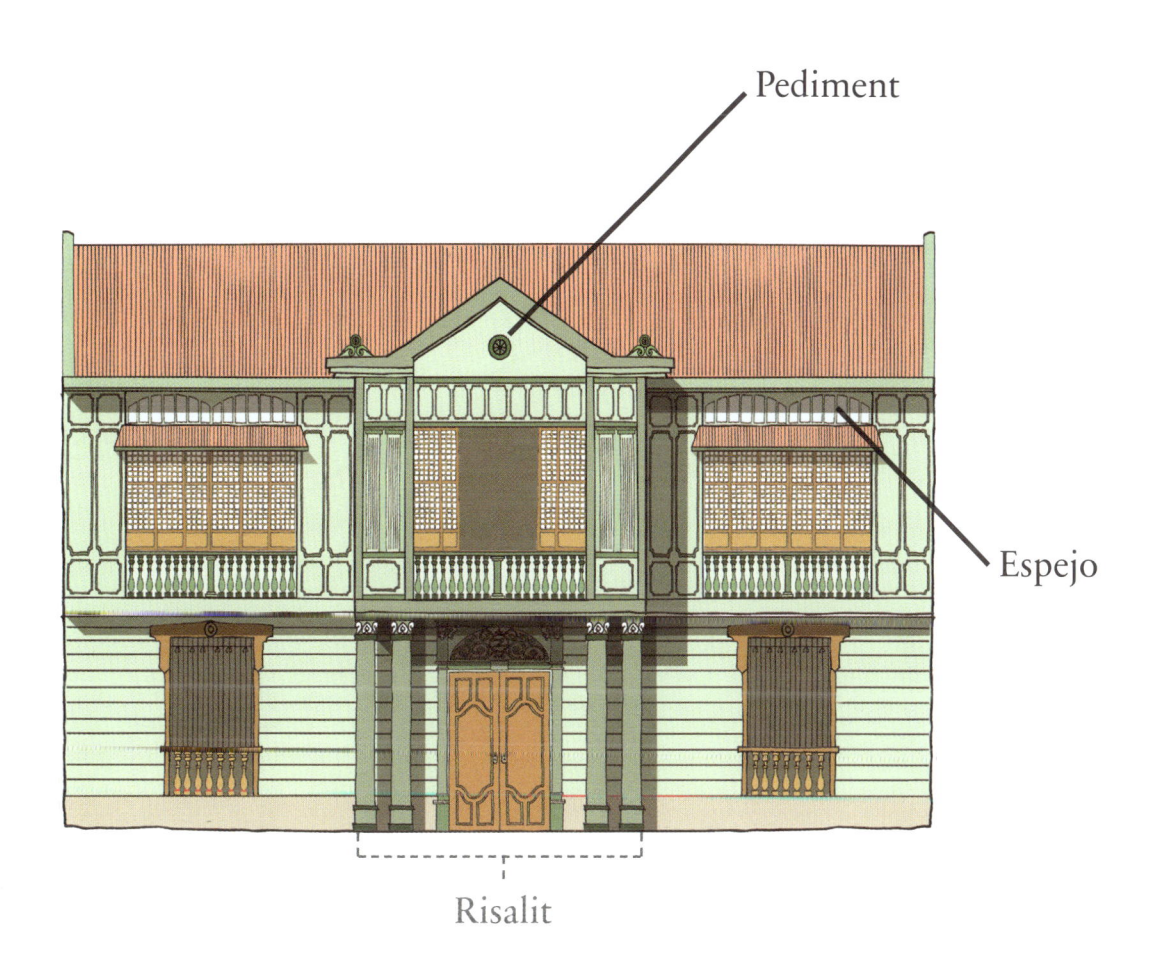

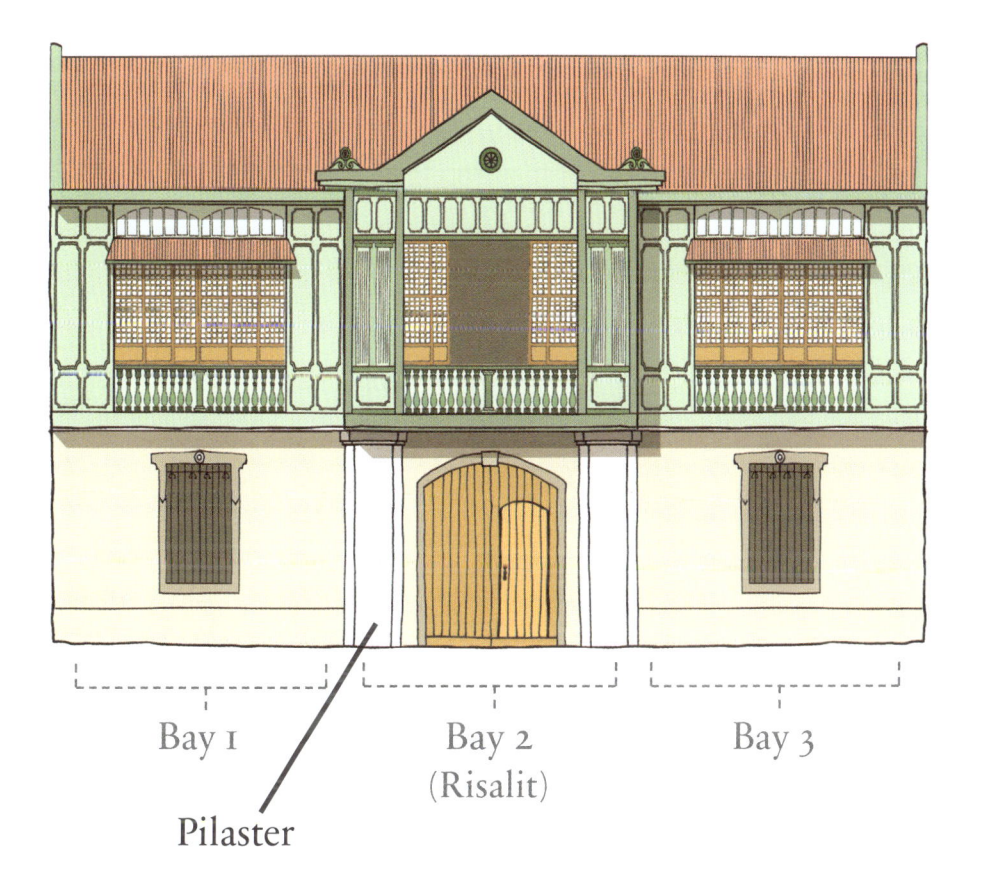

- Pediment
- Espejo
- Risalit
- Bay 1
- Bay 2 (Risalit)
- Bay 3
- Pilaster

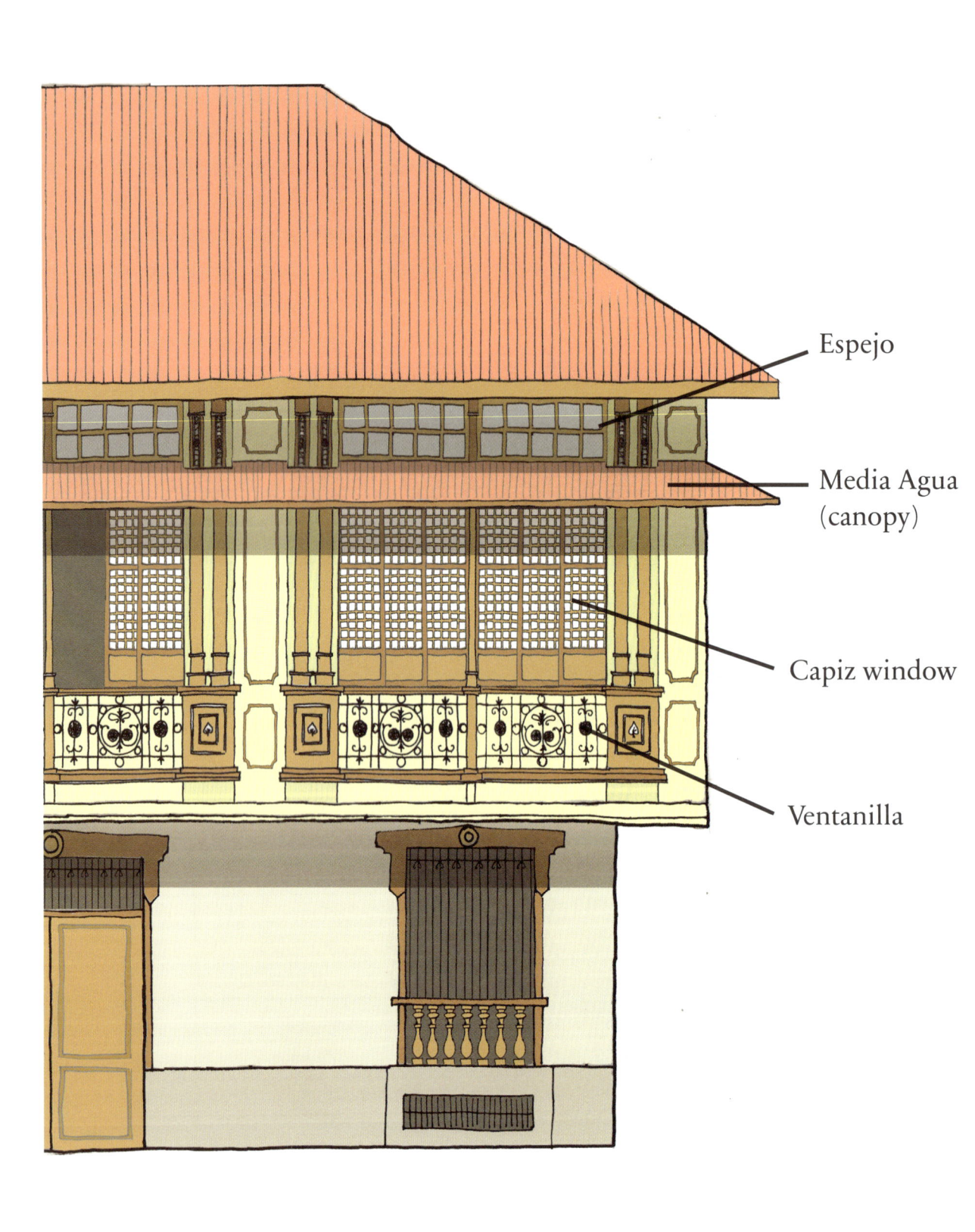

- Espejo
- Media Agua (canopy)
- Capiz window
- Ventanilla

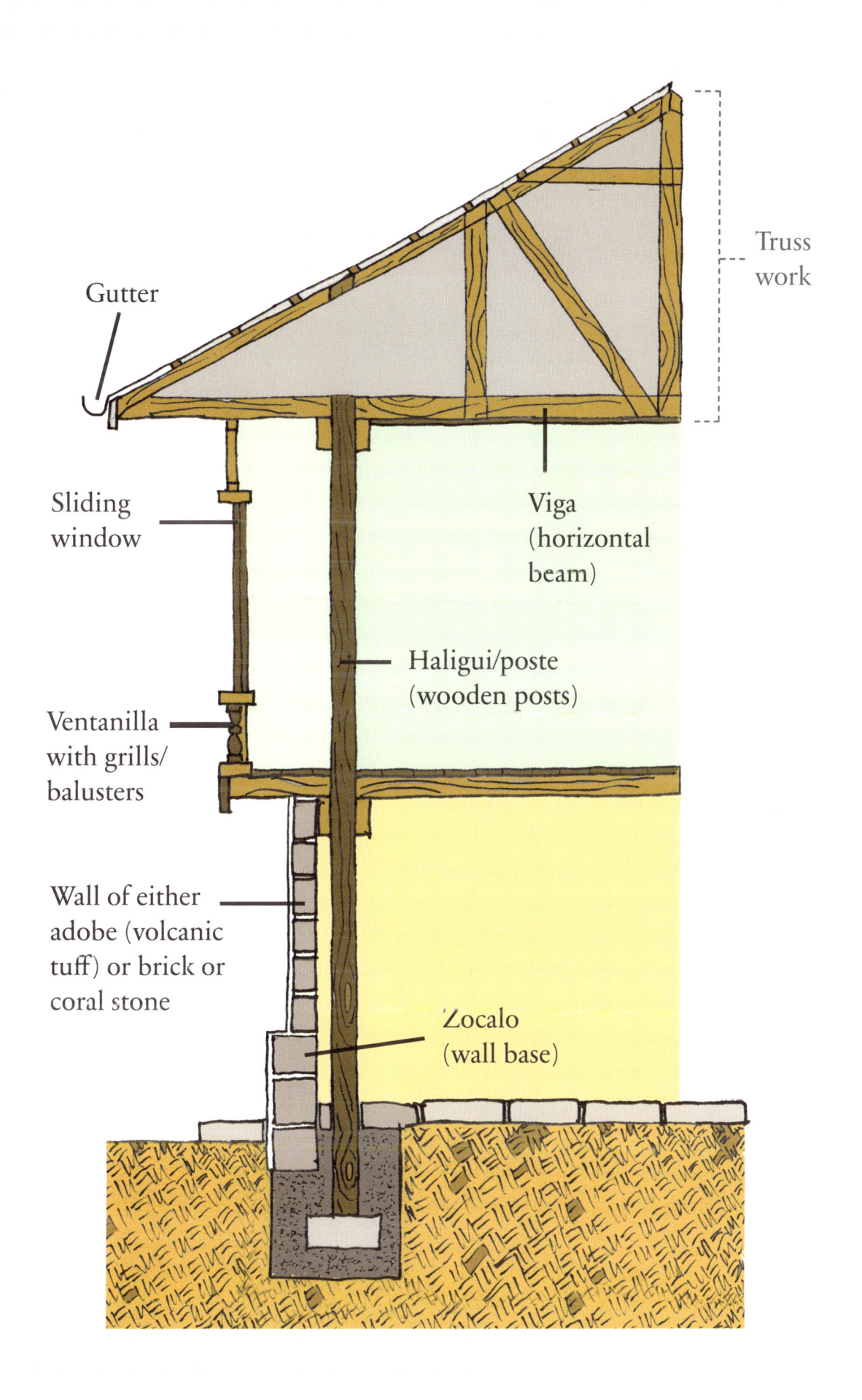

- Truss work
- Gutter
- Sliding window
- Viga (horizontal beam)
- Haligui/poste (wooden posts)
- Ventanilla with grills/balusters
- Wall of either adobe (volcanic tuff) or brick or coral stone
- Zocalo (wall base)

Burda/Calado

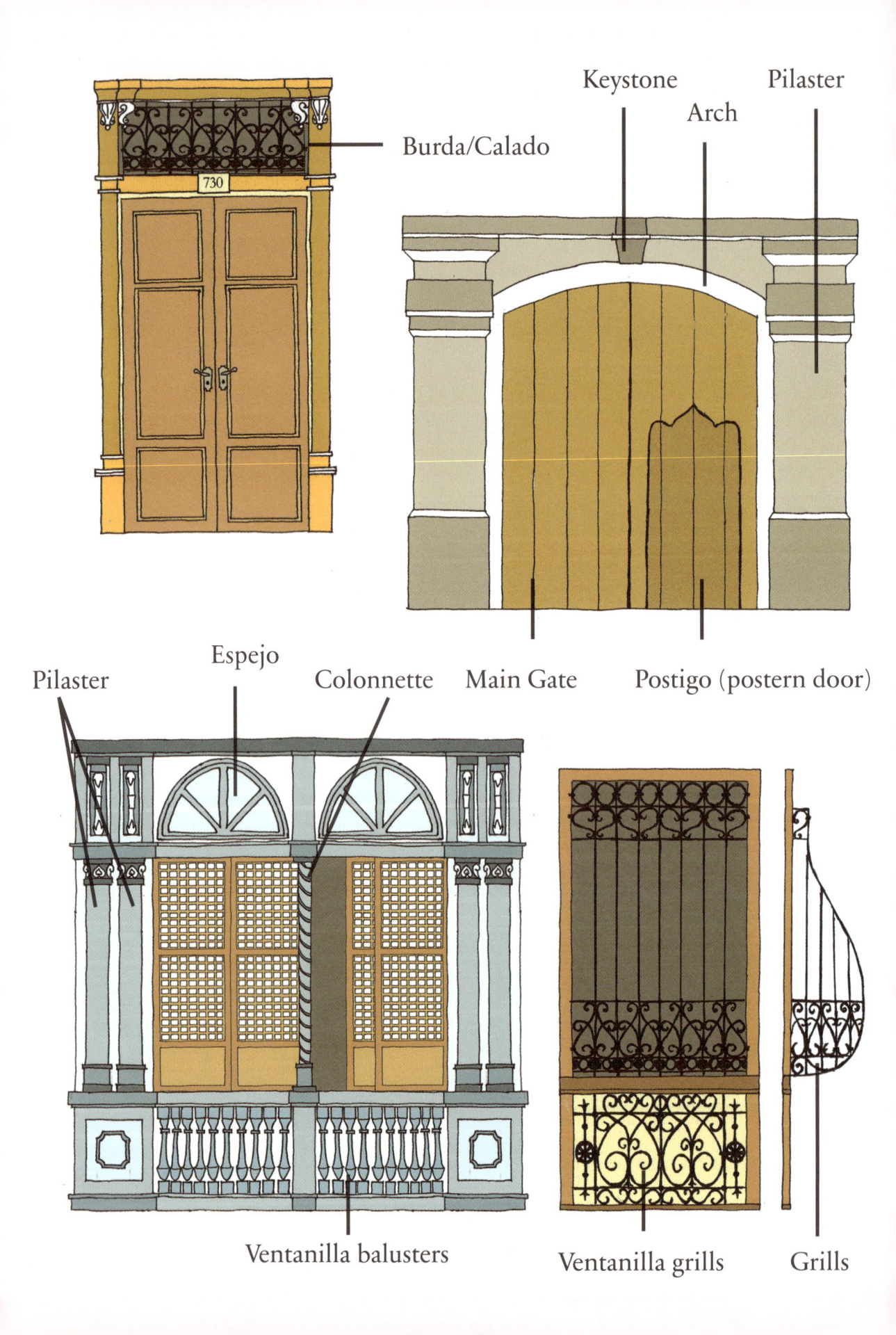

Keystone
Arch
Pilaster

Pilaster
Espejo
Colonnette
Main Gate
Postigo (postern door)

Ventanilla balusters
Ventanilla grills
Grills

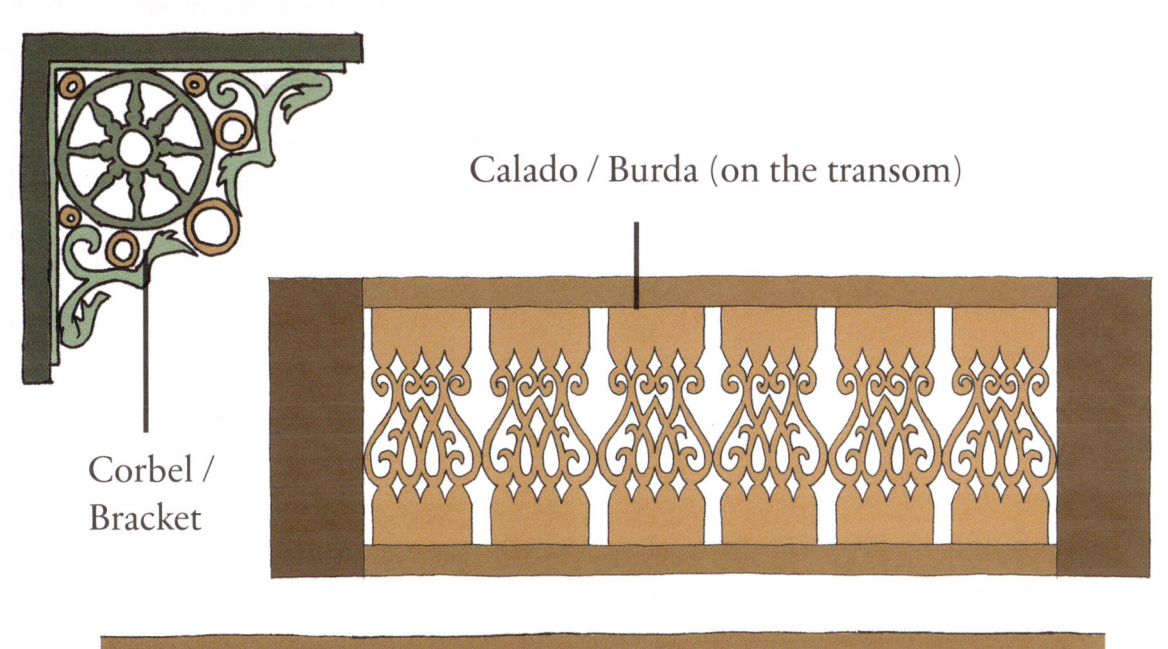

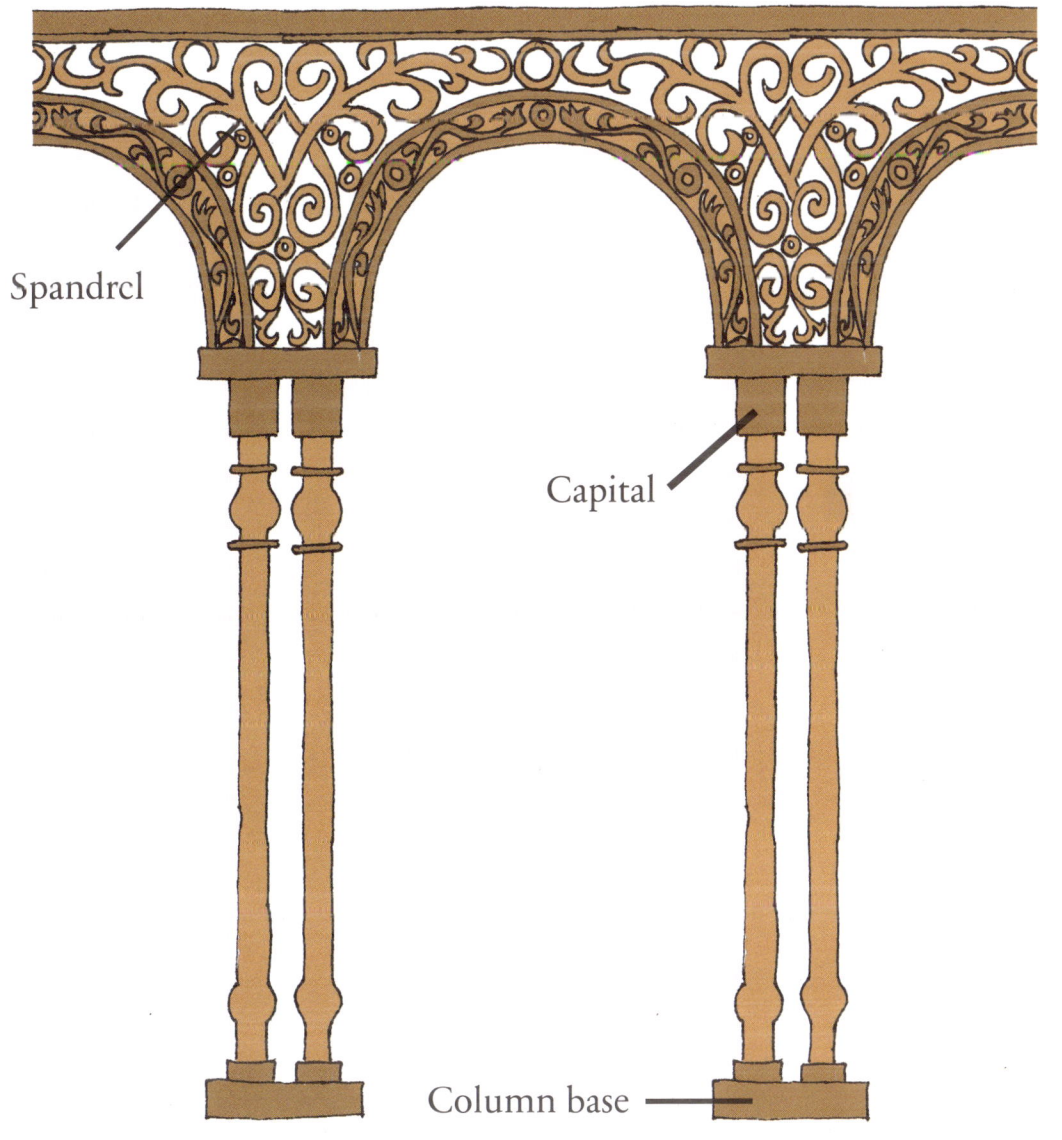

Corbel / Bracket

Calado / Burda (on the transom)

Spandrel

Capital

Column base

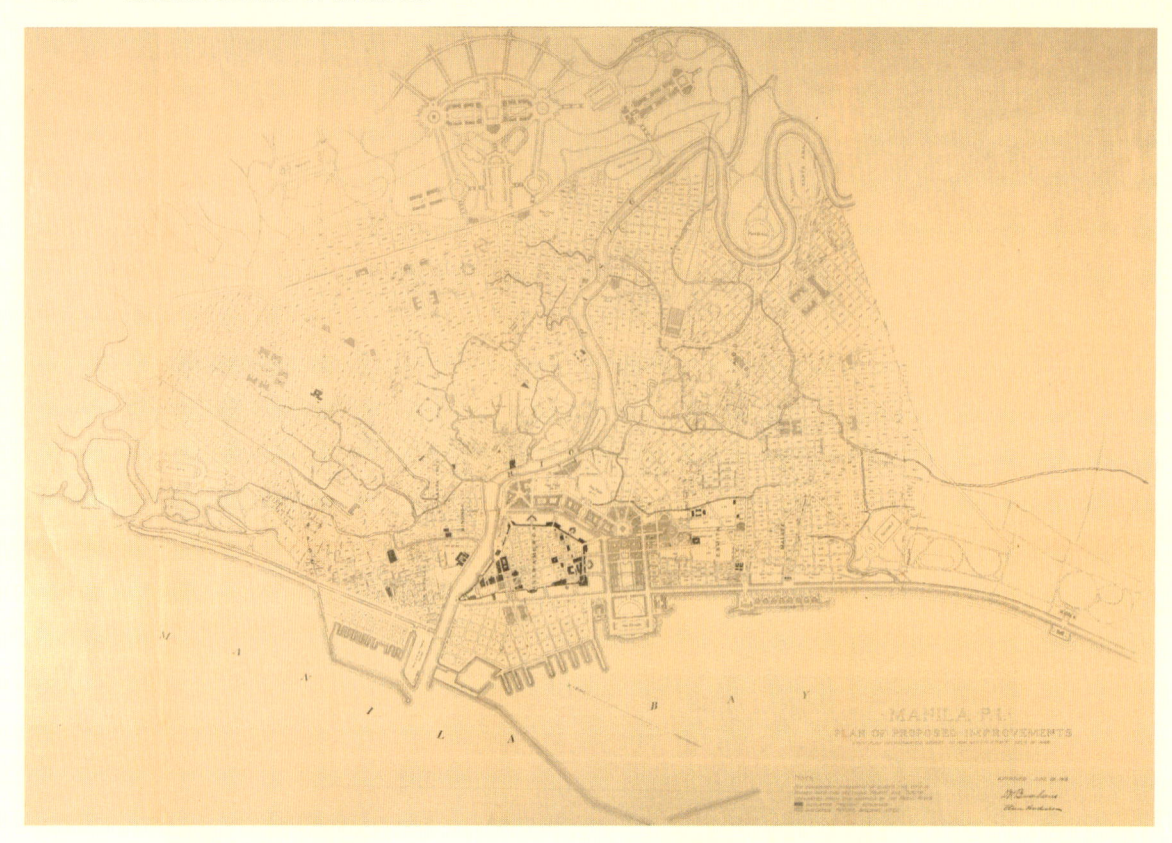

FIG. 6. Daniel Burnham's plan for Manila, 1905

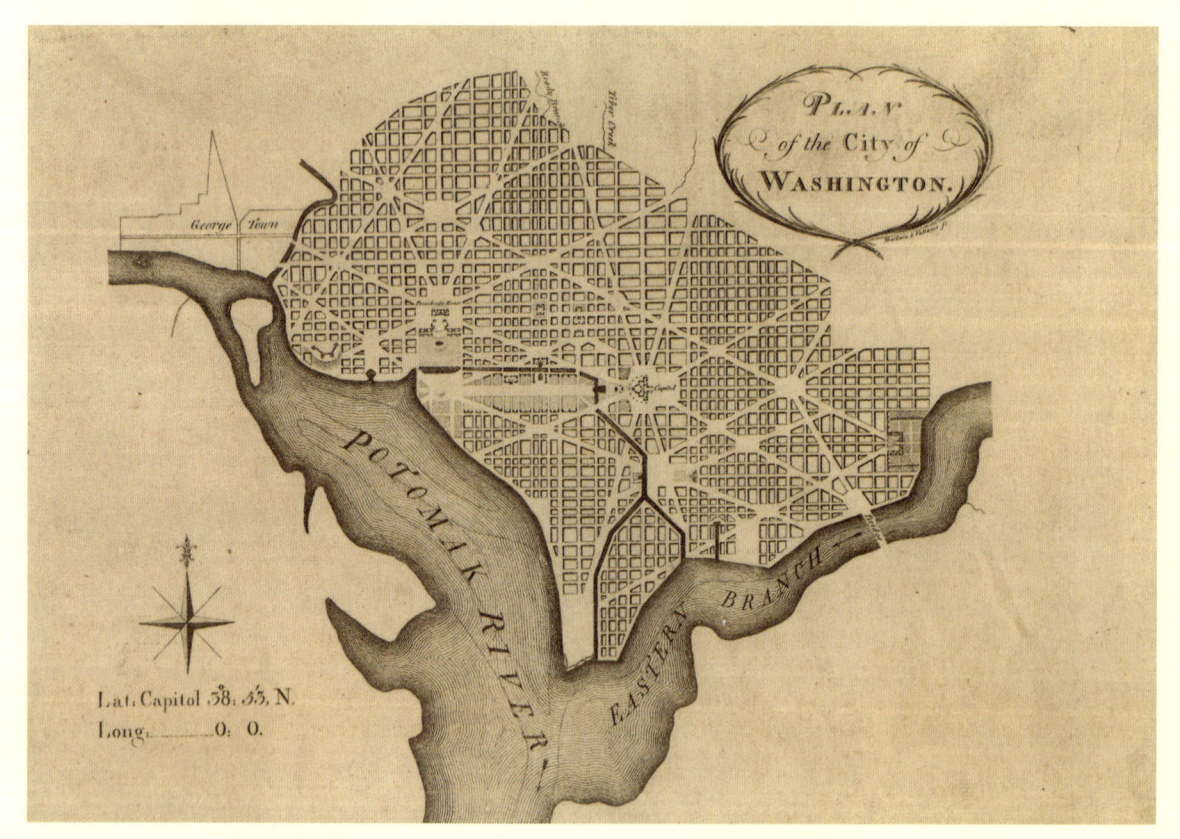

FIG. 7. Pierre L' Enfant's plan for Washington D.C. (revised by Andrew Ellicott), 1792.
Image licensed under Creative Commons Public Domain Mark 1.0, see p. 394.

General Issues: Revitalization of Historic Districts in Manila

VICTOR VENIDA

In general the theme is to locate the restoration of the antique buildings of Manila within a general strategy or vision of urban development along economically progressive, socially equitable, and environmentally sustainable lines. The proposals for individual districts will be in separate chapters. This will largely focus on issues for the city at large since in general, the success of the renewal and preservation of historic buildings and districts relies on its integration with a general program of urban development and on the participation of organized and concerned citizen organizations.[1]

OVERVIEW

It was said that, after the inauguration of US President John F. Kennedy, while on the traditional drive down Pennsylvania Avenue to the White House, he noticed ("was appalled" was the phrase often used) the shabbiness of what has been the main ceremonial road of the US and thought that he might need to do something about it.[2] In 1962, he ordered the formation of the Presidential Advisory Council on Pennsylvania Avenue which further expanded to the completion of an Integrated Master Plan in 1966 for the redevelopment of Pennsylvania Avenue and the Washington Mall. This was called the Owings Plan, after the lead architect Nathaniel Owings.

Indeed the present beauty of Washington, DC is a function of urban renewal plans being continually devised to enhance existing structures and districts, especially the heritage buildings; correct visual eyesores; and identify strategic directions for various districts well into the future. This subsequently explains the huge numbers of tourists and sums of investments that it attracts.

The L'Enfant Plan of 1791 was considered among the grandest city plans ever devised in Western planning history. It was designed to realize the vision of grandeur for a democratic republic's national capital. It followed many of the principles of

Baroque city planning in Europe, such as for Rome and Versailles, but focused on the splendour not of an absolute ruler but that of a democratically elected government. This was the reason behind the prominent location of the US Congress and what would become the White House. Diagonal boulevards intersecting the grids would allow for the location of monuments on strategic crossroads or intersection points. These would have created magnificent vistas for the capital city.[3]

But urban plans can only go so far: by the end of the nineteenth century, railroad tracks had crossed the Mall towards the main train station located right on the northern perimeter of the Mall itself, along 6th Street. Many of the original L'Enfant proposals could not be fully implemented throughout the century because of government budget constraints, the ambivalence of property owners, and the lack of priority to urban aesthetics.[4] There was indeed the Andrew Jackson Downing Plan in 1851, an attempt at a new landscape design for the Mall (inspired by the success of Frederic Law Olmstead for Central Park in New York). But by the turn of the twentieth century, the capital was deemed to be so unsightly that in 1900, the US Congress had to commission a new urban plan, to regain the L'Enfant Plan's lost splendour and restore dignity to the capital city. The result was the McMillan Commission Plan (named after Sen. James McMillan, the main sponsor of the bill, while the lead architect was Daniel Burnham) which used the L'Enfant Plan as the main template and proposed changes to the existing land-use and structures so that aspects of the 1791 Plan could be recovered and realized. Among these were the relocation of the train station to its present site as Union Station, the removal of the train tracks along the Mall which then received a new landscape design and building plan. The Plan also proposed design guidelines for new building construction so that until the 1940s government buildings followed the Neoclassical style as symbolic of modern democracy. These

FIG. 8. Columbus Circle in front of Union Station, Washington, D.C., opened 1907 (From the Lopez Memorial Museum Collection)

include the memorials to Thomas Jefferson and Abraham Lincoln, the National Archives, the Department of Justice and the Supreme Court (which received its own building after decades of sharing quarters with the Congress since the L'Enfant Plan did not provide a specific site for this third branch of government.)[5] Many aspects, like for any city plan, were not implemented, such as the proposed Neoclassical bathhouses and clubs where the Jefferson Memorial was instead located. Maryland Avenue to this day remains a nondescript roadway and has never been redeveloped to be the southerly complement to Pennsylvania Avenue as the radiating diagonal from the Capitol. The other important example was the grandiose colonnade around the front of Union Station which would have made the arrival to the city an experience of splendor but which was also deemed to be too extravagant.[6]

Again social and economic forces would intervene such that by the Kennedy administration the aesthetics of the capital became an issue once again. This was also during the period of steady postwar economic expansion that, among other things, encouraged the destruction of large numbers of old buildings, from private residences to grand public structures (New York's Pennsylvania Station being one of the most notorious cases), for the construction of new expressways, more modern buildings, and new structures with higher commercial real estate value.[7] The blight did scar the capital, like most other cities, and this motivated the government to thus come up with a new urban Plan. The Owings Plan not only addressed design and density issues but also attempted to identify the other districts in the immediate vicinity of the Mall and Pennsylvania Avenue for long-term development. As examples, it identified the Anacostia area to the south of the Mall as dominantly residential but mixed use district, mainly for middle-income households, and the area immediately to the north of Pennsylvania Avenue to be the capital's main commercial and business district. And it

FIG. 9. Washington, D.C., and Potomac River, McMillan Plan, 1907 (From the Lopez Memorial Museum Collection)

proposed the expansion of the open space, parklands, and parkways. The Owings Plan attempted to at least go beyond the main design and aesthetic issues that were the sole focus of the L'Enfant and McMillan Plans to cover locations for various social and economic activities, especially low-income housing, and the development of a viable urban mass transit system.[8]

Manila can thus learn from the experience of Washington, DC. After all, the Philippine capital city itself was largely modelled after Washington, DC, when the Americans made it the showcase of their new colony in the Far East. It was the subject of the famous Burnham Plan of 1905, which was modified later by Burnham's protégé William Parsons whose street plan was largely realized in today's city.[9] The main civic center of the capital was located in Ermita and indeed many of the government and institutional structures are still being utilized in their existing locations. Perhaps it may now be high time for an updated Plan for the City to be undertaken. A starting point for city managers would be the Comprehensive Land-Use Plan and Zoning Ordinance (CLUPZO). There are several available design and development proposals (such as those developed by Palafox and Associates and Arch. Paulo Alcazaren), a number of unrealized building plans (such as those of Juan Arellano), and several heritage structures and districts that can be integrated into this proposed new Plan for Manila.[10]

There also are available plans for the redevelopment of the Pasig River and Manila Bay. These can all be incorporated in an updated and expanded Burnham Plan for the twenty-first century, one that will also determine the strategic directions for the city's long-term economic expansion and the residential requirements of the various social classes that reside in the city. A number of specific infrastructure projects will need to be included for the long term to enhance the capital's visual aspects and attract greater economic activities to the city. The Plan indeed should be designed not just for aesthetics alone but also for long-term social and economic development, with aesthetics as the anchor image for the capital city. Indeed, the experience of most European capital cities has been that heritage preservation has been more successful if integrated in an overall urban development plan and the old structures provided design ideas and guidelines that gave these cities their particular image and identity.[11]

The preservation of the old buildings in the city and the determination of design guidelines for new building construction and renovation of the post-1940s buildings will be necessary to create a sense of place and a distinctive image that is unique and identifiable to Manila. These old buildings need some form of economic use to survive and one will need to identify a range of economic activities that can be accommodated not just in the old buildings but also in entire districts so that heritage preservation becomes integral to an overall strategy of local area development.

INFRASTRUCTURE

To realize the potential for any district as a thriving center of economic activity, whether it has heritage structures or not, there is a need to develop the basic infrastructure. There is a need for street-level improvement to cover paving, sidewalk or curb improvement, and provision for streetlights, lampposts and street signage (preferably the large tile signage placed on walls like the ones in Intramuros, Binondo, and San Nicolas). With regards to street signage, it is also suggested that the old names of streets be indicated under the current names to encourage a sense of historical appreciation and sharpen the sense of place. Ideally new lines for electricity and communication cables would be underground to replace the unsightly overhead ones. Installation of new water lines, sewers and storm drains will also be necessary. There would thus be a need to design the standard location for the electric cables, fiber optic cables, water lines, sewers and storm drains and the construction of these would need to be coordinated among the different utility firms like Meralco, Maynilad, PLDT and Bayantel. Renovation and restoration of old buildings will need to consider environmentally sustainable technologies and materials that have been developed recently. These also add to a district's attraction for tourists, future high-income residents, and investors. The old buildings have already been designed for ideal passive lighting and ventilation. These can be reinforced by features and facilities currently deemed to be ecologically sustainable. It is suggested that good insulating materials be used for the roofs and external walls without, however, compromising the historic façades. The old *aljibe* technology can be re-adapted for the collection and storage of rainwater, and interior courtyards can be redesigned as water gardens, with trees with primary roots

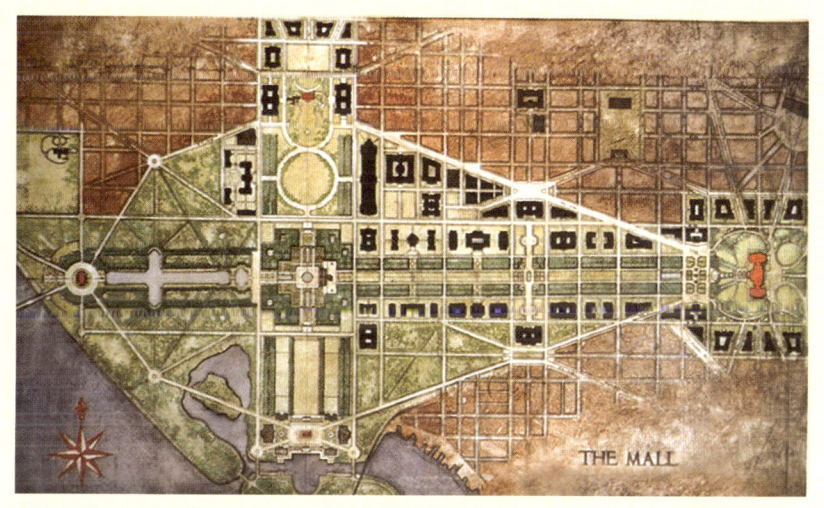

FIG. 10. Civic core of Washington, D.C., McMillan Plan, 1907. By the National Capital Planning Commission, image in the public domain, retrieved from Wikimedia Commons, see p. 394.

to absorb rainwater and diminish groundwater depletion. Fluorescent light bulbs and dehumidifiers as indoor air conditioners are also recommended. The installation of solar-collector panels on the roofs can also be explored to encourage the use of solar energy as sources of off-grid electricity especially on the sunny days. Indoor plumbing facilities would include low-flush toilets, spray faucets, and water-saving shower jets. The city can also encourage the adoption of electric jeeps, buses, and utility vehicles, as these will reduce pollution emissions. Many of the city's beautiful buildings actually just need regular cleaning to look truly beautiful but this has been very expensive because of the severe pollution caused largely by vehicle emissions. Adoption of electric vehicles for mass transit will not only make the air cleaner but will also make buildings look cleaner, less covered with soot, thus more attractive to look at.

The city can initiate long-term plans including a thorough clean-up of the esteros and a redevelopment of the setbacks as walkways and parks to realize the original vision of the Burnham Plan. A completed example is the stretch of the Estero de San Miguel from the LRT-Legarda station to the Estero de Uli-uli. Another is the recently completed clean-up of the estero around the Paco Public Market. These can be replicated in the rest of the city specially if integrated with the development of a new city-wide sewerage system so that the esteros can become more of what they used to be: as outlets for floodwaters in the monsoon and pleasant addition to the open spaces for the rest of the year.

It is also suggested that in the absence of a city-wide sewage treatment facility, a community-level sewage treatment facility be installed. This can discharge treated sewage water and also produce organic fertilizer and bio-gas, which can earn revenue for the operation of the facility. There is also a need to install garbage receptacles and develop a regular system of collection of garbage to minimize the dumping of waste and trash into the river. But for the long term, the city and the entire National Capital Region would thus require investment in a complete sewerage system starting in the heritage districts, and sewage treatment plants to ensure the cleanliness of waterways and the environment well into the future.

The elevated LRT can be reconstructed as an underground subway train system, much like the subway lines in Manhattan and the railway line in Washington, DC. These both started out as being aboveground and so unsightly that in time, the Manhattan trains and the Washington railway lines were reconstructed as underground transport lines.[12] Reconstructing the LRT systems as underground lines will substantially re-create the vistas that were originally proposed in the Burnham Plan, especially those along Taft Avenue and Avenida Rizal. This should be undertaken alongside the above-mentioned relocation of the electric and communication cables underground and the laying of new water pipes and sewer lines. There will be a need for design proposals for the subway entrances and possibly even the development of underground spaces for commercial establishments. One can suggest that the former Insular Ice Plant and Cold Storage be reconstructed and redesigned as an integrated transport terminal on Liwasang Bonifacio, as entry and exit to the underground LRT and station for public utility vehicles, with a ferry station on the riverbank.

The tunneling for the LRT, the relocation underground of electric power lines and internet cables and the installation of new water, sewer, and drainage lines can make the city function more efficiently. Underground electric cables have lower system losses, underground internet cables can be larger and provide greater bandwidth, improved water supply and sanitation systems will make for a cleaner urban environment, and urban vistas will be enhanced with the absence of aboveground cable lines. These are all recipes for a city ready to face continued population growth, economic expansion, and global competition well into the distant future.

Other possibilities for improving traffic management and transport in the city are the restoration of the old *Tranvía* (streetcar) system and the development of bicycle lanes. These could definitely discourage the use of private vehicles and reduce vehicle emissions. Apart from being less expensive than the underground rail transit system, the Tranvía system has to be weighed against the fact that it competes for road space with automobiles and can thus contribute to traffic jams. As for the promotion of bicycles as alternative transport mode, unfortunately for commuting office workers and students in a humid tropical city, biking can be inconvenient as they would arrive at the place of work or school sweaty and tired. They would need access to showers and changing rooms which are not widely available. If the city were to encourage this as a regular mode of transport then it would also need to encourage (or even mandate) the installation of shower facilities and changing rooms in schools and work places.

Two major long-term infrastructure decisions would be the relocation of the petroleum depot in Pandacan and the container port in the South Harbor Port Area. The location of these two facilities quite close to the city center would be anachronistic and problematic as the city develops and expands, if the experience of other cities would be a guide.[13] The depot and the container port both need direct access to the expressways for more efficient delivery and to minimize the adverse impact on city traffic. Relocation of the petroleum depot took place in 2015. The container port has alternative options in the Manila International Port terminal (which needs to develop its access to the North Luzon Expressway) and the Batangas City port. New York, Rotterdam, London, and Barcelona have relocated their container ports elsewhere because these generate heavy traffic of huge container trucks in the city streets, thus making the movement of goods to other points in the country more expensive. These relocation activities will free up substantial space that can be used for further redevelopment. These two facilities are also located near major heritage districts so that their operations now and in the future will have a significant bearing on the survival of many old buildings.

The construction of massive underground facilities (for transport, drainage, water supply, sewers, electric and communication cables) will be a major engineering and financial undertaking. In fact one can say this of all the infrastructure proposals here. This will be a special challenge for a city largely below sea level, subject to regular flooding from torrential monsoon rains, with a government (city and national) that has a notoriously inefficient capacity for revenue collection and expenditure. The only possible justification for all this massive infrastructure undertaking would be Burnham's famous remark, "Make no little plans. They have no magic to stir men's blood and probably will not themselves be realized."[14]

DESIGN

New buildings can be encouraged to adhere to the street walls of the district and to the design of the antique houses nearby. Newer buildings can be designed to install the Filipino window (translucent glass on the transom, awning over the window with sliding panes, a ventanilla on the lower panel) as this will give the area greater character and identity and also make the new buildings realize the benefit of passive lighting and ventilation.[15] There might also be a need to consider the encouragement of developers to design and build transitional buildings between the old buildings, which are generally low-density, and the newer developments.

Given the rich historical associations of the capital city, it is also suggested that markers be installed in the old buildings or the sites of demolished antique structures. Street signs can also be engraved in stone like those in the older city centers of Europe. The barangay can also publish and sell a visitor's guide and brochure. And as part of environmental renewal, most of the pedestrian curbs that are not cantilevered can be enhanced by the planting of shade trees.

An important issue is that of low-cost housing for low-income households. Like the rest of the Philippines, informal settlements dominate the cities.[16] In any city, a substantial portion of buildings happen to be housing units so that these contribute to the aesthetic character and visual impact of the metropolis. No matter the elegance and sophistication of institutional, commercial, and office buildings, especially in the central business district and the government centers, the general image of the urban area will have to juxtapose this with the residential areas. Manila and the other cities of the Philippines do not present a pretty sight.

Since the majority of urban residents in Manila belong to the lower-income classes and since economic development as a goal would eventually provide low-cost housing to them, government at some point will need to be involved not just in the financing and development of low-cost housing estates but also inevitably in the design and aesthetics of these residential buildings.

One could consider the experience of Singapore, where the government decided to be involved in the planning, design, construction, and financing of high-rise residential developments for the majority of the population. This has to a degree created the aesthetic nature of the city.[17]

For the long term, Manila can take a leaf out of this experience and consider greater government involvement in mass housing construction. Whether direct construction or in coordination with private sector efforts (such as the ongoing Gawad Kalinga housing program), participation of government in low-cost housing is not only an issue of social justice and social development, of providing decent habitation for a large portion of the population but also of transforming informal settlements into formal ones. With housing, many informal settlers gain secure tenurial rights that allow for investment in home improvements and the buildup of family assets, in terms of household appliances, savings, educational materials, and the like. Housing also means a more organized and rational mechanism for connecting many households to the city infrastructure of transport access, cable and electricity connection, water supply, and sewer system. Not only will more households have secure access to these (which greatly enhance the quality of life) but utility firms will collect bills more efficiently, reduce their systems losses, and provide more effective service. Moreover, the very process of all this housing construction and extension of infrastructure will be creating jobs since these are all labor-intensive activities. Through this process employment is created, poverty is reduced, and development is attained.

An often-overlooked element in the mass housing experience is the aesthetic aspect. Mass housing since the 1940s in most developed countries has involved genuine improvements in living conditions inside modern housing units compared to the traditional ones. In contrast, however, modern mass housing had plain façades compared to its traditional counterpart. While modern mass housing did provide decent shelters to large segments of the population, it also had to consider exterior ornamentation as unnecessary—even extravagant—in order to stretch construction funds. Residents, unfortunately, in the long-run hated the stigma attached to living in mass housing developments identifiable by their very plain, even drab exterior.[18] In other words, on the question of social justice, though decent housing was provided, this involved denying more aesthetically appealing residential quarters.

Amsterdam and Vienna do provide models of viable mass housing developments that also provided attractive ornamentation on the façade.[19] The housing developments incorporated schools, health centers, commercial establishments, parks, and open spaces for a mixed-use residential community. These were located near mass transit connections that would allow residents to commute to jobs and activities elsewhere in the city. But more importantly, the housing units (all multiple dwelling, multi-level structures) had ornamentation on the façade that adapted the designs of the traditional houses. The Karl Marx Hof in Vienna had bas-reliefs, window treatments, arches and the like that echoed the Baroque ornamentation of the city's older buildings, including the city palaces of the aristocracy. The more restrained traditional architecture of Amsterdam was echoed in the bricks, window and door treatments, gable design and heights of the mass housing projects. These were cases of contextual design and, because of the beauty of these structures, residents remained in their units for generations without the stigma of living in low-cost housing. These created stable, well defined and idiosyncratic communities within the larger metropolis.

Something similar can be proposed for a government mass housing program. The units might need to be multiple-dwellings on multiple levels to maximize the use of scarce urban land. But the exterior can be contextualized to adapt surface ornamentation of old buildings nearby. One can envision these dwellings to have high ceilings, with windows composed of frosted glass transoms, wide windows with awnings and sliding panes, and ventanillas. They can have geometric or floral decoration on the wall surfaces, roof eaves, downspouts, and main doorways. Zialcita and Tinio have documented various examples of these ornamentation.[20] These surface decorations do increase the cost of construction, as the experience of Amsterdam and Vienna show. It does, however, create a lot of jobs and most specially keep alive the various artisan crafts that have created these idiosyncratic buildings. One can also argue that it will be money well spent in creating a more aesthetically appealing image of the city and in achieving a sense of social justice in extending visual beauty to low-income communities.

TRAINING

The practice of reconstructing old buildings to recreate the old districts as part of the national heritage has been successfully undertaken in other places, most spectacularly in the reconstruction of Old Warsaw after World War II.[21] Although derided as a form of façadism, the experience of Warsaw has been the renewal of national pride in the achievements of their society in urban architecture and town planning, and the rediscovery and development of old crafts and techniques in construction, design, ornamentation and decoration of antique buildings, their furniture and furnishings. This created a skilled labor force that has been tapped in the country's own design industries, especially in furniture and furnishings, metal casting, glass, construction materials and the like. In fact, by now, Polish artisans, archaeologists, and restorers are famous the world over. A similar program can thus be seen as an investment not just in the country's heritage but also in the tourism, design, and creative industries. The same model has to a degree been done in other places with substantial numbers of heritage structures (e.g., Vigan, Batangas, Bohol). The very labor-intensive nature of these crafts and skills means the possibility of generating sustainable jobs for the long-term is very real.

The proposed institute for the training of skilled workers in traditional crafts (such as Escuela Taller in Intramuros) can be located in one of the existing theaters or the older buildings of Quiapo, especially along Quezon Boulevard or Recto. The nearby colleges and technical institutes can also be encouraged to develop courses along these same lines. Indeed the proposed craft institute can attain greater effectiveness by integrating its activities with the nearby educational institutions. The abundance of old buildings and the presence of a vibrant craft industry in the vicinity will serve as an efficient laboratory and training ground for the institute. Quiapo can serve as setting for the popular design establishments. For the more sophisticated and upscale design community, a similar institute can be housed in any of the available old buildings in Malate, such as those along Taft Avenue or at the Rizal Memorial Sports Complex.

The City government (and perhaps even the national government) might consider, as part of its long-term development program to establish a training and certification institute for craftspeople, similar to the one established in Warsaw after World War II, the Ateliers for the Conservation of Cultural Property, or *Pracownie Konservacji Zabytkow*. The Polish government decided to completely reconstruct the destroyed old city right after the war in a bid to recover the country's heritage and national pride but in doing so, they realized the need to train builders, technicians, and craftspeople in the construction arts, which for old buildings tend to be handmade. These included:

> old wood-building construction; historical methods of fabricating brick, ceramics and terra-cotta; conservation problems of murals, frescoes, polychrome sculpture, and painted architectural interiors; manufacture of artistic furniture, inlaid wood veneers, and elaborate parquet floors; preservation of all sculpture in all media; preservation of paintings; decorative use of exotic materials such as mother-of-pearl, tortoise-shell, inlaid and gilt precious metals, ivory, horn, lacquer, shells and feathers; restoration of historic clocks and old furniture fittings; conservation of paper and books; re-creation of historic textiles;

replication of historic and stained glass; reconstruction of wooden church interior details such as pulpit, pews, confessionals; historical fabrication methods of ferrous metals, copper, bronze, zinc, lead, silver and gold for roofs, bells, wrought-iron doors, gates, fences, firearms, chandeliers and locks; restoration of historic organs; restoration of ethnographic rural architecture and folk art.[22]

These were based on the structures of Poland; some may not be relevant for the Philippines while a number might need to be included. These serve as worthy starting points in organizing and directing the institute. Moreover the institute can provide certificates to participants who will be employed in the restoration program. The certification will professionalize the skill and can be used to find jobs in other industries that will require these crafts, such as the construction and design of luxury homes and hotels, not just in the Philippines but also abroad, and businesses involved in handcrafted items. These will create substantial number of jobs given that they are labor-intensive and focused on the luxury markets that tend to have a more stable growth compared to the other market niches.[23] The Spanish government has expressed interest in providing funds for such a training institute. In fact, one such institute, the Vigan Conservation Complex, has been established in the UNESCO World Heritage city of Vigan. Initiated and funded by the city government in collaboration with Intramuros' Escuela Taller, it was to serve as a combined arts and crafts training center, conservation laboratory and product development and research center, and would issue certificates to its successful graduates.

It is also proposed that the archaeological profession be integrated with the construction and redevelopment programs. The massive diggings involved in these long-term proposals will inevitably uncover substantial quantities of archaeological material that will need to be studied in situ for further research. Construction management will need to be trained to spot possible archaeological material and develop a system of coordination with the archaeological teams. These activities will be worthwhile in enriching the understanding of the city and the nation's history and expand the collection of historical and archaeological artifacts. Inevitably the discovery of archaeological sites will delay construction activities, thus imposing additional costs to developers. The government will need to design a system of severe penalties and some tax write offs to encourage strict compliance with archaeological requirements and still receive some compensation for the delay.

FINANCE

Many proposals for economic renewal can be summarized as a program of functional diversification which has its own unique possibilities and limitations.[24] For financing purposes, a variety of sources will need to be tapped and a measure of creativity would be called for. These proposals will require a combination of subsidy and tax incentive from the local government, support from foundations and private investments with tax inducements from the city government.

Some of the existing large corporations whose original headquarters were in Binondo can be solicited to finance the installation of markers or even the restoration of the old buildings themselves. These include GMA Network (for the Calvo Building),

Bank of the Philippine Islands (BPI), and Citibank. Their expenditure can be granted some measure of tax deduction for their property taxes, or be channeled through their corporate foundations. The expenditure on restoration and adaptive reuse or any additional expenditure required to conform to the proposed density and design regulations can be granted accelerated depreciation for income and/or property tax purposes. The old buildings can also be granted a lower assessment level (ten to twenty percent) for property tax purposes for as long as the owners restore and maintain the buildings according to the suggested design guidelines. The city government can also consider the San Nicolas district and Eastern Intramuros as locations for an experimental social housing program in the old houses for renewal and/or in new construction. This has to be undertaken within the context of a larger social housing project to cover as many households as possible, as mentioned above. Otherwise a social housing project within the historic district will only attract more informal settlers and blight the entire project. This was what happened with the Ilustre Mansion in Quiapo, which started out as social housing for six households, but now hosts dwellers in the hundreds. A punitive tax rate must also be considered for those who would demolish old buildings or defy the proposed density, zoning, and design guidelines. One method is to increase the assessment level to 50 percent or to place a steep fine for these violations.

The city government can minimize its net expenditures by assiduously monitoring and collecting taxes from the existing and new business activities that this proposal can encourage. The expenditures here can be more easily recovered by the city government from the increase in property tax collections, which will be due to the increase in property values and improved tax administration, as well as business permits and taxes.

Thus the need to identify these old structures and declare them for protection is even more acute. They need to be extended the necessary preferential tax treatment, such as lower assessment levels for as long as they are maintained as heritage structures by the owners and/or residents. And the punitive tax rates for destruction need to be designed and publicized to deter even any modification. But the main problem that faces the restoration of these old houses is the lack of financing for the restoration and renovation process itself. The preferred tax treatment with punitive rates will only be effective in maintaining the buildings but not in attracting funds for restoration in the first place.

A novel proposal (which can be considered not just by the city of Manila but also by all urban centers with old structures) will be to encourage real estate developers and construction firms to provide a measure of financing in exchange for granting these firms tax deduction and/or accelerated depreciation for expenditures on heritage renewal. This system will be a form of modification of Transfer Development Rights (TDRS). A developer with an approved permit to construct a high density structure (for as long as it is consistent with the stated land-use and density as set in the CLUPZO) may be encouraged to adopt a nearby old building for restoration and renovation, to the requirements set by the city engineer and by heritage organizations. The developer can then deduct the expenses for tax purposes or claim accelerated depreciation. This will then allow the owners/residents of the old house to finally remain there and maintain it. The city can allow for the developer to install a plaque stating their role in the restoration and the owners would also be required to allow tours for a certain number of days in the year, especially for students, professors, and experts on architecture, art, and interior design. Such a scheme has been done in France, which requires that an old building be accessible to the general public for about eleven days a year in exchange for protection, restoration funds, and preferential tax treatment.[25] To be effective, it will need to identify the location of the old buildings and the location of lots for further high-density commercial development so that applicants for permits to develop the commercial properties can be invited to participate in this scheme.

As a parenthetical remark, this proposal can actually be adopted even nationally. A developer need not provide for the restoration of a nearby heritage building but even one in a faraway town, especially if the development has no heritage structures nearby. For example a firm involved in construction of new buildings in the Cubao area can adopt some of the old buildings in Sariaya, Quezon or even in Loon, Bohol. The tax deduction on property taxes due to Quezon City can be regarded as a form of financial assistance of Quezon City, one of the country's highest-income cities, to the lower-income towns of Sariaya and Loon. Quezon City can claim the goodwill for supporting a worthwhile activity in another part of the country.

GENERAL ADMINISTRATION

To recover its expenditures the city can use this opportunity to update its tax maps and develop a mechanism for efficient tax collection in these districts. The redevelopment is expected to boost tourist, commercial, and residential activities. The improvement in these activities will also raise land values. These are the general strategies that will allow the city to recover its expenditures and contribute to the overall redevelopment of the city and her low-and-middle-income residents and workers.

This can also be an opportunity for the city to clarify the legal issues of ownership of many of the old buildings, such as the Luneta Hotel, the site of the old Jai-Alai Building, the Laperal Mansion, among others. Development of many sites not just in the city but even in the whole country has been hampered by questions of ownership, conflicting claims, and associated litigation. Updating the tax maps should also be undertaken as a mechanism for a speedy legal resolution of these property issues so that renewal and redevelopment can proceed.

The legal resolution would also cover large tracts of land currently occupied by informal settlers. In many instances the city can expropriate these lands which can thus be an opportunity for on-site development of low-cost housing for the existing residents to integrate them into the general formal economy and society. It has been suggested that this can then free up a lot of the capital of informal settlers: with secure tenurial rights over their residences, they can now be encouraged to invest more of their earnings in home improvement and in family businesses. These can in the long run generate substantial revenues from business and property taxes to recover the cost of expropriation and housing development. Thus a more vibrant economy and urban society can then be realized.[26]

Managing these vending activities will need to follow similar protocols to what was applied along Carriedo, but with minimal congestion. The city or barangay can assign specific lots and charge a rental fee with the proceeds from these fees used to

FIG. 11. Malate Church undergoing restoration by Escuela Taller, 2013

collect garbage on a regular basis in these areas. The city can also consider adapting the regulations on food safety and hygiene that the city of Bangkok implements on ambulant and sidewalk food vendors. This will encourage greater business for these food sellers who also happen to provide more authentic local recipes and food items than the larger establishments and eating places in the vicinity. Their market will increase and more income will be redistributed from the apparently more hygienic large food establishments.

The barangay can also publish and sell a visitor's guide and brochure; the tourist center can be located on Plaza del Carmen, in one of the stalls in the Lacson Underpass and along Plaza Miranda. These offices can also produce and sell souvenir brochures or guidebooks for special events, such as the Quiapo fiesta, and the Holy Week celebrations.

Finally part of the exhibits in the planned Museo ng Maynila (whenever this could be realized, like most of the proposals here) could include a permanent one on the history of planning and management of the City of Manila. These plans, proposals, programs, and projects developed through the decades will need to be made available to the general public so that they can develop a greater appreciation for the complexities of urban management and development and encourage the percolation of ideas as part of the regular administration and strategic management of the city.

NOTES

1. Anthony M. Tung, *Preserving the World's Great Cities: The Destruction and Renewal of the Historic Metropolis* (New York: Clarkson Potter Publisher, 2001), 389-96.

2. Joseph Judge, "New Grandeur for Flowering Washington," *National Geographic* 131 (4 April 1967): 500-39; Frederick Gutheim, *Worthy of the Nation: The History of Planning for the National Capital* (Washington, DC: Smithsonian Institution Press, 1976); Bernard Weisberger, *The District of Columbia* (New York: Time-Life Books, 1968), 47-57.

3. Spiro Kostof, *The City Shaped: Urban Patterns and Meanings through History* (Toronto: Bulfinch Press, 1991); John W. Reps, *Washington on View: The Nation's Capital since 1790* (Chapel Hill: University of North Carolina Press, 1991).

4. Gutheim, *Worthy of the Nation*; Weisberger, *The District of Columbia*, 47-57.

5. Jeffrey F. Meyer, *Myths in Stone: Religious Dimensions of Washington DC* (Berkeley: University of California Press, 2001), 51-98; Pamela Scott, *Temple of Liberty: Building a Capital for the New Nation* (New York: Oxford University Press, 1995), 10-34.

6. Weisberger, *The District of Columbia*, 47-57.

7. John H. Stubbs, *Time Honored: A Global View of Architectural Conservation* (Hoboken, NJ: John Wiley and Sons, 2009), 93-120.

8. Judge, "New Grandeur for Flowering Washington," 500-39; Scott, *Temple of Liberty*, 10-34.

9. Winand Klassen, *Architecture in the Philippines: Filipino Building in a Cross-Cultural Context* (Cebu: University of San Carlos, 1986), 156-60; Thomas S. Hines, *Burnham of Chicago: Architect and Planner* (New York: Oxford University Press, 1974), 1-20.

10. Klassen, *Architecture in the Philippines*, 156-60; Reynaldo Alejandro and Alfred Yuson, *Pasig: River of Life* (Manila: Unilever Philippines, 2000); Palafox Associates, *Architecture, Planning and Design: Palafox Associates the First Twenty Years* (Manila: Palafox Assciates, 2010).

11. Stubbs, *Time Honored*, 93-120; Tung, *Preserving the World's Great Cities,* 389-96.

12. Sir Peter Hall, *Cities in Civilization* (New York: Pantheon Books, 1998).

13. Meyer, *Myths in Stone: Religious Dimensions of Washington DC*; Han Meyer, *City and Port: Transformation of Port Cities, London, Barcelona, New York, Rotterdam* (Utrecht: International Books, 1999).

14. Charles Moore, *Daniel H. Burnham, Architect, Planner of Cities,* volume 2 (Boston, Massachusetts: Houghton Mifflin, 1921), cited in Hines *Burnham of Chicago*, xix.

15. Fernando Nakpil-Zialcita and Martin Tinio, *Philippine Ancestral Houses* (Manila: GCF Books, 1980).

16. Paulo Alcazaren, Luis Ferrer, and Benvenuto Icamina, *Lungsod Iskwater: The Evolution of Informality as Dominant Pattern in Philippine Cities* (Manila: Luis A Yulo Foundation for Sustainable Development, 1991).

17. Martin Perry, Lily Kong, and Brenda Yeoh, *Singapore: A Developmental City-State* (New York: John Wiley and Sons, 1997).

18. Nancy Stieber, *Housing Design and Society in Amsterdam: Reconfiguring Urban Order and Identity* (Chicago: University of Chicago Press, 1998); Tung, *Preserving the World's Great Cities*, 190-247.

19. Eva Blau, *The Architecture of Red Vienna, 1919-1934* (Cambridge. MA: MIT Press, 1999); Stieber, *Housing Design and Society in Amsterdam*; Tung, *Preserving the World's Great Cities*, 190-247.

20. Zialcita and Tinio, *Philippine Ancestral Houses* (Manila: GCF Books, 1980), 162-71.

21. Tung, *Preserving the World's Great Cities*, 73-95.

22. Tung, *Preserving the World's Great Cities*, 87-88.

23. Robb Report, various issues (2007).

24. Victor Venida, "Economic Uses for Quiapo's Antique Mansions," in *Quiapo: The Heart of Manila*, edited by Fernando Nakpil-Zialcita (Manila: Metropolitan Museum and Ateneo de Manila University, 2006), 404-24.

25. Robert Lacey, *Aristocrats*, (London: Hutchinson and Co [Publishers] Ltd., 1983), 35.

26. Hernando De Soto, *The Mystery of Capital: Why Capitalism Triumphs in the West and Fails Everywhere Else* (New York: Basic Books, 2000).

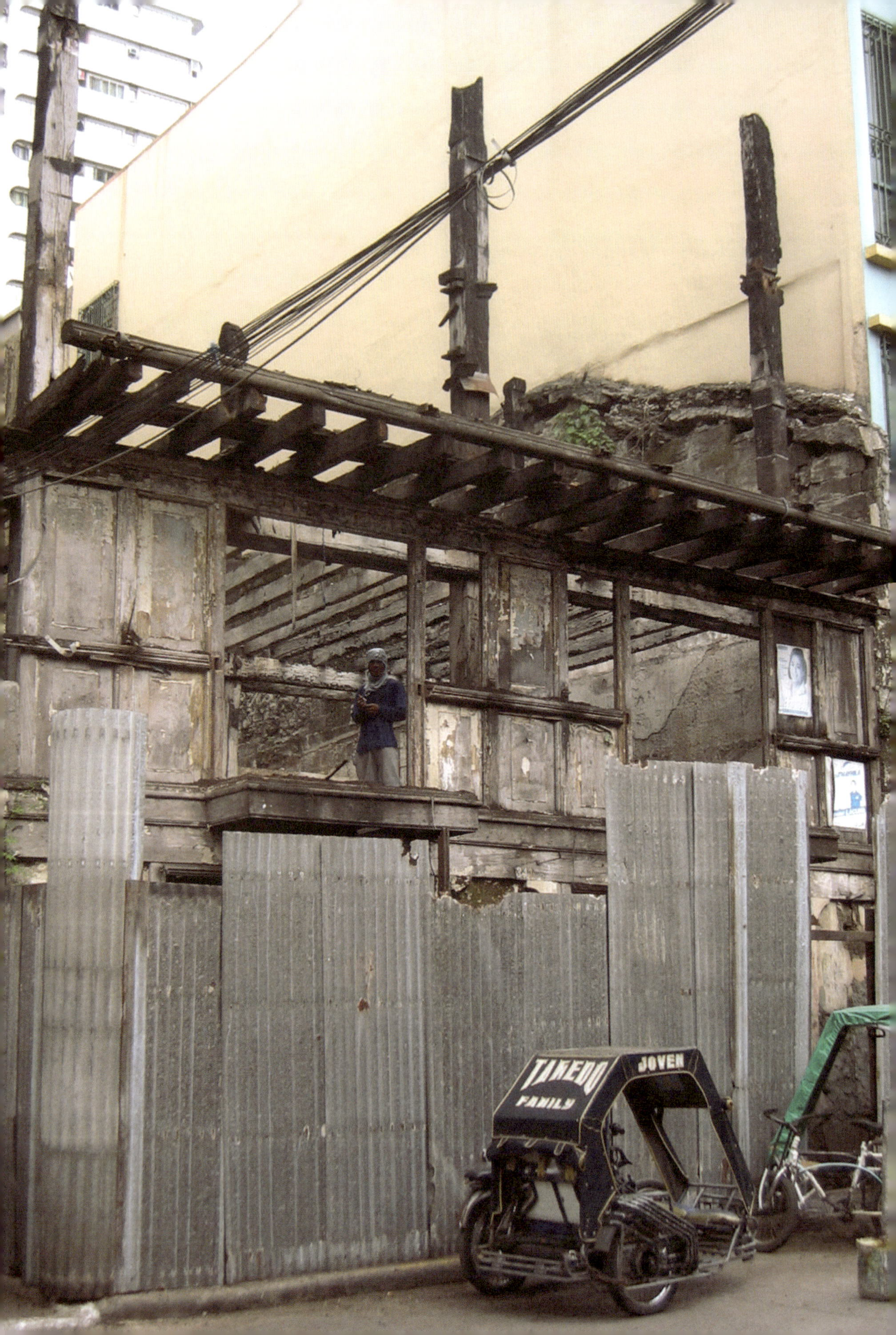
JOVEN
FAMILY

Endangered Splendor: Manila's Disappearing Heritage

ERIK AKPEDONU

ALTHOUGH MANILA IS OFTEN CITED AS THE SECOND-MOST destroyed capital city of World War II (after Warsaw, Poland), actually only the portions south of the Pasig River—including its historic core, Intramuros—were almost completely eradicated. Large parts of the districts north of the Pasig, as well as the district of Sta. Ana in the south, escaped the ravages of war largely intact.

Ironically, although the loss of "Old Manila" has since been mourned endlessly by many sectors of society, the surviving heritage on both banks of the Pasig River has ever since been allowed to be eroded and demolished bit by bit in the name of "progress" and "modernity." As early as 1977, Luning Ira and Isagani Medina in their landmark book *Streets of Manila* urged the preservation as a historic quarter of, for example, San Nicolas, where "the rate the old houses are being torn down accelerates by the day." They further state "Many Manilans feel that what San Nicolas needs is not the demolition squad, but the historical conservation team." Ira and Medina conjured an image of what San Nicolas could be: "Think of the ambience: townhouses along streets steeped in history . . . and a period atmosphere no landscape artist can ever muster."[1]

Yet, nothing happened, and more than four decades later, the situation has deteriorated dramatically: old houses in the district continue to be demolished unabated at an alarming rate, a process that has since wiped out most of the old buildings that survived the Second World War.

DETERIORATION OF MANILA'S OLD HOUSES

Rate of Loss. One of the first systematic surveys of historic buildings in Manila was conducted by Lorelei de Viana for the National Historical Institute from 1985 to

1986, particularly in Binondo and neighboring San Nicolas, which still contains the highest concentration of vintage houses in the metropolis, as well as its oldest. When the Ateneo's Manila Architectural Inventory Project revisited both districts in 2008 it found that of 159 houses documented in San Nicolas by De Viana, 101 had since been demolished, representing a loss of almost two-thirds (64 percent) over a 23-year period. Of 42 houses documented by her in Binondo, 19 had since been demolished, a loss of 45 percent.[2] As already noted by De Viana, it is no small irony that while the loss of Intramuros during World War II is mourned to this day, the demolition of authentic Spanish-era houses just across the river has been allowed to proceed unhindered for decades.

In 2000–2001 a team led by Maria Quimpo on behalf of the National Commission for Culture and the Arts (NCCA) photo-surveyed several hundred old structures in Manila City. Starting in 2008, the Ateneo team revisited those earlier documented sites, enabling it to assess the loss of heritage that has since taken place. For example, of 64 buildings listed in San Nicolas in 2000, 11 percent had been lost eight years later. Worse, the rate of loss has since accelerated significantly: by 2014 almost one-third (31 percent) of those 64 buildings had been lost to fires and demolitions.

In 2008, the Ateneo team surveyed an additional 97 vintage buildings in San Nicolas. Of the thus 161 buildings surveyed since 2000 almost a quarter (24 percent) had vanished only fourteen years later.

Although the rate of heritage loss varies significantly from district to district, it is overall dramatic. The highest loss of vintage structures was recorded in the district of Quiapo, where over a quarter (27 percent) of the buildings documented in 2000 had disappeared eight years later.

Less dramatic, albeit still alarming, is the situation in Sta. Ana and Sampaloc/Sta. Mesa, where 16 percent and 15 percent respectively of vintage structures have disappeared in the same time period. This is closely followed by Tondo and Sta. Cruz, where 13 percent of old buildings were since lost, and by San Andres-Singalong (11 percent). Paco lost one out of ten houses documented in 2000, similar to Pandacan.

Between 2000 and 2008 about 8 percent of heritage buildings were lost in the elegant district of San Miguel, around Malacañang Palace. However, most vintage structures here are in excellent state of preservation, and many are in fact occupied by diverse government agencies. Furthermore, the proximity of the presidential palace and its security requirements, like height restrictions, limit the potential of the district for speculative re-development, unlike in other parts of the city.

The areas south of the Pasig, ravaged by World War II, contain far fewer remaining vintage buildings. These are generally of more recent construction, larger, and mostly built of durable concrete; there is a lower reported rate of loss, with 6 percent in Malate and 5 percent in Ermita, respectively.

By 2008 Binondo, north of the Pasig River, had lost only about 3 percent of the buildings documented in 2000. This may be due to the fact that the majority of vintage structures in that district already fell victim to the wrecker's ball in the 1980s and 1990s, while the remaining ones are comparatively large and, thus, economically more viable concrete buildings.

No loss of heritage structures was recorded in the district of Intramuros, which, having been almost entirely destroyed during the war contains only few original structures to begin with. Instead, it is the only district where the number of "vintage" buildings is actually increasing, in the form of semi-authentic reconstructions (e.g., Beaterio de la Compañía, Ayuntamiento, Maestranza Wall, San Ignacio Church). Most of the ostensibly old buildings in Intramuros today are reconstructions from the 1970s and 1980s onwards.

Threats. A random sample of 355 vintage buildings in Metro Manila, taken from the database of the Ateneo's Manila Architectural Inventory, found that almost 11 percent of them are in poor or extremely poor physical condition, while another 32 percent showed major signs of decay and neglect.[3]

In 43 percent of the above buildings, their continued existence was under threat as stated by key informants or based on ocular observation. Where such a danger was identified, by far the largest threat was that of apparent neglect (51 percent), while flooding and rising street levels (14 percent) were particularly common in Malabon.

Other potential threats to vintage structures in Metro Manila are the plans their owners have for the future, as stated by 226 respondents (out of the above 355). While the vast majority of owners (59 percent) plan to preserve and maintain their house as is (that is, frequent repairs and maintenance works as funds permit), only 8 percent of them do so for sentimental reasons (remembrance of the ancestors, family heirloom, etc.) or because they recognize the historic value of the building. In the vast majority of cases, it is primarily done for practical reasons.

However, 18 percent of respondents plan to demolish their house in the near future, while another 11 percent plan to sell theirs, which by experience frequently also leads to subsequent demolition by the buyer. Thus, almost 30 percent of all vintage buildings may likely be demolished in the near future (as of 2014).

Only 1 percent of owners plan to restore their structure, while 4 percent intend to "renovate" it, and another 1 percent plan to remodel it. Thus, only 6 percent of vintage house owners intend to "improve" their building, whereby it remains unclear in how far these interventions will affect the historic character of their buildings. From experience, the words "restoration" and "renovation" are not always used correctly and can mean many different things to different persons, ranging from meticulous restoration to outright demolition and construction of a new building.[4] Another 5 percent mention passing on their house to the next generation, whereby it is unclear what they intend to do with the structure in the future. Less than 1 percent plan to translocate their building to another site.

Remarkably, of the 355 houses sampled, only 2 percent were officially recognized as heritage structures by the National Historical Commission of the Philippines (NHCP), the National Museum, or a local government unit. Overall, of the circa 3,800 buildings surveyed in Metro Manila, only about 150 are in any way marked or declared by any national cultural agency (NHCP, National Museum, NCCA) or by a local government unit, that is, less than 4 percent. Of these 50 percent are religious buildings (mostly churches), and another 49 percent vintage military structures (bastions and gates).

FIG. 13-15. Old houses can easily be demolished in a few days. (Quiapo, 2009)

Only circa 0.5 percent of all inventoried private residences and commercial buildings have been declared or carry a marker. While the majority of these may indeed not merit such, neither architecturally nor historically, there seems to be room for improvement here.

The current threats to Manila's remaining heritage architecture are manifold, but most can be summarized as follows:

1. Threat of **total loss** by demolition (for diverse motives) and through fires (usually followed by redevelopment of the site).

2. Threat of **partial loss**, due to partial demolition for various reasons, total or partial remodeling, reconstruction, renovation, and misunderstood "restoration."

3. Threat of **translocation**. Although the physical structure or most of it is not actually lost, it nevertheless is lost to the public sphere and to the district's historic fabric.

4. Threat of **dilapidation** to the point of structural failure or demolition order by the city engineer, caused by decades-long neglect and lack of maintenance, extreme overcrowding, and constant makeshift add-ons to an already overburdened structure.

5. Although not an existential danger, a number of historic buildings are under threat of becoming (or already have become) **invisible** to the general public, especially in the government district of San Miguel, where some of the finest mansions of the country have disappeared from public view behind high walls and sealed fences.

FIG. 16-17. Bay-by-bay demoliton and re-development of vintages houses is common (left: Sampaloc, 2000; right: same house in 2009). (Source of fig. 16: Mia Quimpo/Dewey Sergio/NCCA)

Demolition. The districts most affected by demolition and subsequent redevelopments are currently Sampaloc, Sta. Cruz, and San Nicolas. This process of re-development continues on a daily basis without the general public or heritage advocates taking much notice. This is because most buildings affected are not very well-known and thus receive little or no media coverage, unlike more prominent ones, such as the Jai-Alai Building in 2000, or, more recently, the MERALCO Building in Ermita and the Alberto House in Biñan, Laguna.

The demolition of an old house in Quiapo (see FIG. 13–15) is a typical case: Probably one of the oldest nineteenth-century houses in Quiapo, it was issued a demolition permit and was subsequently dismantled in 2009. Its demolition went (almost) entirely unnoticed by heritage advocates, except for a lone entry in an internet blog. An old wooden house can easily be demolished within a day or two, thus escaping the attention of city officials or heritage advocates. According to one architect involved in heritage preservation, about fifty old houses nationwide are thus lost every month.[5]

A variation of outright complete demolition is the widespread partial demolition of a vintage structure. It is particularly common, though not very obvious, with row-houses. It also occasionally happens to single-detached homes, with dramatic visual effect. Thus, a house can be demolished bay-by-bay, becoming smaller every couple of years, until the last remaining bay finally falls to the wrecker's ball. Partial demolition is typically the result of a house inherited by multiple parties, who subdivide the building among themselves, with each party doing with their portion as they deem fit. In cases of multiple joint ownership, on the other hand, sale and complete demolition is an easy way of equally sharing a real estate inheritance. Row-houses or *accessorias* in particular lend themselves to partial demolition due to their functional and structural makeup. Many historic row houses still extant in Quiapo, Sta. Cruz, and San Nicolas once used to be much larger than today, as seen in this row house in Sampaloc (see FIG. 16–17). Still intact in 2001, by 2009 three bays have been replaced with a new and larger concrete structure.

Fire. A constant threat to most vintage houses is the omnipresent danger of fire. With most vintage houses built largely or entirely of wood, they are particularly prone to

FIG. 18-20. Fires have consumed innumerable vintage buildings. Most wooden houses are destroyed beyond repair. (Top: San Nicolas, 2009; below: Quiapo, 2008)

conflagrations, a situation confounded by the fact that many of these houses are badly overcrowded and poorly maintained. Many fine vintage houses have fallen victim to fire disasters, especially in San Nicolas and Quiapo.

Common causes for fire outbreaks are illegal connections to the electric grid, widespread in buildings occupied by poor families or informal settlers. Others have overloaded internal wiring due to overcrowding, outdated or unmaintained internal electric wiring, amateurish repairs, and poorly-maintained electric appliances, such as electric fans and air-conditioning units.

Other often-claimed causes include arson by owners to evict tenants and/or squatters, fireworks (which a few years ago destroyed many old Quiapo houses on New Year's Eve), cooking in rooms, and leaving lit candles inside rooms (e.g., during brownouts).

A significant recent loss to fire, for example, was the Padilla Accessoria, the largest remaining old storehouse in San Nicolas. Converted to residential use it became an overcrowded slum, and was destroyed by fire in November 2007. It was subsequently demolished.

Neglect. Closely connected to overcrowding is the poor physical condition of many vintage houses especially in Quiapo, San Nicolas, and Sta. Cruz. Neglect and overcrowding lead to the fast deterioration of a building's fabric, weakness of its structure, and the decline of its internal infrastructure (e.g., toilets, electric wiring, plumbing, etc.). On the other hand, in the same districts (especially San Nicolas) many vintage houses are either partially or completely vacant, which has the same effect: vacant buildings likewise deteriorate fast, as no more maintenance is undertaken, and critical

FIG. 21-22. Many old houses have been subdivided and become overcrowded. (Left: Quiapo, 2009; right: San Nicolas, 2009)

damages remain undetected and thus unrepaired, resulting in fast decay, especially of wooden structures.

Aside from vacancies and overcrowding, neglect is typically the result of simple lack of interest on the part of the owners; high costs of maintenance, particularly of wooden structures; ownership disputes and court cases where decisions about maintenance—or demolition—are deferred until the case is settled; complex ownership structures (e.g., multiple joint ownership, absentee, or even overseas owners preventing investment and maintenance); inheritance arrangements, and others.

The former Ilustre Mansion in Quiapo drastically illustrates how a once "fabulous" mansion rapidly degenerated into an overcrowded slum (see FIG. 25–26). Once one of the most elegant houses in Quiapo, it became a social housing project in the 1980s, starting with only three families, but today is said to house 120 to 150 families. Even if these figures may be exaggerated, as nobody knows the exact number of residents, the entire building is hopelessly overcrowded. Additional floors have been added and makeshift extensions affixed

FIG. 23-24.
Many historic buildings are in a deplorable state of neglect. (Left: Quiapo, 2009; right: Sampaloc, 2009)

FIG. 25-26. The Ilustre Mansion in Quiapo exemplifies the fall of many once grand houses: in 1980 (left) and in 2009 (right). Source of fig. 25: Zialcita, Fernando N. and Martin I. Tinio Jr., *Philippine Ancestral Houses* (Quezon City: GFC Books, 1980).

to all exterior walls. The barangay hall in front of the house, where a fountain used to be, now extends over the sidewalk. All these have rendered this once beautiful mansion unrecognizable today. Similarly overcrowded and neglected dwellings can be found in many parts of Manila.

Renovation and Remodeling. Vintage buildings, when not outright demolished or neglected, still come under the threat of one-time or gradual remodeling, often termed "renovation." Although the physical structure remains, the building suddenly or gradually loses its historic look and character, ultimately becoming indistinguishable from more recent constructions. Again one of the districts most affected by remodeling is San Nicolas, where many heritage preservation problems come together at the same time, as under a magnifying glass.

Most commonly, upper floor façades are replaced with contemporary, often inexpensive and cheap-looking

FIG. 27-29. Many vintage buildings are much older than they look. The continuous replacement of original materials gradually eradicates their historic character. (San Nicolas, 2009)

materials, such as corrugated iron sheets, Hardiflex boards, or plywood, usually in combination with new "modern" windows. New roofs of corrugated and galvanized iron sheets have today displaced all Spanish-era tile roofs except three (two in San Nicolas). Ground floor walls of adobe or brick are usually replaced with concrete hollow blocks and steel gates.

Gradual remodeling is common: significant architectural elements are replaced by contemporary ones piece by piece over a prolonged period of time, with the building gradually losing more and more of its historic character until it is entirely wiped out. The process may start with the roof, then proceed with new façade boards and windows, followed by the covering of the *espejos*, and perhaps *ventanilla* grills, and finalized with new ground floor walls and gates, ultimately rendering the building's look to either "brand-new" or a "hodge-podge" of incoherent and unharmonious materials. In either case, the historic character is lost.

Similarly, the often well-intentioned enlargement or improvement of churches, or their reconstruction after World War II, can lead to the irreversible loss of historic fabric and character. For example, the structural columns of the central nave in the Binondo and Quiapo churches were removed in the 1960s and 1970s, respectively. This allowed the altar to be visible from all seats, but it also gave both structures the dull feel of a gymnasium rather than that of a sacred edifice. Oversized, brightly colored ceiling paintings, illogical details, and poor proportions also make the new Binondo Church—as many others—a visual agony. Another popular trend is the erection of massive porte-cochères in front of carefully proportioned Baroque facades, and the cladding of old buildings with tiles, as seen recently in the church of Sta. Cruz. Here, brightly colored concrete tiles spoil the original careful balance between richly ornamented portions of the façade and bell tower, and plain unadorned walls. The use of overly bright colors remains a perennial problem in many church renovation projects, be it overdecorated retablos, shiny floor tiles, or garish murals.

FIG. 30–31. Arcades, which separate the central nave from the side aisles, create spacial focus and orientation. Left: Quiapo Church, before remodeling (image courtesy of Ar. Gerard Lico); right: Quiapo Church today (photograph by Judgefloro, image in the public domain, retrieved from Wikimedia Commons, see p. 394)

Restoration. A rather unexpected threat to heritage buildings comes from poorly perceived and executed "restorations." A professional restoration is an expensive, multidisciplinary process that requires thorough understanding of a building's history, its fabric and structure, and knowledge of many related fields, such as painting, chemistry, carpentry, etc. It also requires the thorough documentation of the structure before the intervention, during the restoration process, and thereafter. Unfortunately, in the past (and sometimes up to now) many "restorations" were done with best intentions, but little regard for those requirements, resulting in more harm than good done to the building. A typical case is the "restoration" of the Sta. Ana Church and convent in the 1970s, which involved the removal from the external walls of the *paletada*, the protective lime plaster applied on top of the adobe walls. Without the plaster, the porous and soft adobe stones absorb much more water, and start pulverizing quickly. Sometimes cement is applied as plaster instead, which, however, is much denser than paletada. Once water manages to seep into the masonry, it becomes trapped there instead of gradually evaporating, thus likewise hastening the deterioration of the adobe stone underneath. Then there is the problem of invisible loss of original fabric, such as when original wooden rafters and girders are replaced with modern ones of steel, as happened in Tuguegarao and Malabon, or when adobe walls are replaced with plastered cement blocks. Being "living heritage" churches need to constantly adapt to ever-growing parish populations, thus necessitating constant extensions with the resultant loss of original fabric.

FIG. 32–33.
Without its protective lime plaster, adobe stone quickly deteriorates. (Left: house in San Nicolas; right: Sta. Ana convent)

Translocation. While the occasional relocation of individual traditional houses has been common practice in the Philippines for centuries, translocation has recently taken on a new dimension as many significant historic structures are relocated from their original plots to new sites within or outside the metropolis. Wealthy individuals have transplanted a good number of important historic houses out of Manila in recent years, for private or for commercial use. The districts affected thus far are San Nicolas, Quiapo, and Sampaloc.

In 2006, one of the most impressive houses in Quiapo, the Enriquez Mansion along Hidalgo Street, was disassembled piece by piece, and rebuilt in Bagac, Bataan. Two row houses from San Nicolas had earlier been transported to the same site. Likewise, in 2009, the most famous mansion of San Nicolas, the three-storey *Casa Bizantina* was dismantled and resurrected in Bagac (see FIG. 34–35). The recent controversy about the partial relocation of the historic Alberto House from Biñan, Laguna to Bagac has again directed attention to this new trend, which is controversially debated among heritage advocates (see chapter "Curse or Blessing?—Moving Immovable Heritage" on p. 309).

The threat to Manila's heritage is not limited to individual buildings, but also to its urban layout. Long cherished vistas are threatened by new developments, such as condominiums rising in the line-of-sight of important landmarks like the Rizal Monument in Rizal Park, or the planned reclamations that will forever alter the fabled view of Manila Bay. As early as the 1980s, the construction of the MRT ruined the sweeping vistas of Avenida Rizal in Sta. Cruz, and Acacia-lined Taft Avenue in Ermita and Malate. Today, pylons of fast-food outlets dominate many ancient vistas, such as in Sta. Ana. High-rise condominiums and office towers now hover over skylines, which were marked, for centuries, by the domes and bell towers of ancient churches. The consolidation of small lots into larger ones for large-scale redevelopments alters the fabric of previously small-scale quarters and neighborhoods. Road widening projects threaten to slice off historic facades, while monstrous flyovers are built atop historic vistas, plazas, and parks, as recently in Paco. Parking space in front of buildings alters narrow historic streetscapes even in the absence of historic buildings, as in Intramuros. Small-scale loss of heritage also constantly happens, such as when metal letters on tombs (Roxas Tomb), bronze plaques and parts of statuary (Legazpi-Urdaneta Monument), and even entire cannons (as in Intramuros) disappear, apparently stolen to be sold to antique dealers or to junk yards as scrap metal.

The many threats to Manila's heritage even include its intangible elements, such as historic street names that are frequently changed to honor politicians or national heroes, thereby eradicating parts of the urban narrative that evolved over centuries. The same effects are caused by the alteration of historic boundaries of ancient districts, as in Malate and Singalong, which erode the emotional attachment of residents to their neighborhoods. The loss of Manila's heritage continues unabated, as seen in the wave of demolitions in 2014, aptly termed the "September Massacre" by then

FIG. 34-35. Translocation: Threat or Blessing? Enriquez Mansion from Quiapo rebuilt in Bagac, Bataan (below). In contrast, an increasing number of buildings in Bagac are rather fanciful reconstructions of long-vanished historic buildings from Manila, such as the Hotel de Oriente (above).

HCS president Ivan Henares, when three significant heritage structures were touched within one month.

As of 2020, the fate of many other historic buildings hangs in the balance, such as the Manila Veterans Hospital and Quezon Institute in Quezon City, the Fabella Memorial Hospital in Sta. Cruz, the historic Sunico Foundry in San Nicolas, the Modernist PhilamLife Building in Ermita, and even the iconic El Hogar Building in Binondo.

In whatever manner it comes, Manila seems destined to continue losing its heritage. Without authentic, tangible and intangible witnesses to its history and past artistic and cultural achievements the city will continue to lose its identity, its unique character, its "sense of place." Today, Manila is in danger of quickly becoming a nondescript, interchangeable "somewhere" in a "geography of nowhere."[6]

NOTES

1. Luning B. Ira and Isagani R. Medina, *Streets of Manila* (Manila: GCF Books, 1977), 69, 71.
2. Lorelei de Viana, NHI Study 1987, unpublished. The extensive and detailed material is available in the archives of the National Historical Commission of the Philippines.
3. A fifth of all houses were in excellent condition (20 percent), while the remaining houses (38 percent) were in good condition, with only slight signs of "wear and tear."
4. Erik Akpedonu and Czarina Saloma, *Casa Boholana: Vintage Houses of Bohol* (Quezon City: Ateneo de Manila University Press, 2011), 103.
5. Ivan Henares, "Discussions on the Bagac Project," *Heritage Conservation Society*, last updated 17 August 2008, http://heritageconservation.multiply.com/journal/Item/28›.&show_interstitial=1&u=%2Fjournal%2Fite.
6. James Howard Kunstler, *The Geography of Nowhere. Decline of America's Man-made Landscape* (New York: Simon and Schuster, 1993).

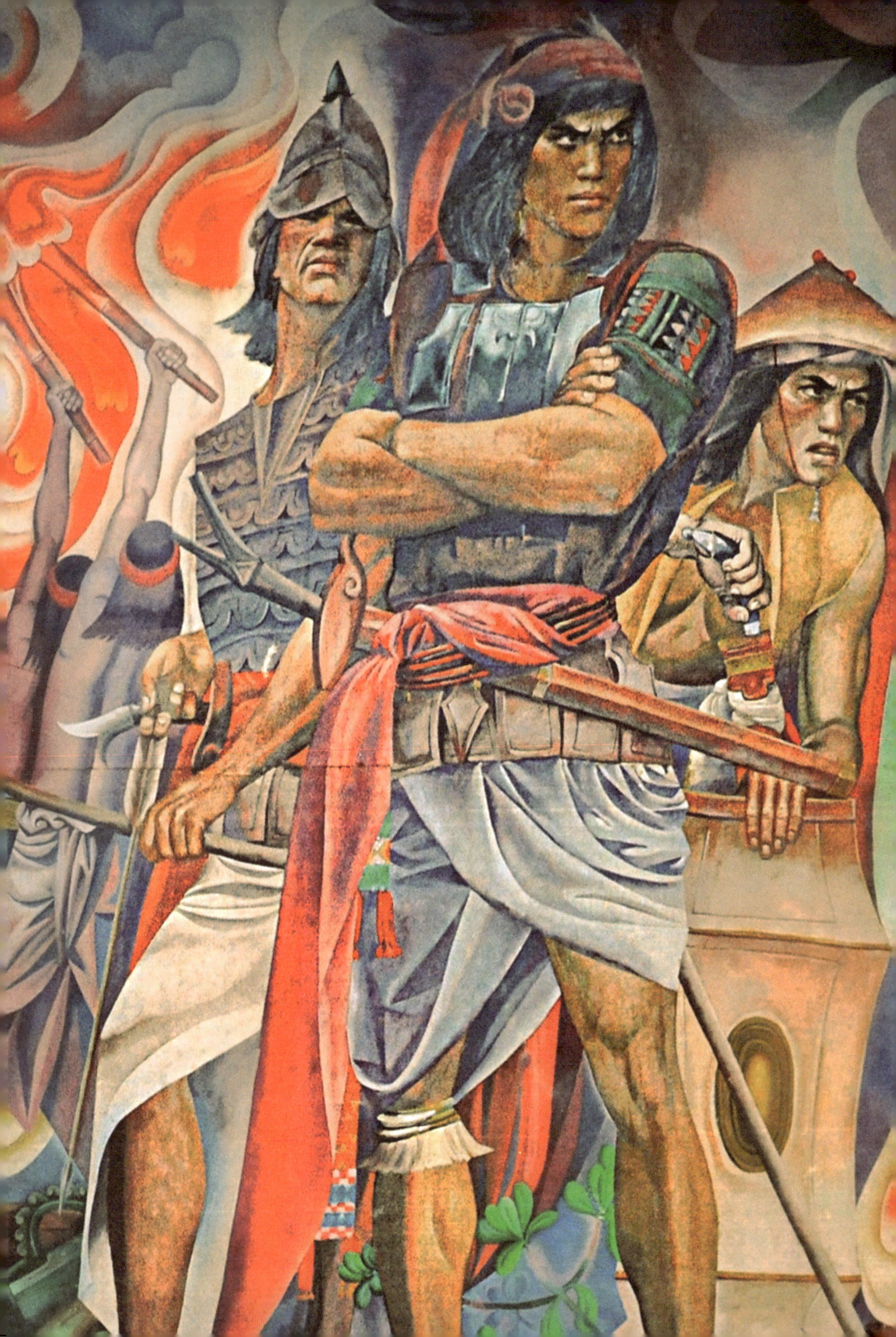

INTRAMUROS
Mother City

FERNANDO N. ZIALCITA

PRESENT-DAY MANILA IS MADE UP OF DISTRICTS. TONDO, ITS biggest, is actually older than the district of Intramuros where Manila began as a trading settlement in the early sixteenth century. The tenth-century copperplate fragment found in Pila, Laguna mentions "Tundun" along with some other settlements in the Tagalog area. There is no mention of Manila.[1]

If urbanism is the criterion, Jolo in Sulu may well be the oldest in the entire archipelago. Nonetheless, post-1571 Manila or, more specifically, Intramuros before the twentieth century, can claim to have mothered many of the Philippines' cities. It can even claim to have mothered the political unity that we call "Philippines." And if we are talking of stone structures, Intramuros has the oldest of these in the islands, for here began building in stone after the fire of 1583, as will be seen. When discussing Intramuros, particular issues inevitably arise. Firstly, that there were already cities in Luzon and Visayas even before Spanish Manila was founded. Secondly, that Intramuros was only for Spaniards, not native Filipinos, down to the close of Spanish rule.

SUPRABARANGAY OR CITY?

Robert Reed is an urban geographer who has specialized in studying the beginnings of urbanism in Java and Luzon. In his third book on Manila, he notes that when Westerners entered Southeast Asia for the first time, there were already ancient cities: Malacca (Malay Peninsula), Ayutthaya (Thailand), Majapahit (Java), Ava (Burma/Myanmar). However, "At the dawn of the sixteenth century an indigenous urban tradition was wanting only in the Philippines."[2] He regards indigenous Manila and Cebu as "suprabarangays" rather than as true cities. Nonetheless, he says, they manifested urbanizing tendencies, and were on the road to becoming truly urban.[3]

What features distinguish a city or urban center from a farming or fishing settlement?[4] This has been much discussed by urban geographers, sociologists, and anthropologists.[5] Firstly, a city is a type of settlement where most residents do not directly engage in farming or fishing as their livelihood. While they may own farms and fisheries, they engage others to do the planting and fishing for them. They devote themselves on a full-time basis to non-agricultural pursuits such as commerce, manufacture, arts and crafts, the sciences, teaching, the service of religion, and administration. Hence the variety of experiences and expertise associated with the city. Secondly, with urbanism, a radical break appears in the social fabric. Class differences become sharper. While most earn a living through manual work, others, such as teachers, merchants, and government officials, are engaged in mental work where physical exertion is not needed. Furthermore, while vertical divisions are sharpened in the city, on the other hand, a broader feeling of sympathy develops horizontally. In contrast to those who live in rural villages, city-dwellers are compelled to think and feel for those who are not even their kin, for now they must live and work with strangers. Lastly, making the city possible is the existence of the State—a polity where either a ruling body or an individual can levy taxes on a continuous basis, control the use of weapons and violence with the help of an armed force, and pass and implement laws.

These characteristics of the city or urban center are particularly relevant for our book, for they help explain why with the formation of true cities, monumental architecture, particularly of stone, finally appeared in Luzon and Visayas in the late sixteenth century. City-dwelling power-holders, such as landholders, wealthy merchants, or state officials, were able to organize, to pay for or even to demand, through taxes, the services of diverse specialists (e.g., woodcutters, masons, carpenters, ironsmiths, scribes, engineers, managers) to build large constructions of stone and wood. A steady supply of food and other provisions was assured by the control exerted by these power-holders over farmers in the countryside. The spread of an organized religion via priests and theologians, ascribing wondrous powers to the rulers and bringing together unrelated individuals into one worshipping congregation, further consolidated the power-holders' authority. It also made it easier to raise complex stone structures. In Brahmanic kingdoms, the king was the incarnation of the god Vishnu; in Buddhist kingdoms, the king was the protector of Buddha's teachings; in sultanates, the ruler claimed descent from the Prophet Mohammed; in Catholic Spain, the king was regarded as the guardian of the Faith. In the name of these beings endowed with uncanny powers and with their contributions, large stone edifices were reared.

FIG. 37. Statue of King Philip II of Spain in front of the Aduana, Intramuros

One deterrent to the formation of true urban centers in pre-hispanic Luzon and Visayas, according to Reed, was the prevalent food technology. Around bodies of fresh water, such as the great lake we now call Laguna de Bay, wet rice cultivation was easy to practice because the waters overflowed annually. One could sow from the boats. While the technology for wet rice cultivation

FIG. 38. Manila ca. 1584–1600 (recent estimate by art historian Dr. Pedro Luengo), painting on a Mexican wooden chest. Courtesy of Museo José Luís Bello y González, Puebla, Mexico.

was known by many Filipinos, conditions for practicing it were often not favorable. Forests were thick and the topography often rugged. The common norm in the Visayas was thus shifting cultivation or *kaingin*: Burn and cut a patch of the forest to plant a garden of many crops for two or three years and then move to another part of the forest. Inevitably settlements, called the *barangay*, tended to be dispersed and at times impermanent.[6] The pre-hispanic barangay was small; it was organized around a ruling kin group and its followers. Conflicts could erupt between neighboring barangay and would be unresolved because the barangay heads, the *datus*, could choose not to defer to a higher authority.[7] Sometimes the barangay sat by itself among the farms; at other times it clustered together with other barangays, as among the Tagalogs, to form a *bayan*.[8] But who would rule a cluster of, say, four barangays, four kin groups and their followers? Who would be the paramount chief? In the absence of a fixed protocol, conflicts could break out.

Highlighting the significance of the pre-modern city and its partner, the predemocratic state, should not blind us to its injustices. Today, democracy is indeed the universal ideal. Nonetheless we have to see past social phenomena in their historical context. On the one hand the pre-modern city all over the world indeed widened the gap between rich and poor, between the well-connected few and the many with limited networks. On the other hand, the great advances of humankind in the arts, sciences, and philosophy over the past six thousand years were facilitated by urban centers. Let us be wary of judging pre-twentieth century Manila and other cities solely by today's democratic standards. Neither Manila nor other cities in pre-twentieth century Asia and Europe could possibly measure up.

Before 1571, noble families had consolidated their rule over wide swaths of settlements between the River Pasig and Laguna de Bay. In what is now Sta. Ana, there ruled Lakan Tagkan and his wife Buan whose domain reached down to Pasay. Tondo then included what we now call Binondo, and thus extended down to the Pasig. It was ruled by Lakan Dula, also called Raha Dula.[9] What about Manila? The renowned expert on

Philippine prehistory, William Henry Scott, claims that "the chiefdom of Manila ... was probably founded as a Bornean trading colony about 1500, with a royal prince marrying into the local ruling family."[10] This was a common avenue through which Islam spread throughout insular Southeast Asia. He adds that Rajah Matanda, whose real name was Ache, was the grandson of Sultan Bulkeiah of Brunei who is identified by Brunei folk history as Nakhoda Ragam—he who had "taken Manila" with a legendary cannon called Si-Gantar Alam (Earthshaking Thunderer).[11] Rajah Soliman was Rajah Ache's nephew. Both were related to the princely families of Sulu and Borneo.[12] As was the custom then, authority was shared between two rulers, the Rajah Mura or "the young ruler," and the Rajah Matanda or "the old ruler." Their fortified settlement controlled the trade between the bay and the upstream settlements. Soliman had developed alliances with the rulers of Lubao and Macabebe in Pampanga. Most likely his authority would have covered much of the southern curve of Manila Bay. But his hold seemed recent and precarious, for Chinese traders complained to the invading Martin de Goiti in 1570 that Soliman compelled them to pay a fee at the risk of having their rudders removed. Indigenous residents also complained of his exactions.[13] His authority seemed not to have been recognized as yet by some sectors.

Nonetheless, under Soliman and his uncle, "Manila was the main entrepôt in the archipelago: here exports were accumulated and imports redistributed."[14] While some of the goods were carried by local entrepreneurs, most were handled by foreigners: "Malay, Bornean, Chinese, Japanese, Siamese, or Cambodian, even Portuguese."[15] Exports were not limited to those from the islands, which were mostly forest products such as wax, honey, dyewoods, deerskins, civet and heavy timber, they also included the resale of merchandise from elsewhere, such as Timor sandalwood, Bornean camphor, Siamese rhinoceros horns, and slaves from Siam and Borneo.[16] For local consumption, articles imported were largely manufactured goods such as "silk and cotton textiles, porcelain and crockery, fine mats, hardware, gongs, kettles, and swords."[17]

In 1571, thanks to intimidation and superior weaponry, Miguel Lopez de Legazpi took possession of the dominion of Soliman and his followers. The latter were relocated down south along the bay to what is now Malate. Indeed this was naked aggression.[18] On the other hand, it was Legazpi who transformed Manila into a city that became a major trading emporium in Asia and the capital of a state (to be precise, an extension of the Spanish empire) that embraced the archipelago from Batanes to Mindanao.[19]

I personally am against war and the use of weaponry. I also prefer to settle disputes by listening to the various sides. However, the reality is that in the pre-democratic, pre-nineteenth century world, most states, regardless of culture, emerged on the basis of coercion. It was also through coercion, tempered by negotiation, that new dominions were added. Over time, coercion would be rationalized as legitimate authority—especially if a common religion and world view were shared. Many Filipinos admire the Java-based Majapahit Empire (1293–1527) which extended from the Malay Peninsula and Sumatra all the way to Timor—and wish we were part of it. But how did its rulers add territory and subjects to their realm? Through bitter conquest. For outsiders like us, it seems natural that the Javanese-speaking rulers of Majapahit should rule over non-Javanese like the Sundanese who live in Western Java where Jakarta is located. But the Sundanese anthropologist Budi Gunawan told me that

FIG. 39. Map of Manila by Antonio Fernandez Rojas, ca. 1713 (Courtesy of Ortigas Foundation Library)

the memory of the bloody massacre of their lords by the imperial forces led by the counselor Gajah Mada rankles even today. Gajah Mada may be a hero to the Central Javanese but not to them.[20] How did the emperors of early Japan establish their sway over the hundreds of local chiefs of the archipelago during the fifth to seventh centuries AD? Again through subjugation.[21] In Hawaii, where I studied anthropology, Kamehameha I is admired as the great chief who finally unified the archipelago. But how did he do it? In 1795, his forces landed on Oahu—which we think of as naturally part of Hawaii but was then a separate realm—pursued the resisting forces to the Nuuanu Cliffs and pushed hundreds of them over the precipice.[22] And finally how was Spain herself integrated as one? After two centuries of warfare, the Romans finally succeeded in the first century BC in uniting the different polities into a province called Hispania.[23]

Nick Joaquin, famous for his historical essays, has two insights that are relevant for our evaluation of Spanish Manila. First, the unification of the archipelago could not have been done solely by a few Spanish soldiers. They needed allies, particularly the Pampangos and Tagalogs. Second, the Filipino's identity is that of a twin. On the one hand, like Humabon of Cebu, who received Magellan and baptism, we have accepted and modified Western influences; on the other hand, like Lapu-Lapu who slew Magellan, we have been the perpetual rebel. Yes, we accept Christianity; but no, we are also skeptical and anti-clerical. Indeed we continue to harbor pagan beliefs and practices.[24]

FIG. 40. Plaza de Armas, 1847, Biblioteca National de España

AT THE CORE

Intramuros de Manila speeded up the making of the Philippines as a distinct nation-state. The boundaries of modern Philippines extending from Batanes to Tawi-Tawi are a direct product of Spanish rule. Over the centuries what integrated the entire archipelago was an administrative structure whose smallest units, the *barrio* (now called once again the barangay), were clustered into the *pueblo* (today the municipality), which in turn were integrated into a *provincia* (now called province). This came from Spain. So likewise did our legal tradition which is based on civil law and not on the Chinese or Indian or Islamic.

Spanish missionaries set forth to create urban settlements which were permanent in character, nucleated, with buildings of solid materials, and embracing hitherto unrelated kin groups. To create concentrated settlements, the missionaries popularized the plow (*arado*), though in its Chinese, not European form.[25] They organized pueblos centered on a plaza where loomed the place of worship and the government building and near where one could shop at a market. The scheme drew on at least a millennium and a half of urban experience in the Mediterranean world. To keep fires from spreading, major buildings were built of stone. After the fire of 1583 consumed the thatch and bamboo structures of Spanish Manila, a newly arrived Jesuit, Antonio Sedeño, introduced the art of building in stone. In this, of course, he was aided by the Chinese who had a tradition of stone construction even older than that of the Spaniards.[26]

INTRAMUROS: MOTHER CITY 65

FIG. 41. Puente de España, ca. 1858, from the Karuth Album (courtesy of Alejandro Padilla y Zobel and Georgina Padilla Zobel de MacCrohon)

FIG. 42. Old Sto. Domingo Church, ca. 1858, from the Karuth Album (courtesy of Alejandro Padilla y Zobel and Georgina Padilla Zobel de MacCrohon)

FIG. 43. Pasig River and Manila Harbor, ca. 1858, from the Karuth Album (courtesy of Alejandro Padilla y Zobel and Georgina Padilla Zobel de MacCrohon)

FIG. 44. Courtyard of the Zobel House, ca. 1858, from the Karuth Album (courtesy of Alejandro Padilla y Zobel and Georgina Padilla Zobel de MacCrohon)

Plow agriculture made it easier to bring barangays (*barrio* in Spanish) together into one bayan under a determinate structure. So likewise did the periodic municipal elections ordained by Manila. The heads of the barangays (*cabezas de barangay*) elected someone from among themselves to head the town as the gobernadorcillo or mayor. From Intramuros de Manila radiated Christianity, a new world view, which offered an alternative vision of the world where—theoretically—all men and women, being children of One God, were equal in dignity. Every year, the community expressed its solidarity during Christmas, Holy Week and the town or district fiesta through the churches and plazas all over the island. While many of us are anticlerical or even Masonic, we remain influenced by Spain, for our brand of anticlericalism and Masonry is Latin. Our social customs incorporate many Spanish elements. To show respect to our friends and relatives we kiss (*beso*) them; we serenade (*jarana*) the fiancée (*novia*); we throw a farewell party for the bride-to-be (*despedida de soltera*); and we insist on a proper and festive church wedding (*boda*).

All these practices emanated from Intramuros de Manila which was the political, religious, educational, social, and cultural center of the Philippines. Because these practices became common in the lowlands, it was easier to visualize the entire archipelago as a vast home called "Filipinas." In turn this expression became the basis for nationalist feelings at the close of the nineteenth century. Though *bayan* originally referred to a settlement consisting of one or more barangays, by 1896, it had come to mean the entire archipelago.

During the late Spanish period, Binondo and Sta. Cruz were the commercial centers. But these outlying suburbs, hitherto independent municipalities, were absorbed into Manila as Manila became *extramuros*. Under the Americans, the outward growth of Manila beyond the Walled City accelerated. In the process, government offices and schools, such as Ateneo de Manila and the University of Santo Tomás, moved outside the walls. Nick Joaquin said, however, that before 1945, the festivities of Intramuros from January to December gave it a special place in the Manileño's life:

> In October all Manila assembled intra muros to glorify the Santo Rosario and La Naval de Manila. In November the Augustinians celebrated a novena for the souls in Purgatory; and the Recollects came up with the their biggest fiesta of the year: the pageant in honor of the nuptials of Mary and Joseph. In December the Immaculate Conception was feasted by the Jesuits, the Franciscans, the Cathedral and all Intramuros, which hung out white and blue flags and illuminated itself on the eve of the Purísima.[27]

But World War II dawned on Manila on 8 December, on the Feast of the Immaculate Conception.

FIG. 45. Aerial photograph of Intramuros in the 1920s

THE DESTRUCTION

First destroyed by Japanese raids in 1941 was Sto. Domingo Church. In February 1945, it was most of the Walled City. The Japanese Naval Forces under Rear Admiral Iwabuchi decided to deny the returning Americans the nearby port facilities and to take a last stand in "Fortress Intramuros" and in Ermita and Malate. At the same time the Americans surrounded them completely, without allowing a chance to retreat from the heavily populated areas. They pounded Southern Manila with artillery. According to some British scholars, "in their overwhelming desire to minimize infantry casualties the Americans lost sight of the need to protect the Filipino population."[28] Meanwhile the Japanese went on a rampage south of the river, killing civilians, especially the men, and raping women before bayoneting them. In one instance, 125 men, including priests, were herded into shelters before the Cathedral. Then the Japanese lobbed grenades through the air holes. Miraculously six survived.[29]

When at last Intramuros and the rest of southern Manila were liberated, many houses, schools and churches had lost their roofs, but still had relatively intact walls, as indicated by aerial photos. Recounted a Spanish priest of the ordeal, "what survived Japanese dynamite soon fell before the chains and the hammers of the Yankee army." The intent was "to create space for tented accommodation and supplies."[30] Francisco Gonzalez, who survived the horrors, recounts in an interview[31] that his house had indeed burned down. But the walls still stood. When he came back a week later,

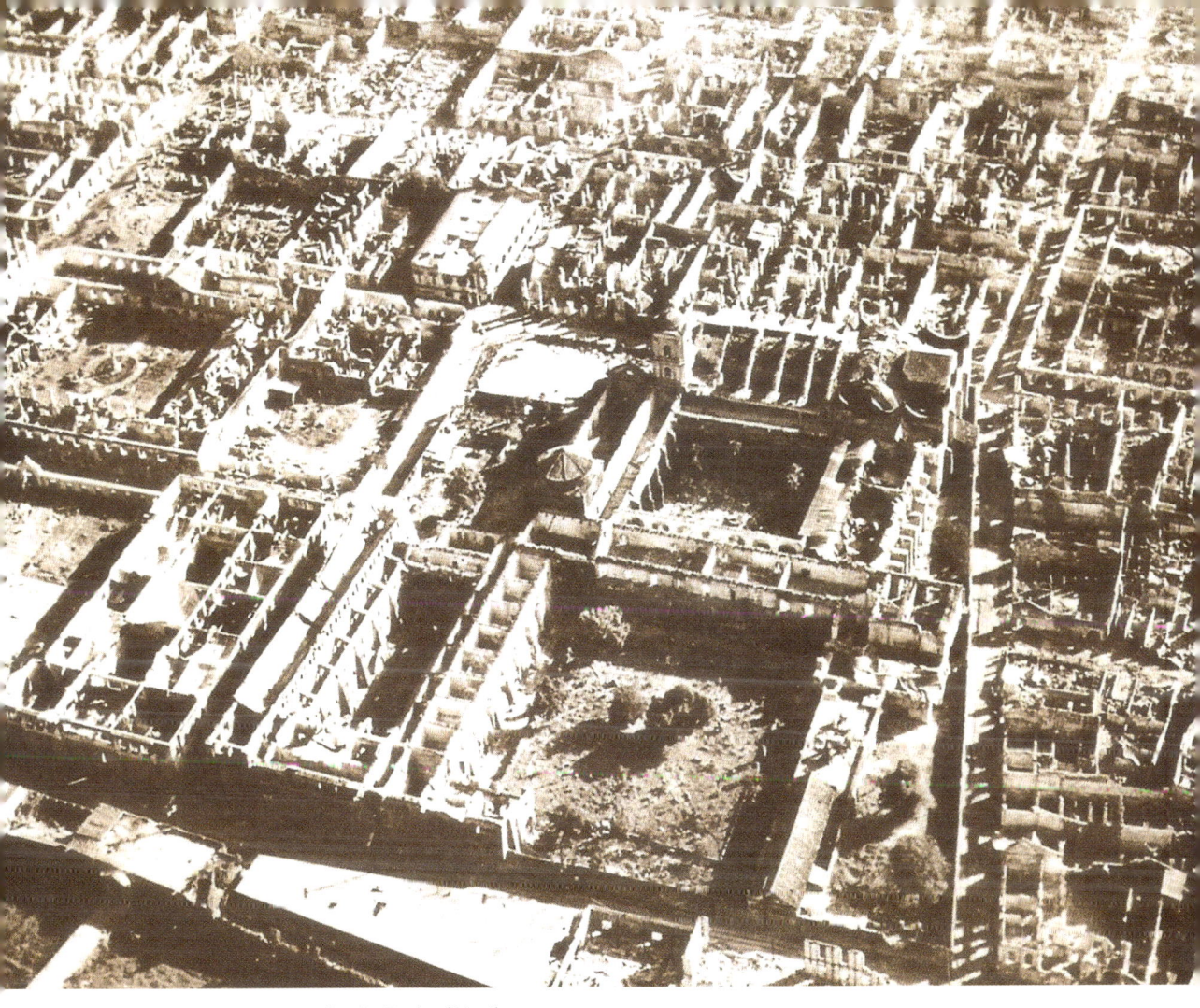

FIG. 46. Intramuros after the Battle of Manila, 1945

the walls had been cleared by American bulldozers. Apparently the beauty and the grandeur of the Walled City did not matter to key generals in the US military. Wrote General Beightler in a report on his division:

> We used these shells and plastered the Walled City until it was a mess.... We made a churned-up pile of dust and scrap out of the imposing, classic government buildings.... If I could have had those dive bombers too, I might have made the big rubble into little rubble. So much for Manila. It is a ruined city—unhealthy, depressing, poverty stricken. Let us thank God our cities have been spared such a state.[32]

After the rubble had been cleared, much of Intramuros became a huge slum area and a location for shipping companies. Churches, like the Recoletos, could have been restored for the thick walls still stood well into the 1950s. Unfortunately they were bought and torn down. Belatedly, under P.D. No. 1616 of President Ferdinand Marcos, an Intramuros Administration was created in the 1970s to oversee the development of the area.[33] The defensive walls were restored. A complex of houses was built fronting the plaza of San Agustin to give visitors an idea of what Intramuros houses were like.

Design guidelines were decreed. However, many lots in Intramuros—and even houses built over the last twenty years—are deserted.

As problematic as the loss of physical structures is, the widespread lack of appreciation for the spirit of traditional Filipino architecture that combines over two thousand years of Mediterranean urbanism, centuries-long lessons from the Chinese, and long-standing indigenous practices had far worse repercussions. Design-wise, many of the houses, especially post-1990s, show a lack of familiarity with historic Intramuros architecture. Many buildings do not provide interior parking, as was the custom pre-1945. As a result they are set back three meters or more away from the street in order to provide parking for the cars. This very American habit destroys the profile of the street and discourages people from walking on the sidewalk because they have to compete with cars parking on the sidewalks.

A serious threat too is the never-ending complaint that "Intramuros excluded the *indio*, the native Filipino. So why preserve it?" Without the software, that is, without pride and sympathy, it is impossible to guarantee that the hardware will endure. But was it really only for the *kastila* down to 1898?

INITIAL SEPARATION, EVENTUAL FUSION

Racial and ethnic relations in the Spanish realm differed from those in the traditional, pre-1960s Anglo-American realm. Commenting on racial relations in seventeenth century Mexico City, the Mexican historian Gonzalbo Aizpuru notes that what prevailed was separation rather than strict segregation. While indios and Spaniards had their assigned quarters in the city, this was not rigidly followed. Spaniards rented out part of their large mansion to indios, while living in some apartments. Over time, they would become friends and *compadres*.[34] Moreover, no laws forbade interracial marriages. Indeed as early as 1503, the Spanish king, Fernando of Aragon, recognized interracial unions as legitimate when formalized in church.[35] In 1537 the Pope published a Bull, *Sublimis Deus*, recognizing that the Indians of the New World were "true human beings" capable therefore of receiving the Faith.[36] Intermarriage and a shared religion bridged social distance both in Hispanic America and in the Philippines.

But what about the Spanish concern for *limpieza de sangre* (purity of blood)? Did this not inhibit mixed marriages? From the sixteenth century onward, according to Pablo Chami, a scholar from a Jewish Argentine research institute, the Spanish Crown enacted statutes that forbade descendants of Jews from assuming positions in Church and State. These prohibitions were extended to descendants of Moslems, Protestants, and those tried by the Inquisition. These were abrogated only in the middle of the nineteenth century.[37] Spaniards had to prove they had a "clean" ancestry lest they be accused of possible heresy. Looking closely, we can surmise why these paranoid statutes were enacted. Following the Fall of Constantinople in 1453, the Moslem Turks used the Mediterranean as a highway for attacking the Christian kingdoms. Spaniards feared that Moslem warriors, aided by Jews, would invade their shores. Meanwhile in Northern Europe, Protestants revolted against the Papacy, and could win converts in the Peninsula. But it was one thing to be a potential heretic; it was another to be a baptized non-Spaniard who accepted Catholic dogma and ritual. Thus while in 1501 Fernando, King of Spain, forbade descendants of heretics from assuming public office, in 1503, as we saw, he encouraged Spaniards to marry non-Spaniards in the overseas possessions.

True, social hierarchy, based on family pedigree, race, and ethnicity, existed in the Spanish empire. But so likewise did it in British, Dutch, and Indian-ruled states before the worldwide triumph of democratic ideals during the second half of the twentieth century. In other states, like Imperial China, race may not have been an issue, but ethnicity was. The Qing dynasty that ruled China in 1644–1911 was Manchu in origin. It favored fellow Manchus and ordered the Han Chinese men to wear pigtails as a sign of servitude. (Landing in Manila, Han Chinese could finally cut off their pigtails if they wanted.) In particular states in democratic US, laws were passed and were strictly observed as late as the middle of the twentieth century forbidding intermarriage between Whites and Blacks,[38] or between Whites and Orientals, such as Filipinos,[39] under pain of imprisonment or lynching. The British historian Arnold Toynbee, an agnostic, observed that, unlike Catholicism, Protestantism initially was not interested in baptizing non-Whites. It would start doing so only in the late eighteenth century. Hence, Catholic colonies were ahead of the Protestant ones in accepting interracial mixing.[40] Significant too was that Catholics revered icons that were dark-skinned. The dusky Our Lady of Guadalupe, Patroness of Spanish America and of the Philippines (down to the 1900s), was venerated by Whites and non-Whites alike. Even darker were the Crucified Christs at Chalma and Otatitlan in Mexico, and Esquipulas in Guatemala. They were black!

Turning to Manila: a report to the King and Council at the close of the sixteenth century by Francisco Tellez, a Manila resident, indicated that even as Spanish women began arriving, Spanish men in Cebu were marrying native women.[41] His report also informs us that in Manila "there are in the city 50 Spaniards married to Spanish women and others are married to native women".[42] Note the word "married"—these were not concubines but rather spouses recognized by Church and State alike. The ancestors of the Aranetas and Legardas may have arrived in Manila as White Basques, but in the course of the nineteenth century, they intermarried with the descendants of Antonio Tuason, a Chinese mestizo.[43] Tuason made his fortune in the galleon trade and was reputedly the wealthiest merchant in the islands in the late eighteenth century.[44] For sure, conflict existed between the racial and ethnic groups in Manila. This is dramatized by the bitter arguments at the table of Kapitan Tiago in José Rizal's *Noli Me Tangere*.

Nonetheless remarkable is that peninsular, creole, mestizo, and indio all sat together at the same table.[45] Earlier in 1859, Sir John Bowring, the British consul of Hong Kong, wrote that, in Manila, the lines of separation between ranks and classes were "less marked and impassable than in most Oriental countries."[46] Indeed "I have seen at the same table Spaniard, mestizo and Indian—priest, civilian and soldier."[47] And while the high-born had their favored locations in the churches, all worshiped at the same altars. Icons, like the Black Nazarene (originally lodged at the Church of the Recollects in Intramuros before transferring to Quiapo) or the Brown Virgin of Ermita (for many generations housed at the Cathedral before being returned to its home), were venerated across color lines. It is a big mistake to translate "*mestizo*" as "halfbreed" or "half-caste." Those English terms have a pejorative connotation even

FIG. 47. The walls of Intramuros de Manila. Courtesy of Paulo Alcazaren.

now, which mestizo does not. It comes from the Latin *mixtus*—meaning "mixed." In Rizal's *Noli*, the heroine Maria Clara is indeed the bastard offspring of Fray Damaso and Doña Pía. But the hero Crisostomo Ibarra is the legitimate grandson of a Basque who married a native woman. In the Spanish language, both are technically mestizos.

There was mixing in schools even if snobbery was rife. As early as 1640, there were student interns of Letran College not of Spanish blood. In the chapter on Sampaloc we will discuss the presence of Indio and Chinese mestizo students at the University of Santo Tomas by the 1760s. An 1840 government report states that half of the residents of the Walled City were Indios and Chinese mestizos. They had more than a hundred houses and were in the colleges, the Conciliar Seminary, sixteen holdings and four lots where they were packed together.[48] When Andrés Bonifacio raised the standard of revolution against Spain in 1896, his ultimate goal was not merely to shout in the wilderness, but to march to the Walled City and attempt to seize it.[49] He was not foolish, as many think today. After cutting off the water supply and seizing the powder house at hilly San Juan, he probably expected the population of the Walled City, by then with a large percentage of Chinese mestizos and Indios, to rally to his cause.

FIG. 48. Tower of Nuestra Señora de Guía

THE WALLS

The protective stone walls of Intramuros were built over the course of centuries from the sixteenth to the nineteenth centuries. The ruler of pre-Hispanic Manila, Rajah Soliman, had a palisade of timber and earthenworks on what is now Fort Santiago. After the Spaniards displaced him, the fortified perimeter became an irregular pentagon 3.7 kilometers long and enclosing sixty-seven hectares.[50] At the other end of the city overlooking the area of the present-day Ermita, Fr. Antonio Sedeño, who came in with the first batch of Jesuits, built a stone tower at a corner of the fortifications in 1584–1590. It thus carried the name of the patroness of Ermita, Nuestra Señora de Guía (Our Lady of Guidance).[51] This tower was defended with culverins.[52] Initially Fort Santiago and this tower fort formed a pair that defended Manila. Sedeño's tower was round and had to be buttressed with four cavaliers. From the start it was criticized for being archaic in concept. Engineering advances had shown the advantages of multi-angled, many-sided bastions over round ones in the face of artillery. Eventually the tower was enclosed by the massive Baluarte de San Diego whose shape was an ace-of-spades. Excavations by the Intramuros Administration have permanently exposed the round tower which consists of three concentric circles. The innermost circle contained a cistern. The third and outermost circle has a diameter of thirty-two meters and a thickness of three meters.[53]

FIG. 49-50. The reconstructed Maestranza Wall (top, left and right)

FIG. 51. View from Ravelin de San Pedro towards Baluarte de San Diego and Ermita

FIG. 52-54. Ramparts of Intramuros (top); carromata inside the walled city (bottom left); old gateway in the Baluarte de San Diego (bottom right)

FIG. 55–57. Puerta Real (top); Puerta de Santa Lucía (bottom left); Puerta Isabel II (bottom right)

During the seventeenth century, successive governors-general raised thick curtain stone walls, created bastions at intervals, and protected the gates with ravelins (*revellín* in Spanish)—triangular advance posts of stone like the rest of the fortifications. In line with innovations by Western engineers in the seventeenth century, the footprint of the new bastions was a polygon to better resist artillery fire. In 1663, fearing an attack by the Chinese rebel and invader Koxinga, Governor-General Sabiniano Manrique de Lara introduced polygonal fortlets to reinforce sections of the walls.[54] Moats were dug on the land side of the fortifications. However, the successful British invasion of 1762 revealed that the walls were not as impregnable as they seemed.

FIG. 58. Puerta del Parian (Courtesy of John Arcilla)

With the return of Spanish rule in 1764, urgently needed improvements in defense were made. First, the defensive perimeter of the walls was extended. Within a determined radius outside the walls, no stone structures, not even churches, were allowed. As the British invasion had shown, these outlying stone structures were easily transformed into refuges for the enemy. Second, the moat was deepened and extended and repairs made in the walls. Improvements by Tomás Sanz in 1781–1787 gave the walls their shape which has endured to this day.[55] In the twilight of Spanish rule, the walls had eight main gates: **Puerta Real** (Royal Gate), **Puerta de Santa Lucía**, **Puerta de los Almacenes** (Storehouses), **Puerta de la Aduana** (Customs), **Puerta de Sto. Domingo**, **Puerta de Isabel II**, **Postigo del Palacio** (Postern), and **Puerta del Parian** (the Chinese quarter).

After the Americans took over, Daniel Burnham, a world-renowned urban planner, generously proposed preserving Intramuros and its walls. However, for purposes of sanitation, the moats needed to be filled in. Moreover, the walls had to be breached at particular points to connect Intramuros to the rest of Manila outside the walls.

How were the walls built? A common view is that they were built with forced (*corvee*) labor. Granted that this were so, this would not have been unusual in the pre-capitalist, pre-nineteenth century world. Money then was scarce in all countries. People fulfilled their obligations by paying in kind (eggs, chicken, salt, etc.), in money, or in labor. It is odd to hear people wish we had an Angkor Wat (which was built through corvee labor) in this country, but at the same time denounce the Spaniards for using corvee labor. But was corvee labor really used in building the walls? A document from the early seventeenth century, examined by the historian Luis Merino OSA,

FIG. 59. Cuartel de Santa Lucia

Quentas de Su Magestad (An accounting to His Majesty) details expenses paid for their construction. The maestro called Jusep received fifty pieces of gold a month while the peon receive one *tomin*, or gold real, a week plus rice ration.[56] Most likely, Jusep was a native Filipino because, like many islanders before the nineteenth century, he did not have a family name.

Under the Americans, the walls were transformed into attractive landmarks for what became one of the most beautiful and most modern cities in Asia. The moats became a fashionable golf course. My father, Dr. Hilario Zialcita, went to school at the Ateneo de Manila within the walls. He recalls visiting the fairs celebrated on top of those walls under the shadow of trees. In 1945, these were pounded by American artillery. Wide sections were reduced to rubble. Under President Ferdinand Marcos, the walls and the gates were restored, making it possible to walk or jog on top of the walls, or to hold parties and stage events at the ravelins. Baluarte San Diego today is a wide expanse that gives a good view of nearby Rizal Park and Manila Hotel, and it has become very popular for outdoor receptions.

From another perspective, equally nationalist, the walls may be regarded as one of the symbols of Manila. Here was where Manila, no longer just a mere trading town but the capital of an archipelago-wide state called Filipinas, emerged.

Here, our Manila, as a city of schools and churches, first developed. Although General Emilio Aguinaldo, leader of the Philippine revolutionary forces, had much of the archipelago and the rest of Manila in his hands by 1898, his failure to capture the Walled City doomed his epic struggle, wrote Nick Joaquin in his eulogy of the Revolution.[57] Aguinaldo could not claim to have captured the capital city, and therefore the center of the archipelago, unless he had won Intramuros.

Close to Puerta de Santa Lucía and parallel to the Walls facing the sea is an odd reconstruction that was undertaken by the Intramuros Administration around 2003 (according to a marker in 1998). Called the **Cuartél de Santa Lucía**, this supposed reconstruction of a 1781 structure designed by engineer Tomas Sanz used to house the Spanish artillery regiment and the office of the Guardia Civil Veterana. In the late nineteenth century, the latter was the hated arm of the colonial government. According to the inscription, in 1901 this became the headquarters of the newly constituted Philippine Constabulary. A school was opened in 1904 which moved to Baguio in 1908 to become the Philippine Military Academy, the training school for the country's military officers. Subsequently another government office took over the site. The building was destroyed in 1945.

FIG. 60. Miguel Lopez de Legaspi and Andrés Urdaneta Monument

The present reconstruction is odd because the design clearly does not match in any way the exhibited photograph of the ruins that was taken after the Battle of Manila. In 1945, the ruins had a chamfered corner to the south, a pediment over the central bay with volutes, and a projecting stone balcony, again with volutes. The current reconstruction, using part of the remaining adobe walls, pretends to be a ruin—walls with no roof—but has altered the configuration of the original ruins. While the southern corner has a conventional sharp corner, the pediment over the central bay has a plain triangular outline with a circular oculus below it. Clearly the architect was influenced by the Postmodernist style of the 1990s which revived elements from previous styles, reduced them to their basics, and used them as decoration. As for the balcony, its present version is a stiff concrete box that lunges forward. What the Intramuros Administration should do is install another inscription stating that this

FIG. 61. Moat and main gate of Fort Santiago

cement reconstruction in no way attempts a faithful rendering, being but a twenty-first century shell intended to commemorate a memory.

Outside Intramuros, in front of the corner bastion of San Diego and at the corner of Burgos Drive and Bonifacio Drive rises a monument honoring **Miguel Lopez de Legazpi and Andrés Urdaneta, OSA**, both in bronze. The monument was cast in 1891, but due to the political turmoil at the time, it was not erected until 1929 in its current location. The monument was made by Barcelona artist Agustin Querol y Subirals; it shows Legazpi extending a baton with his right hand while his left clutches a staff with the Spanish banner unfurling in the wind. Beside him Urdaneta raises high the cross with his right hand while his left holds a wide-open book. Both stand on a pedestal with a beautifully rendered column at each corner. On the pedestal's side facing Burgos Drive are a compass, a rope, a laurel wreath and the words "Urdaneta, 1568." The friar-sailor had discovered the return route to the Americas. Facing the Baluarte de San Diego is the national motto of Spain: *"Ne Plus Ultra."* Though literally meaning "Do not venture beyond this point," it can also be taken as a "Willingness to Surpass Boundaries." Before the Age of Explorations in the fifteenth century, the sea that lay beyond the Pillars of Gibraltar, now known as the Straits of Gibraltar, was regarded as the boundary of the world. Only the foolhardy would dare traverse it. Facing Manila Bay are a crown, a helmet, oak, palm leaves and the inscription: "Legazpi 1572." The symbols here are martial and exalt strength, as in the oak. On the pedestal side facing the Luneta across the street is a seated woman, also in bronze, with a laurel wreath on her head. Her right hand points upward to the inscription: "Junio 24, 1571" when Spanish Manila was founded.[58] Sadly, some of the historic bronze plates were recently stolen, probably by scrap metal scavengers.

Legazpi and Urdaneta look across in the direction of the Luneta, also called Rizal Park. The unintended narrative is very suggestive. It sums up 1565—the beginning of the Spanish colonization—until 1898, a few years after Jose Rizal's execution. A small obelisk in the park commemorates the site where Padre Burgos, Padre Gomez, and Padre Zamora were executed in 1872. A few meters away stood the monument to Dr. Jose Rizal. These symbols unified hitherto separate ethnic groups into one people under the cross. The Filipinos began to see themselves as a nation with the right to rule itself following the Terror of 1872, and the execution of Rizal in 1896.

Unfortunately, statues that were raised in the late 2000s by the City of Manila to honor Jaime Cardinal Sin, Senator Benigno Aquino Jr. and President Corazon Aquino interrupted this narrative. The bronze statues do not form a unified ensemble. Standing on separate oversized pedestals, they gesture past each other. In addition, their location would have been more meaningful at a corner of Rizal Park's Quirino Grandstand, for enormous rallies and holy masses were held there in protest against the Marcos Dictatorship and in celebration of its fall in 1986. Proper siting matters!

FORT SANTIAGO

The clasp binding the walls together is Fort Santiago, formerly The Royal Fort of Santiago (Real Fuerza de Santiago). The citadel stands at the junction of the Pasig River and Manila Bay. Because land during the twentieth century was reclaimed for the Port Area, the bay has since receded into the distance.

Manila enjoyed a strategic advantage because it controlled the trade between coastal communities and inland communities via the river. At that time, rivers and bodies of water were the highways. Moreover, because the river slants as it enters the bay, there was a tongue of land at the junction of bay and river that was relatively easy to seal off and transform into a fortification. The neighboring chiefdom of Tondo did not have this locational advantage.

Soliman was no ordinary ruler, as we have seen. He was related to the ruling families of Sulu and Brunei, by then powerful in their own domains. He fortified his stronghold with earthenworks and a wooden palisade. Because of Manila's strategic location, he and his settlement had become prosperous. It would seem that what his stronghold occupied was part of the perimeter of Fort Santiago. Beyond that was marshland that needed to be drained and whose soft ground would threaten future constructions in Intramuros.

The fort built by Miguel Lopez de Legazpi in 1571 was of wood. Under Governor-General Perez Dasmariñas, the construction of a fort in adobe began in 1591. During the following century, platforms and parapets were constructed. A bulwark commanded the river; a second one commanded the sea. A moat was dug to separate the fort from the city. Barracks were installed to house the soldiers. Imprisoned and tortured in the chambers of the fort were those whom the state regarded as enemies. They included some Spanish governors-general and one archbishop, and Filipinos fighting for equal rights from the 1870s down to the 1896 Revolution. The most famous of these was José Rizal, who was arrested in 1896 on charges of inspiring the ongoing armed Revolution.[59] It was here that he wrote his last poem, "*Mi último adios*" (My Last Farewell): "*Adios patria adorada, region del sol querida*" (Farewell my revered Motherland, region loved by the sun.)

The Americans sent their enemies instead to Bilibid Prison in the district of Sta. Cruz, Manila. They transformed Fort Santiago into the headquarters of the Philippine Division of the US Military,[60] eventually into the headquarters of the United States Armed Forces of the Far East (USAFFE).[61] The fort was graced with gardens and became a pleasant destination even for civilians.[62] But the Americans were forced to leave the fort in late December, 1941 as Manila was about to fall to the Japanese. Upon the latter's entry, they made the fort the headquarters of the dreaded Kempei-tai or military police. Hundreds of Filipinos were brought there to be tortured and executed.[63]

Being in the front line of Japanese defenses during the Battle of Manila in 1945, the fort was destroyed by American artillery. However, under the newly independent Republic, the Fort, declared a National Shrine on 6 March 1951,[64] was restored in stages and enhanced with gardens. Before the fort is the **Plaza de Moriones** which has been landscaped with trees. On the east side is the partially reconstructed **Almacenes Reales** (the Royal Storehouses), built at the turn of the seventeenth century, which kept goods destined for the city. On the west side are the **Baluartillo de San Francisco Javier** (1663) and the **Reducto de San Francisco Javier** (1773) which house

FIG. 62. Almacenes Reales

FIG. 63. Spanish-era cannon on Plaza de Moriones

FIG. 64. Main gate of Fort Santiago, with wooden relief of Santiago "Matamoros," National Saint of Spain

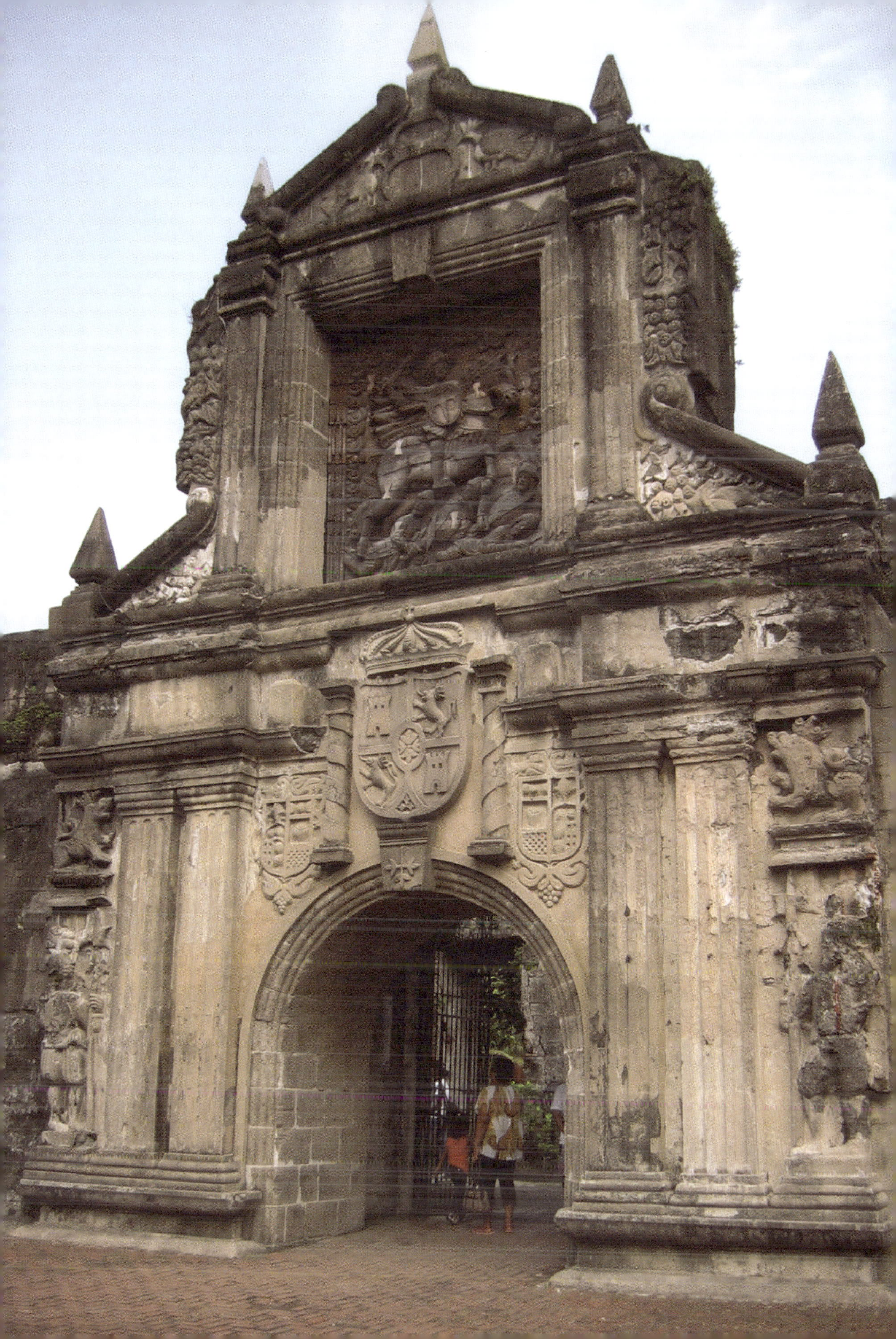

FIG. 65-67. Former Artillery Barracks, now Rizal Shrine (top); main gate (bottom left); Former Artillery Compound (bottom right)

FIG. 68. Cuarto Escuela, now Dulaang Raha Sulayman

the Intramuros Visitors' Center.[65] Connected to these fortifications is the ruin of the **Barracks** which used to house US Military before 1942. The two-story building with seven bays is made of adobe, and was probably built in the second half of the nineteenth century. However, the front porch over a porte cochère is of concrete and dates from the American period.

A moat separates the fort proper from the Plaza de Moriones. The stone gate has become one of Manila's icons. Over the doorway is a wooden bas-relief representing the Spanish coat-of-arms and above it Santiago "*Matamoros*" (St. James the Great), patron saint of Spain, overcoming his (Muslim) enemies in battle. It is an irony of history that the Spaniards, after having reached the opposite end of the world, would again meet their main foes from the Spanish peninsula, namely the "Moors," as all Muslims were then generally called. Hence the significance of the patron saint and the bas-relief. Guarding the doorway are statues of *moriones* (soldiers). A triangular pediment tops the gate. The stiff style of both the doorway and the statues identifies it as dating from

FIG. 69. Artillery Barracks/Rizal Shrine

FIG. 70. Sentry post, Baluarte de Sta. Barbara

the early seventeenth century. The visitor enters the triangular-shaped **Plaza de Armas**. This was most likely the site of Raha Sulayman's palisade. On the northeast side are the ruins of two **former barracks.** The ruins of the eighteenth-century Cuarto Escuela barracks was converted into an outdoor theater, **Dulaang Raha Sulayman,** where the Philippine Educational Theater Association (PETA) used to stage spectacular plays before opening its own theater in Quezon City. On the western side, part of the former **Artillery Barracks** from 1824 was rebuilt to house the two-story **Rizal Shrine**. José Rizal's memorabilia are on display. A room replicates his prison cell and includes a life-sized representation, for he was imprisoned in this building. Translations of his poem into several languages are on the walls.

Fronting the river (and formerly the bay) is the **Baluarte de Sta. Barbara** whose massive chambers formerly stored gunpowder. We are told that tales about prisoners being kept here to drown at high tide cannot be true because the floor is way above the water level,[66] for it stored ammunition. Romeo Galang Jr., a scholar who has delved into Intramuros's history for his thesis, says that the so-called dungeons are part of the cellar of the Casa del Castellano (House of the Castle-Commander) which once stood next to the gunpowder chambers. The baluarte has a ramp, the **Media Naranja** (meaning "half-orange" because of the shape) with a commanding view of the river.

The Intramuros Administration recently reconstructed a section of the wall facing the Pasig River, which was demolished in 1903 by the Americans to create space for a wharf and modern warehouses. Known as the **Maestranza Wall** because of the nearby former cannon foundry and weapons arsenal, it is to house exhibitions and a planned museum of the Galleon Trade within its extensive vaults in the future. The Maestranza wall, which faced the river, was initially built at the turn of the eighteenth century to serve as both a defensive wall and a warehouse. The old gate originally located here was accordingly called *Puerta de Almacenes*. The wall was rebuilt at the turn of the nineteenth century and was demolished a hundred years later; a century after demolition, it was rebuilt again albeit of different materials. Although of contemporary construction—with pre-cast concrete panels faced with bricklets for the vaults, adobe cladding, and hollow space in-between the walls—the result is quite convincing and offers an impressive perspective though its dozens of chambers. All that is missing are the museum exhibits and the replica of an ancient sailing vessel anchored along the muelle to complete the picture.

THE GATES

The gates that survived were all remodeled after the British invasion and mostly date from between 1781 to 1791. They are Puerta Real, Puerta de Santa Lucía, Puerta de Isabel II, Postigo del Palacio, and Puerta del Parian. They have since been restored. Under the directorship of Ana Maria Harper, the Intramuros Administration enhanced the gardens in each gate and bastion, and fostered a specialty. For instance, Puerta del Parian became an oasis of palms of different species, while Baluarte de San Diego became a riot of flowers.

Puerta de Isabel II became more meaningful after the government relocated the bronze **statue of Queen Isabel II** after which it was named and opened in 1861. The queen reigned from 1833 until 1868. Her reign was stormy. Her uncle, Carlos, attempted to seize the throne on the grounds that ancient customary law did not allow a woman to sit on the throne. A civil war broke out which ended in 1839. Under her watch, the monarchy became less absolutist and more constitutional. She ceded more powers to parliament. However, she played favorites with the conservative factions against the liberals. The unrest led to an uprising that resulted in her abdication and the inauguration of a short-lived republic.[67]

FIG. 71. Statue of Queen Isabel II

Nonetheless, during her reign, Spain and likewise the Philippines steadily modernized. Free public education on the elementary level was introduced in Spain in 1857 and shortly after, in 1863, in the Philippines.[68] This made the Philippines a pioneer in Asia, along with Japan.[69] In Spain, various banks fused together to become the Banco de España in 1856.[70] In the Philippines, the Banco Español-Filipino de Isabel II was founded in 1851 and was allowed to print Philippine currency, rather than Mexican.[71] This bank is now Bank of the Philippine Islands, one of the country's most trusted banks.

The queen's statue is of bronze and stands on a marble pedestal with inscriptions stating that it was installed by the Ayuntamiento of Manila in 1860. She stands holding a scepter in her right hand and a document in her left. The flounced layers of her crinoline dress have lacework which is rendered in detail. Her famously ample bosom is enveloped by a large lace fichu from which a royal cape falls and drapes in rich folds over the edge of the pedestal. The statue was made by a Spanish sculptor, Ponciano Ponzano.[72]

The statue formerly stood in the nearby Plaza de Arroceros (now Liwasang Bonifacio), but was taken down after Governor-General Carlos de la Torre, who represented the Spanish Republic, arrived in 1869. It was moved in 1896 to the plaza in front of Malate Church.[73] Another inscription says it was installed in its present site in 1974. The relocation is just as well. Ironically, the queen, who was notorious for her lovers, once stood in front of Malate Church where passersby sometimes mistook her for the Virgin Mary!

On the same street by the Pasig used to stand a column decorated with "an anchor, a cable, a cross, oak leaves, ears of wheat, grapes and pomegranate."[74] All in stone, this **monument to Hernando Magallanes** was erected in 1848 to honor the man who captained the expedition that completed the first circumnavigation of the world. Sebastian Elcano took over after his death in Mactan in 1521. Being by the river, the column was a casualty during the Battle of 1945, its remains dumped into the Pasig River.

FIG. 72. Anda Monument

Both Puerta del Postigo and Puerta de Santa Lucía used to open with a view of the bay and the promenade called the Malecón (sea promenade). Beginning in 1880, this part of the bay was dredged and transformed into a port. The Malecón became Bonifacio Drive. However, a landmark remains, the **monument honouring Simón de Anda** on a rotunda.

As Manila was about to fall into British hands on 4 October 1762 during the Seven Years War, Anda escaped to Bulacan with forty documents and PHP 500. From there he moved to Bacolor, Pampanga where he launched attacks against the British and confined them to Manila. After the 1763 Treaty of Paris handed back the islands to Madrid, he was recognized as the interim governor-general. He returned to Madrid in 1767. Sent back to Manila in 1770, as the new governor-general, he fortified the walls, built a fleet of warships, and established a chamber of commerce.[75]

An obelisk was raised in his honor, topped with a spherical sun with rays. On its pedestal are lion heads with spouts, with the surrounding fountain recently rebuilt.

An inscription says that, at the insistence of Governor-General Carlos de la Torre, public gratitude built the monument in 1871. Originally located near the Pasig River, the monument was moved to its present location in the center of a large roundabout after the war. Luckily, plans in 2014 to translocate the monument again to ease traffic on Bonifacio Drive have thus far not materialized.[76] With the move, Intramuros (and the adjacent South Harbor) would lose yet another grand entry to the walled city in the name of "progress."

Across Puerta de Santa Lucia and its filled up moat is a small plaza that honors the Mexican Connection and is easily seen from Bonifacio Drive. The bronze figure of Padre Miguel Hidalgo standing on a pedestal towers over the garden plaza. He launched a revolution on 15 September 1810 that was one of several armed uprisings that ultimately destroyed the Spanish empire in all of mainland America. Though this statue was raised in 1964, it merits attention because it dominates this garden where another Mexican monument stands—that was dedicated in September 1945 shortly after the close of the Pacific War on 15 August 1945.

FIG. 73. Magallanes Monument

To the rear of Hidalgo is a small, modest stone monument. On top is a carving of an eagle perched on a cactus, with its beak on a large snake that is fighting back. Originally this was the symbol of the Aztec Indians and their empire. Today this is the seal of Mexico, which also appears on their flag. On a tablet below is a dedication written by members of Mexico's Air Combat Squadron 201, which fought in the Luzon theatre to free the Philippines from the Japanese. It is addressed to the Mexican pilots who fell in combat: Second Captain P. Rivas Martinez, Lieutenant J. Espinoza Fuentes, Lieutenant H. Espinoza Galvan, Sub-Lieutenant A. M. Lopez Portillo, Sub-Lieutenant T. Vega Santander. Why did Mexican pilots choose to fight for the Philippines? My father met a Mexican pilot—a survivor of the war then taking higher studies—while taking post-graduate studies at Ann Arbor, Michigan in 1946. When asked why the Mexican pilots chose to fight for the Philippines, the pilot said, "if we were to die, we might as well die for a brother country."

AN ADVANCED STREET PLAN

Manila, like other overseas cities of the Spanish empire, originally had more advanced planning than peninsular cities like Madrid itself during the sixteenth and early seventeenth centuries. During the Middle Ages and down to the late sixteenth century, cities in Spain, like their peers in the rest of Europe, had developed haphazardly with no guiding plan. However, with the revival of interest in Classical antiquity during the Renaissance and a respect for rational planning, a new vision of the city appeared.

Planners urged that streets be lined with buildings of similar heights and designs that harmonized with each other, be laid out at right angles, and end in a dramatic vista. They emphasized the need for visual dignity and for better ease of communication between different points within the city.[77] It was easier to implement this conception in the new overseas cities that were rising up on empty spaces rather than in Europe itself where ancient cities already stood.

Most streets in Intramuros are thus laid on a grid. Before 1945, many used to end in a plaza or to pass a small garden park. Today, because of the war's destruction, there are only a few plazas left with a monumental structure. Many streets, however, do end in a view unique not only to the Philippines but also to the region, that is, walls with ramparts.

FIG. 74. Streets in Intramuros are traditionally very narrow. (Calle Urdaneta)

The streets of Intramuros were deliberately narrow, not because of a monkish preoccupation with gloom, but because of a practical consideration—the need for protection against the tropical sun. The Laws of the Indies, which dictated what the new cities were to be like, were quite explicit. They stated that while in cold countries streets should be wide, in countries with plenty of sun, streets should be narrow.[78] "But why couldn't the Spaniards have combined wide streets in seventeenth-century Intramuros with rows and rows of trees—as in late nineteenth-century Sydney?" Or so went a question innocently raised by a Filipina tourist when marveling at Sydney. The answer, of course is that seventeenth-century Spaniards, like their contemporaries in Britain, France or Italy, could not have anticipated the late nineteenth century vision of the city as a garden. In the second half of the nineteenth century, Westerners envisioned the city, now connected by the newly invented street cars, as blocks of buildings connected by treelined avenues and large swaths of wooded public parks. The idea soon spread and resulted in greener cities, as seen in the avenues and parks of London, Paris, Berlin, Madrid, and Barcelona. This also explains the appearance of avenues outside the Walls of Manila that were wide and lined with greenery like the unique and now vanished bamboo-bordered Paseo de Azcarraga (which is that section of Recto passing through Divisoria), or the acacia-lined avenues of San Miguel and Ermita-Malate. Like the railroad car, electricity, telegraph, and democratic freedoms, the Garden City was a nineteenth-century invention.

FIG. 75-76. Statue of King Carlos IV (left); Plaza Roma before World War II (right)

PLAZA ROMA

During the Spanish period, this was the Plaza Mayor (Grand Plaza). Today it is named after Rome, the seat of Catholicism. From 1571 to the 1930s, this was the center of power in the entire archipelago. On the east side was the Ayuntamiento, earlier called the *Casas Consistoriales*, where city and later national government offices were located. On the west side was the governor-general's palace which was wrecked by the severe earthquakes of 1863 and 1880. On the south side, dominating the plaza by its sheer height was the cathedral where the chief prelate of the islands sat—the archbishop of Manila.

In the middle of the plaza is a **bronze statue honoring Carlos IV**, King of Spain (reigned 1788–1808).[79] Unlike his reformist father Carlos III, he was an ineffectual ruler, and was satirized by the painter Goya for being dull. However, he did his overseas possessions a good turn. Smallpox epidemics were then frequent in many parts of the world and were particularly fatal to children. To stop this, he sent samples of the newly invented anti-smallpox vaccine to the cities of his empire. But how was the vaccine to be stored? Cold storage had not yet been invented. Spanish children were inoculated with the vaccine and sent overseas to the Americas in 1803, under the supervision of Dr. Francisco Javier de Balmis. Needles were then stuck into them to extract the vaccine. From Mexico, other children were sent to Manila in 1805 where the same procedure was repeated. After Manila, they left for China for the same purpose.[80] The plaque thanks the king. However, a study by the historian Pedro Luengo using material in the Archivo General de Indias and the National Archives of the Philippines indicates that the statue had been planned since 1796.

FIG. 77. Ayuntamiento

The bronze statue shows a slim Carlos IV, far different from the rotund version that Goya mocked. Dressed in breeches and jacket, he wears a late eighteenth-century wig with a queue. His right hand wields a scepter while his left hand is held akimbo. His magnificent cape, decorated with royal insignia, sweeps to the right in the wind. The statue was designed in Spain by Juan Adán, but executed in Manila under Ambrocio Casas.[81] Per Luengo, the team had Spanish foundry hands, and native and Chinese sculptors. The pedestal inscription indicates that the statue and the marble pedestal were raised in 1824.

Ayuntamiento. One of the most important buildings in Intramuros, this was the original Cabildo (city hall), then after 1907 the seat of the Philippine Assembly and later of the Supreme Court during the American era. The original design, which we know from sketches by the artists of the 1792 Malaspina Expedition and from a pre-1863 photo, shows a two-story government building in stone with overhanging grill balconies. The palace, with its decorative center turret, was heavily damaged in the 1863 earthquake. It was consequently reconstructed as a Neoclassical building with a ceremonial staircase in Y-shape between 1879 and 1886, designed by military engineer Eduardo Lopez Navarro. Exterior ornamentation came from the simple massing of Ionic pilasters. Vintage photos suggest that this was one of the grandest buildings in the islands, but the shelling of 1945 gutted the interior. After lying in ruins for over six decades, the building was recently rebuilt by the Bureau of the Treasury as its office.

For practical purposes, only the main halls have been originally reconstructed. These are the Lobby, the Marble Hall and the Office of the Governor-General. The rest

FIG. 78. Ayuntamiento, Salon de Fiestas y Actos Públicos (Marble Hall), session hall of the first Philippine Assembly (after 1907) and of the House of Representatives (after 1916)

of the building has been allotted to offices designed in a contemporary style. Two large inner patios flank Marble Hall. The Bureau of Treasury should be congratulated for insisting on reconstructing at least the exterior and the two halls mentioned above.

Something of the grandeur of the prewar lobby is conveyed by the wide Y-shaped staircase that welcomes the visitor. Four lions, each with a paw on an orb, stride pedestals enclosing the first landing. These represent Spain whose coat-of-arms features a lion rampant. At the top of the first landing stands Juan Sebastian Elcano who captained the only surviving ship of Magellan's fleet back to the Peninsula in 1522, and thus became the first man to have sailed continuously around the globe. During a soft opening in November 2012, Elcano and the tall jars decorating the lobby were of a dark brown metal. Supposedly these are temporary. Originally the statue was of marble and the Oriental jars of porcelain. In order to convey grandeur, the lions and the stair railings have been painted with gold. Unfortunately, the gold has too yellow a luster, and thus looks more Chinese rather than Spanish.

There are two doors on either side that lead to the Marble Hall. The hypnotic quality of the checkerboard black-and-white marble floor is echoed by the flat ceiling that has been divided into over a hundred coffers. The walls rise in two stories. The openings of the tall lower story are framed by Ionic pilasters and a panel displaying the silhouetted busts of Spanish heroes, too many to enumerate. For grandeur, the capitals, the cartouches and floral bouquets of the pilasters are gilt with gold. Once again the gold seems too yellow. Pairs of rectangular windows on the clerestory of the second story give the entire composition a lifting quality.

FIG. 79–80. Ayuntamiento, Grand Staircase (left); Sala de Sesiones: Office of the Governor-General, after 1916 session hall of the Philippine Senate, and after 1926 of the Supreme Court (right)

Back at the first landing, the two arms of the staircase together lead to the former Office of the Governor-General. For Arch. Michael Manalo of the Escuela Taller, an expert in heritage research, the lobby-hall-office is really the climax of the ensemble. Notable is the well-reconstructed wooden desk, the symbol of the governor-general's authority. On the coffered ceiling are figures representing Philip II on horseback and, on either side, the first century of Spanish rule in Magellan and Legazpi, and the last century in Isabella II and Alfonso XII. The mural was painted by artists from the town of Angono, Rizal. I have problems both with the painterly style and the content. First, the chosen style seems too cautious and uninspired. Despite the use of chiaroscuro, the murals seem flat. Secondly, did the pre-1945 ceiling really narrate such an allegory? Or is this merely a supposition? An extant pre-1941 photograph in *Intramuros of Memory*, hints that the overhead murals may not have carried these personalities. Third, too much of Spain's political rule is celebrated.[82] In all the reconstructed public spaces, we should celebrate as well the birth of the Philippines as a nation-state. Two murals in the Marble Hall, one depicting the story of the Philippine Assembly, the other of the Philippine Judiciary, would make us feel the relevance of the building and of Intramuros to our story as a sovereign people. An example is what the Mexicans continue to do since their Social Revolution of 1910. They paint scenes from Mexican history and culture, from a Mexican perspective, on the walls and ceilings of eighteenth to nineteenth century convents and palaces in a dynamic style that is of today. The juxtaposition of styles is exciting while the imposition of a nationalistic Mexican perspective makes the structure more meaningful to ordinary citizens.

The Ayuntamiento's importance for the Philippines is best summed up by Nick Joaquin:

> In Intramuros sat the first Philippine Assembly, which determined a new direction for the development of the Filipino people.... In Intramuros were enthroned Osmeña at the Ayuntamiento and Quezon at the Intendencia as heads of the First Philippine Legislature that resumed our experiment in representative government.[83]

FIG. 81. Palace of the Governor-General, ca. 1850

Palacio del Gobernador. The original two-story palace, built in several stages between 1733 and 1850, was severely damaged by the earthquakes of 1863 and 1880, compelling the governor-general to transfer residence outside the walls to an estate by the river, Malacañang.

Under Imelda Marcos, the governor of Metro Manila, a modern building was raised on its site in 1978. It was called "Palacio del Gobernador." In fact, it made no attempt to replicate, or at least connect with, the style of the preceding palace. The eight-story tower destroyed forever the symmetry of the plaza. Moreover, the style tried to replicate the unique architectural style of Madrid, not that of Intramuros. It has those corner towers plus rose-colored surfaces characteristic of sixteenth to early seventeenth-century government buildings in Madrid. But because the proportions are not the same (save for the corner towers, Madrid buildings of that period do not go beyond three stories), and the context is different (this is Manila, not Madrid) the effect is bizarre. At least it had one good effect: it prompted the creation of the Intramuros Administration, which has held office therein ever since.

Manila Cathedral. The cathedral is dedicated to the Immaculate Conception, patroness of the Philippines. The first cathedral was of wood, bamboo, and nipa but burned down in a fire that swept Manila in 1583. A cathedral of stone was built starting in 1603 but was severely damaged in the great earthquake of 1645. A third cathedral began in 1659. This was thoroughly rebuilt and completed, as a fourth cathedral, in 1792. Following its collapse in the 1863 earthquake, a fifth cathedral was begun in 1872. The cathedral mutated visibly with each new reconstruction. Thus in 1792, its resemblance to the Baroque Church of the Gesú in Rome is striking: the façade has no towers and is topped by a triangular pediment. On both sides of the central bay are scrolls. However in 1872, the inspiration clearly became *romano-bizantino* (Romanesque-Byzantine) as its architect Vicente Romano declared.[84] Romanesque would be the

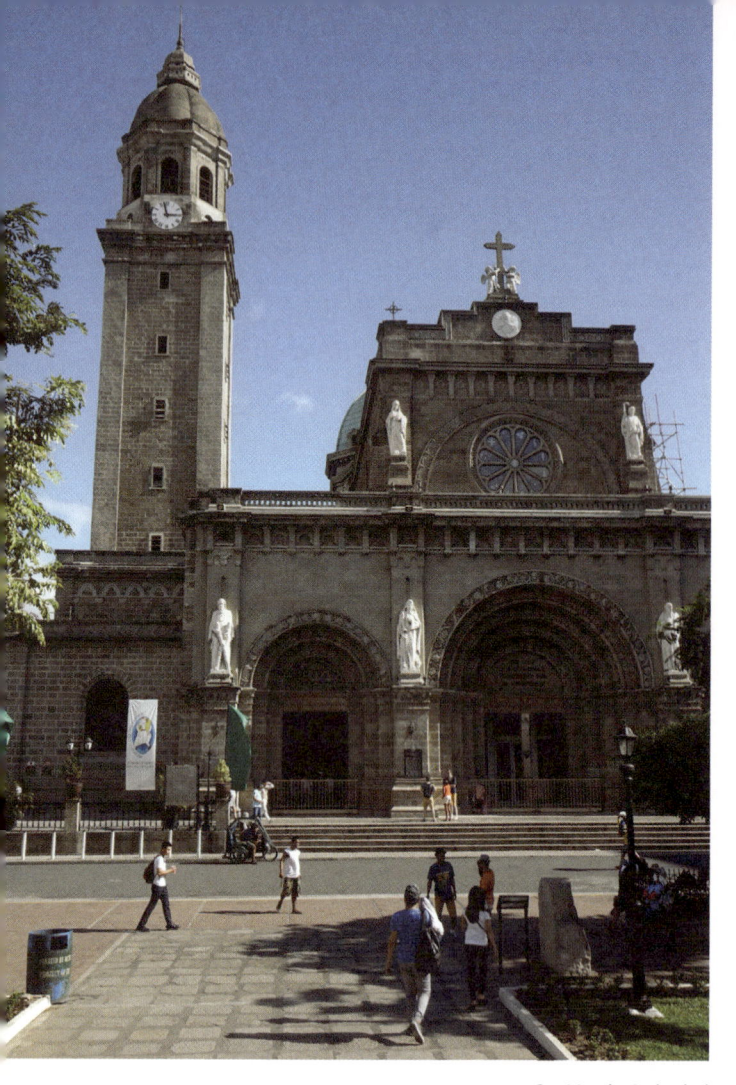

FIG. 82. Manila Cathedral

recessed portals, that is, the arches of the doorway form a series of arches that diminish as they reach the door, and the rose window over the central bay; Byzantine would be the simple shape of the cupola. A feature shared by all the variations on the cathedral since 1792 is the separation of bell tower from the church proper. This may have resulted from a fear of earthquakes. Moreover the tower rose in tiers as an eight-sided tower. A polygonal shape, most often in eight sides, is common in eighteenth and nineteenth century Philippine bell towers. This may be an unconscious homage to Chinese pagodas since masons, in this case Dionisio Saplan, could be of Chinese descent.[85] The cathedral was damaged by American artillery in 1945.

A bulldozing unit of the Armed Forces of the US was tasked to level off the cathedral's shell, along with the remaining ruins of Manila, but Santiago Picornell, a Manileño with a profound love for his city, heard of this and convinced the American officer not to do it.[86] The sixth cathedral arose in 1954–1958 with Fernando Ocampo as the architect. The shell of the fifth cathedral was retained and rebuilt. Retained too, according to Javellana, were the cruciform and the triple nave plan of the fourth cathedral.[87] The overall design, using reinforced concrete faced with adobe stones, is Neo-Romanesque though in a stylized contemporary manner. On the façade is a small rose window. The arches of the three portals are recessed. The interior has groined vaults resting on pairs of columns with capitals carved into exuberant foliage. All these are typical of Romanesque. Travertine and marble are used lavishly. But the tower is now four-sided and rises straight until it becomes a belfry, while the deambulatory behind the main altar is lit up by stained glass in tall, three-story windows. These high tower and windows, unaided by buttresses on the exterior, exist thanks to modern technology. Chapels open along the side aisles. When inaugurated in 1958, the cathedral had a glorious set of stained glass windows celebrating the works of mercy, images of famous Madonnas of the Philippines, and the emblems of the Philippine Republic and of the Archdiocese of Manila. These were designed by Galo B. Ocampo. There was a side chapel, dedicated

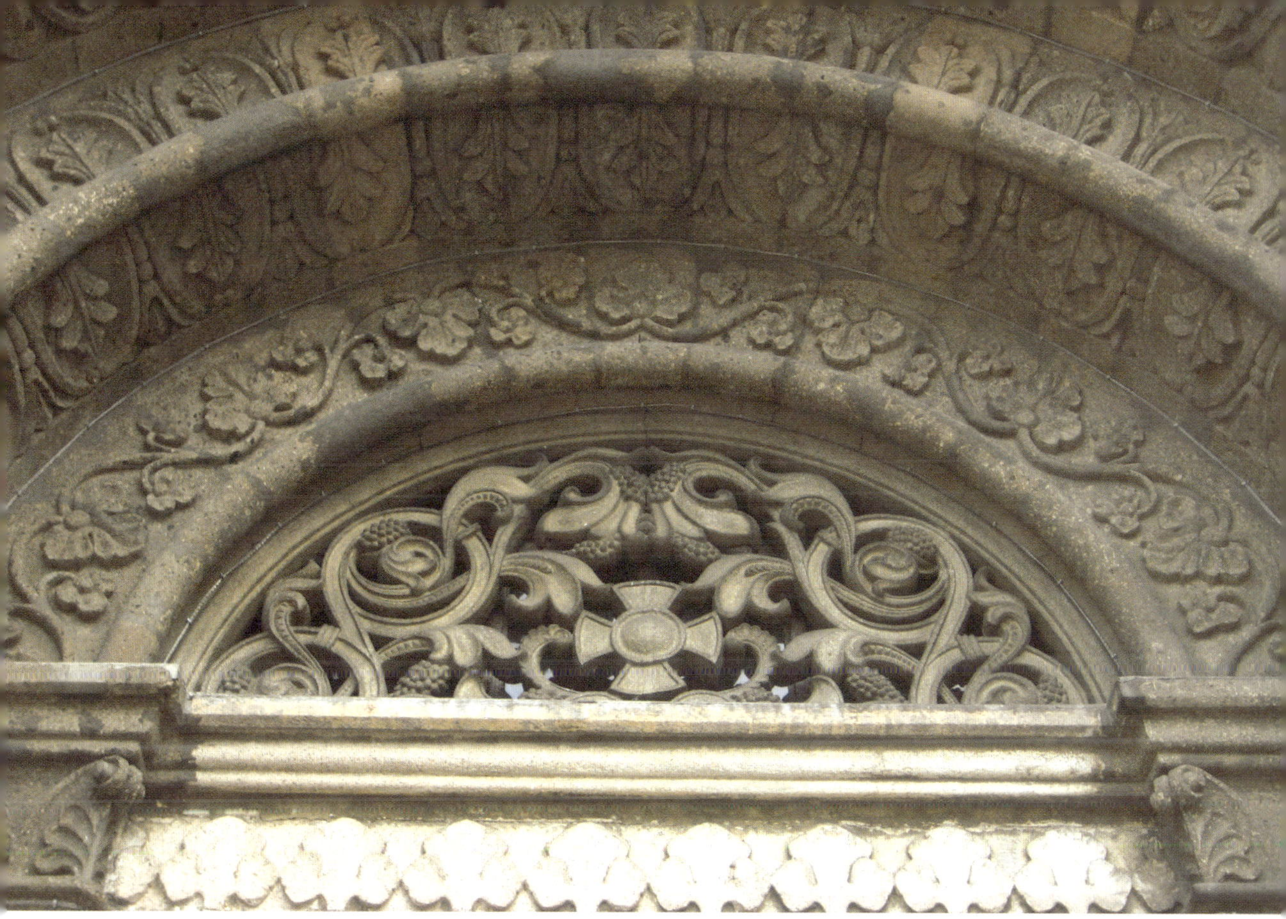
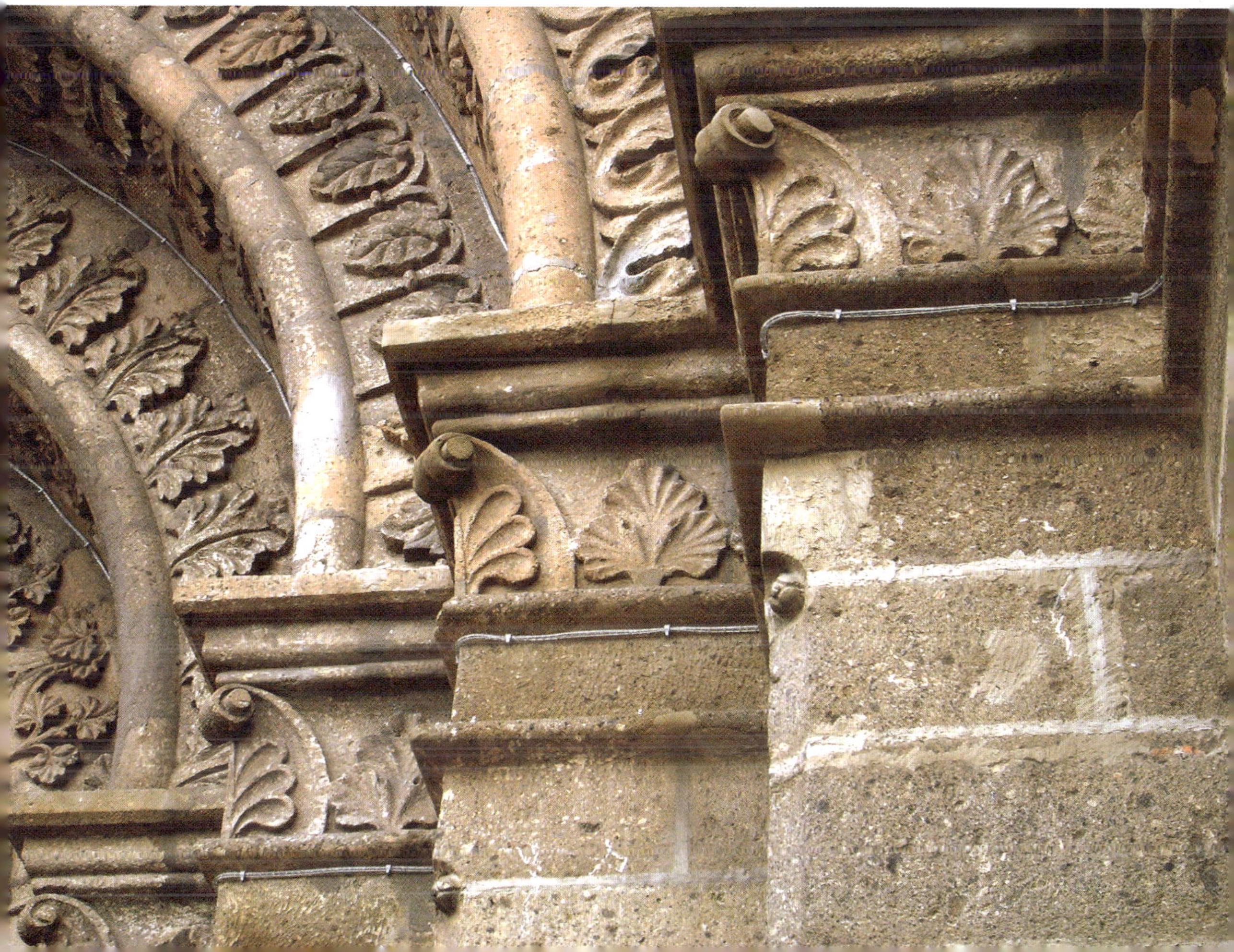

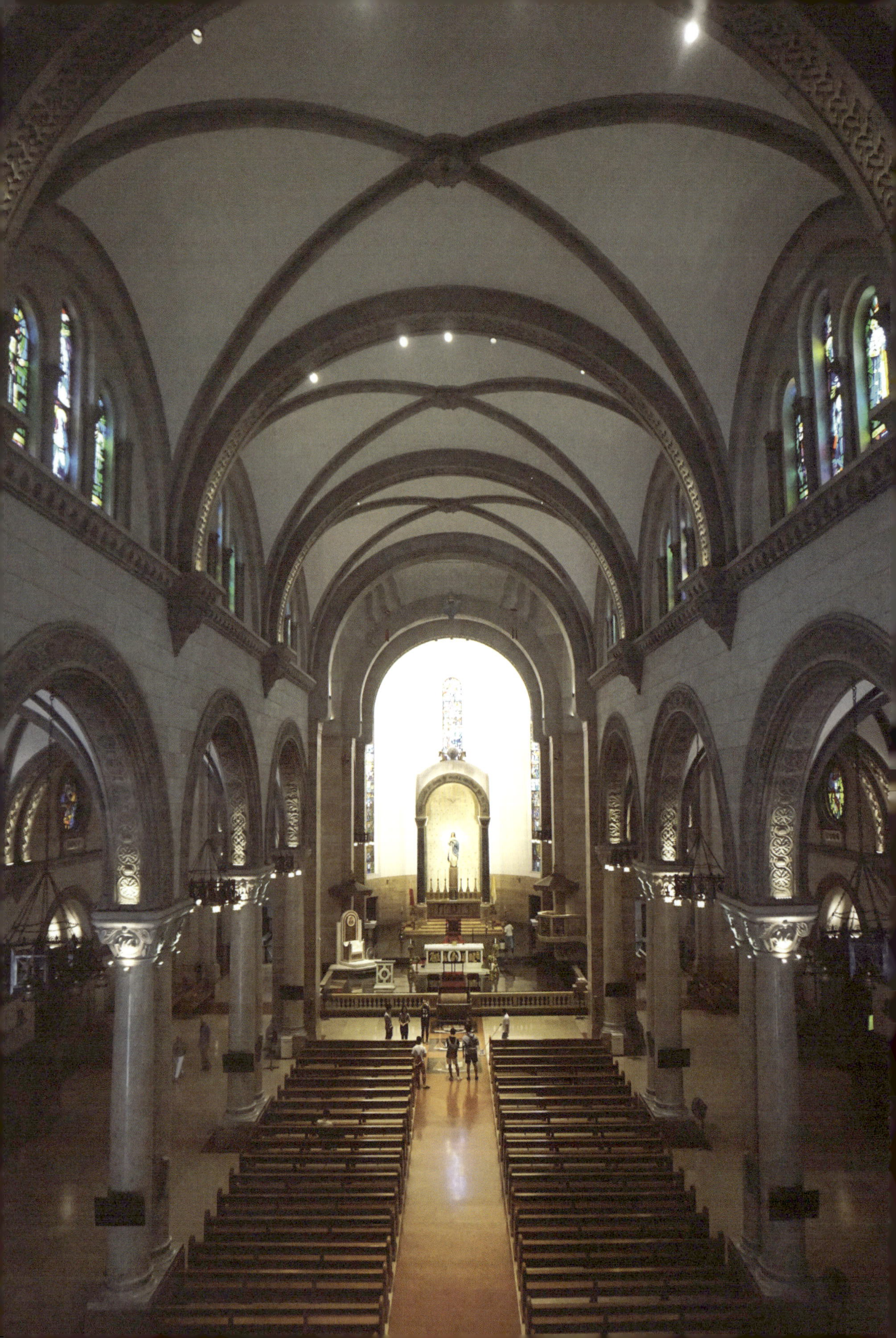

to Our Lady of the Pillar, which was donated by Spain. The windows blazed with red colors. Unfortunately some of the windows, including those of this particular chapel, were shattered by strong typhoons and were replaced by acrylic windows with poor drawing and an incoherent management of colors. One of the attractions of the cathedral are the bronze doors, cast in Italy, which depict the symbols of Mary and the history of the cathedral.[88] A panel on the Battle of Manila in 1945 shows the Angel of Death swinging a fierce scythe.

Having been at the center of power, the cathedral witnessed important scenes in the unfolding of Philippine history. Two key figures in the emerging nationalism of the nineteenth century were located here as assistants to the archbishop: Fathers Pedro Pelaez and José Burgos. Though creoles (Philippine-born of Spanish ancestry), both of them fought for the rights of all Filipino priests—whether native, mestizo, or creole—to administer the parishes. Unfortunately, Pelaez was killed by falling masonry in 1863. Burgos, his successor, was the leading light in the campaign for Filipinization of the parishes but was executed on false charges in 1872.[89]

Along Aduana—A. Soriano, are three prewar office buildings. All appear in 1945 photos of Intramuros as war-damaged. The Shipping Center Building even bears an inscription: "1940" in its gable. Though they are not built in any of the nineteenth century styles and are not architecturally significant taken individually, nonetheless they form a harmonious streetscape that enhances Plaza Roma. Most certainly they look better than the monstrous Palacio del Gobernador and the towering Banco Filipino Condominium (built on the site of the Universidad de Sto. Tomás) standing alongside the Ayuntamiento. The buildings are the **Shipping Center Building** from 1940, the **FEMII** Building (built sometime between 1935 and 1945) and the former **Army and Navy YMCA** from 1926, which later housed the offices of the Chronicle newspaper. Each occupies most of a block and has a merciful limit of only four stories. The idiom is typical of its time—whitewashed reinforced concrete, with some "Spanish" touches, such as metal balconies and a door frame decorated with volutes. Of the three, the most commonsensical is the first—which faces the Cathedral. This is because its simple grill balconies have a functional purpose. They are platforms onto which glass doors open and not cages to conceal air conditioning units.

REAL

Down into the 1960s, the main street in Filipino towns was called "Calle Real"—the King's Street. The origin of all these King's Streets in the Philippines was this street.

Along with the cathedral, **San Agustin Church and Convent** was the first church built in Luzon.[90] As the Roman empire collapsed in the fifth century, St. Augustine enjoined like-minded colleagues to give away their possessions and lead a life of prayer and reflection. During the chaos of the following centuries, men and women followed his exhortations. In the thirteenth century, the Augustinian Order was formally constituted. The order was the first to enter the Philippines, thanks to Andres de Urdaneta who accompanied Miguel Lopez de Legazpi. A former sailor, he discovered how to return to Mexico from the Philippines by exploring the Japanese current. One of the charisms of the Augustinian order has been scholarship and the arts. During the nineteenth century, it was a confrere in Austria, Gregor Mendel, who discovered the laws

FIG. 85. Cathedral, central nave (adjacent page)

FIG. 86. Shipping Center Building

of heredity by observing plants. In the Philippines, Manuel Blanco, OSA wrote *Flora de Filipinas*, a pioneering study of Philippine plants that helped lay the foundation for Philippine botany as a science.[91] In the arts, many of the churches in the Philippines from the Spanish period were built under the care of the Augustinians.

Popularly called "San Agustín," its patron saint is in fact St. Paul, the first missionary. The original structures of wood, thatch, and bamboo burned down in 1574, 1583, and 1586. In 1587, the construction of a church and convent in adobe was begun under the guidance of Juan Macías, a Spaniard,[92] and was completed twenty years later. It was a difficult project considering that stone construction was new in the islands, and adobe is actually quite a soft stone. Moreover, funds had to be raised to pay the workers. Appeals were made for contributions which came in the form of "money, chickens, rice, bamboo canes, and rattan."[93] Appeals were also made to the King of Spain for a contribution.[94]

The current façade, ornamented solely by pairs of columns flanking the door and a window above, dates only from the nineteenth century said the historian Luengo in a May 2020 webinar for the Intramuros Administration. Here and at another door

FIG. 87. Army and Navy YMCA in the 1920s.

on the north side is an intricately carved wooden door in an earthy, Filipino version of Rococo, a style associated in Europe with courtly daintiness. Flanking the church door are two pairs of Chinese lions for good luck. Only in the Philippines do such lions guard churches. Two bell towers were added by Luciano Oliver in 1861, but one cracked badly in the earthquakes of 1863 and 1880 and had to be torn down.[95]

A unique feature of the church is the extensive use of stone. For fear of earthquakes, most pre-twentieth century Philippine churches restricted the use of stone to the walls and preferred wooden trusses and ceilings. In contrast, San Agustin has a stone barrel vault over the entire nave. So how are the supporting walls kept from buckling? The nave has side chapels on both sides whose dividing walls, in-between the side chapels, are in fact concealed buttresses.[96] So sturdy is this system that the church survived severe earthquakes in 1645, 1863, 1880, and the heavy bombing in 1945. In 1875, two traveling Italian painters, Cesare Alberoni and Giovanni Dibella, were hired to decorate the interior with trompe l'oeil paintings that relieve the massiveness of the barrel vault. Cutting open the vault into windows or carving bas-reliefs into it would have weakened the fabric. Thanks to the expert draftsmanship of the

FIG. 88. San Agustin Church and Convent

two painters, false windows, simulated coffers, and painted garlands break up the vast space of the vault.

In the side chapels are ornate Baroque altars with twisting columns. Adjoining the church is the **First Monastery,** built together with the church, with a courtyard in the center. Again barrel vaulting was used for the cloister and for the surrounding rooms, for instance the former reception room, the various sacristies, the former refectory, and the ossuary. Save for the ossuary, these rooms have been transformed into a museum of ecclesiastical art featuring masterpieces like ornately carved chests-of-drawers, silver vessels, and exquisite ivories like one crucifix by the eighteenth century Filipino master Juan de los Santos.

Connecting the ground to the upper story is a magnificent Renaissance-style stone floor stairway that ascends in stages under a stone dome. A contribution of the Spanish Renaissance to Western art was to take the stairwell from conceal-

FIG. 89-92. San Agustin, Rococo gate (top left); "Foo Dog" (top right); main altar and retablo (bottom left); pulpit (bottom right)

104 ENDANGERED SPLENDOR

INTRAMUROS: MOTHER CITY 105

FIG. 94. First Monastery, courtyard and cloister

ment, expand it and transform it into a grand setting for ceremonial entries. San Agustín's circular dome, built by Luciano Oliver after 1863 is the highest part of this convent complex and is kept in place by thick buttresses applied to the external surface.[97] The buttresses slant, and make the exterior look sculptural.

The Augustinians combine an active apostolate with prayer in common. At certain hours of the day, they come together to chant the Divine Office. At San Agustin the choir is located above the entry. It has a large set of choir stalls of molave with delicately carved arabesques that date back to the seventeenth century. From the same period dates a choir fascistol that may have come from Macao[98] and is supported by very Chinese-looking angels.

San Agustin has witnessed important events in Philippine history. Miguel Lopez de Legazpi and the patriot-painter Juan Luna were buried at San Agustin. The first church council and the first synod of bishops in the late sixteenth century were also held there. In the sacristy in 1898, plans were discussed for the surrender of Manila to the invading Americans.[99] In February 1945, seven thousand civilians and religious crowded the entire church complex. But the Japanese military plucked the men, whether lay or religious, whether rich or poor, herded them to a shelter in front of the cathedral and massacred them.[100] A monument in the ossuary honors the victims of this atrocity. Shelling by the Americans hammered San Agustin with "300 bombs per day" despite white flags hoisted over the church.[101] This destroyed the **Second Monastery** from 1623 along Real and Santa Lucia streets.[102] Almost all that remains of this building today is the massive three-story adobe-and-brick wall facing Calle Real del Parian, part of an additional wing of the second monastery built sometime between 1713 and 1828.

In 1968–1969, San Agustin underwent extensive transformation in the name of "restoration."[103] The lime plaster was peeled off from the exterior, the cloister, and the adjacent rooms. The goal was to reveal the texture of uncovered adobe. This was the heyday of the Swiss architect Le Corbusier who had delighted the world by revealing the rough beauty of unpainted concrete. Forgotten was that adobe is not concrete. It is porous and, when exposed to the air, either pulverizes or absorbs water. Stripped of its protective lime covering, it becomes sickly-looking. Many uncovered stones of San Agustin began to turn into powder. In the 2000s, the Augustinians woke up to

FIG. 93. Inside San Agustin Church

FIG. 95. San Agustín, Renaissance-style Grand Staircase with dome

FIG. 96. Second Monastery ruins along Calle Real

the threat. Slowly, with the help of architects specializing in conservation, the lime plaster was reapplied. Meanwhile, permanent damage was inflicted. Following the example of Puebla and other Mexican convents of the seventeenth century, there must have been painted murals on the lime cover, as suggested by the remains of such a mural in the former refectory of San Agustin. But the ancient lime cover in the halls has disappeared forever. Even worse, churches all over the country, including Sta. Ana in Manila, copied San Agustin's example. Lime was peeled off from bricks and adobe, thus hastening their deterioration.

A **new monastery** has recently been built west of the existing ancient monastery. Unfortunately, the qualities of traditional upper stories in Intramuros buildings, particularly those of San Agustin's wood-and-stone second monastery from 1623–1668 or the refectory of 1894 have not been incorporated into the new design despite the available photos. Unlike those upper stories, this new monastery's upper story does not cantilever gracefully beyond the ground story walls. Cornices were attached to

FIG. 97. Oscar Ledesma Building

the upper story's bottom part. They are inexplicably wide and thick; they look heavy. It seems that people have the notion that "If it's old and Spanish, it must look heavy" and did not carefully examine surviving structures in Manila and the provinces.

Despite all these changes, San Agustin, along with Paoay, Sta. Maria in Ilocos and Miag-ao, were recognized by the UNESCO as part of the World Heritage List in 1993.

Across from San Agustin and its patio is the privately owned **Oscar Ledesma Building** from 1933 at the corner of Real and Luna. It is of two stories and reinforced concrete and has Art Deco-like parabolas.[104] Though the building looks heavy, the mere fact that its walls survived both American artillery fire and bulldozers is noteworthy.

ARZOBISPO

This street leads from the Archbishop's Palace to San Agustín and is thus named after the Archbishop.

Here were located the nineteenth-century **Ateneo de Manila** before World War II (its ruins exist no more) and **San Ignacio Church** (whose ruins remained). Ignatius of Loyola founded the Society of Jesus in 1540. The Protestant Reformation questioned the authority of the Pope, while the Italian Renaissance questioned all authority that was not backed by reason and observation. In response, the Jesuits opened schools that prized reasoning and thus emphasized mathematics, grammar, and rhetoric. Also emphasized was education in the classics, that is, exposure to the works of the best minds, for eloquence is only a channel for wisdom. Above all students were encouraged to meditate in silence on the life of Christ. This was Christian humanism at its best—a spirituality grounded in the Gospel, but rational and open to the currents of the age.

There were several San Ignacios. The first was begun by Antonio Sedeño, SJ and completed in stone in 1596, thanks to donations given by Manila residents. It was described as being not only of stone but also as having a cross vault (*boveda de arista*).[105] Surely this was a major step for architecture in the islands. In addition, an eyewitness claims that it was the best Jesuit church in all of New Spain[106] but the 1599 earthquake destroyed the vault. Eventually the entire church had to be replaced.[107] A **new one** was raised in 1626–1632 by Gianantonio Campioni, SJ and was located at a site now occupied by the Pamantasan ng Lungsod ng Maynila.[108] It had a nave and two aisles. At its crossing was an eight-sided cupola with "an airy lantern tower

FIG. 98. Old Ateneo de Manila

topped by a pineapple." To resist earthquakes, the ceiling was of wood, and the arches segmented (*arco escarzano*) rather than semi-circular.[109] Unfortunately, after the Jesuits were expelled, years of neglect weakened the stone fabric. Earthquakes in 1852 and 1863 destroyed the church.[110] The **third San Ignacio** was begun in 1878 at its present site on Arzobispo.

This church served as the college chapel of the Ateneo de Manila; here therefore prayed its students, many of whom became the leaders of the Philippines. Felix Roxas was the architect at the start; upon his death Francisco Riera, a Jesuit brother, took over. The Neoclassical façade was made of bricks, marble and cut coral from the Visayas.[111] Let us recall that this style became popular in the nineteenth-century West because it offered a relief from Baroque and Rococo excesses. The exterior of San Ignacio was adorned with a central triangular pediment supported by twin columns: Corinthian for the second story, Ionic for the ground story. In accordance with the Neoclassical aesthetic, these elements were correctly rendered. Because of the frequent tremors, the two bell towers were made of iron sheets and were designed by José Fuentes,

FIG. 99. Ateneo de Manila, main entrance

FIG. 100. Ruins of the second San Ignacio Church

a government engineer. The interior had a nave and two side aisles. On both sides of the nave rose galleries on the second floor that connected with the choir loft and the entrance. San Ignacio's glory was its coffered ceiling decorated with wooden carvings by the renowned Isabelo Tampinco and his artisans. "The ceiling was ornamented with acanthus leaves enclosed in boxes with ropelike designs."[112] The round arches and galleries of the interior recalled Renaissance models. According to Fr. Rene Javellana, at the spot where a cupola was to have been raised but was not, an octahedron was formed with reliefs of Jesuit saints. But the coffered wooden ceiling, particularly the octahedron, does not evoke a Renaissance interior. Instead, with its eight sides and its ornate but carefully measured carving, it evokes the interior of a Chinese temple.

The high altar, composed of correctly rendered Corinthian columns, had a single niche with a statue of San Ignacio carved by Crispulo Hocson, father-in-law of the famous Tampinco. The pulpit, carved from hardwood, had images from the Bible and the symbols of faith, hope and charity.[113]

In 1945, the church became another casualty of the battle. Together with the lot, the shell was sold to a business company which fortunately did not tear it down. It was eventually bought by the government and given to the care of the Intramuros Administration. Since 2013 the church has been undergoing reconstruction as a museum to house the Administration's extensive collection of ecclesiastical art. While the exterior is being rebuilt close to the original design, the reconstruction of the exquisite interior may be done in a later phase due to the high costs of recreating Tampinco's carved masterpiece.

Adjoining the church is the reconstructed offices of the **Archdiocese of Manila.** Fortunately the archbishops of Manila did not sell what remained of their property.

FIG. 101-104. San Ignacio, door screen of main entrance (now at Rizal Library, Ateneo de Manila University, top left); Third San Ignacio Church (top right); Building plans (bottom left and right)

FIG. 105. Third San Ignacio Church, nave and altar

FIG. 106-108. Third San Ignacio Church, ceiling panels (left and center), side portal (right)

This building houses the archdiocesan archives, a museum, and offices. It is a new building from the 1980s, though designed to look like a nineteenth-century one. A problem is that the building is not forthright about it being of three rather than two stories. Because the continuous wall of the ground story hides the first two stories, the extremely tall windows of the ground story seem out of proportion. The better solution would have been honesty: two rows of windows in the ground story. Or: retain the ground story (that has only one story in it) and let the two additional stories rise above. Another problem: the existing upper story barely juts out over the lower story. The overall look of the exterior lacks the generous, horizontal expanse of traditional urban Filipino houses.

FIG. 109. Ruins of the third San Ignacio Church before reconstruction

By the Puerta del Postigo is a miracle—the **Araullo Building**—because it survived the Battle of 1945 largely intact. According to an 1859 plan of the Intramuros Administration, the building started out as a single story cuartel (garrison) with stables. Modified during the American period, the concrete upper story does not cantilever. Instead, it is differentiated from the lower story by a narrow cornice. The thick ground floor walls indicate Spanish-era origins as the site was previously part of the archbishop's palace or the San Carlos Seminary. Even in the upper story, the windows of glass are tall and narrow rather than long and horizontal. As an afterthought, a continuous metal canopy was installed over the windows of both stories. Decorations center on the middle bay: over the main entry, a triangular pediment rests on two pilasters with rosettes as capitals. Above it, an American eagle presides over the oblong seal of the City of Manila, the original owner of the building, which was remodeled to its current appearance from 1915–1916 and was then known as the Postigo Building. Today named after esteemed Chief Justice Manuel Araullo (served 1921–1924) and adjacent to the former Supreme Court facing Plaza Roma, the Araullo Building was part of the former Supreme Court complex in Intramuros before the court moved to its present location in Ermita. After the war it became the headquarters of the National Bureau of Investigation (NBI), founded as the Division of Investigation in 1936.

The Commission on Elections, which manages the entire electoral process of the Philippines, began in 1940 in the third floor of the Manila City Hall. After the war,

FIG. 110. Araullo Building

it moved to the reconstructed Aduana Building, together with the Bureau of the Treasury.[114] However, after a mysterious fire burned the structure, the COMELEC moved into a building adjacent to the Araullo. The latter was designated as the COMELEC Annex in 1960.[115] But another mysterious fire struck the COMELEC's Main Office, forcing it to move again. Araullo remains its annex, hopefully not to be burned for mere short-term political gain, after having survived the epic Battle of Manila.

ADUANA

The street is named after the Customs House which was formerly located here. It was renamed after A. Soriano, Secretary of the Philippine government-in-exile in the US in 1941–1945 under President M. Quezon. The Central Bank thus fell under his watch. After Liberation the Central Bank held office in the Aduana before it moved to its present location on Roxas Boulevard.[116] Still, street names, like Aduana, that have been in existence for several generations should be respected. Constant changes sow confusion.

Till the early nineteenth century, Manila's customs house was the eight-sided Alcaicería de San Fernando located north of the Pasig in what is now the district of San Nicolas (see the chapter on San Nicolas). Unfortunately, this encouraged merchants to live outside the city walls rather than within them. Government instructions in 1796 ordered that a customs house be built within the city walls.[117]

FIG. 111. Aduana Building

The structure, built in 1828–1829 to a design by Spanish engineer Tomas Cortes, was of adobe in all stories and was faced with lime. Luis Merino, OSA quotes a report of the period stating that the building had three principal entrances, two courtyards, and two principal staircases.[118] The inspiration was not the traditional Filipino Wood-and-Stone building but Western models of its period. A quest for simplicity arose in reaction against the opulence of the Baroque. Greek and Roman buildings were extolled as models of dignity and simplicity. The silhouette of the building rises sheer from the street and is interrupted halfway by projecting balconies with lace-like iron grills. French windows open into these balconies. The main entry is defined by three arched doors. Above these are French windows separated from each other by pilasters with fanciful Ionic capitals. Corner bays are emphasized by sets of pilasters. The building was damaged by the 1863 earthquake. Reconstruction was begun by Luis Perez Yap-Sionjue while the little-acknowledged architect was Juan Rom. The 1874 construction was supervised by Luis Cespedes who made some modifications to make the building stronger.[119] Here were lodged no longer the customs but rather the offices of Finance, Accounting, and Treasury, of the Regulation of Payments, and of the Central Administration of Revenues.[120] The involvement of a Yap-Sionjue is significant, for it lays to rest the notion that the construction of all these buildings was directed solely by Spaniards.

Then came the great earthquake of 1880. Because the building had taken proper account of the qualities of local stone and wood and was well-constructed, it had only a few minor damages.[121] However, the building was destroyed once more during the fighting in 1945. It was reconstructed and housed the Central Bank of the Philippines, the Office of the Treasury and the Commission on Elections. Unfortunately, one of those mysterious Manila fires consumed it in 1979. Under President Fidel Ramos, there were plans to relocate the National Archives here. Restoration work began in 1998.[122] However, this was halted and has not resumed up to today.

MURALLA

This street running along the Walls of Intramuros is aptly called such—the Spanish for "wall."

In 1620, Juan Alonso Geronimo Guerrero, a retired Spanish soldier who led the life of a hermit, gathered orphans—the sons of soldiers. He converted his house into a refuge and taught them religion, basic arithmetic, and grammar.[123] This became the Colegio de Niños Huerfanos de San Juan de Letrán (College of the Orphan Boys of San Juan de Letrán)[124] now known as the **Colegio de San Juan de Letrán**. It was named after the Basilica of St. John Lateran in Rome—Letrán in Spanish. Informed of the poverty of Geronimo and his wards, in 1623, Philip IV endowed them with a steady means of support.[125] Meanwhile Brother Diego de Sta. Maria, OP arrived in 1632. Moved likewise by the condition of poor orphans, he asked his fellow Dominicans' permission for the orphans to stay in their convent.[126] In 1640, Juan Geronimo turned over his college to the Dominicans, and then joined the order.[127] Was Letran only for the Spanish-born? So claims the popular cliché today. But under Geronimo's care was the famous native Filipino Andrés Malong, who entered in 1629 at age nine, as an orphan. He became Maestre del Campo in the Spanish army, but deserted in 1660 to rebel against Spain.[128] Cristoval Punsalan, obviously Pampango, was born in Guagua in 1638, and entered in 1645. After finishing secondary education, he joined the military and became the Capitán de Infantería, and eventually Alcalde Mayor (Governor) of Panay and Leyte.[129]

FIG. 112. Colegio de San Juan de Letran

FIG. 113. Colegio de San Juan de Letran, Portal

By 1640–1655, there were more than 590 students in Letran. They came from all over the Philippines, as can be gleaned from this list of their places of origin: Apalit, Bacolor, Bagumbayan, Betis, Cagayan, Caraga, Cavite, Orani (Bataan), Cebu, Ilocos, Lingayen, Longos (Bulacan), Lubao, Macabebe, Parañaque, Tayabas. They also came from other countries: Acapulco, Pachuca (Mexico); Los Angeles (now in California but used to be a part of Mexico); Avila, Canarias, Madrid, Seville (Spain); Chalco, Lima (Peru); Nagasaki, Osaka (Japan). The list also mentions Dilao (now Paco) which was then a Japanese settlement.[130] Letran was thus a school that was truly island-wide in its reach, and at the same time international. It was the first of its kind.

During the following centuries, Letran nurtured men who would lead the emerging Filipino nation: Fr. José Burgos, Marcelo del Pilar, Emilio Jacinto, Apolinario Mabini, and Emilio Aguinaldo.

In 1933–1937, a new complex of buildings that were taller, larger, and made of reinforced concrete replaced the previous one of Wood-and-Stone.[131] Though destroyed in 1945, it was rebuilt with four floors following the original design: two risalits at both corners of the principal façade, and a major risalit at the entry; decorative though very simplified pilasters connecting the floors; cartouches at the top of all three risalits to give a noble flourish, especially at the middle where the college seal is displayed.

VANISHED VISTAS

In other localities, we can easily ignore vintage structures and sites that have long since vanished. Not so in Intramuros where their spirit has a vivid presence even today.

Let us begin with plazas and patios that create expansive spaces. Perhaps more memorable even than the Plaza Mayor (now Plaza Roma) in front of the Cathedral was the magnificent **Plaza de Sto. Tomás**—an island of greenery bounded on the north by the Neo-Gothic nave, lantern tower and twin entry towers of **Sto. Domingo Church**, on the west by the **Universidad de Sto. Tomás**, on the east by the **Colegio de Sta. Rosa**.[132] In the middle grew rows of stately royal palms whose pointed curves rhymed with the Gothic arches of the nearby church. Below were two simple round fountains flanking the statue of Fr. Benavidez, founder of UST. Another memorable patio was that one bounded on the one side by the **Church of San Francisco** and on the other by the 1723–1734 **Chapel of the Venerable Orden Tercera** (Venerable Third Order of St. Francis). No greenery here, but it must have been a sight to see two churches, both Baroque and monumental, partnering to form an angle at this open space. The site is now occupied by Mapua Institute of Technology. Finally there was that patio that was not quadrangular but rather an L-shape bending around the corner of the tall, mullioned tower of the Recollects. The site is now the location of *Manila Bulletin*.

Churches and convents abounded. Mention was already made of **Sto. Domingo Church**. The 1864–1868 version was designed by local architect Felix Roxas as a robust tropical version of Gothic: two low façade towers without spires and with interior wooden vaulting. Its main treasure was the image of Nuestra Señora del Santíssimo Rosario, popularly called La Naval de Manila because of the victories attributed to

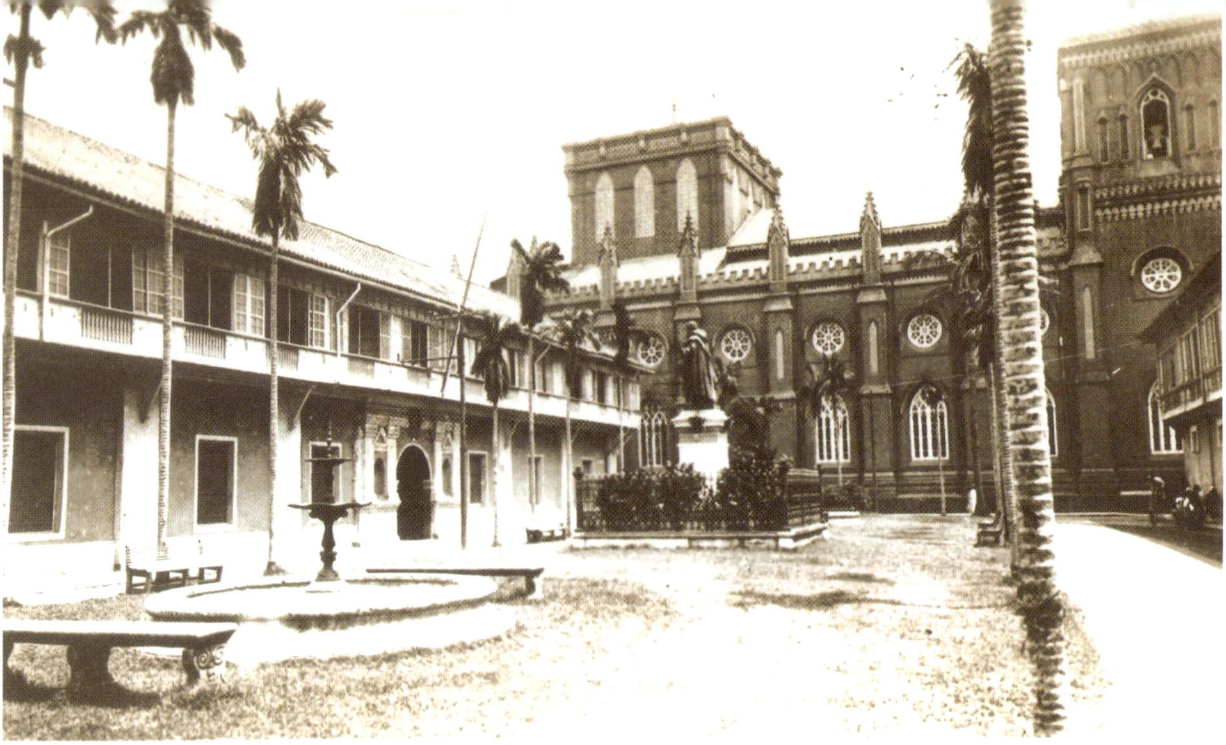
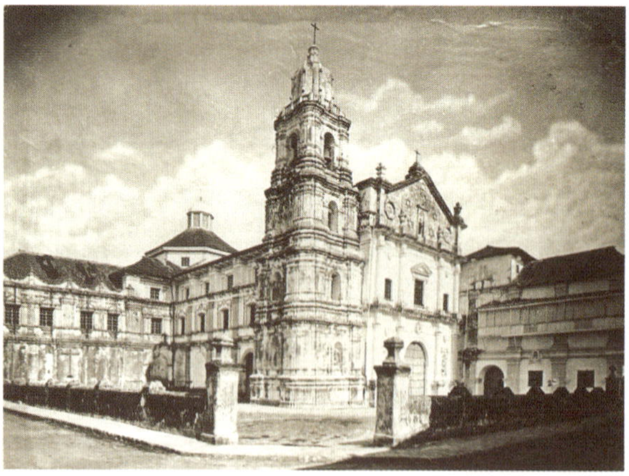
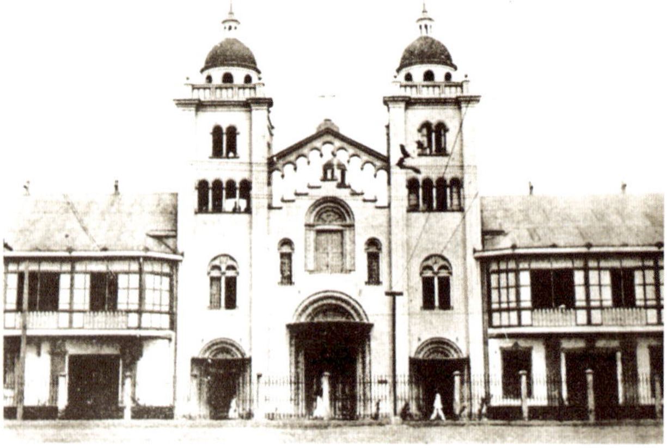
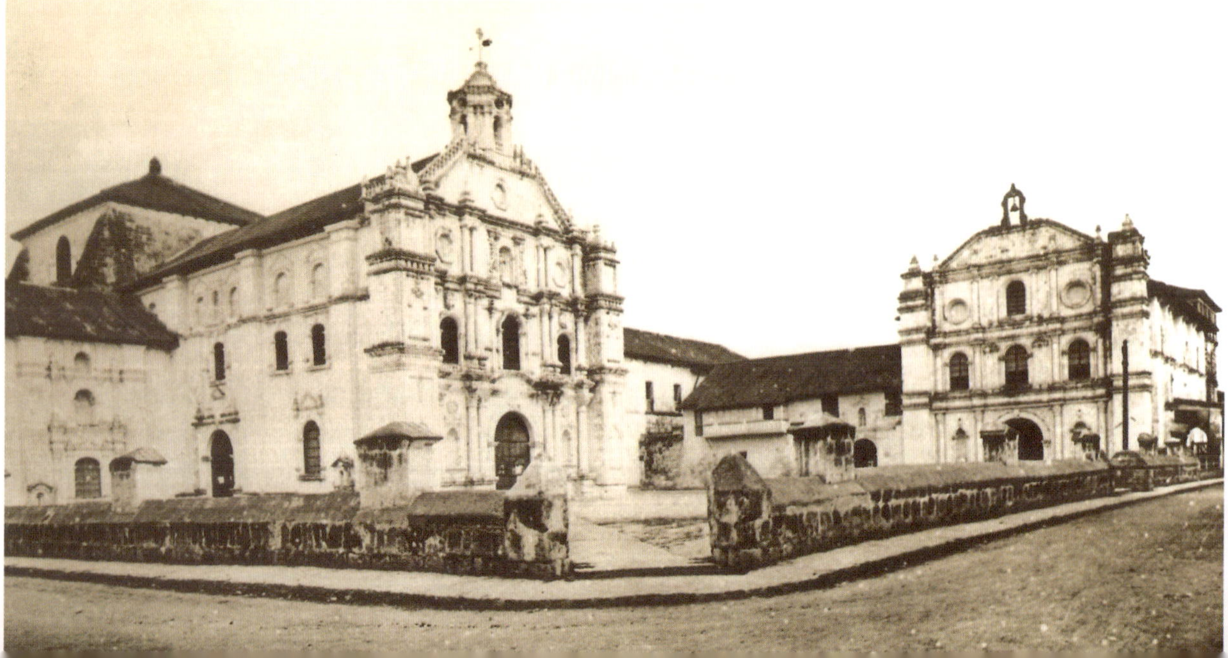

FIG. 114-117. Adjacent page: Plaza Sto. Tomas with Sto. Domingo Church (top, right side) and Universidad de Sto. Tomás (top, left side) with Statue of Miguel de Benavides, OP (today replaced with a replica);

San Nicolas de Tolentino Church (middle left); Nuestra Señora de Lourdes Church (middle right);

San Francisco Church (bottom, left side) and Chapel of the Venerable Orden Tercera (bottom, right side)

her intercession during five seabattles with the Dutch in 1646. The Franciscan church of **Nuestra Señora de los Angeles** was a Baroque composition sans belfry of paired columns, arches and octagons dating from 1739–1750. The 1781 Recollect church of **San Nicolas de Tolentino** had a lone tower whose four corners curved gracefully because of clusters of pilasters. The interior boasted of a tall Baroque retablo with twisting columns. It was also famous for its pipe organ. **San Ignacio**, as described earlier, was built after the return of the Jesuits in 1859. Most recent of all was the Capuchin church of **Nuestra Señora de Lourdes** built 1894–1898 in a somewhat stiff rendering of Neo-Romanesque. Attached to these churches were the respective convents of the Recollects, Franciscans, Dominicans, and the Jesuits. Pious women had their sacred enclosures too: **Monasterio de Sta. Clara** (founded 1658), **Beaterio de la Compañía** (founded 1684), **Beaterio de Sta. Catalina** (founded 1696), and the **Convents** of the nuns teaching at the **Colegio de Sta. Isabel** and the **Colegio de Sta. Rosa**. Most if not all of these residences had private chapels, libraries, archives, vestments, and sacred objects used for worship. Most of these treasures perished in 1945.

FIG. 118. Sto. Domingo Church

There were several schools. For men: **Colegio de San Juan de Letrán, Colegio de San José,** established 1601, **Ateneo de Manila** founded in 1859, **Universidad de Sto. Tomás,** founded 1619. For women: **Colegio de Sta. Isabel** established 1632 and **Colegio de Sta. Rosa**. Many of these were repaired or rebuilt after the 1863 and 1880 earthquakes. Although their style springs from Intramuros' tradition of building in wood-and-stone since the late seventeenth century, they often looked more monumental than private houses. They had many bays and sometimes had three stories. Their entrances were highlighted by columns, and ornately carved arches. Their ornateness created a dramatic contrast with the simplicity of the rest of the exterior which featured a rhythmic series of windows and, occasionally, pilasters. Most outstanding was the UST. Its lofty entrance lobby led to a magnificent central stairway of stone. On the lobby's walls were reproductions of the works of the great Spanish

FIG. 119. Colegio de Sta. Isabel

FIG. 120. Beaterio de Sta. Catalina

FIG. 121. Palacio de Sta. Potenciana

FIG. 122. Colegio de San José

painter Velasquez. Adjacent garden patios opened the mass of the building with wells of air and greenery.

The **Hospital de San Juan de Dios,** rebuilt in 1876 after the devastating earthquake of 1863 had a unique exterior. Over the main entry was a long, flat terrace of several bays. The second story rose behind the terrace. At the corners of the hospital were two-story stone pavilions from which self-contained wooden window galleries (*galerias voladas*) jutted out and seemed to defy gravity. Though the windows were of capiz, they recalled the famous cantilevered wooden galleries of Viceregal Lima of Peru and of Arab cities like Cairo and Jeddah. This hospital began in 1577 at the porter gate of the Franciscan convent of Manila where poor Filipinos would go seeking a cure. In 1656 the hospital passed on to the Brothers Hospitallers of San Juan de Dios.[133] Its successor is the Hospital of San Juan de Dios on Roxas Boulevard, Pasay City.

In addition to the Ayuntamiento described above, Intramuros had another palace—the **Palacio Arzobispal** (Archbishop's Palace) which was located beside San Ignacio Church. Its throne room rose three stories high and was hung with chandeliers. Rows of tall, uninterrupted columns flanked the hall and emphasized the height.

The **Colegio de Sta. Potenciana**, observes art historian Romeo Galang Jr., was another palace. Located on the present street of Sta. Potenciana where the Knights of Columbus are now located, it was founded in 1589 as the oldest girls' school in the country, and was last rebuilt in 1885 as an office of the Governor-General.

FIG. 123. Hospital de San Juan de Dios

Flanking many of these important institutional buildings were houses of ordinary citizens, some obviously wealthy, others poor. Although built at different historical periods, they harmonized with their neighbours because of similar proportions and silhouettes: cantilevered upper stories over lower stories of stone. Pre-1945 Intramuros had a wealth of Renaissance vistas—rows of buildings with windows and doors receding into the distance. Particularly elegant were the curving corners of cantilevered upper stories.

A unique feature of the Walled City were the occasional bridges connecting second stories with each other. The most salient joined the Augustinian convent with the office of the Augustinian Provincial (now the Cojuangco Building). The covered bridge had a gallery of open windows under transoms decorated with Stars of David, for one of the titles of Our Lady's Litany honors her status as a wife to a descendant of King David.

NOTABLE RECONSTRUCTIONS

To rationalize the development of Intramuros, President Ferdinand Marcos created the Intramuros Administration as an administrative unit separate from the City of Manila and directly under the national government. The district was placed under the Ministry of Human Settlements (MHS). After the MHS was abolished by President Corazon Aquino, Intramuros passed over to the custody of the Department of Tourism where it so remains to this day.

Though the Marcos government committed grievous mistakes in terms of urban planning, like allowing the monstrous high-rise called the Palacio del Gobernador to tower over the cathedral and the plaza, it should be credited for eventually imposing a height restriction and for promoting the construction of new buildings that tried to accord with the area's previous architecture. True, the result's quality has been mixed. Very often, there is little appreciation for the functional features of traditional urban Filipino houses. Thus, instead of creating authentic ventanillas that can be opened to let in much breeze, fancy iron grills are affixed to the wall below the windows to simulate a ventanilla. And instead of vents with grills on the bottom pedestal of the entire house to allow air to enter and dry the basement, another fancy grill is screwed on to

FIG. 124. Along Calle Sta. Clara

the wall to simulate a vent. The recently "restored" Almacenes Reales exemplify the lack of attention to historical accuracy. The wall bricks were exposed; in between the red bricks, gray cement rather than white lime was applied. The effect is ghastly. Moreover, the supposed French windows, being higher than the balcony railings in front, cannot open into them. The effect can only be described as visually illogical. Seventeenth- to eighteenth-century windows opened into railings and were not located above them. Traditional island architecture was logical: every major component had a functional role to play.

The graceful, leaping profile of traditional Manila architecture is now often ignored. The steep slope of the roof, its wide eaves plus its moderately sized gutter pulled the cantilevering wooden upper story forward beyond the stone walls of the lower story. The result was a buoyant, floating feeling which reprised the same feeling of the native house on stilts, though in stronger materials and in a more complex way. This buoyancy is lost in the present tendency to thicken both the roof edge and the bottom edge of the cantilevered upper story.

However, there have been efforts to retain the architectural character of the district. We should count our blessings. What Intramuros needs is a style book that will guide future builders and developers in designing their structures. Here are three notable buildings constructed beginning in 1981.[134]

Barrio San Luis Complex. This 1980s complex occupies one whole block on the north side of San Agustin's plaza. It includes a lifestyle museum, a restaurant, an exhibition hall, a hotel, and a bevy of specialty shops. All of these use late-twentieth-century building technology but with adobe cladding.

Casa Manila is a museum that recreates the ambience of a grand, late nineteenth-century mansion. The furniture pieces are authentic examples of Filipino craftsmanship of that period at its best.

Stylistically, Casa Manila is more typical of Binondo and San Nicolas across the river in that it has three storeys of which the middle has projecting balconies. Moreover, its use of adobe sans lime plaster has created a bad example for other subsequent reconstructions. At least, together with its neighbours in Barrio San Luis,

FIG. 125. Casa Manila: Sala (main living room)

FIG. 126. Casa Manila: Oratorio (chapel), former Hidalgo House, Quiapo

FIG. 127. Casa Manila: Comedor (dining room), with manually-operated cloth fans

FIG. 128. Casa Manila: Cusina (kitchen) with horno (oven) and irons

FIG. 129. Casa Manila: Ice-operated refrigerator (before the advent of electricity)

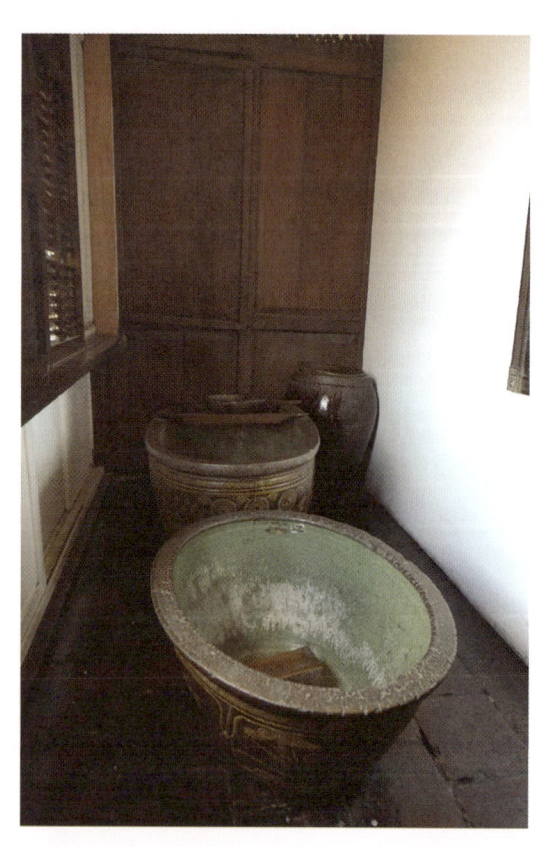

FIG. 130. Casa Manila: Banyo (bathroom) with bathtubs

FIG. 131. Casa Manila: Latrina (comfort room) with double-seater toilet

it protects this very important plaza from intrusions like high-rises. The houses in this complex create an engaging ensemble.

The second reconstructed building is **Los Hidalgos** which houses the restaurant Barbara's and various shops. This design is unusual for Intramuros. The two-story walls are both of adobe and rise sheer with no cantilevering. Projecting forward from the second story's French doors is a row of stone balconies. Its design is based on a photo of a building that existed in the Walled City before 1945 (and is believed to date from the mid–eighteenth century). The style, more Peninsular Spanish than Filipino, may well be what was common in Manila before the earthquake of 1645 levelled multi-story buildings of adobe. Beside Los Hidalgos is **El Hogar Filipino** which communicates the exuberant Filipino style at the turn of the nineteenth century: a fondness for dividing wall spaces into bordered panels patterned with flowers within some of the panels, floral iron grills, and ornate brackets under roof eaves and a cantilevered second story. The house is modelled after the ancestral House of the Cuyugan family at M. H. del Pilar Street in Ermita, and was reconstructed based on old drawings in the National Archives.[135] This building serves as reception area for events. Behind Calle Urdaneta are two buildings: **Casa Urdaneta** and **Casa Blanca**. The former houses a hotel and was designed by Augusto Villalon, a restoration architect and foremost advocate of heritage preservation. Another style, more typical of the Caribbean, is evoked by the hotel: one where a continuous balcony hangs in front of the exterior inviting the occupants to spend their afternoons on lazy chairs overlooking the street. When it was still new, the balcony was white against a subtle old rose wall: the building exuded charm. It has, however, been recently renovated. The sixth building (Casa Blanca) in this complex is called such because it is completely in white. At the upper story of the main exterior facing Urdaneta is a continuous row of capiz windows and ventanillas with a mixture of wooden balusters and iron grilles; below is a street door with a flat arch. The uses of this building have varied over time. Sometimes it has been used for superb exhibits

FIG. 132. Casa Los Hidalgos patio, San Luis Complex

of art. Beside it is the remarkable **Casa Ruiz** whose stately row of Ionic columns faces Calle Real del Parian. It was modelled after the nineteenth-century house of Teniente Coronel Felix D. Ruiz, whose plans were found in the National Archives.

The roof eaves-and-gutter, as well as the cornice of the projecting second story, have been thickened unnecessarily on these buildings. As a result the house profile looks a bit heavy. Moreover, must the windows always be closed? Still taken together, they communicate

FIG. 133-134. Casa Manila courtyard with fountain (top); Casa Los Hidalgos (bottom)

something of the charm of a bygone era. Moreover, their most picturesque interior patios connected together by arches and galleries encourage exploration.

Eduardo Cojuangco Building. Fronting the convent of San Agustin on Real corner Arzobispo is this remarkable building from 1989. Originally there was a building here that was the Augustinian Provincial's House (built 1894–1898) and connected to the convent with a beautiful bridge, somewhat reminiscent of Venice's Bridge of Sighs. Both the bridge and the house were destroyed in the 1932 fire which also gutted the old Ateneo de Manila and part of Sta. Isabel College. The present building recreates its former Neo-Mudejar magnificence. It is built entirely of reinforced concrete, and skilled craftsmen created bas-reliefs in the upper two stories that are carved with care. Memorable are the Stars of David that appear in circles over the windows of the upper story. The "Star of David," a popular title of Mary in her litany, alludes to Joseph, her husband, who came from that noble line.

El Amanecer Building. This is the location of Silahis Arts and Crafts which began in 1966, but the building itself arose after the Intramuros Administration began. Before 1945, the Capuchin church of Our Lady of Lourdes stood on this site, and is commemorated by photos within the building complex. Fronting the street is a long building whose ground story is of reinforced concrete clad with adobe blocks and whose upper story is of brown wood with capiz windows and balustered ventanillas. Behind is a patio with a well, and farther behind a restaurant specializing in traditional Filipino cuisine. El Amanecer, the long building, is designed simply and looks dignified. Thankfully the upper story cantilevers generously. It is also the only privately owned building in all of Intramuros that actually uses wood for the upper floor, instead of the omnipresent concrete which replaced the traditionally-used wood after the war.

FIG. 135-136. Casa El Hogar Filipino

FIG. 137. Casa Ruiz, home of Instituto Cervantes Library

FIG. 138-139. Casa Urdaneta (left); Casa Blanca (right)

FIG. 140. Eduardo Cojuangco Building/Augustinian Casa Provincial

It was awarded by the Intramuros Administration as an outstanding conforming building in 1985. My main concern is that the designer chose to expose the adobe blocks and thus highlight their greyness, while painting the wooden upper story a dark brown. A gloomy mood hangs over the exterior. I grew up in a 1914 house (the Nakpil in Quiapo) and often explored houses and neighbourhoods in San Nicolas, Manila, Taal, and San Miguel de Mayumo before the craze for the grey and brown finish became prevalent in the 1980s. Untampered, the traditional pastel colors of pre-1940 houses looked cheerful.

Colegio de Sta. Rosa. It fronts what used to be a beautiful plaza dominated by the towers of Sto. Domingo, and should also be thanked for attempting to follow the original, pre-1945 design of its three-story school after initially rebuilding in Modernist style.

Beaterio de la Compañía. Another well-reconstructed building is the former nineteenth-century Motherhouse of the Beaterio de la Compañía which was rebuilt in 2003 to accommodate a Light-and-Sound Museum. The exterior's austere silhouette is dominated at one end by the triangular shape of the chapel's gable roof rising over

FIG. 141. El Amanecer Building

an entry framed by pilasters and a beautifully rounded arch-pediment. The rest of the façade is a rectangular wall with three stories from which a gallery gently cantilevers.

A century after the coming of the Faith to Manila in 1571, some devout women felt the need to live the Gospel with more intensity. While some entered the Franciscan Monasterio de Sta. Clara, others formed the *beaterio*. A *beata* was a woman who, together with like-minded women, wished to live a life dedicated to prayer and charity. They wore a habit, could live either at home or together, and placed themselves under the guidance of a priest. Such a community was called a beaterio.[136] Madre Ignacia del Espiritú Santo, a Chinese mestiza, founded such a community for Chinese mestizas and native Filipinas who were not admitted into Sta. Clara which was strictly for Spanish women only. Instead of just a vow of chastity, Madre Ignacia and her beatas also assumed a vow of poverty, and placed themselves under the guidance of a Jesuit. By 1684, Madre Ignacia had opened a house that welcomed women, whether Spanish or native, who wished to live a life of recollection.[137] The Beaterio eventually specialized in conducting spiritual retreats in the Ignatian manner among the women.[138] Much impressed were the archbishop and the governor-general, and the Marquis de Obando, whose own wife had benefited from these retreats in the Beaterio, conducted by the non-Spanish beatas.[139] There was indeed separation between ethnic groups in Spanish Manila, for each had its own legal identity, but not segregation. Moreover, such a separation could be subverted by a commonly held Faith.

Today this mission of teaching in schools and conducting retreats is continued by the beaterio's successor, the Religious of the Virgin Mary, the first Filipino congregation for women.

WHY PRESERVE WHAT IS WHOLLY NEGATIVE?

Inaugurated in 2003 by the Department of Tourism, the reconstructed Beaterio houses a Light-and-Sound Museum that narrates the history of Intramuros down to the execution of Rizal. The narrative is all about the abuses of the Spaniards. We should ask: if Intramuros is all about negativities, why preserve and reconstruct it? Is this merely to attract tourists?

FIG. 142. Colegio de Sta. Rosa

Errors and clichés abound in the Light-and-Sound Museum, aptly nicknamed "the Museum of Horrors." As usual the claim is that the Walls were built with forced labor and that Intramuros was only for Spanish residents. I answered those charges earlier in this chapter. That all the learning and the developments in the arts were only for Spaniards is a strange claim the museum makes. So what were Rizal and other native-born Filipinos doing in Ateneo de Manila learning not only Spanish, English, and French, but also Latin and Greek; studying not only mathematics and literature but also painting, sculpture, and music? The same can be asked of students in Letran, among them Emilio Jacinto and Emilio Aguinaldo, who were exposed to a very classical education with even greater emphasis on music—for Letran was renowned for its music school. In lectures at the University of the Philippines and the Ateneo de Manila, William Summers, a musical historian from Dartmouth, New Jersey specializing in Hispanic Manila, warned in a public lecture at the Ateneo de Manila against the tendency towards black propaganda. Nineteenth-century Manila, according to him, had a very lively opera season that lasted for almost three months every year.

FIG. 143. Beaterio de la Compañía

FIG. 144. Carromata

Spanish and Italian companies made Manila and its suburbs their regular stopover. Such a season would have been impossible if only the numerically few Spaniards went to the theater.

MAGALLANES DRIVE

This, of course, is named after the explorer Magallanes.

Outside the walls but within the district of Intramuros is the **Chamber of Commerce** by Juan Arellano. It is well-described by Reuben Ramas Cañete as:

> A gem of a structure with its restrained Palladian-style blocking of elements. Its only concessions to ornateness are the sculpture frieze surrounding the main hall's arched windows, and the window mouldings on the west and east ends, with ceremonial urn finials.[140]

Though the original building from the 1930s was built during the American period and was heavily damaged in 1945, it seems to have been restored well except for the grand double staircase that, like in a Baroque palace, led to the grand entrance but was removed during a later renovation.

The **National Press Club of the Philippines** was inspired by the Bauhaus; this four-story building has a circular, glass-enclosed stairwell that gives commanding views of the Walls, the Post Office, the Pasig, and part of the Escolta as one ascends the stairs. It used to have a witty mural by Vicente Manansala. The elegant, minimalist design is typical of Angel Nakpil. It was built in 1954–1955.[141]

FIG. 145. Chamber of Commerce Building and Statue of Queen Isabel II

LIVING IN INTRAMUROS

"Oh, Manila! My last thoughts shall be of you! (*O, Manille! A toi sera ma dernière pensée!*). Thus wrote Jean Mallat in 1846, a Frenchman who had lived in the Philippines for almost a decade and knew the Walled City well.[142] He found it "charming"; in it abounded a "goodness of heart" and an "enthusiastic friendliness" that made a man's home the home of others as well. In it there were no "differences of rank and fortune."[143] Almost as similar a refrain would be heard from the visiting Sir John Bowring thirteen years later.[144]

Fast forward: At first blush, the Walled City today seems to be an unattractive place to live in. There are large colonies of informal settlers at its core. There is no mall, no movie house. Yet, a different picture is given by the recently deceased Randolph de Jesus, a history professor who lived there since 1993 in a townhouse. The district is easily accessible by jeepney or a walk across the bridges to Quiapo and Sta. Cruz.

There are several good restaurants within the walls and a bank. While there is no mall, nearby malls in Ermita are just a few minutes' walk away. Intramuros seems "unsafe," yet de Jesus felt safe because he and his family made friends with their neighbours in a nearby informal settlement. While their neighbours do love to sing between seven and nine p.m., they stop by ten. He loved the "mystique" of the place. As a student in nearby Letran, they rehearsed for their school plays at Puerta Isabel II. Today students like to roam on top of the walls in the afternoon. Monuments are close by. On Sundays he and his family went to the cathedral. Throughout the day, bells mark the hour. On the Sunday before 8 December, streets are closed and cleaned in preparation for the annual procession that many of the residents wait for in anticipation. Lavishly decorated statues of Mary are taken out on the Feast of the Immaculate Conception and paraded around the district. On Holy Thursday evening, there is a different buzz. The streets are crowded with devotees, most of them from the rest of Manila, who are there to visit San Agustin and the Cathedral as part of the "Visita Iglesia." Vendors line General Luna Street which connects the two churches.

FIG. 146. National Press Club of the Philippines

But what about ordinary residents of Intramuros? What do they think of the place? In 2010, I interviewed some of the poor residents of the place.

A common and unexpected answer was that the poorer residents feel "protected by the Walls." "Outside the Walls," they said, "there is criminality. Here we feel safe." In their youth, they would play in the gardens of Fort Santiago. Now married, they tend to spend their afternoons within their neighborhood, that is, on the streets, while some still bring their children to the gardens of the fort. Sundays they go to San Agustin or to the Basilica of the Nazarene in nearby Quiapo. Contrary to expectation, poorer residents do visit the various museums because they say they like to look at old furniture and garments. Of course, they cannot do this often because of the cost but, at least, these are nearby.

FIG. 147. Manila Cathedral and Plaza Roma at night

That the poor residents feel rooted is borne out by the fact they now celebrate their own fiesta, the Feast of Our Lady of Lourdes. In 1890, the Capuchins raised a church in honor of Our Lady of Lourdes. The church was another casualty of 1945. No matter. The residents, some of whom are third-generation inhabitants, love to celebrate this feast with feasting in their neighbourhoods. "Just because we are poor does not mean we cannot spend for a fiesta."

NOTES

1. Antoon Postma, 1992, "The Laguna Copper Plate Inscription: Text and Commentary," *Philippine Studies* 40, no. 2: 183–203.

2. Robert R. Reed, *Colonial Manila: The Context of Hispanic Urbanism and Process of Morphogenesis* (Berkeley, California: University of California Press, 1978), 1.

3. Reed, *Colonial Manila*, 3.

4. City comes from the Latin *civitas* which can mean either city or state. *Urban* is derived from the Latin *urbs*—another term for city. There is an extensive literature in sociology and anthropology on what makes a "city" or an "urban settlement" different from other types of settlement. This has nothing to do with population or with what a government, like the Philippine, recognizes as "city." Examples of such studies are Lewis Mumford, *The City in History: Its Origins, Its Transformations and Its Prospects* (San Diego: Harcourt Inc., 1961); Gideon Sjoberg, *The Preindustrial City, Past and Present* (New York: Free Press, 1960); Anthony Giddens, *A Contemporary Critique of Historical Materialism, Vol. 1: Power, Property and the State* (London: The Macmillan Press, 1981). Such studies cannot be regarded as "Western-centric," for they examine examples from all the continents, and in fact show that urbanism in Western Europe appeared much later than in the Near East. A running theme is the presence of institutions, such as full-time division of labor, and the division of this into mental and manual labor. Discussions of when urbanism began in pre-nineteenth century

Philippines should take such studies into account.

5   In addition to the above, these are relevant: Robert R. Reed, *Hispanic Urbanism in the Philippines: A Study of the Impact of Church and State* (Manila: University of Manila, 1967); Reed, *Origins of the Philippine City: A Comparative Inquiry Concerning Indigenous Southeast Asian Settlements and Spanish Colonial Urbanism* (Berkeley, California: University of California Press,1971); Robert Redfield, *The Primitive World and Its Transformations* (Ithaca, New York: Cornell University Press, 1953); Robert Mcormick Adams, *The Evolution of Urban Society: Early Mesopotamia and Pre-Hispanic Mexico* (Chicago: Aldine Press, 1966).

6   Reed, *Colonial Manila*, 7-9.

7   See for instance: the Author of the Boxer Codex, "The manners, customs and beliefs of the Philippine inhabitants of long ago, being chapters of 'A late sixteenth century Manila manuscript,'" transcribed, translated and annotated by Carlos Quirino and Mauro Garcia, *The Philippine Journal of Science* 87, no. 4: 325-453; Pedro de Chirino SJ, *Relación de las Islas Filipinas/ The Philippines in 1600* (Manila: Historical Conservation Society, 1969), 89, 328; Antonio Morga, *Sucesos de las Islas Filipinas,* edited and with commentary by Wenceslao E. Retana (Madrid: Librería General de Victoriano Suárez, [1609] 1910), 193.

8   Chirino, *Relación de las Islas Filipinas/ The Philippines in 1600*, 24, 256.

9   Luis Dery, *A History of the Inarticulate: Local History, Prostitution and Other Views from the Bottom* (Quezon City: New Day Publishers, 2001), 5, 7.

10 William Henry Scott, *Barangay: Sixteenth-Century Philippine Culture and Society* (Quezon City: Ateneo de Manila University Press, 1994), 191.

11 Ibid.

12 Luciano Santiago, "The Houses of Lakandula, Matanda and Soliman (1571-1898): Genealogy and Group Identity," *Philippine Quarterly of Culture and Society* 18 (1990): 39-73; Luis Dery, *A History of the Inarticulate,* 4, 22.

13 Anonymous Author of 1570, 1903, "Relation of the Voyage to Luzon, June 1570," in *The Philippine Islands 1493-1803*, vol. 3, by Emma Blair and James Robertson (Cleveland, Ohio: A.H. Clark, [1903-1909]); "Conquest of the Island of Luzon, Manila, 20 April 1572", *The Philippine Islands*, vol. 3 by Blair and Robertson.

14 Scott, *Barangay*, 207.

15 Ibid.

16 Ibid.

17 Ibid., 208.

18 One common view is that the conquest of the Philippines was a relatively peaceful one. However, a more recent perspective highlights the violence and the resulting decrease in population. See Olivia Newson, *Conquest and Pestilence in the Early Philippines* (Honolulu: University of Hawai'i, 1999).

19 Robert R. Reed, examined the origins of urbanism in Manila in a sequence of three books mentioned in footnote 3. His perspective, being that of a cultural geographer, is valuable.

20 This is described by Bernard H. Vlekke, *Nusantara: A History of the East Indian Archipelago* (Cambridge: Massachusetts, Harvard University Press, 1945), 56-57.

21 Joan Piggott, *The Emergence of Japanese Kingship* (Stanford: Stanford University Press, 1997).

22 There is a description of this event at the outlook point at Nuuanu Cliffs. Plus popular tales about ghost armies roaming the area at night keep this memory alive.

23 Edward Spenser Bouchier, *Spain under the Roman Empire* (Oxford: Blackwell, 1914), 21.

24 Nick Joaquin, "Lapu-Lapu and Humabon: The Filipino as twins," *Philippine Quarterly of Culture and Society* 7, (March-June 1979), nos. 1-2: 51-57.

25 Some of the Spanish missionaries themselves came from a rural background and thus knew how to plow and harrow. They taught these methods to their parishioners, according to the priest Antonio Mozo, in *Noticia histórico-natural de los gloriosos triumphos y felices adelantamientos conseguidos en el presente siglo por los religiosos del orden de N.P.S. Agustín en las missiones que tienen a su cargo en las islas Philipinas, y en el grande imperio de la China* (Madrid: Andrés Ortega, 1763).

26 Chirino, *Relación de las Islas Filipinas/ The Philippines in 1600*, 15, 37, 247, 270.

27 Nick Joaquín, "Introduction," *Intramuros of Memory*, with Jaime C. Laya and Esperanza B. Gatbonton (Manila: Ministry of Human Settlements, 1983), 8.

28 Richard Connaughton, John Pimlott and Duncan Anderson, *The Battle for Manila* (Makati City: Platypus Publishing, 1995), 183.

29 Ibid., 156-57.

30 Ibid., 163.

31 Francisco Gonzalez was a former resident of Intramuros and now lives in Paco, Manila. Francisco Gonzalez, interview by Isaac Donoso and Guillermo Gómez Rivera, February 2009.

32 Ibid., 163.

33 The Dictatorship was harsh, cruel, and greedy. Many were its victims, not least the Philippines as a whole which contracted a huge foreign debt that was only fully repaid during the first decade of the twenty-first century during the presidency of Gloria Macapagal Arroyo. Nonetheless we should credit Marcos for at least having a strategic plan for revitalizing a part of Manila. This cannot be said of his successors who have not presented any such strategies.

34 Pilar Gonzalbo Aizpuru, "Convivencia, segregación y promiscuidad en la capital de la Nueva España," in *Actas del Tercer Congreso Internacional Mediadores Culturales. Ciudades mestizas: Intercambios y continuidades en la expansión occidental Siglos XVI a XIX* (Mexico, D.F.: Centro de Estudios de Historia de México, 2001), 123-38.

35 According to the king's order to Governor Ovando, Spaniards should marry indios so that the latter would become "people of reason" (*gente de razón*). In 1514, Fernando the Catholic gave his formal authorization to mixed unions. See Agustin F. Basave Benitez, *México mestizo: análisis del nacionalismo mexicano en torno a la mestizofilia de Andrés Molina Enriquez* (México, D.F.: Fondo de Cultura Económica, 1992), 17.

36 Alfredo Jimenez Nuñez, "Los habitantes, mestizaje, población actual," *Gran Enciclopedia de España y América* 2 (Madrid, Gela S.A.: Espasa-Calpe/ Argantonio, 1989).

37 Pablo Chami, "Estatutos de Limpieza de Sangre," (lecture given at the Centro de Investigación y Difusión de la Cultura Sefardi, October 2000, modified in 2007), accessed 26 June 2011, http://www.pachami.com/Inquisicion/LimpiezaSangre.html.

38 W.A. Plecker, "Shall America remain White?" *Virginia Health Bulletin* (November 1925), 17, extra no. 12, accessed 23 November 2008, http://198.66.252.234/powell5.html.

39 Leti Volpp, "Constructing Latcrit Theory: Diversity, Commonality, and Identity: American Mestizo: Filipinos and Antimiscegenation Laws in California," *The Regents of the University of California, U.C. Davis Law Review* (2000), accessed 23 November 2008, http://biblioteca.uprrp.edu/LatCritCD/Publications/PublishedSymposium/LCIVUCDavis(2000>./4LCIVLetiVolpp.p.

40 Arnold Toynbee, *A Study of History* (London: Oxford University Press, 1948-1961, 12 vols.), 1, 211.

41 Luis Merino OSA, *The Cabildo Secular or Municipal Government of Manila* (Iloilo, Research Center: University of San Agustín, Iloilo, 1980), 60.

42 Ibid., 61.

43 Aside from having Chinese mestizo ancestors such as the Tuasons, the Aranetas also have native Filipino ancestors. Thus the brown features of famous scions like Senator Mariano Roxas and Margarita Fores. As for their relatives, the Legardas, a renowned ancestor is Benito Legarda y Tuason (1853-1915) who was the Philippines' First Resident Commissioner to the US.

44 Benito Legarda, *After the Galleons: Foreign Trade, Economic Change and Entrepreneurship in the Nineteenth-Century Philippines* (Quezon City: Ateneo de Manila University Press, 1999), 230.

45 José Rizal, *Noli Me Tangere*, (Manila, Comisión Nacional del Centenario, [1887] 1961), 11 ff.

46 Sir John Bowring, *A Visit to the Philippine Islands* (London: Smith, Elder and Co., 1859), 18-19.

47 Ibid.

48 Merino OSA, *Arquitectura y urbanismo*, 12.

49 Zeus Salazar, *Agosto 29-30, 1896: Ang Pagsalakay ni Bonifacio sa Maynila* (Quezon City: Miranda Bookstore, 1994), 19 ff.

50 The basic reference for the history of many of the structures of Intramuros is María Lourdes Diaz-Trechuelo Spinola, *Arquitectura española en Filipinas, 1565-1800*, prologue by Diego Angulo Iñiguez, Sevilla, Escuela de Estudios Hispano-Americanos de Sevilla, 1959. This is heavily documented with references to primary sources not available in the Philippines and comes with maps, plans and illustrations from that period. For laymen, there is a series of brief, well-written, and well-researched articles by Rene Javellana on different structures in Intramuros. See for instance his "Intramuros walls," in *CCP Encyclopedia of the Arts 3, Architecture*, 234-36.

51 Pedro de Chirino, *op. cit.*

52 An excellent study of the bastion's history and present-day reconstruction is in Esperanza Gatbonton, *Bastion de San Diego*, [Manila] Intramuros, Ministry of Human Settlements, 1985.

53 Ibid., 37

54 Rene Javellana, *Fortress of Empire* (Makati: Bookmark), 59.

55 Ibid.

56 Luis Merino OSA, *Arquitectura y urbanismo en el siglo XIX: Introducción general y monografías* (Manila: Centro Cultural de España and The Intramuros Administration, 1987), 50-51. This makes use of primary sources, reproduces some of them, and has plans and illustrations.

57 Nick Joaquin, *A Question of Heroes: Essays in Criticism on Ten Key Figures of Philippine History* (Makati, Metro Manila: [Filipinas Foundation], 1977).

58 This description is based partly on that made by A. E. W. Salt and H. O. S. Heistand, "Monuments and Inscriptions of Old Manila," in Mauro Garcia and C. O. Resurrección, eds., *Focus on Old Manila: A Volume Issued to Commemorate the Fourth Centenary of the City of Manila* (Manila: Philippine Historical Institute, 1971), 432-35.

59 National Centennial Commission, *Fort Santiago and the Rizal Shrine in Intramuros, Manila, Philippines* (Manila: National Historical Commission, 1972); Encarnación Alzona, *Rizal in Fort Santiago: A History of Fort Santiago* (Pasay City: Epifanio de los Santos College Press, 1967); José Rizal National Centennial Commission, *Fort Santiago: The Heroic Fort* (Manila: Bureau of Printing, 1958).

60 Leonard Wood, Major General, Commanding, *Roster and Directory: United States Troops Serving in the Philippine Division, Stations of Troops, List of Garrisoned Towns and Telegraph Stations* (Manila: Fort Santiago Headquarters, 1907), 15.

61 National Centennial Commission, *Fort Santiago and the Rizal Shrine in Intramuros, Manila, Philippines*, 5.

62 Alzona, *Rizal in Fort Santiago*, 46-47.

63 National Centennial Commission, *Fort Santiago and the Rizal Shrine in Intramuros, Manila, Philippines*, 5; José Rizal National Centennial Commission, *Fort Santiago: The Heroic Fort* (Manila: Bureau of Printing, 1958).

64 Ibid.

65 Intramuros Administration, "Fort Santiago," (Intramuros, 2009), accessed 25 May 2010, http://www.intramurosadministration.com/aduana.htm.

66 Ibid.

67 Salt and Heistand, "Monuments and Inscriptions of Old Manila," 431.

68 Alma Mater Hispalense (de la universidad de Sevilla), "La Ley Moyano de 1857," *Alma Mater Hispalense*, accessed 23 July 2011, http://personal.us.es/alporu/historia/ley_moyano.htm.

69 The observation was made by the famous Swedish economist Gunnar Myrdal in his three-volume *Asian Drama: An Inquiry into the Poverty of Nations*, principal assistants: William J. Bander and others (New York: Pantheon, 1968), 3, 1632-34. He concludes with this after making a lengthy comparison of the educational systems in China, Siam, Japan, Spanish Philippines, British India, Dutch East Indies, and French Indo-China during the nineteenth century.

70 Wikipedia: *La Encyclopedia Libre*, "Banco de España," *Wikipedia: La Encyclopedia Libre*, accessed 23 July 2011, http://es.wikipedia.org/wiki/Banco_de_Espana.

71 Funding Universe, "Bank of the Philippine Islands," Funding Universe, accessed 23 July 2011, http://www.fundinguniverse.com/company-histories/Bank-of-the-Philippine-Islands-Company-History.html.

72 Salt and Heistand, "Monuments and Inscriptions of Old Manila," 429-30.

73 Ibid.

74 Ibid., 435.

75 Ibid., 400, 402 ff.

76 "DPWH to remove Spanish-era Anda Circle in Manila to ease traffic woes", *GMA Network,* 8 September 2014 (based on a report by J. P. Soriano on *News To Go*), http://www.gmanetwork.com/news/story/378253/lifestyle/design/dpwh-to-remove-spanish-era-anda-circle-in-manila-to-ease-traffic-woes.

77 Carlos Chanfon Olmos, *Historia de la arquitectura y urbanismos mexicanos: el periodo virreinal: el encuentro de dos universos culturales*, México, DF, Facultad de Arquitectura, División de Estudios de Posgrado, Universidad Autónoma de México 1997; Fernando Marías, "Arquitectura y urbanismo. Rejería y orfebrería," *Historia de España Menendez Pidal: La cultura del Renacimiento (1480-1580)*, 31, directed by José María Jover Zamora, (Madrid: Espasa Calpe S.A., 1999), 394-96.

78 Consejo de la Hispanidad, *Recopilacion de las Leyes de los Reynos de las Indias* 2 (Madrid: Consejo de la Hispanidad, 1943), 21.

79 Salt and Heistand, "Monuments and Inscriptions of Old Manila," 413-14.

80 Luís Miguél Ariza, "La Odisea del doctor Balmis," El País.com (24 January 2011), accessed 9 July 2011, http://www.elpais.com/articulo/portada/odisea/doctor/Balmis/elpepusoceps/20100124elpepspor_3/Tes.

81 Regalado Trota-Jose, *Of War and Peace: Lantakas and Bells: In Search for Foundations of the Philippines, Part 2: Bagting: The Valuation of Time and Money in Spanish Colonial Philippines* (Manila, UST Publishing House, 2009), 180-183.

82 Joaquin, Intramuros, 94.

83 Ibid., 11

84 Here is a concise essay by Rene Javellana, "Manila cathedral," *CCP Encyclopedia of the Arts*, vol. 3, Architecture, 247-50. For a lengthier narrative, there is the book by Ruperto C. Santos, *Manila Cathedral: Basilica of the Immaculate Conception* (Manila: The Archdiocesan Archives of Manila).

85 Diaz-Trechuelo, *Arquitectura española en Filipinas, 1565-1800*, 197.

86 Manila Metropolitan Cathedral, *Souvenir Program (of the) Solemn Inauguration of the Metropolitan Cathedral of Manila, 3-9 December 1958*, (Manila: Manila Metropolitan Cathedral, 1958), 39.

87 Santos, *Manila Cathedral*.

88 Ibid.

89 Fidel Villaroel, *Father Jose Burgos, University Student* (Manila: University of Santo Tomas, 1971),118-119.

90 Pedro G. Galende and Regalado Trota-Jose, *San Agustín Art and History 1571-2000*, s.l. (San Agustín Museum, 2000), 11, 14.

91 Another comprehensive book on the church and convent is Pedro G. Galende OSA, *San Agustín: Noble Stone Shrine* (Metro Manila: Formoso, 1989).

92 Galende, *San Agustin*; Rene Javellana, "San Agustín Church and Convent," *CCP Encyclopedia of the Arts 3, Architecture*, 270-71.

93 Galende, *San Agustin: Noble Stone Shrine*, 24.

94 Ibid.

95 Javellana, "San Agustin Church and Convent," 270-71.

96 Ibid.

97 Galende and Trota-Jose, *San Agustin Art and History 1571-2000*, 120.

98 Ibid., 136-37.

99 Javellana, "San Agustin Church and Convent," 271.

100 Galende, *San Agustin*, 98.

101 Ibid.

102 Ibid.

103 Galende and Trota-Jose, *San Agustin Art and History 1571-2000*, 37.

104 Dr. Victor Torres, historian formerly with Intramuros Administration and now with De La Salle University, tells me that there was in fact a date of 1933 or so on the façade. But this was erased during a recent renovation.

105 Diaz-Trechuelo, *Arquitectura española en Filipinas, 1565-1800*, 233.

106 Ibid.

107 Ibid.

108 Rene Javellana SJ, *Wood-and-Stone for God's Greater Glory: Jesuit Art and Architecture in the Philippines* (Quezon City: Ateneo de Manila University Press, 1991), 32. This book describes in well-documented detail the various structures reared by the Jesuits from the beginning.

109 Diaz-Trechuelo, *Arquitectura española en Filipinas*, 235.

110 Javellana, *Wood-and-Stone for God's Greater Glory*, 34.

111 A shorter version of the description of the third San Ignacio is in Rene Javellana, "San Ignacio church," *CCP Encyclopedia of the Arts 3, Architecture*, 272-73.

112 Ibid., 273.

113 Ibid.

114 This is according to data kindly shared with me by Ms. Myrna Segundo, COMELEC Librarian, 19 July 2011.

115 Ibid.

116 The Aduana should not be called the Intendencia, according to Luis Merino, OSA in his exhaustive study of the building's history in "La Aduana de Manila, antecedents del Edificio y el Proyecto de su Reconstrucción," *Arquitectura y urbanismo en el siglo XIX*, 201, 207.

117 Merino, *Arquitectura y urbanismo en el siglo XIX*, 185. A good summary in English of the history of the Aduana was done by Rene Javellana, "Aduana," *CCP Encyclopedia of the Arts, 3, Architecture*, 210.

118 Merino, *Arquitectura y urbanismo en el siglo XIX*, 186.

119 Ibid.,189, 194-95, 206-7.

120 Ibid., 201

121 Ibid., 204

122 Intramuros Administration, "Aduana," (Intramuros, 2009), accessed 25 May 2010, http://www.intramurosadministration.com/aduana.htm.

123 E. Bazaco OP, *Historia documentada del Real Colegio de San Juan de Letrán* (Manila: Imprenta de la Universidad de Sto. Tomas, 1933), 10.

124 In a discussion on Intramuros in April, 2010, Rene Javellana, SJ noted that at that time a "collegium" was not yet what it has come to mean since, that is, a school of higher learning on the tertiary level. Then it was simply an association with a legal personality; in this case, one devoted to educating the young of all ages.

125 Bazaco, *Historia documentada del Real Colegio de San Juan de Letrán*, 13.

126 Ibid., 18

127 Ibid., 26-27.

128 Ibid., 216

129 Ibid., 222

130 Ibid., 51-52.

131 The source for this is Mr. Mario Zamora, the Head of Letran's Intramuros Studies Program.

132 Photos I have seen reveal the first three structures. Romeo Galang Jr., who studied Sto. Domingo's history, informed me of house structures on the plaza as well.

133 Felix de Huerta OFM, *Estado geográfico, topográfico, estadístico, histórico-religioso de la Santa y Apostólica Provincia de San Gregorio Magno de Religiosos Menores Descalzos de la Regula y Mas Estrecha Observancia de N.S.P.S. Francisco en las Islas Filipinas* (Binondo: Imprenta de M. Sanchez y Compañía, 1863), 553.

134 It was in 1981 that the first buildings of Barrio San Luis were raised. See Asteya M. Santiago, *The Restoration of Historic Intramuros: A Case Study in Plan Implementation* (Diliman, Quezon City, School of Urban and Regional Planning (SURP), University of the Philippines, Diliman, and the UP Planning and Development Research Foundation, Inc., 2003), 134.

135 Comment by Jaime Laya in Facebook group "Ancestral Houses of the Philippines", 28 June 2014.

136 Sister Maria Rita C. Ferraris RVM, *A History of the Congregation of the Sisters of the Blessed Virgin Mary of the Philippines: the First Filipino Congregation for Religious Women* (Quezon City: R.V.M. Publicity Committee of the Philippines, 1969), 4-5.

137 Ibid., 6-8.

138 Ibid., 15

139 Ibid., 16.

140 Reuben Ramas Cañete, "Building National Masterpieces: The Architecture of Juan M. Arellano," *BluPrint*, special issue on January 2011, 88-96.

141 The National Press Club of the Philippines, "The National Press Club of the Philippines," accessed 3 May 2011, http://national pressclub.org.ph.

142 Jean Mallat de Bassilan (1808-1863), *Les Philippines: histoire, géographie, mœurs, agriculture, industrie et commerce des colonies espagnoles dans l'Océanie* 1 (Paris : Bertrand, 1846), 168-69.

143 Ibid.

144 Bowring, *A Visit to the Islands*, 18-19.

Economic Uses for Intramuros
VICTOR S. VENIDA

INTRAMUROS BY ITSELF ALREADY ATTRACTS SUBSTANTIAL TOURISM and investor interest as it is the definitive historic center of the capital and the Republic. Fort Santiago, the Cathedral, San Agustin Church and Monastery, the Barrio San Luis Complex, and the walls or Muralla are all heritage structures that have thrived as centers of tourism. However, the district can still stand substantial improvement and its unique assets still need to be underscored and fully realized. Since it already attracts significant commercial interest anyway, there is a need to convert the district into a more inhabited and vibrant community as it was for centuries.

There still are several vacant lots and open spaces in this district and there still are unsightly slum areas, specially in the east side vicinities of Letran, Mapua, and the Lyceum. These open spaces and slums can be converted into mixed-use, low-income multiple dwelling units as part of a low-cost housing program in line with the 1992 development plan for Intramuros. The structures can go as high as three stories so that they can remain as low-density structures and not fracture the historic skyline. It is suggested that the ground floor areas be set aside as rentable, low-cost commercial units, with the residential units on the upper floors or on the interior ground floor areas. These buildings can be designed following the architectural designs of old Intramuros houses which can still be obtained from existing photos and building plans. What has worked for restaurants and tourism-oriented establishments in the Barrio San Luis complex can now be replicated in restorations for mixed-use dominantly residential development for the low-income residents. They can be housed in reconstructed *accesorias* with all the modern infrastructure features. This can create a vibrant resident community that can maintain the historic district as an integral and significant contributor to the urban economy. It is also suggested that a functioning public school with a social service center also be constructed for the residents and again be designed to harmonize with the rest of the proposed structures.

The former Augustinian Procurator's building on the west side is a model of a successful reconstruction with a contemporary use, and several other buildings have also been designed with similar design and ornamentation. It must then be necessary to, as much as possible, reconstruct what can still be realized so that as much of the old city can be revived, much as what happened with the historic district of Warsaw after World War II.[1] There are proposals to reconstruct the old Ateneo de Manila and the third San Ignacio Church is already undergoing reconstruction. An example of a successful reconstruction is the chapel and convent of the Beaterio de la Compañía, now the site of the Light and Sound Museum. The Santo Domingo church can still be reconstructed as its site is underutilized. There have been plans for the Aduana for twenty years now and the reconstruction of the Ayuntamiento has been completed recently. There is also the possibility that the Palacio del Gobernador of 1863 (before the earthquake) can replace the existing one but this would remain a dream given the massive costs and loss of investment it would entail. Another high-rise has recently been extensively renovated into a hotel and restaurant-school, so that Intramuros Administration (IA) would be careful about taking up such a drastic matter. One would need to find some contemporary uses for these buildings.

The Aduana can be used as extensions of the National Museum and/or the National Archives (since there is an existing plan for the Aduana to be such). The reconstructed Ayuntamiento now houses the Bureau of the Treasury and this is an enlightened approach by government to house its offices in heritage structures, whether reconstructed or renovated. The old Ateneo de Manila would also look stunning as a museum or art gallery. The fact that these are all near each other would create a cluster of museums on the northwestern side that can encourage the location to the nearby buildings of tourism-oriented establishments like restaurants, coffee shops, souvenir shops, book stores, even inexpensive hotels. These can complement the mixed-use dominantly residential development proposed for the block in the eastern side near Letran, Lyceum, and Mapua. It is noteworthy that a substantial portion of the collections of the National Museum lack space for display. These reconstructions can create more space and can also entice some of the private collections to be on public display here as well.

These proposed reconstructions would be a recreation of what were well-known gems of Philippine architecture, sculpture, and interior design. One can also suggest that, as alternative use, these be shrines for devotions that can be popularized. The success of the National Shrine of the Divine Mercy in Marilao, Bulacan and the Kamay ng Diyos shrine in Lukban, Quezon are both instructive. Each has attracted a stream of pilgrims and devotees and has created substantial business in the surrounding communities. Perhaps a religious organization (the El Shaddai can be one) with a substantial following can be encouraged to turn the reconstructed Santo Domingo into their main devotional center, especially since the site of the old church and convent of Sto. Domingo is occupied by the vacant former head office of the defunct Far East Bank. The popular devotion to the Sacred Heart can once again be located at the San Ignacio where it was originally located in the first place.[2] The old Beaterio de la

Compañía can be the shrine for Ignacia Incua del Espiritu Santo (alongside the Light and Sound Museum) whose beatification and canonization will stir not only national pride but also devotional fervor which will need a physical location for expression.

The district has its unique infrastructure requirements. It is a compact area so that tourists and pilgrims can be expected to do a lot of walking. Thus it is proposed that a parking building be constructed in one of the vacant lots near the Puerta Real. The design again will need to harmonize with the nearby buildings but this can be problematic, as a viable parking garage would have to be either large or tall enough as to be out of scale with the comparatively small-scale developments in the neighborhood. The typical design requirements for a parking garage will also have to avoid "façadism." A radical proposal would be to construct a massive underground parking area in the open space surrounding the walled city but this would be very expensive given the high water table in the area. This can be done in coordination with the proposal to convert the LRT into a subterranean rail transit network (see General Issues) and convert the road network in the Liwasang Bonifacio to the underground to create a vast open space in front of the Post Office and the Metropolitan Theater (see the chapter on Ermita). If this tremendous project can be realized, then the theatrical activities now ongoing at the Raha Sulayman theatre can be relocated to the Metropolitan Theater and the entire Fort Santiago can be reconstructed to create more exhibit space for an expanded museum.

An alternative proposal would be to provide a small street car line, a revived "tranvía" connecting Intramuros with the nearest LRT station (e.g., Central or UN). Intramuros used to be connected to the rest of the city by tranvía before the war, but is totally disconnected today. Walking there from any of the existing LRT stations is extremely unpleasant because of all the highways that need to be crossed. This can also allow for a reconstruction of the demolished Insular Ice Plant, which has the dimensions of a contemporary art museum, along the lines of Tate Modern in London. In this way, the proposed museums of the reconstructed government buildings in Intramuros (including the expanded Fort Santiago museum) can be integrated with the exhibit area of the restored Insular Ice Plant. With the nearby Metropolitan Theater, this can be the nucleus of a pedestrian-accessible and truly mass-based center for the arts and culture. This would also interface with the nearby existing Philippine National Museum for Art (former Legislative Building), the Museum of the Filipino People (former Finance Building), and the recently opened Museum of Natural History (former Department of Agriculture Building), thus creating a vast museum zone.

This area already has substantial business activity because of the presence of government buildings and their employees, namely the Post Office, and the Bureau of Immigration and Naturalization among others. The National Commission on Culture and the Arts (NCCA), the Commission on Elections (or the Araullo Building, the only institutional building in Intramuros to survive World War II), and the Department of Education occupy rather unsightly buildings (except Araullo) within Intramuros but their buildings can be redesigned to harmonize with the rest of the district, in terms of density and ornamentation.

There have been various proposals for the conversion of the stately old Post Office building, including its conversion to a hotel like the Fullerton Hotel in Singapore.

However, the location does not make it attractive to the higher income hotel patrons (unlike the Luneta Hotel). Given the majestic façade and its dominating location, it would have been ideal for a major government institution, like the Supreme Court, as a physical embodiment of the majesty of the law. The other equally attractive possibility would be its incorporation into the National Museum complex (as discussed above), such as a museum for the decorative arts or an exhibition hall for arts and crafts.

The other infrastructure requirements would involve the necessity for buildings to have interior parking spaces for vehicles to minimize the use of the already narrow streets as parking areas. Sidewalks need to be properly designed and constructed to precisely encourage pedestrian traffic to minimize the need for vehicular use (specially those for mass transit) within the district. It is also suggested that street signs use the old style already applied in the vicinities of the Cathedral, San Agustin, and Barrio San Luis, and that old-style lampposts be installed in all the streets to recreate the peculiar atmosphere of the old city. Historic markers are also to be installed in the applicable locations. This can encourage themed walking tours.

On the longer term, the further development and renewal of the walled city will depend crucially on developments in the Port Area. The road system of the walled city is subject to tremendous stress by container trucks that pass through and from the port district. If one were to consider developments in other cities such as London, Barcelona, New York, and Rotterdam, at some point the port area would need to be moved to another location as a truly modern container port with direct access to the country's expressway network for faster and more efficient movement of cargo and other goods.[3] In its current location, expansion is limited and the transport of goods is hampered by the distance to the expressways; the movement of container trucks through the city center contributes to the massive traffic jams.

To repeat what was mentioned in the General Issues, it is thus proposed that at some point, the container port functions need to be fully transferred to another location, perhaps to the Manila International Port Terminal (which needs an expressway connection to the North Luzon Expressway) and the Batangas City container port. The current port can thus be opened mainly to passenger boats, cruise ships, and even marinas. These can relieve the stress on the road network and the old buildings in the vicinity. The entire district can then be redeveloped for mixed-use commercial, residential, and tourism activities, along the lines of the Fanueil Hall Marketplace in Boston and Baltimore Harborplace, as realized by the famed developer James W. Rouse.[4] There also are existing office buildings in the area, the Manila Hotel and across the Luneta, the site of the recently renovated Army and Navy Club, and the old Elks Club. With the National Museum complex to the east, the entire district has the potential to be the premier center for arts, culture, tourism, and churchly devotion, all located in renewed heritage structures and modern buildings that harmonize in design with the old ones. The Port Area also has space to allow for the construction of harmoniously designed parking buildings for the expected traffic of patrons and residents.

If the buildings in the Port Area are to be encouraged to have at least six floors (as many already are and even exceed these) then there would also be additional space for low-income housing, alongside the higher-income residential developments. This mixing of the social classes is necessary for a stable and vibrant city center. The low-income families are the main labor supply for the various service establishments that are part of any district of leisure, arts, and tourism. They will be needed in restaurants, hotels and lodging places, retail and other service establishments, and repair activities, all essential in a district of this nature. The higher-income households will benefit by the access to inexpensive labor and goods. These resident households will also be the market for all the establishments that can be attracted to locate in the district, and they will also be the main clients of schools, hospitals and social service centers, and the potential parishioners for religious establishments in the Walled City.

These proposals thus aim to create a diverse but balanced set of uses for the district and its vicinity. This can create greater economic value for the expenditure on reconstruction, restoration, and renewal of the old buildings and the redesign of the newer ones (specially the existing government buildings). They can also prevent undue commercial redevelopment with the creation of vibrant museum, arts and theatre districts, and pilgrimage destinations. The presence of a stable and viable residential community with its own commercial and social centers will also enhance this very vibrancy. It will create a renewed image and identity for the city as all these proposed uses will be consistent with the history of this ancient locale.

NOTES

1. Anthony M. Tung, *Preserving the World's Great Cities: The Destruction and Renewal of the Historic Metropolis* (New York: Clarkson Potter Publisher, 2001), 73-95.

2. Rene Javellana, *Wood and Stone for God's Greater Glory: Jesuit Art and Architecture in the Philippines* (Manila: Ateneo de Manila University, 1991), 147-50.

3. Han Meyer, *City and Port: Transformation of Port Cities, London, Barcelona, New York, Rotterdam* (Utrecht: International Books, 1999).

4. Nicholas Dagen Bloom, *Merchant of Illusion: James Rouse, America's Salesman of the Businessman's Utopia* (Columbus: Ohio State University Press, 2004).

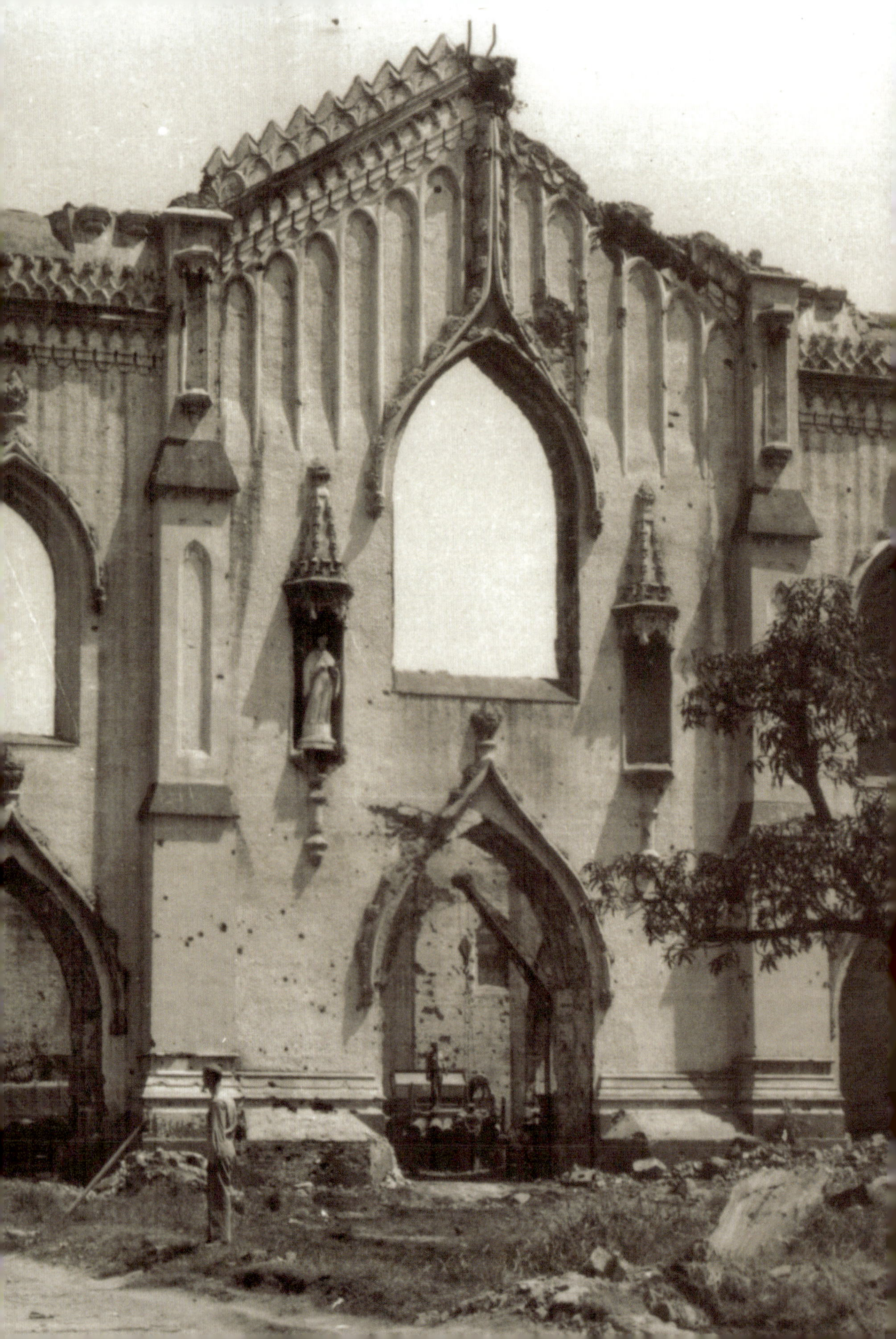

Whose Heritage? The Ideological Dimension of Postwar Reconstruction

ERIK AKPEDONU

WHILE HERITAGE BUILDINGS MAY BE MERELY OF TOURISTIC, aesthetic, historic, or scientific interest to outsiders, for locals they can be (and often are) highly ideologically and politically charged: Historic buildings can underpin a group's or nation's claim to ancient lands, as seen in Israel/Palestine (e.g., Temple Mountain in Jerusalem). They can likewise symbolize a group's longing for independence (Iolani Palace, Honolulu, Hawaii) and its perceived or real cultural repression, such as Christian Churches in the Middle East. Historic religious buildings may be seen as symbols of one religion triumphing over or repressing another, thus exposing them to the danger of destruction and/or replacement by the sacral buildings of a competing faith, as seen in Ayodhya, India in 1992 (the destruction of a Mughal-era mosque to rebuild a former Hindu temple on the same site) or in the Bamiyan Valley, Afghanistan (dynamiting of two sixth-century Buddha statues by the Taliban in 2001).

Often historic buildings or their ruins are employed to legitimize political power, as in the case of antique Babylon's partial reconstruction by Saddam Hussein in the 1980s, which sought to depict him as the successor to the great Babylonian king, Nebuchadnezzar II. However, built heritage can also play an important role in nation building and reconciliation, as pointed out by Patricia Gonzalez, Heritage Management scholar. Examples she mentions include efforts in Singapore and

FIG. 148. Ruins of Sto. Domingo Church, Intramuros, 1945; image courtesy of Conrado Bugayong (adjacent page)

Penang, Malaysia, to give cultural representation to each ethnic group, its history, and its contribution to the development of the city. Others are Cape Town's District Six, a symbol of South Africa's post-apartheid reconciliation efforts among its various ethnic groups. Also noteworthy is Beirut's conservation area and its Heritage Trail, which aims to "celebrate the multi-layers of Beirut's rich heritage" after decades of civil war and which gives credit to all groups which have shaped the history of the Lebanese capital from Phoenician times to the present, including Roman, Ottoman, and French colonizers.

Photos of Intramuros taken immediately after the liberation in February 1945 show the entire district totally destroyed by Japanese arson and American artillery fire, leaving almost all its historic buildings in ruins. It is commonly claimed that Manila was the second-most devastated major city of World War II, after Warsaw in Poland, with particularly massive destruction inside Intramuros, its historic core. Yet surprisingly, many of the walled city's destroyed landmarks, such as the San Nicolas de Tolentino, Sto. Domingo, and Lourdes churches, actually survived as abandoned ruins long into the late 1940s and 1950s, as evidenced by numerous postwar photographs. However, the lots on which they were located were one-by-one sold by the religious orders who had decided to move out of Intramuros. Subsequently, the remaining ruins were eventually demolished one-by-one by the new owners, with the last being the ruins of the San Nicolas de Tolentino Church in 1959.

It appears from these photographs that most of these ruins could probably have been saved and rebuilt after the war. Many historical buildings, especially churches, similarly or even more destroyed than those in Intramuros, were repaired or rebuilt in Europe after 1945 (e.g., the Monte Cassino monastery in Italy), or were at least preserved as ruins, such as Coventry Cathedral in England. Substantial portions of Intramuros' historic churches survived the fires and bombardment. While its nave had been leveled, the ornate façade of the San Francisco Church had remained largely intact, as had the bell tower of San Nicolas de Tolentino. Half of the latter's nave was likewise still largely complete, as was its façade. Even though the Sto. Domingo church was a burned-out shell, its perimeter walls were still standing, as were those of Lourdes Church.

Although fire, bombardment, and year-long exposure to the elements must have caused significant structural damage, comparable ruins of adobe, brick, or cement that have survived to the present (e.g., the second monastery of San Agustin, the Fort Santiago barracks, or the Oscar Ledesma Building) indicate the possibility of rebuilding or at least preservation of the ruins. In fact, the remnants of the Manila Cathedral, as much destroyed as almost all other churches in the area, were saved from bulldozing by concerned citizens, and have since been integrated into the new cathedral. Likewise, all that remained of the Binondo Church after 1945 was its ornate façade and bell tower, both of which were saved and integrated into a new church building.

Intramuros had been destroyed many times in its 400-year history, by fires and earthquakes, and each time had been rebuilt immediately, ensuring the site's permanent habitation and the continuation of its traditions and lifestyle. Yet this was not the case after 1945, when the walled city was practically abandoned and taken over by warehouses and informal settlers. Why then is it that the historic city was not

FIG. 149-150.
Warsaw 1945 (left, by M.Świerczyński) and today (right, by Shalom Alechem). Both images in the public domain, retrieved from Wikimedia Commons, see p. 394.

rebuilt after 1945? Why were its ruined monuments bulldozed, and the rest left to weather away for almost a quarter of a century? What happened in other places where World War II had left historic city cores in ruins or wiped them out completely, as in Intramuros?

In European countries affected by World War II, rebuilding of destroyed historic city cores took a wide spectrum of forms, ranging from meticulously faithful reconstruction to outright complete demolition and rebuilding in modern, contemporary form and concept. Often, such decisions were based, among others, on then-dominant political ideologies, notions of national or local identity, and new developments in urban planning and design, and not least economic opportunities.

In Warsaw, often mentioned in connection with Manila, the historic core, which had been completely and systematically obliterated by the German occupation forces in 1944, was faithfully reconstructed to its previous form, using traditional materials, methods, and crafts. In fact, so meticulous was the reconstruction carried out that the restoration skills honed and developed during the process gave Polish restorers a world-class reputation, and culminated in the inscription of Warsaw's historic core as a UNESCO World Heritage site in 1980. Remarkably, inscription was based not on what the reconstructed core represents—centuries of Polish art and history—but on the actual site itself being an outstanding example of large-scale historic reconstruction.[1]

Works started immediately after the war in 1945 and were largely completed by 1980, but continue to the present day. The motivation for the reconstruction of Old Warsaw was as much ideologically motivated as its destruction: the German attempt to wipe out Polish history, culture, and thus identity was countered by Polish nationalist determination to resurrect this very history and culture. Thus, even churches and royal palaces were faithfully rebuilt, although Poland was then under a communist regime, whose ideology promulgated atheism and the overcoming of feudalism and

FIG. 151–152.
Prewar Koenigsberg (left, image in the public domain, retrieved from Wikimedia Commons, see p. 394), and Kaliningrad today (right, by Georgy Dolgopsky, licensed under Creative Commons Attribution-Share Alike 3.0 Unported, see p. 394)

capitalism, including its architectural relics and forms (which were to be replaced first, by Socialist Realism architecture, and later by Modernist, industrialized mass housing without any reference whatsoever to the feudal and capitalist past).

A similar approach was taken in Gdansk, a formerly German city which became Polish after 1945. Its historic core, destroyed during the war as in Warsaw, was similarly carefully reconstructed from the 1950s to 1960s. Again, nationalist ideology was at play here: in the reconstruction the period from 1793 to 1920, when the city was under Prussian (German) rule was ignored. Instead emphasis was given to pre-1793 architectural forms, when it was under Polish sovereignty.[2]

Prime examples of the opposite extreme are communist Kaliningrad, Russia, and capitalist Rotterdam in the Netherlands. The historic center of Kaliningrad, formerly German Koenigsberg, was totally wiped out in the closing days of World War II, and entirely rebuilt by the new Soviet rulers with socialist mass housing, complete with uniform, industrially-produced concrete apartment blocks along wide avenues and boulevards. Not only were almost all war-damaged ruins bulldozed, culminating in the demolition in 1969 of the ruined royal palace, once the residence of the Prussian/German rulers, but the entire urban layout was altered along socialist models of urbanism. Thus, a dual ideological motivation was at work here: First, the deliberate and systematic eradication of all traces of the 700-year German history of the city (complete with the deportation of the remaining German population and their replacement with Russians). Second, the implementation of an ideal socialist model city, planned and built along Modernist principles, without any traces whatsoever of historic precedents and evolution.[3]

A similar approach, though under entirely different ideological presages was taken in Rotterdam, whose historic old town was annihilated in 1940. Here, the local authorities likewise decided not to rebuild the vanished past, but to use the opportunity for

WHOSE HERITAGE? THE IDEOLOGICAL DIMENSION OF POSTWAR RECONSTRUCTION

FIG. 153. Prinzipalmarkt, Muenster. By Rüdiger Wölk, image licensed under Creative Commons Attribution-Share Alike 2.0 Germany, see p. 394.

a large-scale experiment in avant-garde modernist urbanism. Hence they completely removed all war ruins (to the point of even digging up all water and canalization pipes) and bought out the original lot owners to create a clean slate for rebuilding along Western Modernist ideas of architecture, housing, and traffic management. Only the medieval church marking the former city center was retained, although it was initially also scheduled for demolition. Today, the center of Rotterdam is dominated by huge office blocks and wide traffic arteries, and almost entirely without traces of its 800-year-old history. In few city centers in postwar Europe were new concepts executed as radically as in Rotterdam, which was perhaps so pre-destined since even before the war it was already an experimental ground for innovative forms of architecture and urbanism (e.g., Van Nelle Factory).[4]

FIG. 154-155. Rotterdam after 1940 (left, from Rijksdienst voor het Cultureel Erfgoed, licensed under Creative Commons Attribution-Share Alike 4.0 International, see p. 394), and today (right)

FIG. 156. Nicolai Quarter, Berlin

In Coventry (Great Britain) whose medieval core was also destroyed in 1940, reconstruction in the 1950s took a similar path as in Rotterdam, though not as comprehensively, as at least the few surviving old buildings were retained. The city was rebuilt in modern style and form, with separation of the different uses of the city and of vehicular and pedestrian traffic. Subsequently, Coventry and Rotterdam were the first European cities with pedestrian zones.

Most postwar city centers in Western Europe, especially in Germany, adopted a mix of the above extremes, usually the relatively faithful reconstruction of major monuments such as churches, town halls, palaces, and other landmarks, while at the same time introducing to varying degrees contemporary concepts of urban planning and traffic management with accompanying modernist architecture and design, especially for residential and commercial buildings. Closer to home, in postwar Japan, major monuments destroyed during the war such as wooden castles and temples were likewise faithfully reconstructed, although usually in concrete.[5] While attempts were made to update the urban fabric, there were no large-scale reconstructions of entire historic wooden districts due to the existing legal frameworks as well as practical constraints and safety (fire risk) considerations.[6]

Today considered one of the most remarkable examples of 1950s reconstruction architecture is the historic core of Muenster, a major city in central Germany. Its medieval *Prinzipalmarkt* (main market square), totally destroyed in 1943 was, upon pressure from the local population, rebuilt from 1947 to 1958 not as faithful reconstructions of the original merchant houses, but rather as a simplified and somewhat standardized reinterpretation.[7] Using typical local materials and urban forms on the original footprint, it is a compromise between the quest for contemporary form and the desire to preserve local identity. The solution manages to encapsulate the historic ambience of the originals so well that most tourists who today visit the city in large numbers are not aware that all those "historic" buildings in reality are significantly modified postwar structures.

Perhaps closer to the situation in Intramuros today is the 1980s reconstruction of the Nicolai Quarter, Berlin's medieval core, with a mix of relatively faithful reconstructions, more "loose" historic interpretations, and post-modern infill architecture, often built with prefabricated concrete panels.[8] The result, as similar projects in neighboring quarters, was and still is highly controversial, with common criticism of "Disneyland" and "Kitsch," but apparently very popular with locals and tourists.[9]

As can be seen, in Europe, issues of political ideology, nationalism, local identity, and Modernist philosophy, among others, played a significant role in deciding which path to rebuilding should be taken, with dramatically varying results. How did these factors play out in the rebuilding of Intramuros?

Political ideology. It seems that Intramuros was unfortunate to have been destroyed at a most vulnerable point in its history: the year after its destruction came independence, and with it a critical reevaluation of the colonial past, coupled with disinterest in and disregard for the built relics of colonialism. The demonizing of the Spanish era, propagated by the new American colonizers for obvious political reasons (the so-called *Black Legend*) culminated in the notion that Intramuros was not Filipino. Thus wrote a prominent Filipino historian: "The history of Intramuros in the centuries of Spanish rule is part of the history of Spain in her overseas colonial possessions and not of the Filipinos in their own country."[10] Subsequently, the Philippine Historical Committee, a government agency composed of leading historians in 1964 strongly objected to plans of the mayor of Manila to restore the walls of Intramuros, arguing that they were a "hated symbol which must have been a source of humiliation and despair to our forebears."[11] Luckily, the suggestions by some historians then to even demolish the walls once and for all did not materialize.[12]

It is remarkable that the systematic rebuilding of old city cores in Europe started immediately after the war, but languished in Intramuros (though notably not in the rest of Manila) until the 1970s, as if authorities were ambivalent and undecided as to what to do with it, given all that it embodied. It required a gradual positive change in attitude towards and renewed interest in the Spanish colonial past, as promoted during the Marcos regime with its emphasis on art and culture, to finally work out a comprehensive development plan for the walled city.

Modernist philosophy. At the same time, Filipinos had been primed during the previous half-century by US American values, with their trademark emphasis on the new, modern, and up-to-date, and an accompanying certain disregard for anything deemed old and outdated. Thus, once Intramuros was destroyed, historic preservation or even reconstruction was hardly on anyone's agenda. Moreover, as this was immediately after the war, there were other pressing concerns to address with the very limited funds available. It was also soon after 1945 that Modernist ideology about architectural design, urban planning, zoning, and traffic management according to the Charter of Athens (1933) started their triumphant march around the globe.[14]

Local identity. Unlike, for example, in Muenster, where a long-established local population with a strong sense of local identity demanded the historic image of the city to be retained, there was no such population in Intramuros left after 1945. Already before the end of Spanish rule its inhabitants had started the move to the suburbs of Binondo and Quiapo, and later under American rule, to Ermita and Malate. By the 1930s, most inhabitants were already boarders and rural migrants. The remaining old-time families were either killed during the liberation or, not least because of the trauma suffered during the liberation, emigrated after the war to the new suburbs or even overseas, to be replaced by a wave of informal settlers from the provinces. With most of the monastic orders, so vital to Intramuros' religious life and local traditions, moving out, the last traditional dwellers of the walled city left the place, never to return. As Nick Joaquin pointed out in his essay "Sa Loob ng Maynila" ("Inside Manila"), the essence of Intramuros was not primarily its buildings and walls, but the spirit it embodied: "Destroyed again and again, it kept rising from the ashes because there was a will to persist and the spirit to continue. . . . Since what mattered was not the style or shape of the vessel, but what it carried."[15]

The reasons why the ruins left behind were not saved are, of course, manifold, and not only ideological. For example, one aspect often forgotten is that in 1945, many Intramuros churches, convents, and houses which today would be considered historic were then merely sixty to eighty years old, having been rebuilt after the 1863 and 1880 earthquakes, and thus not particularly "antique" or historically significant. Similar to the little qualms we might have in demolishing fifty to sixty years old buildings today, the Manileños—let alone the US military that bulldozed the ruins—did not foresee how much the witnesses of the past would be missed today, when the postwar era and Modernism promised a brave new world.

Yet in a way, Intramuros was at least lucky not to have been sacrificed to modernist urban renewal, including demolishing the remaining walls, as some had suggested after 1945. The few Modernist structures that did get built in the 1950s to 1970s show little regard for their historic environment. Intramuros becoming a haven for informal settlers saved it insofar as it retained the option for future historic revival: Their presence for a long time prevented the buildup of most of the area with permanent concrete structures, which would have been prohibitively expensive to remove later when conditions had changed in the late 1960s and early 1970s.[16]

The reconstruction of important historic buildings lost to World War II still continues to the present, more than seventy-five years after the end of the war. It notably picked up pace again in the 1990s following the overthrow of communism in Eastern Europe and the ideological reorientation towards the West. At the same time the advent of post-modernism shed Modernist and Socialist concepts of urbanism, and provided a fertile environment for the reevaluation of the past and its embrace. In Dresden, the Cathedral of the Holy Trinity was faithfully reconstructed, and its surroundings rebuilt with modernized versions of historic Baroque townhouses.[17] In Berlin and in Potsdam, the historic city palaces have been reconstructed at huge expense, while in Polish Stettin/Szezecin, many wounds of war are gradually being filled up with more or less accurate reproductions of historic prewar houses. Even in Russian Kaliningrad similar plans of reconstructing parts of the German past are

WHOSE HERITAGE? THE IDEOLOGICAL DIMENSION OF POSTWAR RECONSTRUCTION 155

FIG. 157-158. Japanese Government-General Building in Seoul (left, from 門田房太郎; image in the public domain, retrieved from Wikimedia Commons, see p. 394); Gyeongbokgung Palace Gate (right, image courtesy of Ryan Indon).

currently being discussed and have been partially executed already (i.e., the Fischdorf project).[18]

Closer to home, the royal palace of Mandalay, Burma (destroyed in 1945) was rebuilt in the 1990s, while elsewhere in Asia, losses to conflicts or conquests other than World War II have likewise been reconstructed of late, from Vietnam (Hue Citadel, destroyed 1968) to South Korea: Here, in a remarkable act of architectural re-writing of history the Government-General Building in Seoul, seat of the Japanese colonial administration (but also of the Korean National Assembly, and later the National Museum) was demolished in 1995. This was to enable the reconstruction of the main gate of the Gyeongbokgung Palace, which had previously been demolished by the Japanese to erect the Government-General Building and to thus symbolically take the place of the monarchy and epitomize their domination over Korea.[19] In China, the old Summer Palace, destroyed in 1860 during the Opium Wars, was reconstructed and opened in 2015, albeit not in its original location near Beijing, but in Dongyang, more than a thousand kilometers away. According to the developer the rebuilt palace is to present the glory of the past to reinforce patriotism among the young generation.[20] In Malacca, Malaysia, even the former sultan's palace destroyed 500 years ago by Portuguese invaders, was replicated in 1984 as part of an effort of the national government to reemphasize the "Malay" origin and heritage of the city. As the Malacca of today consists mostly of Chinese shop houses and Portuguese, Dutch, and British colonial architecture, the reconstructed palace is to "preserve for posterity the period of the Melaka Sultanate which forms an integral part of the historical heritage of the Malay race."[21]

FIG. 159. Souq Waqif, Doha, Qatar

This wave of reconstructions is not merely limited to historic structures

FIG. 160. Sultan's Palace, Malacca. By Adiput, image in the public domain, retrieved from Wikimedia Commons, see p. 394.

lost to war, but also such lost to modern development, as exemplified by the recent reconstruction of Dejima Island in Nagasaki, Japan, a seventeenth-century Dutch trading post. In Doha, Qatar, the Old Souq (market) is actually a faithful if enlarged replica of the ancient market, demolished during the heydays of the petro-dollar real estate boom. Rebuilt upon the explicit wish of the country's ruler Sheik Hamad bin Khalifa al-Thani to recreate the memories of his youth, it became an instant success with locals and tourists alike.[22]

In Intramuros, the recent wave of reconstructions of major monuments, such as the Ayuntamiento (former City Council) for the Bureau of the Treasury, the Maestranza Wall as a future exhibition ground, and the Jesuit San Ignacio Church as an ecclesiastical art museum, put the district firmly in line with such global trends.

The reasons for this wave of reconstructions and replicas, often criticized as Façadism, Disneyfication, falsification of history, or pure sentimentalism, are manifold, and commonly revolve around notions of nation-building and ethnic/national identity as in Malaysia, local identities (e.g., in Germany), and promotion of commercialism and tourism.

The popularity of historic reconstructions, just as the global spread of Post-Modernism closely related to it, can also be seen as a general and widespread alienation from and rejection of Modernist design philosophy and dogma, varyingly being viewed as cold, banal, soul-less and un-rooted.[23] Apparently, there is a deeply-ingrained longing for the beautiful and meaningful, connecting to one's real, imagined, or adopted past. History, culture, and sense and pride of place matter, not only to governments, business, and tourists, but also to ordinary people. Thus, in a fast-changing world old buildings, whether authentic or reconstructed, provide virtual memories and a feeling of nostalgia and continuity.[24]

Destroyed and neglected for decades, Intramuros has finally awakened, albeit with much delay, to its immense historical, cultural, and national significance, and its huge, though still vastly underutilized tourist potential. Today it is one of the few places in the country (and perhaps the only one in Manila) with a hopeful outlook for the preservation of its built heritage, whether original or reconstructed.

NOTES

1. UNESCO, "Historic Centre of Warsaw," *UNESCO*, accessed 10 September 2012, whc.unesco.org/en/list/30.

2. Konstanty Kalinowski, "Rueckgriff auf die Geschichte: Der Wiederaufbau der Altstaedte in Polen—das Beispiel Danzig," in *Die Schleifung—Zerstörung und Wiederaufbau historischer Bauten in Deutschland und Polen*, edited by Dieter Bingen and Hans-Martin Hinz (Darmstadt: Deutsches Polen- Institut, Harrassowitz Verlag, 2005), 80–96.

3. Bert Hoppe, "Auf den Trümmern von Königsberg: Kaliningrad 1946–1970," in *Schriftenreihe der Vierteljahreshefte fuer Zeitgeschichte* (Muenchen: Oldenbourg Verlag, 2000), 32–74.

4. "Rotterdam's City Planning," *Macalester College*, accessed 10 September 2012, http://www.macalester.edu/courses/g eog261/Otte_Rotterdam>. Rotterdam%20City%20Planning.html.

5. Cherie Wendelken, "Aesthetics and Reconstruction: Japanese Architectural Culture in the 1950s," in *Rebuilding Urban Japan After 1945*, edited by Carola Hein, Jeffry M. Diefendorf, and Ishida Yorifusa (Palgrave Macmillan, 2003), 202.

6. Jeffry M. Diefendorf, "War and Reconstruction in Germany and Japan," in *Rebuilding Urban Japan After 1945*, edited by Carola Hein, Jeffry M. Diefendorf, and Ishida Yorifusa (Palgrave Macmillan, 2003), 210–35.

7. Norbert Huse (ed.), *Denkmalpflege. Deutsche Texte aus drei Jahrhunderten* (Muenchen: C. H. Beck Verlag, 2006), 188-90.

8. Wohnungsbaugesellschaft Berlin-Mitte mbH, "Architektur: Die vielen Jahrhunderte ...," *Nikolaiviertel 1237: Berlin von Anfang an*, accessed 10 September 2012, www.nikolaiviertel-berlin.de/nikolaiviertel-berlin/cms/de/.

9. Lars Klaaßen, "Das Nikolaiviertel: Historizismus mit Tradition," *Berliner Mieterverein e.V.*, last modified September 2007, https://www.berliner-mieterverein.de/magazin/online/mm0907/090724.htm.

10. Carmencita H. Acosta, "Symbol of Oppression: Historians Oppose Manila Mayor's Plan to Restore Walls of Intramuros," *Philippines Free Press* 57 (7) (February 15, 1964), 10.

11. Ibid., 70.

12. Ibid., 71.

14. The Charter of Athens, named after the 4th Congress Internationaux d'Architecture Moderne (CIAM) in 1933 and published by Le Corbusier in 1943, had immense worldwide impact on urban planning after World War II. It advocated the "functional city," based on high-rise mass housing surrounded by open green space, separation of zones of different functions such as commercial centers and suburbs, and their interconnection through free-flowing automobile traffic on wide highways.

15. Nick Joaquin, "Sa Loob ng Maynila," in *Intramuros*, edited by Nick Joaquin (Manila: Philippine Daily Inquirer Inc., 1988), 125–26.

16. Gerard Lico, *Edifice Complex: Power, Myth, and Marcos State Architecture* (Quezon City: Ateneo de Manila University Press, 2003), 61–62.

17. Städtebaulich-gestalterisches Konzept für den Neumarkt," *Gesellschaft Historischer Neumarkt Dresden e.V.*, accessed 10 September 2012, www.neumarkt-dresden.de.

18. Thoralf Plath, "Kaliningrad: Zentrum Königsbergs soll neu entstehen," *Russland Aktuell*, 5 February 2008, http://www.kaliningrad.aktuell.ru/kaliningrad/stadtnews/kaliningrad_zentrum_koenigsbergs_soll_neu_entstehen_296.htm.

19. Ronan Thomas, "The Capitol, Seoul," *History Today* 47 (1), 1997, https://www.historytoday.com/archive/capitol-seoul.

20. sto/AFP, "Historische Stätte: China eröffnet Nachbau des Alten Sommerpalastes," *Spiegel Online Reise*, 11 May 2015, http://www.spiegel.de/reise/fernweh/china-alter-sommerpalast-als-kopie-a-1033208.html#js-article-comments-box-page.

21. Virtual Museum Melaka, "Melaka Sultanate Palace," *Virtual Museum Melaka*, accessed 12 May 2014, http://www.virtualmuseummelaka.com/cultural.htm.

22. Helge Sobik, "Basar in Katar: Der Souk ist abgefahren," *Spiegel Online Reise*, 29 January 2013, http://www.spiegel.de/reise/fernweh/souk-wakif-in-doha-aus-neu-mach-alt-a 880103.html#spcommentsboxpage.

23. James Howard Kunstler, *The Geography of Nowhere: Decline of America's Man-made Landscape* (New York: Simon and Schuster, 1993), 80, 84.

24. Michael Petzet, "International Principles of Preservation," *International Council on Monuments and Sites* (Hendrik Baessler Verlag: Berlin, 2009), 42.

AD SPACE
0918.9390511
JUAN LUNA PLACE
HERITAGE BUILDING WITH ATTRACTIVE LEASE OPTIONS
AVAIL OF THE FREE RENTAL AND PROMO PACKAGES!!!
MOEN

BINONDO
Pivot of the Pacific

FERNANDO N. ZIALCITA

FOR THE FIRST TIME IN WORLD HISTORY, THE GALLEON TRADE (1565–1815) linked four continents together—Africa, Asia, America, and Europe. This was not yet "globalization" strictly speaking, as the economic historian, Benito Legarda y Fernandez, has pointed out in his lectures on the Galleon Trade.[1] "Globalization" refers to the worldwide convergence of prices that has occurred today as capital travels easily from one country to the next. The Galleon Trade can be viewed as a "precursor" because it facilitated trade and exchanges between four continents. The pivot was the city along the Pasig.

Silks, porcelain, embroideries and precious stones from China, spices from the Moluccas, costly textiles from India, and carpets from Persia were sold in Manila and paid for with silver currency.[2] After Spain annexed Portugal in 1580,

> Manila took the place of "Golden Goa" as the seat of a united Hispanic power that reached from Ormuz around to Macao. For a glorious season, she was the foremost city of the Eastern Indies, capital of a proud empire and emporium for trade, not only with China, but with the surrounding archipelagoes from Japan to Java and with Malacca and the Indo-Chinese kingdoms of the mainland. Never again was Manila to know such greatness.[3]

According to the French economic historian Pierre Chaunu, during the seventeenth century, a truly worldwide economic network emerged with the galleon trade as its stimulus.[4] Coins hitherto minted in East Asia were of copper which devalued

FIG. 161. Binondo Riverfront along the Pasig River

FIG. 162. Puente de España, 1824. (Source: Museo de América, Madrid. Photography: Gonzalo Cases Ortega)

over time. In contrast pesos minted in Lima and Mexico were of high-quality silver.[5] Also called "*dolares*" (dollars), Mexican pesos were a highly prized currency around the Pacific, including the young United States—until the close of the nineteenth century. In Asia, Hispanic Manila was the principal source of the precious silver. While it is true that, before 1571, Chinese ships called on Manila, the historian William Henry Scott claimed that "native Philippine products were of limited variety and value, and handling them was not enough to attract a resident Chinese colony."[6] The few Chinese encountered by the Spaniards in 1570 were "political refugees and recent arrivals."[7] But the entry of Mexican silver pesos of high quality changed the situation dramatically. By 1603, the Chinese population in Manila "was estimated at 20,000—in contrast to perhaps 1,000 Spaniards."[8] There were also Japanese who migrated because they wanted to practice freely their Christian faith. Received admiringly by the clergy for their commitment to the Faith, they were invited to perform their dances and music in church festivities.[9] Africans came either as slaves or indentured sailors. Some taught vocal music to Tagalog parishioners.[10]

David R.M. Irving, an Oxford music historian, claims that "Manila was the world's first global city."[11] By "global," he meant more than "international." Rome under the Caesars, Beijing under the Mongols, and Malacca under the Sultans were international cities but they were not global. Their network did not yet include the Americas. In contrast, during the 1600s economic, social, and cultural currents from the four continents finally converged in Manila, from which they fanned out to other countries. Thus while musicians from Africa came to Manila, Italian musicians and missionaries in turn passed through it on their way to Imperial Beijing. Here Japanese boys received a Christian and a Western musical formation before travelling to early seventeenth-century New Spain (now the US Southwest, Mexico, and Central America).[12]

These global transactions took place at the Parian[13] which was transferred several times until finally it was relocated in 1758 to Baybay, now San Nicolas but at that time part of Binondo.[14] However, even as early as 1594, Binondo had already become an enclave of the principal actors in the Galleon Trade—the Chinese merchants. Governor Luis Perez Dasmariñas bought the island of Binondo, north of the Pasig River and donated it to the Chinese community as a place where they and their families could

FIG. 163. Escolta in 1884

reside.[15] Its original name was *Binondoc*, meaning "hilly," because of the high ground.[16] The knolls have disappeared, but estuaries (*esteros*) still encircle this island.

During the late eighteenth century, Manila's importance as the premier port of Asia began to wane. The eighteenth-century Enlightenment's critique of mercantilism made free trade increasingly more attractive. Indeed Singapore under Raffles became a free and prosperous port. Meanwhile, the Spanish monopoly over passage through the Pacific Ocean was being broken by French and British incursions. Though the last galleon was docked in 1815, by 1809 Manila had already been opened to English traders. Following the end of the Napoleonic Wars in 1814, European colonial powers agreed that their ports were to be open to all nations and that alien Europeans would be allowed to reside within these ports.[17] Despite these changes, Binondo continued to be the archipelago's commercial center, this time of nascent capitalism, for, in addition to Cavite, Binondo too was Manila's port. Those wide quays (*muelle*) now called Muelle de la Industria and Muelle del Banco Nacional were stone wharfs where goods and passengers were loaded and unloaded by ships that entered the river. Goods were easily transported through the nearby Canal de la Reina which led northward to the esteros of Tondo which in turn connected to the waterways of Central Luzon. The Canal de la Reina also led to the railway station at Tutuban, built from 1887–1897 in Tondo.

FIG. 164. Escolta, c. 1900

British, American, French, German, Indian, Spanish, and Filipino businessmen opened their offices and shops. Wealthy families resided close by, like the Lunas (whose house still stands at Calle Urbiztondo), the Rizals (whose house at Calle Estraude burned down two decades ago), and the Albertos (whose house still stands by the Puente de San Fernando). A guidebook from 1875 declared "because of its importance, Binondo is the premier pueblo after the Capital (Intramuros, which was then all of Manila). Indeed in terms of trade, it is more important than the Capital."[18] Shortly after, Binondo was absorbed by the expanding Capital as another district. But its star shone more brightly. Escolta, Rosario (now Paredes) and their vicinity were the country's center of finance, trade, and consumer retail.[19]

Under the US, Manila from 1899–1941 became a showcase of modernity. Its competitors were other major cities on the Pacific, such as Tokyo, Sydney, Honolulu. Four important developments marked this period. First, despite American restrictions and competition from the Japanese, Chinese traders were able to expand their control of sectors in the retail trade.[20] New wealthy Chinese appeared, capable of commissioning high-rises in that busy island. Second, American enterprises expanded in the newly acquired colony. The locus of these businesses was Binondo. An example was the Pacific Commercial Company which actively engaged in the then-lucrative copra

FIG. 165. Rosario Street, 1920s

and hemp industry and in importing fruits and vegetables. It was regarded as the most important prewar company in the islands.[21] Third, thanks to factors such as the new Philippine National Bank (PNB), wealthy Filipino families who had hitherto derived their wealth from the export of commodities "were quick to participate financially in the extraction of both sugar and coconut oil."[22] At the same time, educated Filipinos filled the ranks of white-collar employment. By 1939, Filipinos made up almost 90 percent of all professionals in the city.[23] The preferred place of work was Binondo. Fourth, Americans such as William Odum introduced concrete buildings to Manila, particularly to Escolta and Dasmariñas.[24] This was appropriate, for the Americans introduced high-rises by daring to use on a large scale, apart from steel frames, modern reinforced concrete which had been invented in 1849 by the Frenchman Joseph Monier.[25] Magnificent office buildings sprang up, as we shall see.

Though part of the district, including the Escolta, was destroyed in the Battle of Manila in 1945, reconstruction led to recovery. Once again Escolta-Dasmariñas were the places to go. However, by the 1970s, traffic tangles made it a chore to commute to work in Binondo. Incredibly, other than the Light Rail Transit (LRT) system, which was installed in 1984, no plans were made to address this issue. Soon developments in the former grassland that was Makati attracted businesses and upper-income residents

FIG. 166. Escolta, 1950s

FIG. 167. Jones Bridge, 1950s. From the American Geographical Society Library, University of Wisconsin-Milwaukee Libraries

away from the district. Today traffic has eased but many office buildings are empty.

The only structure that survives from the era of the galleons is the Binondo Church. Old office buildings that line the district's streets date from the 1900s to the 1960s and exhibit a variety of styles. The Chinese community continues to live in the area to this day, serving as a reminder of Manila's glory days as the entrepot of Asia.

STREETS

In comparison to San Nicolas and Intramuros, the streets in Binondo are not laid out strictly on a grid, for several reasons: Some of them follow the course of the esteros and the Pasig River; Ongpin, the street that connects the churches of Binondo and Sta. Cruz, bends obliquely twice perhaps because it connects the nuclei of two settlements that were once separate municipalities. Another reason may be that while Intramuros was a showcase of empire, Binondo was left to grow at will as a commercial town. Hence a district that was the epitome of modernity in the late nineteenth and early twentieth centuries has streets that are dead ends or that narrow abruptly. Some are alleys, like the aptly named Hormiga (Ant) or Carvajal, which is a picturesque blend of popular eateries and vegetable stalls.

A former characteristic of Binondo houses along the esteros was that they had two entrances—street and waterway. Recall how Crisostomo Ibarra of Rizal's *Noli me Tangere* parted from Maria Clara for the last time at the *azotea* facing the estero, and then ran down the steps to a small boat where Elias waited to row him to the Pasig, and upstream to Laguna de Bay. The house was supposedly located on Calle Anloague, now Juan Luna Street. Office buildings have now replaced such houses. Binondo is unique in that it has quays either by an estero or by the Pasig River. Along the Pasig runs the wide Muelle de la Industria/Muelle del Banco Nacional which has no counterpart elsewhere in Sta. Cruz, Quiapo, and the districts east of Binondo. Though such quays and waterways are now often dirty and occupied by informal settlers, they can and should still be rehabilitated. Even in their current state, the locations create interesting panoramas, particularly of the Pasig River, the Post Office, and the Walled City.

FIG. 168. 18th-century map showing the Isla de Binondo (From the Lopez Memorial Museum Collection)

BINONDO CHURCH

In 1606, under the Dominicans, a church of stone replaced the earlier one built of light materials around 1595–1596. In 1640, the Dominican Diego de Aduarte praised it as "a most beautiful Temple, very spacious, very well-lit and very cheerful, fully of stone."[26] However, in 1740, the church was demolished and a new one constructed in 1740–1749. It is this church whose external walls can still be admired today.[27] How was the new church constructed, then—through forced labor? Records detail how the Indio and Sangley laborers were organized. They were specialists in their task, and not just anyone impressed into labor. Funds came from "the *reserva de tributos*, alms, the Dominican Casa de Binondo, the Dominican Province of the Most Holy Rosary, and donations from sangley, indio, mestizo and Spanish residents."[28]

Much of the church was destroyed in 1945. However, the original façade and bell tower remain and can be admired. Typical of the islands is the use of only two, rather

FIG. 169. Binondo Church

than three, stories as a precaution against earthquakes, and of an eight-sided bell tower. Such towers became popular beginning in the eighteenth century with its Chinese influence for the octagon, like the *ba gua* of feng shui, represents good luck in their lore. The façade decoration is minimal and refined; some Baroque scrolls and angels appear on the façade.

Unfortunately, insensitive rebuilding after 1945 has totally altered the interior and even endangers the exterior shell as well. The new roof was raised well above the façade silhouette. What an awkward sight! Removing the columns dividing the nave from the aisles has destroyed the scale of the interior, so that it now looks like one large gym. Also, churches from the seventeenth to nineteenth centuries usually require a lime plaster cover for the exterior, partly to protect the soft, porous adobe stones and most types of local brick, partly to emphasize the sculptural form of the entire building. Without the lime plaster, the porous volcanic stones are endangered by erosion; they also begin to look dingy. Bas-reliefs of Baroque scrolls and angels on the façade cannot be appreciated today. Since the lime coating of the stonework was peeled off, the curving lines now clash visually with the angular corners of the many

FIG. 170-172. Roadside altar along Ongpin Street (top); tombstone from 1722 in front of main entrance, remnant of a former Chinese cemetery around Binondo Church (bottom left); Chinese Foo dog (guardian lion), Ongpin Street bridge (bottom right)

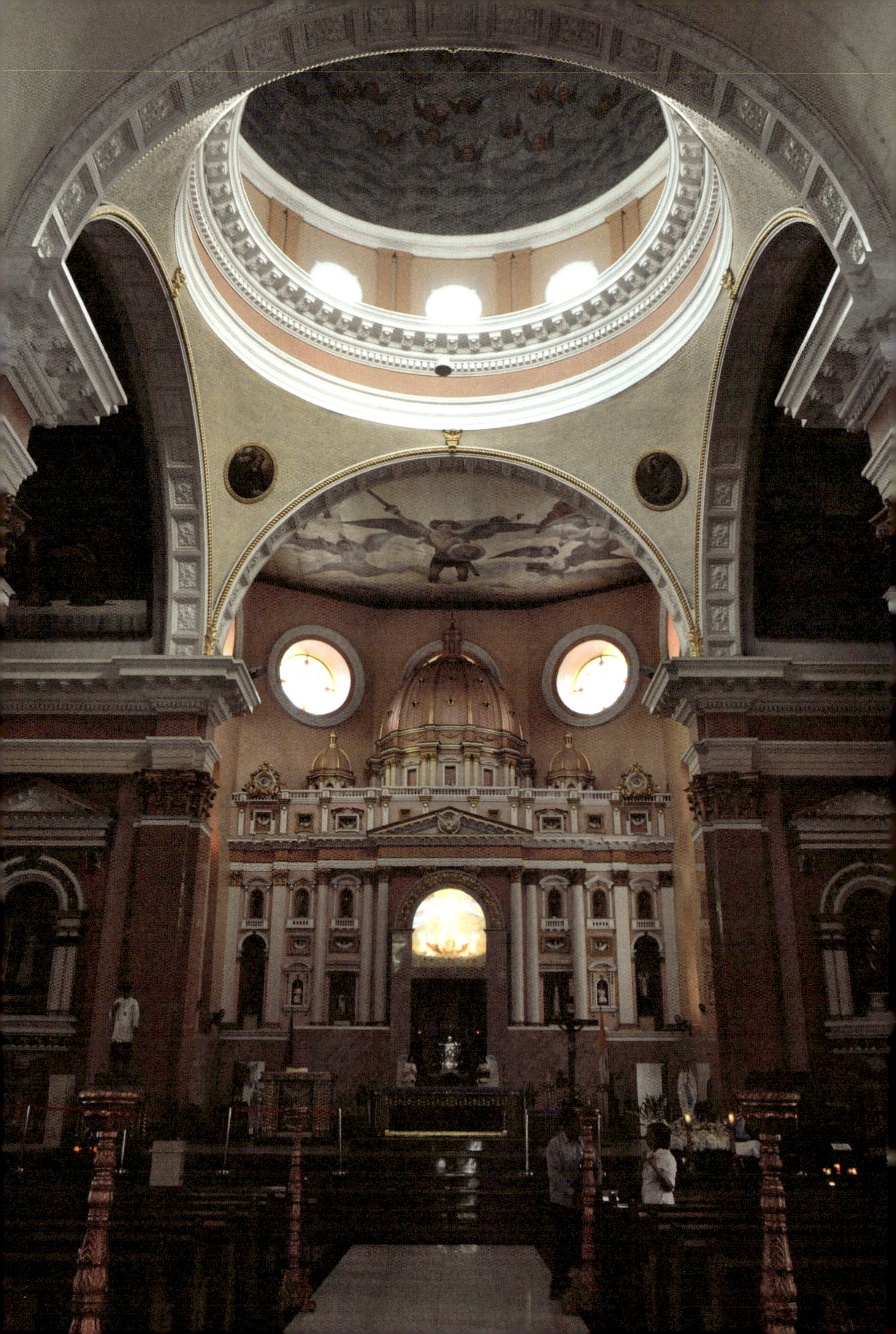

blocks of cut adobe stones. Imagine wearing a flowery shirt over checkered pants! Blank walls, either whitewashed or in pastels, act like a frame that highlights, through contrast, the ornate complexity of the altars.

The late twentieth century paintings on the ceilings above the nave are out of scale: too large for the low height of the ceiling, they seem ready to fall on the devout who gazes upward. Moreover, they are copied from standard religious paintings (*estampitas*) without much skill and vigor. The saints look flat. Although the painted oculi try to imitate the trompe l'oeil oculi of San Agustin, they merely look like gray masses of paint because their creators do not suggest three-dimensional depth through anatomy and drapery on a flat surface. The oversized engaged columns with their golden capitals lack proper architraves, beams, or arches as counterparts and thus look structurally illogical. Finally the altar looks heavy with the metallic gray relief replica of St. Peter's Basilica above it. Why have a literal copy of a basilica? Will this lift the mind and heart to Heaven? Saints and angels at the altar would have been more inspiring.

The church used to be run by the Dominican Order but is now managed by Diocesan priests. Under the Dominicans, the church was placed under the advocacy of **Nuestra Señora del Santísimo Rosario (Our Lady of the Most Holy Rosary)**. Like its peer across the river in the Walled City, Sto. Domingo Church, it celebrated the October feast of the rosary with fanfare, for the **Feast of La Naval (The Navy)** commemorated the Spanish and native Filipino victory on poorly outfitted galleons over the invading, well-armed Dutch warships in 1646.[29] Today the church is officially called the **Minor Basilica of San Lorenzo Ruiz**.

Two treasures are kept here. One is the oldest religious painting in the islands, a small painting on a metal sheet measuring 20 cm by 15 cm, from circa 1588, showing Mary and the Child. Her title is **Nuestra Señora del Pronto Socorro (Our Lady of Immediate Help)**. This is kept in the baptistery. More visible to the public at a side altar in the church is another treasure, the **Santo Cristo de Longos (The Crucifix of Longos)**. We shall return to this crucifix in the chapter on San Nicolas.

PLAZA LORENZO RUIZ (FORMERLY PLAZA CALDERÓN DE LA BARCA)

The recent name honors the first canonized saint of the Philippines: Lorenzo Ruiz who was martyred in seventeenth-century Japan for not renouncing the faith. It was formerly called Calderon de la Barca to honor one of Spain's—and Europe's—greatest playwrights who deeply influenced earlier generations of educated Filipinos.

That this is the largest of Manila's plazas indicates the wealth and importance that Binondo has enjoyed since the seventeenth century. Trees, a rare commodity even at Manila's plazas, give shade to the island at the center. Were the two late nineteenth-century metal **fountains** to gush out water continuously, they would have given added relief. The fountains located at both ends of the island are identical. Their three basins rise as a tier with the first serving as a large pool at whose center Baroque spirals carry wide acanthus leaves rising up to form a column. The second basin is smaller and surrounded by seated boy water spirits while the third basin opens above

FIG. 173. Inside Binondo Church

FIG. 174-175. Tomas Pinpin Monument (left); fountain on Plaza Ruiz (right)

the water spirits to receive the jet. The design may be a common nineteenth-century one, for the exact fountain design can also be found, for example, in Rio de Janeiro, Brasil;[30] nonetheless it is beautiful.

In between the fountains are several monuments. Two are short **obelisks**. One of stone, dating back to 1916, honors Tomas Pinpin with a bas-relief showing his face and with an inscription in Spanish which reads as "The First Filipino Printer 1610." Another **obelisk** commemorates Joaquin de Santa Marina, founder of La Insular Fábrica de Tabaco y Cigarillo (La Insular Factory of Cigars and Cigarettes), 1883. Made of dark purple marble, the surface is badly damaged and the engraved Spanish words eroded. The monument was raised in 1924 by his sister, Doña Emilia vda. (for *viuda*, meaning "widow") de Santa Marina, according to an engraving. A Latin motto, *Labor Omnia Vincit* ("Hard Work Conquers All") is engraved on one face of the obelisk.

Two other monuments on the island are more recent: a monument to Chinese-Filipinos who resisted the Japanese invaders in 1941–1945, and a bronze statue of San Lorenzo Ruiz (circa 1600–1637) who was canonized in the late twentieth century. Ruiz was from Binondo. Noteworthy as all these monuments are, their sheer number is beginning to make the plaza feel crowded.

FIG. 176. Best house in town: Hotel del Oriente (left) and La Insular Cigar and Cigarette Factory (right), established 1883 by Luis Santamaria after the abolition of the tobacco monopoly.

Hotel del Oriente and **La Insular Cigar and Cigarette Factory** are "ghosts" that pass judgment over the current nondescript look of the plaza. Hotel del Oriente was the best hotel of the city and was famous for its French, Spanish, and Indian dishes.[31] Designed by Juan Hervas and inaugurated in 1889,[32] it had two-story-high arches that rested on slender columns to create an attractive arcade for the main exterior. A central pediment with a triangular gable roof over the middle bay gave a dramatic focal point. In 1904, it was converted into government offices.[33] Close by was La Insular Cigar and Cigarette Factory completed in 1894 and likewise designed by Hervas.[34] Once again it had a two-story-high arcade over the entry. The pairs of slender columns rose to support a series of delicate horseshoe Neo-Mudejar arches of varying heights. Both were destroyed during World War II. La Insular perished in 1944[35] but its ruins survived up to the 1950s and formed part of my early childhood recollection of the plaza.

Adjoining the plaza are surviving relics from the eighteenth and nineteenth centuries. The **Puente de Binondo** (**Binondo Bridge**) was built in 1796 to connect the neighborhood called Baybay (now the district of San Nicolas) to the island that is Binondo. It used adobe stones from Meycauayan and Chinese granite for paving.[36] Later on it was renamed **Puente General Blanco.** It is still in use today, for here the important main street of San Fernando passes to enter the plaza. It has been much altered though to look like a Chinese bridge. Two houses stand on the northeast side of the bridge and appear in nineteenth century photos of Binondo's Church and

FIG. 177. Puente de Binondo (General Blanco Bridge)

Plaza. These are the former **Panciteria de Macanista** mentioned in Rizal's *Noli Me Tangere* at **539 San Fernando** and **401 Juan Luna**. The former typifies the three-story house that became widespread in commercialized Binondo during the nineteenth century. The style is contemporaneous with that of the 1850s Luna House that we shall meet in San Nicolas. Not only are the walls of adobe, the capiz and glass windows run continuously as one grid on the upper story while the espejo has capiz in diamond formations, again typical of that era. In between ground floor and third story is a mezzanine with wooden balustered ventanillas. It is now the only original such house left in the whole of Manila, after the demolition of a similar house in San Nicolas and the translocation of another one in the early 2000s. A drawing of the elevation, extant in the National Archives and printed in De Viana's book on Binondo, indicates that this was an accesoria built by Severino Alberto in 1880.[37] Was he a relative of Rizal's mother, Teodora, who was an Alberto? The house adjoining this at the corner of San Fernando and the plaza had only two stories. Formerly the site of **Alhambra Cigars**, it may have dated back to the late nineteenth century, but has been heavily altered to accommodate a bank. It was demolished in 2014. Opposite those two houses sits another, now-rare wooden house. As the block on which the house sits was destroyed in 1945, this must be a postwar reconstruction possibly from recycled materials, which would explain the unusual façade, which mixes elements from various prewar styles (**536 San Fernando**).

FIG. 178. Panciteria de Macanista, 539 San Fernando Street

FIG. 179-180. Marker on former Plaza Calderon de la Barca (left); wooden house at 536 San Fernando (right)

REINA REGENTE

María Cristina reigned as regent from 1885–1903 during the minority of her son Alfonso XIII. It was during her reign that the Filipino bourgeoisie became wealthier but also more vocal and finally rebellious. The estuary, Estero de la Reina, honors her.

This street connects the Plaza San Lorenzo Ruiz to Recto Avenue going north. A few meters away from it is the **Puente de Meisic** (**Meisic Bridge**) which crosses an estero. This narrow nineteenth-century bridge of adobe has a single span. Though eroded in parts, it seems to withstand the heavy volume of traffic passing over it. Going to Reina Regente, we pass a modern building that stands on the former site of the **Cuartel de Caballería de Meisic** (**Headquarters of the Meisic Cavalry**). Here once stood a magnificent stone building for the cavalry soldiers and their horses. After its destruction in 1863, a new building rose on it in 1873 as a cigar factory. Over the course of the twentieth century, it was given various names and uses, such as Jose Abad Santos Elementary School, and the Meisic Police Station. Unfortunately the stones were torn down and a hugely successful mall—11/88—was built on the site. In a half-hearted attempt to commemorate the history of the site, the mall entrance is clad with fake adobe stones with an odd rendition of a nineteenth century house above. Notes Erik Akpedonu, "Right behind it the new Lucky Chinatown Mall opened just recently, complete with a row of old-style facades glued to the boxy mall body. These facades, the 'Chinatown Walk,' are meant to recreate 'the Chinatown of old, complete with Spanish era-inspired architecture,' but ironically are more typical of Straits Settlements shop-houses as found in Georgetown, Malacca (Malaysia), and Singapore."[38] We are often told by some hard-nosed businessmen that "You can't eat heritage." Obviously, some have found out that a fake version of it does help sell a product. Why can they not look around them in Binondo and San Nicolas and appreciate their unique local Filipino-Chinese heritage?

FIG. 181. Puente de Meisic (Meisic Bridge)

PAREDES (FORMERLY ROSARIO)

For centuries this main street was called Rosario in honor of the patroness of Binondo. It was changed in the last decades of the twentieth century to Quentin Paredes after a senator. A long, hallowed tradition of calling the street Rosario ended abruptly. What will it be called next?

This street goes directly from Plaza Moraga, where the north side of Jones Bridge terminates, to the Binondo church and its plaza. It is named after a Franciscan friar who in 1619, upon hearing that Philip III's council advocated abandoning the islands for being an unprofitable, expensive burden, prostrated himself before the king to plead the cause of the baptized who would be abandoned. The king promised to keep the islands.[39]

The building's year of construction, 1938, is clearly stated at the **Hap Hong Building** corner Paredes and Dasmariñas. It was commissioned by Lim Sy Co, a businessman from Xiamen (formerly Amoy), China, and designed by So Eng Suy. The pedestrian is sheltered by street arcades on both sides of this three-story building of reinforced concrete with four by four bays. Over the arcade columns runs a cornice while below the second story windows is a continuous decorative band of bars. Canopies with rounded corners project over the second story windows and seem to float. Integrating the entire composition is a continuous flat canopy and a parapet. Hap Hong Hardware is a well-known hardware business.[40]

The **Hospicio de San Jose Building** at **433 Paredes** is a two-story office building of poured concrete, dating from 1917 and owned by the orphanage, the Real Hospicio de San Jose of San Miguel, Manila. Its style is eclectic: Contemporary but with Neo-Renaissance details. There is a colonnade of Corinthian-type columns on the first story, and seven plaster cast medallions on the walls of the second story. Above the upper floor windows are coffered bandejas. At each corner of the building is a sculptured griffin. Unfortunately the colonnade and the upper story do not quite blend together. There is too much blank wall space in between. Too often charitable and religious organizations are criticized for owning land. But, without investments, how are they to provide free services to the poor?

The **Citibank Building** at **483 Paredes** is a stylized twentieth-century version of the nineteenth-century wooden Filipino house using poured concrete. The ground floor and second story are integrated by pilasters. Note the contrast between the somewhat round arches of the ground floor arcade and the lintels of the second story. Keystones and lintels are stylized to serve as decoration while columns have stylized capitals with decorative bolts. Highlights are the coffered panels below the second floor windows and the pairs of stepped corbels. The resulting look of this 1930s building is a coherent and sculptural design. Thankfully it was tastefully restored a few years ago.

FIG. 182-183. Hap Hong Building (top); Hospicio de San Jose Building, griffin (bottom). A 2020 re-development preserves only the façade of the building.

FIG. 184. Co Ban Kiat Building

FIG. 185. City Chain Trading Building

Built in 1947, according to a retired employee, was the building at **497 Paredes** which was demolished recently. This was owned by **Co Ban Kiat**, a pioneer in the hardware business. The three stories of reinforced concrete are in Streamline Moderne with Chinese overtones. The building's narrowness encourages the eye to go up towards the third floor over which is a tower with a flat, generous eave. Other towers in Binondo office buildings are of Euro-American inspiration, and are located at the corners. This one is located at the central bay. With its wide eaves, it feels Chinese. Also guiding the eye upward are triangular balconies and decorative vertical indentations on the wall panel above the third floor ledge. In counter-balance are the flattened arches of the ground story and the four horizontal Streamline Moderne bands that act as column capitals.

The ziggurat, a favorite Art Deco motif, is cleverly used as the skyline's profile in the **Uy Su Bin Building**, a three-story building with five bays at **537 Paredes.** Of the three bays, the middle bay is the widest, while the south bay is both the tallest and the shortest. This playful movement is picked up by the metal-and-glass windows of the second story which vary in width—the narrowest being that of the south bay, the widest that of the middle bay. During the Depression Years of the 1930s, Classic Art Deco became Streamline Moderne which highlighted even more machine-like parts. On the ziggurat's uppermost step, located on the south bay, is a rectangular panel with flowers in bas-relief. Flanking this on both sides are sets of projecting, floating disks whose otherwise sharp corners become rounded as they approach the panel. Two stories below, the disk motif reappears in the capitals of the columns enclosing the sidewalk arcade. But while the middle columns and their disks are circular, the outermost capitals and their disks are square.[41] A rectangular bas-relief of flowers and streams rendered with a refined Chinese sensibility enlivens a long central panel at the head of the middle bay. According to Ivan Man Dy, a Binondo resident famous for his walking tours, this used to be a hotel. This would explain the attention paid to detail and nuances. Hidden inside is a small restaurant set within a charming Art Deco courtyard.

Closer to Binondo Church, the mood of **561–565 Paredes**, Office of **City Chain Trading**, becomes a modest Art Nouveau. Urns rise at the corners of the parapet running over the third story. Pilasters defining the three bays have narrow decorative insets. Arches enclose the third story glass windows, but in between them on the middle bay is a blind arch for contrast. Below the third story windows, and above and below the second story windows, engravings represent five-leafed clovers. Art Nouveau-inspired volutes decorate the arches' spandrels in the first story. The building may have begun in the 1900s to 1920s.

FIG. 186-187. Uy Su Bin Building (bottom); patio (top). Demolished in 2020 except for the façade.

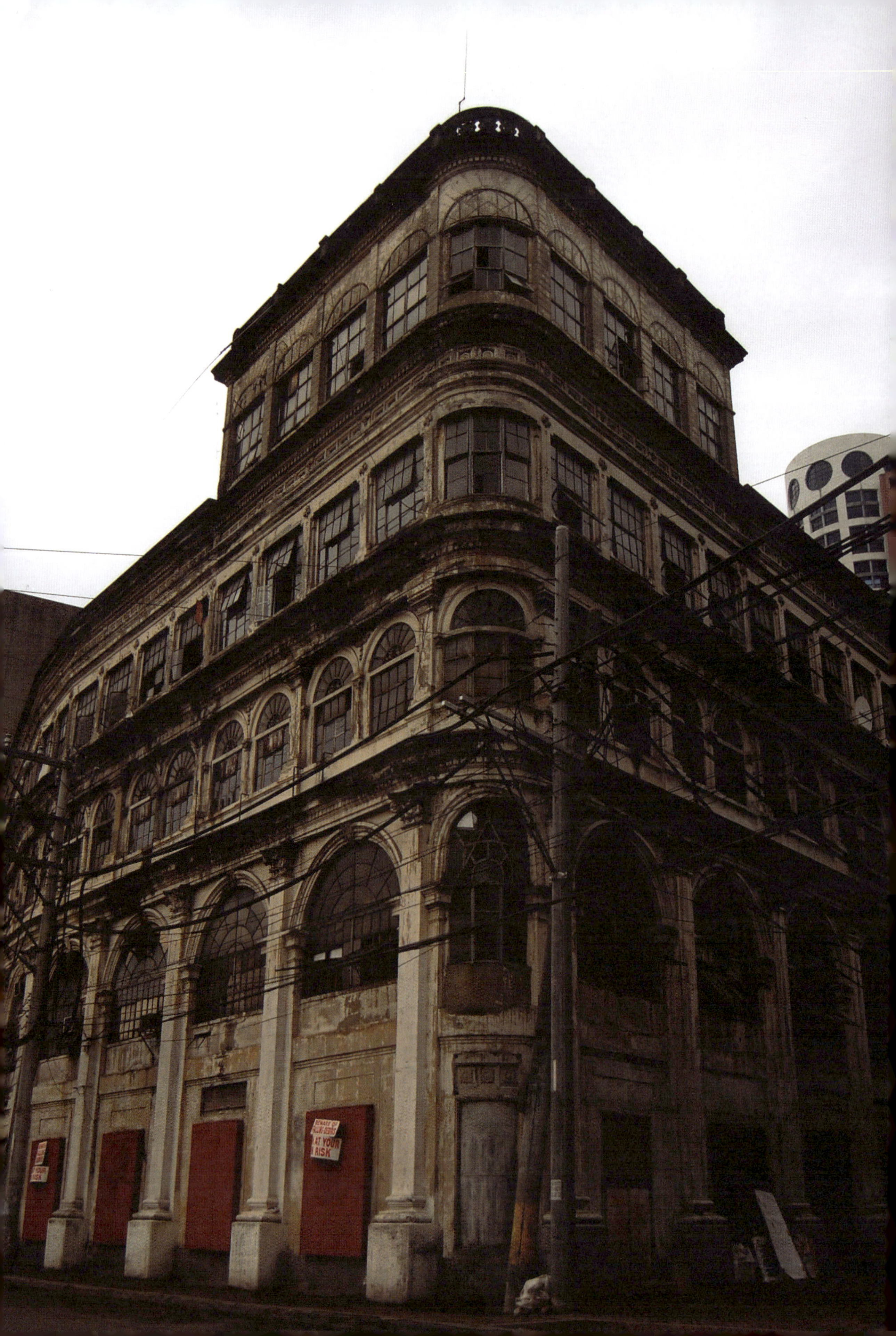
AT YOUR
RISK

JUAN LUNA

Formerly Calle Anloague (meaning "Carpenter Street"). In Rizal's *Noli Me Tangere* this was the address of Capitan Tiago's mansion. Later on the name was changed to Juan Luna. He was of course, the great painter whose awards in Spain directed attention to the Philippines. His *Battle of Lepanto* still hangs at the Spanish Senate. Close by on Urbiztondo Street in San Nicolas is the house where the Lunas once lived.

So optimistic was the era from the 1880s to the 1910s that it was dubbed the *Belle Epoque*—The Splendid Era. Thanks to science, new inventions made life more comfortable. War between the Western powers seemed inconceivable because the monarchs were all relatives to each other. The exceptions were republican France and the US. However, the bitter competition between the imperialist powers ended in World War I in 1914.

Belle Epoque architecture reflects this optimism. The Beaux Arts style originating in Paris made use of the updated version of concrete to endow the structure with a lavish mix of reliefs and sculptures while moulding the surfaces into audacious forms. This can be experienced in the **El Hogar Building** at **Juan Luna corner Muelle de la Industria** and in a directly adjacent building we shall also visit. The El Hogar was built in 1911 by Architects Ramón Irureta Goyena and Francisco Perez Muñoz for Antonio Melia y Pavia, the Count of Peracamps of Spain.[42] His wife was Margarita Zóbel de Ayala. He founded "La Sociedad Mútua de Construcción y Préstamos" (a building and loan association) and "La Casa de Beneficencia" (for employees of associations), and held major administrative posts in San Miguel Brewery, Ayala y Compañia, and Banco de las Islas Filipinas in 1910–1920.[43]

Formerly this was one of the most sought-after addresses in the city. Some of the former tenants were the Consulates of Belgium and France (1925); Smith, Bell and Company; Warner, Barnes and Company; the Japanese Chamber of Commerce, Wrigley's Philippines. Until recently it was owned by El Hogar—which means "home"—Corporation. But, like many of its proud neighbors, it has since fallen on hard times.

Like buildings of the period abroad, it has a corner tower that visually pulls up the structure. Its corner edge subtly curves even as the riverside wall bends obliquely to follow the shape of the quay. This alone, made possible by concrete, is quite an achievement. Two-story-high arches with fan windows, supported by pilasters with Corinthian capitals, create an insistent, vertical rhythm. As our eyes travel upward, we enter into spaces divided into narrower bays with shorter pilasters. Starting with the third floor, the succeeding windows are half the size of those in the floors below. This reduction pulls our eyes upward; it also creates an illusion of height. Instead of pilasters, the fourth floor has bas-reliefs of what seem to be fleur-de-lis while the roofline has a frieze with dentils and embedded medallions consisting of circles within squares. Bouquets divide medallions from each other. Inside the building a grand stairway sweeps downward with grills of curving vines to end in a newel shaped like a metal griffin with flaring wings. An inner, fully-enclosed courtyard brings in light.

The **Pacific Commercial Company Building** on **Juan Luna corner Muelle de la Industria** was designed by Murphy, McGill, and Hamlin of New York and Shanghai, represented on the ground by H. H. Keys and was completed in 1922.[44] The art historian Santiago Pilar says that this building of reinforced concrete featured many firsts in Manila: smooth plastering on the walls, moulded plaster of paris on the ceiling of

FIG. 188. El Hogar Building. Condemned by city engineers in 2015, the building's future is uncertain.

FIG. 189-192. El Hogar Building: inner courtyard (top left); staircase (top right), newel post in the form of a legendary creature (bottom left); medallion of Count de Peracamps Antonio Melian y Pavia (bottom right)

FIG. 193. Pacific Commercial Company Building. Sadly, a massive fire in 2017 damaged the newly renovated building.

FIG. 194. Hongkong and Shanghai Banking Corporation Building

the ground floor, rooms with glass walls, and a special type of window sash. It also had the latest amenities such as modern plumbing and elevators and automatic safety doors.[45] This sober building offers a vivid contrast to the El Hogar Building. It relies for its effect on a procession of three-story-high Ionic columns, six of them facing the river, rising over a ground story with rusticated walls and arched doorways. The reduced scale of the ground floor highlights the monumentality of the columns. This building once housed the National City Bank of New York, perhaps from the 1930s down to the 1970s when the latter joined the exodus of banks to Makati. Recently, it has become the centerpiece of an initiative to revive the Escolta and neighboring area as an IT haven, and was thus recently renovated. From the nearby quay, there is a splendid view of the river and its landmark buildings.

A more modest version of the Beaux Arts style is **117 Juan Luna corner San Gabriel (now Valentin)** which is four stories in reinforced concrete. Formerly the headquarters of the **Hong Kong and Shanghai Banking Corporation (HSBC)**, it was designed by the British architect G. H. Hayward and was completed in 1919–1922.[46] Recently, the fittingly named "1919 Grand Cafe" opened on the ground floor. Tall Ionic pilasters frame the chamfered corner where the grand arch of the main entrance is located. Precast corbels jut over the windows over the main entrance for emphasis. Rectangular medallions appear below the edge of the skyline. Note also the fine turrets on top of the roof facing the corner. Their flattish cupolas seem to have been influenced by the Mughal towers of India, a former British colony and considered the Jewel of their Empire. Sadly, it is now dwarfed by yet another monstrous high-rise condominium rising in front of it.

FIG. 195-199. Manila's former Wall Street: Architrave and Ionic columns, Pacific Commercial Company Building (top left); Corinthian columns of the China Banking Corporation Building (top right); main entrance (middle left) and Ionic pilasters (middle right) of the HSBC Building; Seal of the Hong Kong & Shanghai Bank (bottom)

China Banking Corporation, popularly known as **China Bank** is found at **Juan Luna corner Dasmariñas Street**. To help the Chinese business community, Dee C. Chuan opened this bank in 1920. But the actual management of the bank was entrusted to Albino Sycip and E. E. Wing, an American who managed the bank from 1923 to 1926.[47] The bank stood out, not only locally but in Southeast Asia as well, for being an organization that was both Chinese and modern.[48] As a commercial bank, it hired non-Chinese managers as stated above. It was neither family-controlled nor a closed private institution. Its shares were tradable in the Manila Stock Exchange.[49] As one of the country's biggest banks today, it enjoys a solid reputation for being professional and trustworthy. This building, erected in 1924, and the Pacific Commercial Company Building, two blocks south, form a duet. Both are Beaux Arts-inspired, but while the former is a sober bass, the latter sings a showier baritone. The bare walls of the China Bank's ground story contrast with the monumentality of the upper stories. Three-story-high Corinthian columns separate the windows of the upper stories. These support a slightly projecting fourth floor with a highly articulated entablature whose continuous row of lion heads roar at the two streets below. Bas-reliefs of garlands and cornucopias decorate spaces between windows and on the building corners. Finely carved Greek female faces with tresses look down from above the third floor windows. In between the fourth floor windows are bas-reliefs of winged torches, symbolizing progress, which carry the company's monogram. In contrast with this ornamentation are the austere triangular pediments capping the second story windows. The building's footprint is a six-by-six bay square. A neighborly arcade opens at the ground floor facing Dasmariñas. Unfortunately we cannot appreciate the building's grandeur because of the thick bunches of ugly electrical lines that crisscross at the street corner.

FIG. 200. China Banking Corporation Building

The Fernandez Hermanos, a group of companies that invests in agriculture and real estate, built the **Fernandez Hermanos Building on Juan Luna**. Before 1941, they were preeminent in shipping and the copra trade. The founder of the group of companies was Vicente Fernandez.[50] Rafaél Fernandez was at one time a director in the major company that is San Miguel Brewery. He became mayor of Manila in 1920–1923, and represented the Fourth District in 1923. His brother Ramón was at one time the president of San Miguel Brewery, a director of the Philippine National Bank, and a director of the board of El Hogar Filipino and of the Philippine Engineering Co.[51]

FIG. 201-202. Fernandez Hermanos Building (left); Wilson Building (right)

Most likely this was built in the 1930s. Its four stories in reinforced concrete have Neo-Renaissance reminiscences: restrained Tuscan pilasters with long projecting balconies on the second story and a short balcony for each of the four French windows on the third.

The **Wilson Building** which can be found at **231 Juan Luna corner Nimfa Street corner Muelle de Binondo** was later known as Fil-Am Building, and currently the Co Ban Kiat Building. Because 1920s to 1930s skyscrapers sprouted turrets and gargoyles, their shadowy corners became the preferred setting for the comic book creations of the late 1930s, as in Batman versus psychotic lawbreakers. In that sense, this building is Gotham-like. The former owner of this building, Samuel Wilson, was a US-American who settled in the Philippines in 1923.[52] Being an expert in the new photo-lithographic process, he built up Carmelo and Bauermann as the premier printing establishment before 1941. At the same time, he made money in mining. As a naval reserve officer, he fought in Bataan and Corregidor. After their fall, he joined the guerillas in Mindanao—all the while, his family was interned at the University of Sto. Tomás (UST) by the Japanese.[53] But like the comic strip hero, Sam Wilson triumphed in the end. He joined the American forces that landed in Luzon, and was with the column that rescued the prisoners at UST, including his family.[54]

The Wilson Building was built in 1937.[55] Initially Wilson raised a three-story building that later became nine stories. Its tenants were the Standard and Chartered Bank, the Manila Stock Exchange, and even the Japanese Consulate General[56]—with whose armies Sam would clash. With its two chamfered corners, it extends for eleven bays from Juan Luna to the estero quay. Although visually somewhat incoherent because of window openings in the upper stories, it has a strong presence because of its height and its irregular profile. On the Juan Luna side, it rises to three stories. It halts, then the rest of the nine stories rise at a distance from the street line. A wide Greek fret uncoils on the cornice above the first story. The classical allusion is repeated by the row of palm-shaped acroteria on the cornice of the third story. In between the cornices, are segmented pilasters framing pairs of glass windows. The recessed tower with its bewildering series of windows ends as a sloping, mansard-like concrete roof that has dormers and buttresses. On the quayside, the acroteria appear much higher, being on the cornice of the seventh story, while the segmented pilasters are pulled up for four stories. The verticality here is more pronounced that at the Juan Luna side. Above the acroteria, the walls slope again to form a mansard-like roof

FIG. 203. Traders Building

with flying buttresses that angle forward like spider legs. Thankfully, the building was renovated in 2015.

Traders Building, at **275 Juan Luna corner Ingreso,** is a narrow building (six bays-by-two) and a low one (four stories) in a neighborhood of giants. The most memorable feature is its narrow two-stage balcony into which the third and fourth stories of the chamfered corner open. The colonnettes of the third story balcony carry boxy capitals with eight-petalled floral bursts. These bursts repeat throughout—on the colonnettes' base, though with tassels; on the colonnettes of the fourth story's open porch; and on the rounded corbels supporting the roof. The juxtaposition of the balcony colonnettes is very Art Nouveau, with half-arches supporting the canopy to emphasize the curve of a part. Also typical of that poetic style is the languid, undulating curve of the corbels supporting the balcony. Incongruously, right before this exquisite balcony is noisy Juan Luna. Judging from vintage photographs, the building dates back to the 1920s. Juan Luna goes north towards the Recto Avenue.

Aguinaldo Department Store at **578 Juan Luna** lives up to its present name, Marvel Building. It rises above a busy and congested street that empties into the huge Divisoria Market while proclaiming universal values! Moreover it is in a flashy Art Deco mode that interrupts accustomed rhythms, bringing to mind Jazz music which became popular worldwide in the 1920s. Hence the tall and narrow windows of this six-story building appear in a pair on one bay, on the next in a triple, then in four pairs with a column of niches in between, again in a triple, and finally in a pair with a column of niches in between. The four pilasters dividing the façade have wide vertical tube-shaped pipings (comparable to those of Escolta's Perez-Samanillo Building). The pilaster heads have rectangular medallions with indentations and Nautilus shell

FIG. 204. Aguinaldo Department Store

carvings. Above is another capital head with ziggurat outlines. Eye-catching are the four cement statues standing before the pilasters above the first story: the Statue of Liberty, Bonifacio's Cry at Balintawak in 1896, a Filipina in native costume cradling a baby, and a Filipino brandishing the staff of Asclepius. By 1931, when this building was raised (expanded 1935), Filipinos excitedly looked to the 1935 Commonwealth of the Philippines as the prelude to independence and looked up to the US as the home of freedom. The building, which was originally only half the current size, but was later doubled with an identical wing to the right side, expresses this popular sentiment. At the same time it exalts maternity and health. The conception is kitschy—mixing folksy statues with Art Deco motifs. But kitsch, when done with conviction, becomes surreal and therefore haunting. As another surprise, at the back of the building, overlooking the estero, is a delightful oriel or bay window.

This was originally the home of the then-highly popular Aguinaldo Department Store begun by Leopoldo Aguinaldo.[57] His enterprise grew into a chain after 1945, only to disappear in the 1980s in the face of competition from newcomers. A famous descendant is the painter Lee Aguinaldo, who is one of our best abstract expressionists.

PLAZA CERVANTES

Plaza Cervantes was named after the famous Spanish author Miguel Cervantes, whose work *Don Quixote* is widely regarded as one of the world's greatest literary creations. This plaza offers interesting panoramas that could still be further maximized. Once again, looking over across the river is the Post Office. Depending on where one stands, the visitor gets to see two Baroque churches at the end of a street: Sta. Cruz Church and Binondo Church.

The **Jones Bridge** replaced the **Puente de España**, which was located a few meters to the east. The Bridge of Spain, the first stone bridge in the islands, was built in 1629–1630 with ten spans. For centuries, it was the sole all-weather connection between Manila (then Intramuros) and Binondo. It was destroyed by the 1863 earthquake but was rebuilt with six short stone spans and two central long ones of imported cast iron. The new bridge was inaugurated in 1875.[58] Under the Americans, a new bridge was built which was later called Jones Bridge, in honor of William Jones who authored the Philippine Autonomy Act of 1916 recognizing that Filipinos had to be prepared for

FIG. 205-206. Uy Chaco Building (adjacent page: top and bottom right); Insular Life Building, home of the first Filipino life insurance company (bottom left)

BINONDO: PIVOT OF THE PACIFIC 187

PHILTRUST BANK
BINONDO BRANCH
PHILIPPINE TRUST COMPANY
PHILTRUST BANK
LTRUST BU
BINONDO
非律濱信託銀行

eventual autonomy. This structure was redesigned by Juan Arellano and rebuilt in 1921 as three graceful arches of reinforced concrete resting on massive piers decorated with allegorical statuary.[59] For many, it recalled Paris' daring Pont Alexandre III which had only one long curving span. Unfortunately, the Jones Bridge was destroyed in 1945. The rebuilt version was purely utilitarian: three spans again but the piers are not given any special treatment, nor do they have statues. However, one of the original statues of the old Jones Bridge, the "Madre Filipina," kept in Rizal Park after the war, was recently (2019) reinstalled together with replicas of other statues lost during the war, as part of a major facelift project which also included the installation of new street lights.

Built in 1914 by the architect Samuel C. Rowell at **Plaza Cervantes corner Paredes**, the six-story **Uy Chaco Building** of reinforced concrete is regarded as Manila's first high-rise building. Mariano Uy Chaco built up a hardware business in the Philippines together with José Yutivo. Eventually he returned to China, leaving the business to his son Uy Yet, who was born in Jinjiang, China, and moved to the Philippines at age 11. Uy Yet was originally interested in hardware, and eventually in wholesale, retail, and transportation. Mariano Uy Chaco Sons and Company was incorporated in 1926.[60]

FIG. 208. La Madre Filipina

The building has Neo-Renaissance features such as a rounded corner with a turret crowned with a helmet-like dome. Perhaps because of the latter feature, some mistakenly think that the building is meant to resemble a French chateau. At the same time, as in the Art Nouveau buildings of its time, its balconies undulate like waves—though somewhat stiffly. The building is now owned by Philtrust Bank. Beside this building is another one owned by Philtrust (see Dasmariñas corner Paredes.)

Opposite the Uy Chaco stands the old **Insular Life Building,** with which it once formed a marvelous ensemble guarding the entrance to Binondo. The Insular Life Building, built in 1930 by Andres Luna de San Pedro, won an architectural award as the best-designed office building in Manila. The protruding tower was crowned by a huge eagle. Sadly, a Modernist renovation has rendered the once imposing building virtually unrecognizable and nondescript. Worse, a massive fire in 2017 severely damaged the building which burned out completely.

FIG. 207. Uy Chaco Building

FIG. 209–210. Judge Allison Gibbs Building (left); former American Chamber of Commerce (right). Prime example of "Facadism": Interior gutted in 2017/19 to build a high-rise tower inside.

DASMARIÑAS

Together with Escolta and Rosario, this used to be the location of major shops and offices. Gomez Perez Dasmariñas was governor-general of the Philippines in 1590–1593. After he was killed, he was succeeded by his son Luis Dasmariñas, who served from 1593–1596.

The street has a building style that distinguishes it from other streets, not only of Binondo, but of the rest of Manila as well. For convenience, we can call it the "Columns-and-Canopies" style. The multi-story buildings of reinforced concrete have (or used to have) fixed slanting, umbrella-like canopies over each window in a row. While the canopy was of metal, the supporting brackets, often with a faintly floral profile, were of wood. As an updated version of the *media agua* or canopies of the traditional Filipino house, it had a practical aim—to protect the windows from sun and rain. At the same time, seen together as rows in at least two stories, it had an aesthetic appeal: it broke up the stern profile of the building with rows of diagonals that evoked a sheltering house roof. Moreover, in typical Beaux Arts fashion, very dignified pilasters, which seemed almost like engaged columns, stood on the ridge of the first story, in between the bays, and connected at least two stories. At times the columns were crowned with correctly rendered Ionic or Corinthian capitals. Finally, the skyline was a straight parapet that concealed the roof when looked at from the street. These office buildings thus looked stately—thanks to the columns and parapet, but also approachable—thanks to the canopies and the frequent presence of arcades for pedestrians. Seen as a streetscape looking west, Dasmariñas thus has a distinct ambience that contrasts with Escolta's.

If based on the extensive use of slanting canopies that the multi-story William Parsons-designed Manila Hotel displayed in 1912, the "Columns-and-Canopies" style spread during the late 1910s and all of the 1920s. It was then replaced by Art Deco and Streamline Moderne (see the chapter on Ermita.)

Seen east from the estero and Plaza Sta. Cruz, the office building, built in 1923 for Judge Alison Gibbs by the prominent contractor William James Odum,[61] at **417–425 Dasmariñas corner Banquero and the Estero de la Reina** serves as a sort of landmark and once housed the Manila Machinery Company.[62] Formerly, it seems to have been constructed in the "Columns-and-Canopies" style. After a fire razed the building in the early 1980s, it was rebuilt in a simplified form: The canopies are now in concrete and have been crowned with the mass-manufactured curved roof tiles common since the 1970s. The resulting design is too abrupt and lacks grace. Engaged columns have been replaced by plain vertical divisions separating each bay from the other, which advance so far forward that they almost conceal the slant of the canopies. Only the remaining grills in the crescent tympana of the arcade's round arches evoke the building's former look.

FIG. 211. Leyba-Martinez Corporation Building

Right beside Wilson, at **407 Dasmariñas corner Burke,** is another building erected in 1923 for the same Judge Gibbs.[63] Its well-preserved exterior embodies the "Columns-and-Canopies" style. It once belonged to the Fernandez family and housed the People's Trust Bank.[64] The exterior exudes dignity: between each of the eight bays on Burke and five on Dasmariñas, correctly rendered Ionic pilasters rise above the first story to connect the two upper stories together, and over the windows used to open rows of slanting canopies supported by wooden brackets. The rows project forward rhythmically. The skyline consists of two relatively thin layers of cornices that extend gently less than a meter forward.

The **Leyba-Martinez Corporation** at **385–391 Dasmariñas and Burke** has upper floors composed of shops and offices. On the ground floor, there are shops selling harnesses and chains for unloading cargo. Originally three of the four stories sported rows of slanting canopies as in the buildings above. Unfortunately, these have been torn down as the nails sticking out from the upper frames of the windows indicate. Gone too are the pilasters in between the bays of the second and third stories. Holes in the walls in between the bays suggest they were of pre-cast concrete. There are interesting features: the plain, square capitals of the ground floor arcade are repeated on the topmost story and are accentuated with circular medallions; the parapet on the roofline has abstract Chinese cut-out ceramic flowers. This commercial building probably dates from the late 1910s.[65]

Continuing the former march of columns and pilasters is the **Streamline Corporation Building,** also from the early twentieth century, on **379 Dasmariñas corner Pinpin**. Here, too, engaged columns rise above the first story to connect the two upper stories. They stand in between five bays on Dasmariñas and three on Pinpin. This time they are crowned with Corinthian-style capitals. Formerly the building ended in a free-standing parapet above the third story. However, a fourth story was added. Though the building never had canopies, it blends well with its neighbors because of its articulated columns.

408 Dasmariñas corner Burke is the fourth of four identical buildings built in 1923 for Judge Alison Gibbs.[66] It is located on the south side of Dasmariñas and is in silent dialogue with its twin, the PhilFlex, located across on the north side. It retains those slanting canopies over windows (of the second and third stories) which make its profile exuberant.

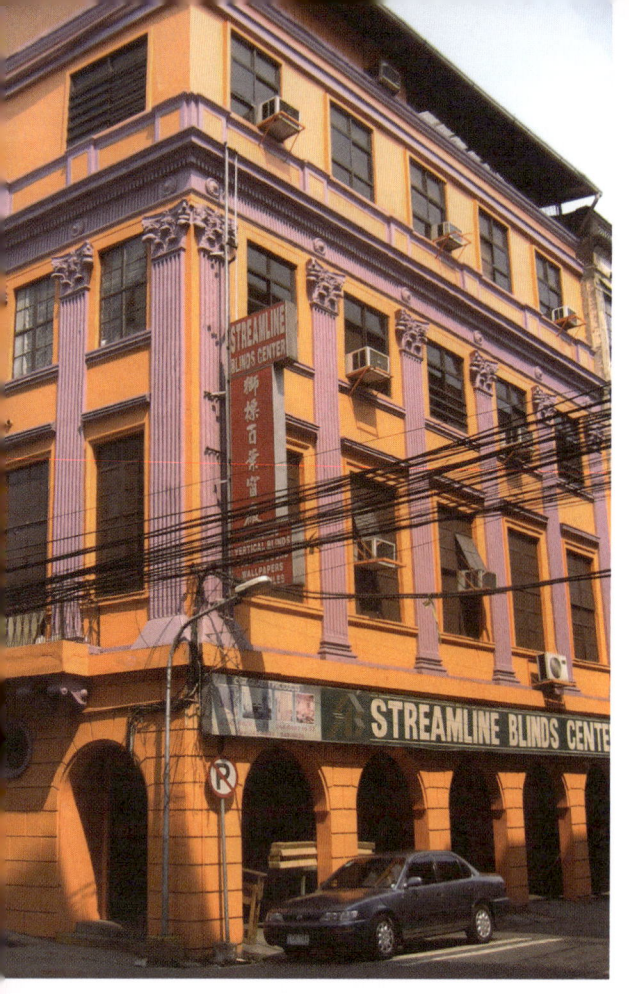

FIG. 212. Streamline Coporation Building

At the same time noble Ionic pilasters divide each of the five bays (on the Dasmariñas side) and eight bays (on the Burke side) from each other. This was the address of the American Chamber of Commerce during the early half of the twentieth century, as indicated by the inscription on its parapet wall (the interior was gutted in 2019).

Dasmariñas corner Yuchengco (formerly **Nueva**) **corner San Vicente. Yutivo Building**. Another building with slanting canopies on this street is the Yutivo Building. If the tempo of the preceding buildings is *con brio*, this one is *vivace*—lively in a refined manner. At the close of the nineteenth century, José Yu Tivo laid the foundation of what became the Yutivo Sons Hardware Company which was registered in 1916 under the care of his eldest son Yu Tiong Siong. The company moved into its present building in 1922. The third generation of Yutivos built the company into "arguably the biggest Chinese hardware firm in the Philippines."[67] Yutivo continues to be a leader in the industry today.

Rising to five floors, on the Dasmariñas side, the building has nine bays and, on the Yuchengco, five. Though it, too, has pilasters between the windows of the upper stories (third and fifth), these are subtly indicated. They are almost flat, consisting solely of three shallow flutings. At the base of each pilaster, the flutings end in a delicate series of incised squares while carved garlands with tassels gently pull each pilaster upward towards parapet brackets that display cartouches. A refined Viennese spirit, which stylizes classical motifs, infuses the exterior. But this building is also practical. It has canopies on the two uppermost rows of windows. On the Dasmariñas side is an arcade with slender columns and grilles in the tympana.

Behind the Yutivo stands the **Kodak Building** from the 1930s, today known as the Siem Kang Building. The Kodak Company moved here in 1928. This building is remarkable for its very reduced, almost abstract ornamentation, as can be seen in the flat geometric capitals that sit atop plain pilasters which unite the third and fourth floors. Ground floor and second floor are articulated by a monumental arcade which offers protection to pedestrians and storefronts. While the façade already hints at Modernism, the protruding turret that dominates the corner of Dasmariñas and Marquina is anchored in the tradition of Beaux Arts.

FIG. 213. Yutivo Building

The **Zuellig Building** at **Paredes** is a reinforced concrete three-story building from 1934. Its eclecticism features both Art Deco and Beaux Arts motifs: decorative soft jags on the skyline, angular forms, rectangular medallions, and an asymmetrical balance. At the same time it has a very Beaux Arts scrolled frieze. Frederick Edward Zuellig embodies an important stream of migrants that few appreciate today because of the mistaken belief that Manila has always been "unattractive" compared to other Asian cities. In fact during the Spanish period, Germans, such as Jakob Zobel, came seeking a better future in this city and ended up liking it here. A German Swiss by birth, Zuellig came to Manila in 1903 to work in a Swiss trading house, Lutz & Company, as an office clerk, became a partner after ten years, and eventually the owner of the company under the name of F. E. Zuellig, Inc.[68] Prewar Manila was very cosmopolitan. Should not our government be concerned that it has ceased to be so?

FIG. 214. Kodak Building

FIG. 215. Zuellig Building

Next to it on the **corner of Dasmariñas and Paredes** stands the former **Cortes-Ochoa Building**, originally with five stories,[69] whose jagged pilasters make it a classic representation of 1930s Ziggurat Art Deco. Together with the Uy Chaco and Zuellig Buildings it today forms part of the Philtrust Bank complex.

At **Dasmariñas corner Juan Luna** we meet once again the **China Bank Building**. Since we have been talking of columns and canopies, it is important to note that according to an old photo,[70] the original China Bank building also had canopies over its fourth and fifth floors but no Corinthian columns in between windows. The Corinthian columns may have been added later in the 20th century—perhaps with more prosperity.

101 **Dasmariñas corner Muelle de Binondo. Guison Building** has three stories in reinforced concrete. There is a contrast between the continuous line of the long window canopy of the third floor and the short window canopies of the second floor. The sidewalk arcade has Art Deco trapezoidal arches that suggest a construction date of the late 1920s. The third story seems to be a later addition. The building has a modest but dignified appearance.

FIG. 216. Detail, Cortes-Ochoa Building

YUCHENGCO (FORMERLY NUEVA)

Nueva means "new" in Spanish and may have been a new street centuries earlier. It has been renamed in honor of Enrique Yuchengco, a migrant from Fujian in the late nineteenth century who founded a line of entrepreneurs responsible for successes such as Malayan Insurance and Rizal Commercial Banking Corporation.

This street connects the Pasig River to Binondo's inland neighborhoods by crossing Dasmariñas, Escolta, Carvajal, and Chinatown's main street Ongpin. Once past Ongpin it passes behind Binondo Church.

FIG. 217. Go Hoc (Ynchausti) Building

The former **Ynchausti Building, 460-484 Yuchengco corner Padilla** (formerly Gandara) is an elegant Streamline Moderne office building from the late 1930s. According to Nikolas Ynchausti-Skalomenos, in a conversation, this was built by the Ynchaustis and served as an office for many years. It was subsequently sold and is today known as the Go Hoc Building. Because this corner lot has a trapezoidal shape, at the building's chamfered corner, the sides of the three-story building fan out like the sides of a ship (the Ynchaustis used to be engaged in shipping.) A recurring motif is the long, thin, continuous ledge running alongside the windows of the nine bays along Yuchengco and the six at Padilla. At particular spots, like a main window or the main door at the junction of the two streets, the ledge rises up abruptly at an angle, bends horizontally, and descends to form a protective box-like overhang. The motif is picked up and dramatized by the thin narrow rectangular ledge that boldly cantilevers high above the building crest over the main door.

Chinese elements are important components of Filipino architecture. However, Chinese style parapets are rare in Manila. An example is that of the **Yu-Tan Building at 515–523 Yuchengco** raised in 1927 according to the inscription. The parapet crowning the third story has a cut out silhouette that suggests the long, flowing curves of two Chinese clouds. In the parapet's middle section is a short round column surmounted by what appears to be a carved peony, symbol of good fortune. At both ends of the parapet are columns topped with lotus flowers—Buddhist symbols of purity. Within the parapet's frame are bas-reliefs representing two phoenixes rising from the flames of destruction. Like houses in the Straits Settlements (Malaysia and Singapore), this building mixes Chinese and Mediterranean elements. Thus over the uppermost windows of the four bays is a decorative, Spanish-inspired row of slender metal grills, round arches, and pillars.

FIG. 218. Yu-Tan Building

FIG. 219. Lam Bee Building

TOMAS PINPIN

Once again the first Filipino printer is honored, this time by a street. This street parallel to Yuchengco has a similar trajectory.

Lam Bee Company Building, a handsome three-story, pastel-colored apartment building at **628–634 Pinpin corner Carvajal**, was constructed in 1938, according to the inscription above the main entry. The lot's trapezoidal shape makes the building's mass seem to fan out from the chamfered corner. On the second and third stories of the apartment's two long sides hang continuous two-story covered balconies where residents can walk freely from one end of the side to the other. Vertical slits open the sides of the balcony balustrades. Over the main entry at the chamfered corner hang two balconies, one over the other. The hanging balcony, a traditional feature of both Hispanic and Middle Eastern cultures, is reinterpreted in a simplified, modern way using a contemporary material—reinforced concrete.

The **Rex Theater** at 744 Ongpin is a 1930s Art Deco Theater, and is one of only two theaters in Binondo (the other was the now demolished King's Theater on Ongpin). Its façade, originally of three floors, is characterized by the flat and sharp reliefs typical of Art Deco with stylized leaves on the former attic. Today the building houses a fine Chinese restaurant.

As we cross Ongpin, a wayside shrine appears on a wall with a replica of the Santo Cristo but sans the figure of Christ. Chinese-Filipinos burn joss sticks and bend three times before the Cross hung with sampaguita garlands. The fusion of Chinese, Spanish, and indigenous traditions is vividly alive. Past this corner, Pinpin narrows abruptly until it becomes a cul-de-sac.

Once again an apartment building with hanging balconies looms before us, the **Sunny Commercial Building** at **628–636 Pinpin**, built, according to an inscription, in 1948. The affinity between this and the Lam Bee Building is striking. But there are differences. This apartment is part of a row, rather than a corner one, and is higher by another floor. The vertical rhythms of the balconies are more pronounced, for the balusters have square footprints while the pillars occur at intervals in pairs. Finally, on the upper part of the central bay, a carved eagle spreads wide its wings.

One side of the cul-de-sac was dominated by the massive hulk of the **Tiong Building, 638–648 Pinpin**. The balcony sides ran continuously across five bays from corner to corner for four floors above the first floor. They were framed at each corner by equally massive pilasters with rectangular bodies, rising on cantilevered supports. The columns tapered into two level ziggurats. This unexpected example of the Streamline Moderne style of the late 1940s to 1950s in a side street bore a remarkable similarity to the Main Building of the Far Eastern University in Sampaloc. Unfortunately it was demolished in 2014.

On Masangkay Street (1015–1023) we find the **Su Kuang Institute,** a Chinese school founded in 1933. The beautiful and restrained Art Deco building dates from 1949. Sadly, it was demolished in 2017.

Also recently demolished, the 1850s to 1870s house at **1223 Soler** was one of the last wood-and-stone houses which once characterized Spanish-era Binondo, and one of the oldest houses that survived in the district. It is said to have at one time housed an infamous night club. Its adobe ground floor walls, in combination with a mind-green wooden upper floor and red windows, made this small house in the midst of a frenetic commercial district a charming reminder of long-vanished, slower-paced times.

FIG. 220. Su Kuang Institute

POBLETE-CLAVERIA

Pascual H. Poblete, a journalist, advocated liberalism for the Philippines and was exiled to Spain in 1895. Upon his return and after Rizal's execution, he campaigned to have a monument in his honor.[71] Narciso Clavería y Zaldúa, governor-general in 1844–1849, reorganized the municipal system in such an effective way that the Americans in the 1900s adopted this system.[72] Down to the 1840s, many Filipinos either had no family names (as in Java to this day) or else had very popular names like Cruz or Santos. He thus published a list of family names drawn from both Spanish and the native languages from which families could choose.

Claveria heads south and ends perpendicular to Poblete. Two small streets—Marquina and Ugalde—go north and end suddenly at Poblete. Such is the unexpected and picturesque layout of streets in this area once associated with modernity.

FIG. 221-223. Sunny Commercial Building, demolished 2019 (top); 1223 Soler (bottom left); 329 Poblete, circular window (bottom right)

307 Claveria corner Poblete. The **Yutivo Warehouse** is a solidly conceived building with four-by-four bays and rising to three stories. Its corner is chamfered. It probably dates from the second decade of the twentieth century. The windows continue to be of capiz, while the roof has a hipped shape. Part of its charm is that it doggedly adhered to a different style of construction in a neighborhood that was eager to be abreast of the latest in the 1910s to 1940s. Its design vocabulary is simple: cornices between the first and second stories and another one between the second and third, T-shaped projections from the lowest cornice, rectangular insets in the walls below windows.

A fragment of a wall at **329 Poblete** that has been incorporated into a two-story repair shop is a mysterious sight. What is this one-story adobe wall, probably dating from the late nineteenth century, doing in a neighborhood that wholeheartedly embraced reinforced concrete in the 1900s, ahead of the rest of the country? Just as intriguing: there are only windows, one on each side of the door. One window is circular, the other an octagon in the classic ba gua of feng shui. They are framed by large carvings whose rectangular projections recall either gears or the spokes of an automobile tire. They also evoke the eight rays of the sun shining on the Philippine flag! Perhaps this was the result of a nationalist impulse. Pilasters on both sides of the entry door repeat the same rectangular projections.

SAN VICENTE

Most likely this was named after San Vicente Ferrer, a Dominican friar (for Binondo was a Dominican parish during the Spanish period) who was prayed to when giving birth.

This is one of those narrow and unexpected side streets in Binondo. Adjacent to the Natividad is the **Tuason Building** on **320 San Vicente**. Recently renovated, this five-story building with ten bays exudes dignity. The rows of plain rectangular glass windows are separated from each other by slender cornices, of which the fourth rests on brackets. Insets under windows have diamond patterns. These elements suggest the late 1900s as the origin.

Going west toward Dasmariñas are two row houses that represent a different Binondo, being more akin to the nearby San Nicolas district. **House 211–215** belongs to **San Juan de Dios Foundation.** Though completely of wood, the upper story cantilevers

FIG. 224. Detail from Tuason Building (before renovation)

forward. The windows in the four bays continue to be of capiz. On the thin bars of the ventanillas are volutes forming Greek crosses. Wooden boards are laid in tongues-and-grooves. An elderly tenant avers that this was only constructed after 1945. Despite the late date, this row house of seven bays has those three stories that appeared in late nineteenth-century Binondo in response to limited space: a first story and a mezzanine and, above, a third story of wood, in this case, in tongue-and-groove. Beside this is **House 217** which again, according to the present owner, dates back to only the postwar period. It burned down in 1945 but was rebuilt by their family in 1948. Ventanilla grills likewise have volutes in clusters of quadruples to accentuate the plain vertical bars.

FIG. 225-226. San Vicente Street: House 211-215 (left); House 217 (right)

ESCOLTA

The Spanish word for "escort" is "Escolta." There are conflicting versions about the origin of the term. The most convincing version states that the governor's escort guards had their outpost on the street.[73]

This was Manila's premier business and shopping address from the nineteenth century till the 1970s.[74] After the Uy-Chaco high-rise was built, other high-rises sprouted on this street. They housed banks, business headquarters, and the most fashionable department stores. Pre–1945 Manileños quipped that Escolta was the longest street in the universe: it began with the Estrella del Norte (North Star) Jewelry Shop at the east end and ended at the Puerta del Sol (Gate of the Sun) Shop at the opposite end. Though destroyed in 1945, many of its buildings were rebuilt. By the 1950s to 1960s, it had recovered its prestige. Unfortunately, in the 1970s, it lost out to Ayala Avenue in Makati. Many buildings are now either half-empty or subsist on low rentals.

FIG. 227. Gateway to Escolta, seen from Plaza Sta. Cruz (adjacent page)

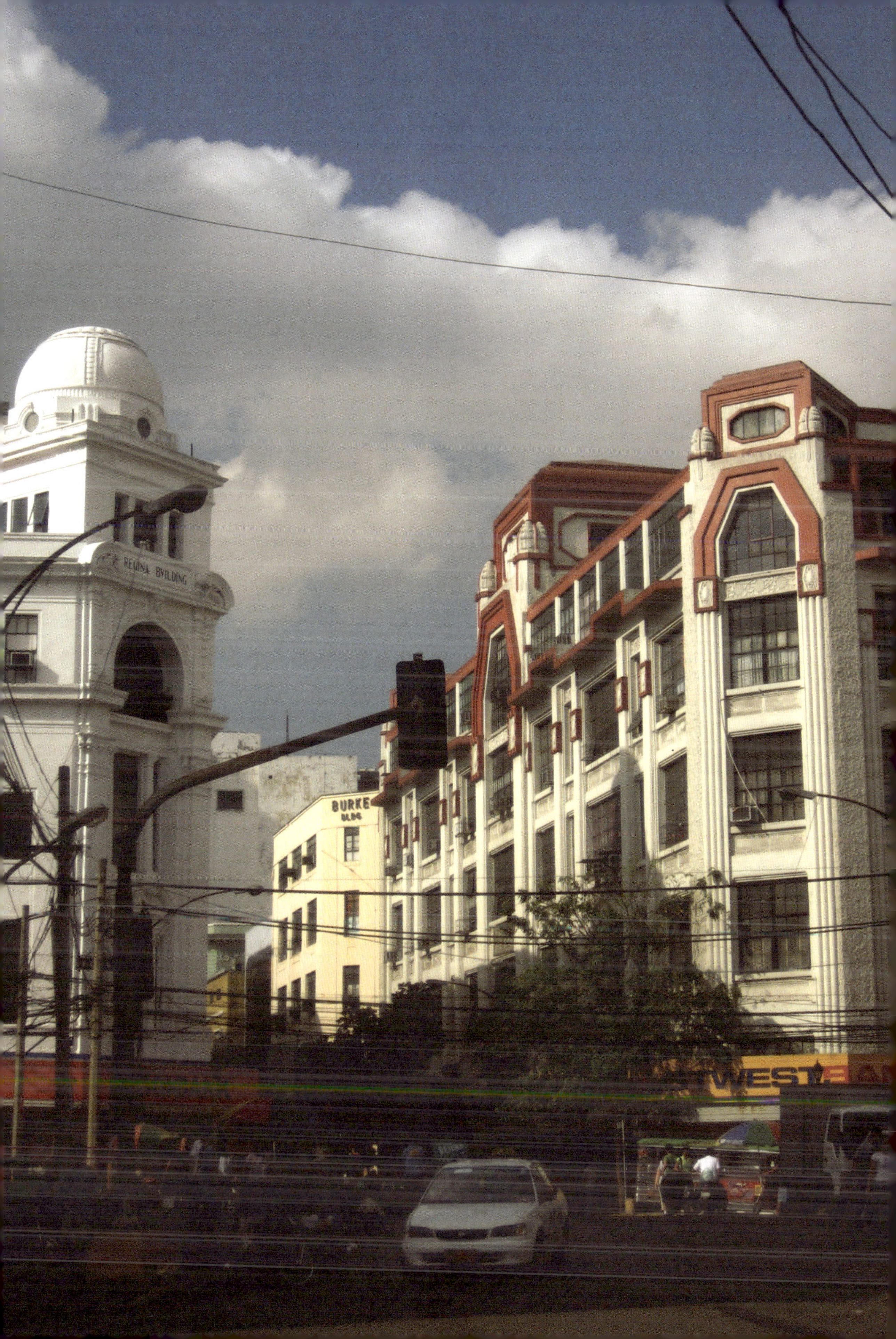
REGINA BVILDING
BURKE
BLDG

Escolta corner Burke corner Estero de la Reina. The **Perez-Samanillo Building** now **Sylianteng Building,** also called **First United**. Built in reinforced concrete, this dates back to around 1928 and was designed by the famous Andrés Luna de San Pedro, the only child of Juan Luna, patriot and painter.[75] Luis and Rafael of the Perez-Samanillo family were merchants of the early twentieth century who were leaders in the construction industry. The building used to be a prestigious address, being home to law firms and to Luna de San Pedro himself.

Like Cubist art of the period, Art Deco consciously embraced the angularity and abruptness of the Industrial Age's machine forms. While bas-relief flowers appear at Perez-Samanillo, these are bottled up in rectangular panels confined to the uppermost story. Moreover they are very stylized, being more like gears and sprockets. These rectangular panels connect the legs of each of the three trapezoid arches that dominate the skyline and that frame glass windows. Pilasters, consisting of tubular-looking pipings, descend continuously across four stories from the trapezoid arches to the top of the first story. Art Deco had another intent as well—to create a World style incorporating non-Western design motifs into a contemporary idiom. Hence the Babylonian-like ziggurats and the trapezoids inspired by Mayan doorways. There are three trapezoid arches here: one for each chamfered corner and a large one for the central bay to highlight the main door. While each trapezoidal arch plugs into

FIG. 228-233. Perez-Samanillo Building (adjacent page: bottom), now Sylianteng Building, also called First United: staircase (top left); newel post (top right); main entrance (bottom left); lobby (bottom center); elevators (bottom right)

FIG. 234. Regina Building

pilasters below it, above it rises a tower enclosing an elongated eight-sided tray within a rectangular arch. At the chamfered corners such trays are windows, while at the middle bay these become a bas-relief with stucco figures. For drama, the tower at the middle bay becomes a ziggurat. The rhythm of the windows as they march across the six bays on the Escolta side is novel. If 1 = narrow window, 2 = wide, 3 = wider, and 4 = widest, the sequence of the widths is as follows: 2+1+3+1+2+4+1+2+3+1+2. During this era the Argentine tango with its mixture of long, seductive melodic lines and sharp turns became the rage internationally.

The building was damaged in February 1945 but was restored. A sixth story was added, cramping the towers. Together with the Regina Building, this office block frames the entry to Escolta, as we come from Sta. Cruz church. Conversely, the two frame Sta. Cruz church. In 2015, a small museum opened honoring businessman Sylianteng, former owner of Berg's Department Store once located on the ground floor.

Escolta corner Burke corner Estero de la Reina corner Muelle del Banco Nacional. The **Regina Building** was owned by Jose J. de Leon, Jr., a pioneer in Pampanga's sugar industry and in the insurance industry in the 1930s.[76] His father was Jose L. de Leon Sr. who was active in both the sugar industry and in the Philippine National Bank.[77] The building began as the Roxas Building in 1921 but was expanded by Andrés Luna de San Pedro and was renamed "Regina" in 1926.[78] The fourth floor addition is by another famous architect, Fernando Ocampo.[79] The building was named after the first wife of Jose de Leon Sr., Regina Joven, the mother of Jose de Leon Jr. "Regina" is the Latin for "queen." With its size (it covers a block at the corner of an estero and the river) and its superb style, this structure is indeed the Queen.

Opened in 1934, the reinforced concrete building is typically Beaux Arts in its dramatic mixture of sculpture and architecture. Located at the chamfered corner at Escolta and the quay, a square-sided tower rises and is crowned with a dome. Below the tower, the building's name is inscribed in between two magnificently carved volutes, whose profile resembles a clam shell rather than the traditional Baroque spiral. Directly below the name is a large rounded arch that hovers over a three-story

FIG. 235-239. Regina Building: turret (top left); façade detail (top right); bronze nameplate (middle left); main entrance (bottom left); arcade (bottom right)

recessed portico. The portico has glass windows and a pair of disengaged colonnettes at the center. The capitals of the two pilasters enclosing the portico reveal maidens' faces amid acanthus leaves. Another maiden's face appears in low relief at the articulated keystone of the large arch to form the apex of this implicit female trinity. The dome's dignity is highlighted by a contrasting dome, which is smaller and was part of the original building prior to 1934. It caps a beveled, five-sided structure that cantilevers somewhat whimsically at the opposite corner on Escolta and Burke. The ground floor arcade which runs on all sides save the Escolta side has trapezoidal Art Deco arches. But how to link this angularity with the round arches of the third story fan windows and their Beaux Arts ambiance? Diagonal striations appear in the spandrels of the trapezoids; these become anemone-like patterns in the bas-relief panels of the story above them. Subtly these finger-tipped anemones wave again in the spandrels of the round arches.

Filipino-owned insurance companies opened at the Escolta in the early twentieth century. Thanks to Jose J. de Leon Jr., pioneers that held office here were National Life Insurance and Provident Insurance Corporation (now Mapfre).

FIG. 240. Burke Building

Escolta corner Burke, Burke Building. The ancestors of the Burkes settled in Manila in 1818, explained Edouard Burke-Miailhe, administrator of the building, in a published interview.[80] In 1873, according to a marker, William Burke was born in San Miguel, Manila. Equipped with a medical degree from the University of Dublin, he taught at the University of Santo Tomas, and installed the first electrocardiograph in the islands. His descendants are the Burke-Miailhes (of French parentage) who are active in both business and cultural projects.

The Burkes owned a building on this same site that survived the great earthquakes of 1863 and 1880. This was replaced in 1919 by a four-story building of reinforced concrete built by William Odum.[81] The country's first elevator was installed here. A famous pre-war tenant was MERALCO (Manila Electric Company). Badly damaged in 1945, the building was rehabilitated after.[82] This five-story building, consisting of three by seven

FIG. 241-244. Windows of Escolta: Calvo Building (top left); Natividad Building (top right); Perez-Samanillo Building (bottom left); Regina Building (bottom right)

bays, of reinforced concrete has a chamfered street corner and clean lines. Simplified pilasters subtly divide each bay from the other. Under each window is a decorative rectangular inset.

Right beside the Burke Building on the corner of Burke Street and Martinez is a four-story building, now called **Blue Horizon** which was probably built in the 1920s or 1930s. Unlike its neighbor, which lost its ornamentation during post-war reconstruction, it is still decorated. Each of the four bays (on Burke) and two (on Martinez) is inset between simply etched pilasters. Where one would expect a capital to appear is a carved cartouche, below which acanthus leaves open out in low relief. In the middle of each pilaster is a long fluting decorated with turned bars. For contrast it is flanked by two equally long but thin and simple flutings.

FIG. 245. Natividad Building (formerly Gaches Building) by Spanish architect Fernando de la Cantera Blondeau

Escolta corner 359 T. Pinpin. The former **Gaches Building,** now commonly known as **Natividad Building.** Together with a corporation, Samuel Gaches, an American businessman married to L.C. Gaches of Spanish ancestry, took over the assets of the Philippines' largest department store, Heacock's, in 1910 at Escolta and David Street.[83] Gaches had the current building raised in 1925. It was sold before World War II to José L. de Leon, a pioneer in Pampanga's sugar industry and President of the Pampanga Sugar Development Corporation (PASUDECO).[84] It was named Natividad after his second wife and the sister of Regina, his first. It is now managed by Leonies Development Corporation. Though destroyed during the war, it was renovated thereafter. It has a sculptural feel because of its chamfered corner and its row of blind arches on the second and fourth floors. The Neo-Renaissance arches are not rendered sharply. Being almost flat, they emphasize the volume of the building. The decorative horizontal frames, found only on the chamfered corner, also emphasize its volume.

FIG. 246-248. Windows of Escolta: Natividad Building (top); Perez-Samanillo Building (bottom left); Regina Building (bottom right)

FIG. 249-250. Calvo Building (left); relief of Capitol Theater (right)

266 Escolta, Calvo Building. In a conversation, Gerardo Teotico, administrator of the building and a Calvo family member, recounted that it was built in 1938 for Angél Calvo, a migrant from Spain who is his ancestor. Originally Luis Fernandez was Angél's partner. This reinforced concrete building of five stories was designed by Arch. Fernando Ocampo and originally had only four stories. The design called for a Beaux Arts look, though with a Neo-Baroque inflection. Each bay has a tall rounded arch in between tall Ionic columns with volutes exaggerated for expressiveness. Garlands in bas-relief and a sculptured cartouche over each arch create a moving space.

The operations of the Philippine Bank of Commerce under Filipino directors began here. The famous Republic Broadcasting System (RBS) under the care of Robert Stewart ("Uncle Bob") was also born here. The radio station was DZBB. Later on in its new headquarters in Quezon City, RBS became the nationwide GMA 7—nicknamed "Kapuso." Inside the building, the owners opened a museum, during the past decade, with old pictures, miniature models of buildings, and maps of Escolta.

Capitol Theater. Escolta was also where movie houses appeared side by side with office buildings during the American period. The heirs of Demetrio Tuason pioneered in show business. They founded the Eastern Theatrical Company which built this

FIG. 251. Capitol Theater. Tower with reliefs by Italian artist Francesco Monti. The remainder of the theater was demolished in 2020.

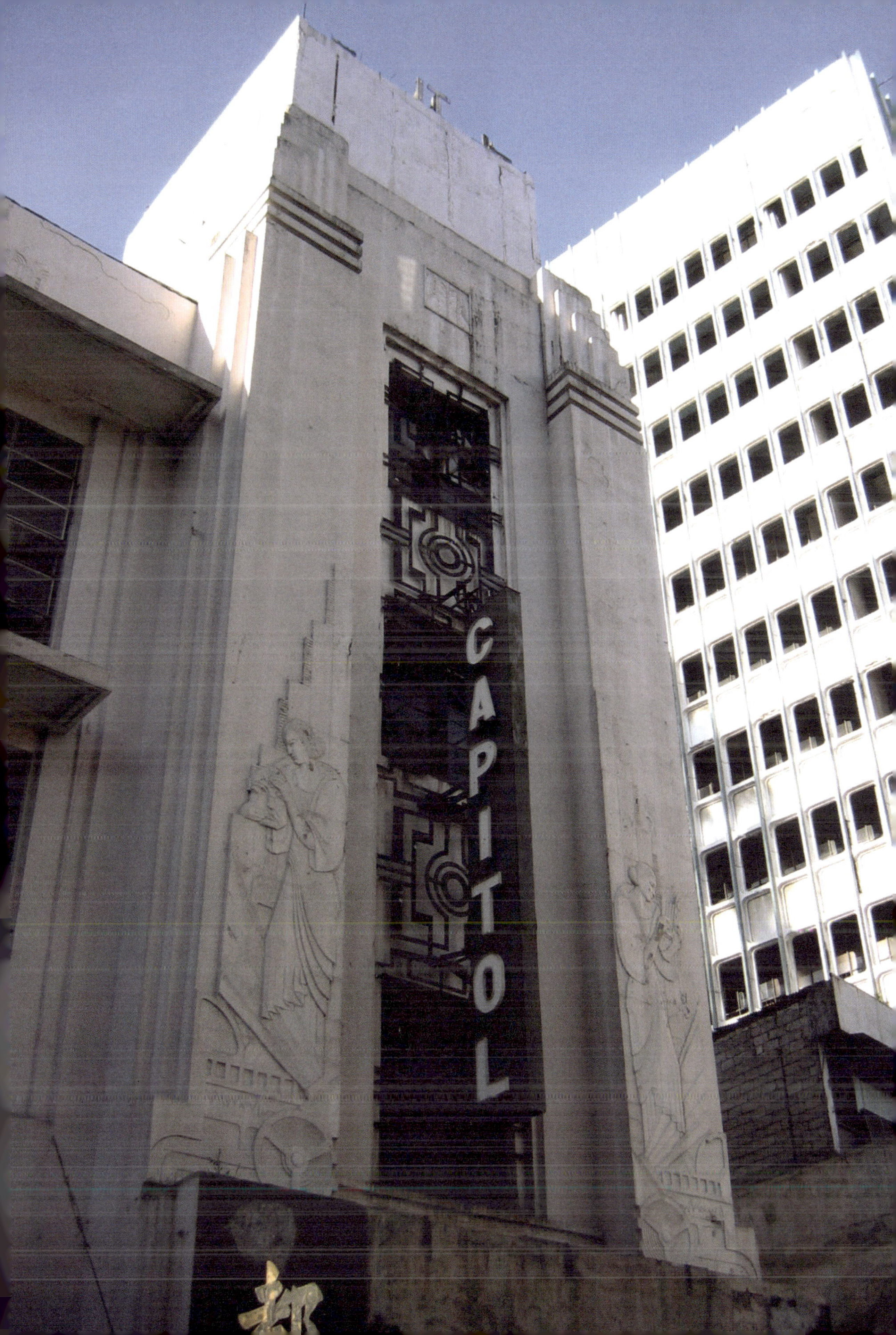
CAPITOL

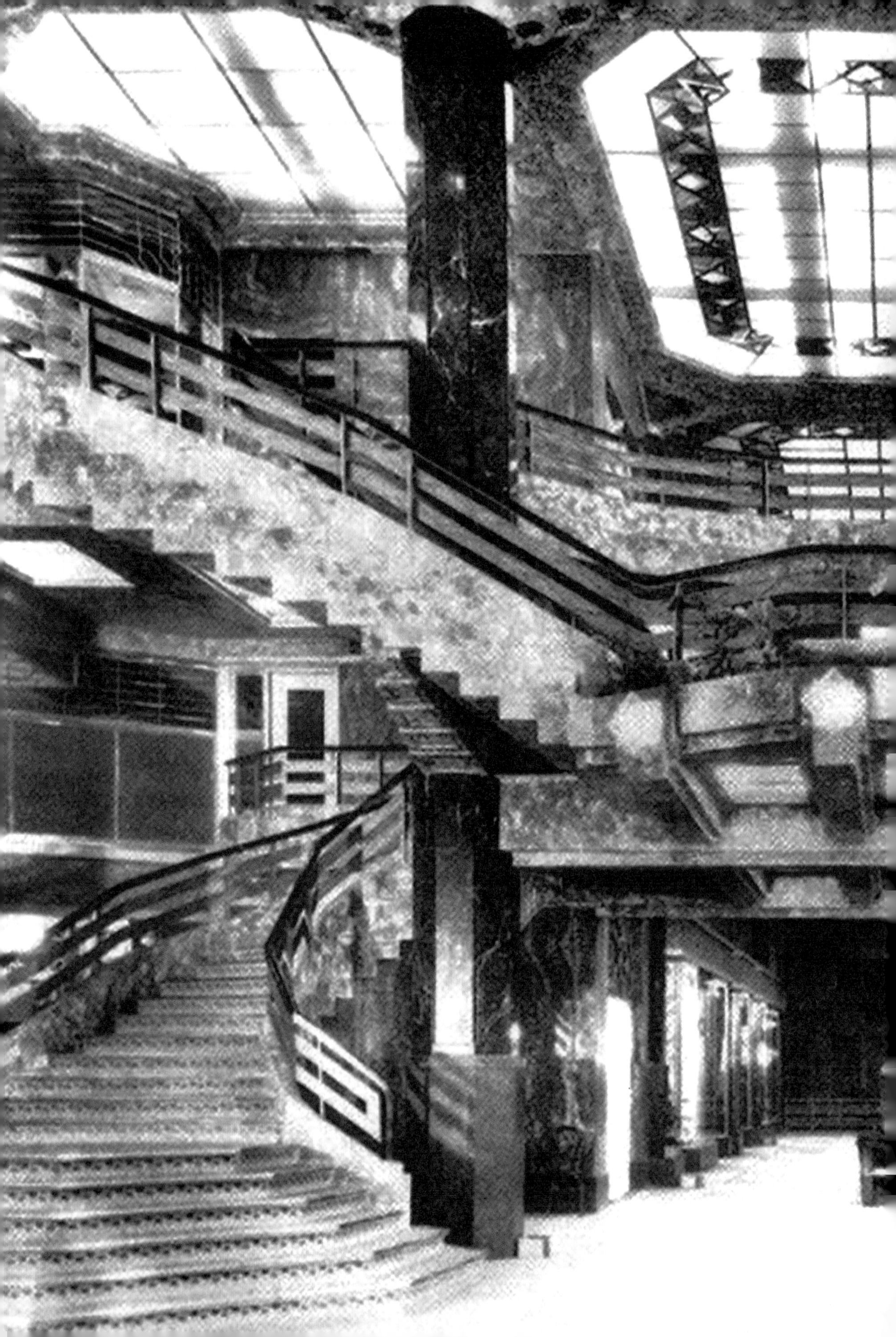

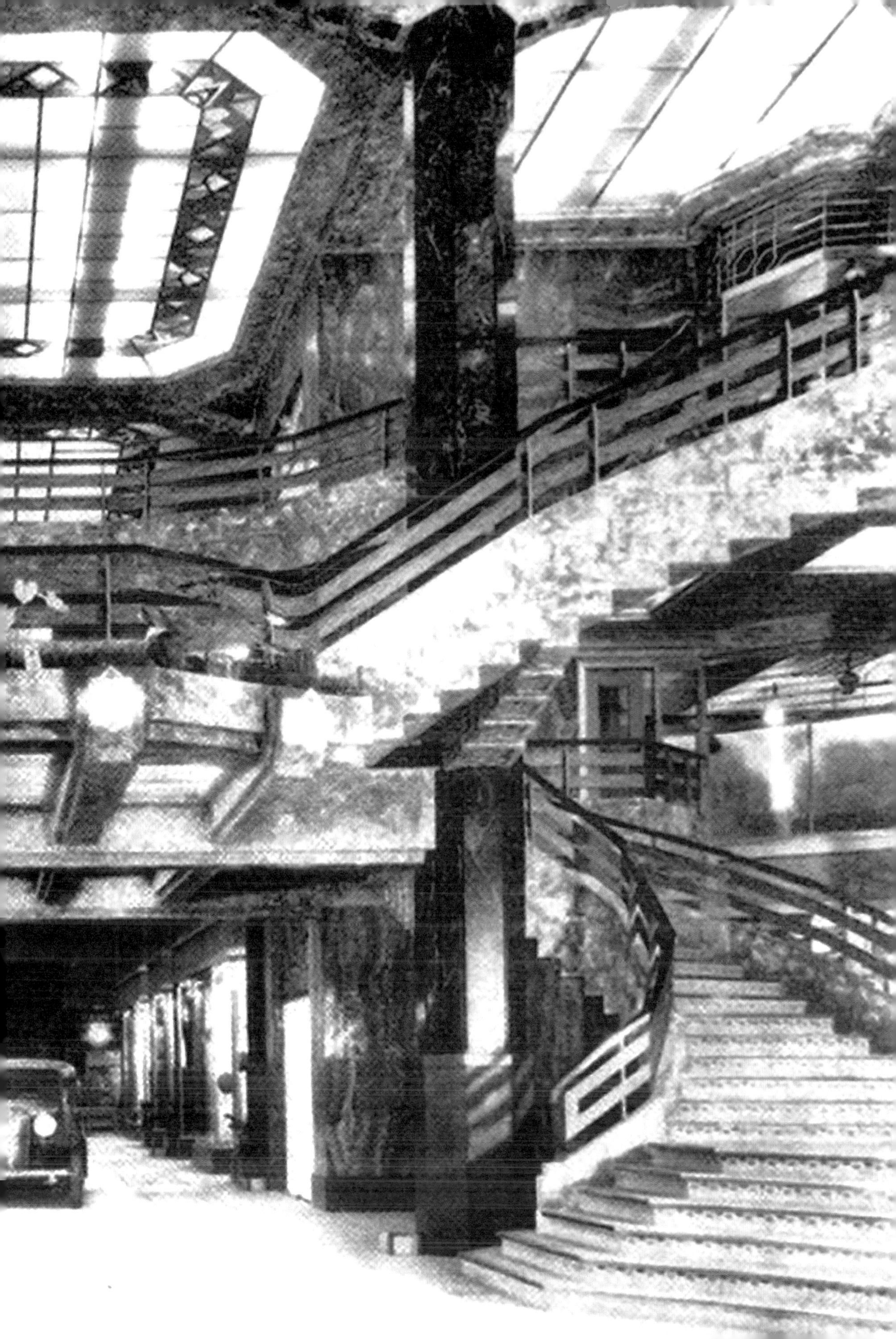

FIG. 252. Crystal Arcade (previous spread), Manila's first air-conditioned shopping mall, which also housed the Philippine Stock Exchange. Provisionally patched up after the war, its ruins were finally demolished in 1966. Image courtesy of John Oren Tewell.

structure designed by Juan Nakpil.[85] The building rises as three floors with six bays. At the east end is a tower whose two pilasters are embellished with bas-reliefs celebrating theater and music: a Filipina in *baro't saya* holding a theater mask and another one playing on a lyre. Below them are spools of film. A ziggurat crowns this 1937 Art Deco building. After it had been vacant for a long time it is currently (2020) being redeveloped with only the historic tower preserved.

Crystal Arcade. Several "ghosts" haunt Escolta. The most notable is this building with shops, offices, and the Manila Stock Exchange, which was regarded as Andres Luna de San Pedro's "masterpiece" and was then admired as the city's most modern building."[86] Old photos reveal a three-story foyer with two symmetrically balanced grand staircases sweeping upwards to form curving, cantilevered stairs that led to the upper stories. Daylight entered the foyer's ceiling through several suspended stained glass skylights that recalled Parisian department stores. The building opened in 1932, but was smashed in the Battle of 1945.

HOLDING OFFICE IN BINONDO

Jose, scion of sugar-producing families, continues to hold office in his vintage building. But much of the Escolta area now slumbers. First the banks left in the 1970s for Makati, eventually the Philippine National Bank transferred in 1995 to its own financial center at Roxas Boulevard in Pasay. The lack of parking deters potential investors. So too do the dirt, the smell of the esteros, and the air of decay. Why stay in this area that is no longer our Wall Street? One reason is "sentimental." His ancestor had the building constructed and passed it on to his descendants. Jose loves the high ceilings, now a rarity in post-1960 buildings, and the look of the structure. For instance, in repairing the elevator, he makes sure that the brass fixtures are either kept or replicated. "When we fix something, we are faithful to the original design." He considers it worthwhile doing these careful repairs, for "You can see where your efforts go into." He also likes to look out of the window over the Pasig, to McArthur Bridge and to the Post Office. "You don't get that panorama in Makati! Sometimes there are seagulls." There is an association of owners of Escolta properties. They are eager for the entire area be regenerated. For this to succeed, the cooperation of the City Government is, of course, needed. In 2014 the National Historical Commission of the Philippines (NHCP) moved to have the area between Dasmariñas and Escolta declared a heritage zone, to protect its architectural heritage while at the same time opening up new business opportunities, such as tourism and the booming call center industry. Six years later (2020) the declaration still has not materialized.

NOTES

1. An important introduction to the trade is given by Benito J. Legarda Jr. in "Two and a half centuries of the Galleon Trade," *Philippine Studies* 3, no. 4 (December 1955), 345-72.
2. William Lytle Schurz, *The Manila Galleon* (New York: E. P. Dutton and Company, 1939), 32-33.
3. Ibid., 30.
4. Pierre Chaunu, *Les Philippines et le Pacifique des Ibériques (XVIe, XVIIe, XVIIIe siecles) : Introduction méthodologique et indices d'activité* (Paris: S.E.V.P.E.N., 1960).
5. Sociedad Estatal para la Acción Cultural Exterior, *Filipinas puerta de Oriente: De Legazpi a Malaspina* (Madrid: Sociedad Estatal para la Acción Cultural Exterior, 2003), 269-70.
6. William Henry Scott, *Barangay: Sixteenth Century Philippine Culture and Society* (Quezon City: Ateneo de Manila University Press, 1994), 207.
7. Ibid.
8. Ibid.
9. David R. M. Irving, *Colonial Counterpoint: Music in Early Modern Manila* (Oxford: Oxford University Press, 2010).
10. Ibid., 42.
11. Ibid., 19.
12. Ibid., cites various examples throughout the book.
13. The Parian and its various locations are discussed in Edgar Wickberg, *The Chinese in Philippine Life 1850-1898* (New Haven: Yale University Press, 1965).
14. Lorelei D.C. de Viana, *Three Centuries of Binondo Architecture 1594-1898: A Socio-historical Perspective* (Manila: University of Sto. Tomás Press), 30.
15. Ibid., 16-17.
16. Ibid., 17. See print by Jakob von Schley.
17. Benito J. Legarda Jr., *After the Galleons: Foreign Trade, Economic Change and Entrepreneurship in the Nineteenth Century Philippines* (Quezon City: Ateneo University Press, 2004), 95.
18. Ramón Gonzalez Fernandez, *Manual del viajero en Filipinas* (Manila: Establecimiento Tipográfico de Sto. Tomás, 1875), 114.
19. Lorelei D.C. de Viana, *Three Centuries of Binondo Architecture 1594-1898*, 50-51.
20. Kwok-Chu Wong, *The Chinese in the Philippine Economy, 1898-1941* (Quezon City: Ateneo de Manila University Press, 1999).
21. Lewis E. Gleeck, *American Business and Philippine Economic Development* (Manila: Carmelo and Bauermann, Inc., 1975), 43.
22. Daniel F. Doeppers, *Manila 1900-1941: Social Change in a Late Colonial Metropolis* (Quezon City: Ateneo de Manila University Press, 1984), 57.
23. Ibid., 64.
24. Lewis E. Gleeck, Jr., *The Manila Americans (1901-1964)* (Manila: Carmelo and Bauermann Inc., 1977), 215.
25. Modern concrete was invented in 1756 by John Smeaton, a British engineer, by adding an aggregate of pebbles and powdered brick into a cement mixture; in 1824, Joseph Aspdin, a British inventor, burned ground limestone and clay together to create a cement with better bonding qualities. See "The History of Concrete and Cement," accessed 16 September 2012, http://inventors.about.com.
26. Cited by María Lourdes Diaz-Trechuelo Spinola, *Arquitectura española en Filipinas, 1565-1800*, prologue by Diego Angulo Iñiguez (Sevilla: Escuela de Estudios Hispano-Americanos de Sevilla, 1959), 33, 282.
27. De Viana, *Three Centuries*, 89; a narrative is likewise given by Rene Javellana, "Binondo Church," *Cultural Center of the Philippines Encyclopedia of the Arts*, vol. 3, "Architecture" (Manila, Cultural Center of the Philippines, 1994).
28. De Viana, *Three Centuries*, 90-91.
29. And likewise in Malolos in Bulacan, and Bacolor in Pampanga.
30. As discovered by famous guide, Ivan Man Dy.
31. De Viana, *Three Centuries*, 139.
32. Ibid., 137.
33. Ibid., 139.
34. Ibid., 122.
35. Ibid, 97-98.
36. Ibid., 109.
37. Ibid., 173.
38. Ana Gonzales, "Lucky Chinatown: Inspiring Lifestyles in Binondo," Anagon, 16 August 2012, http://www.anagonzales.com/2012/08/lucky-chinatown-inspiring-lifestyles-in.html.
39. John Newsome Crossley, *Hernando de los Rios Coronel and the Spanish Philippines in the Golden Age* (Farnham, Surrey: Ashgate Publishing Ltd., 1988), 152.

40 Lorelei D.C. de Viana, "Binondo in the Twentieth Century," in *Manila: Studies in Urban Cultures and Traditions*, edited by José Victor Torres, Bernardita Churchill, Manila Studies Association, and National Commission on Culture and the Arts Committee on Historical Research (Quezon City and Manila: Manila Studies Association; National Commission on Culture and the Arts Committee on Historical Research, 2007), 43-44. The article is a valuable follow-up to the author's earlier *Three Centuries of Binondo Architecture*. Unfortunately, though the bibliography makes use of primary sources, the author does not cite sources within the text, making it difficult to do further investigation on a topic.

41 Versions of such reduced columns and capitals appear in drawings of futuristic cities in the comic strip *Superman* (created in 1938).

42 Santiago Albano Pilar, "El Hogar," *CCP Encyclopedia of the Arts*, vol. 3, 232-33.

43 George F. Nellist, *Men of the Philippines: A Biographical Record of Men of Substantial Achievement in the Philippine Islands Today*, vol. 1 (Manila: The Sugar News Company, 1931), 206-9; Filipinas Compañía de Seguros, 1913-1953.

44 Santiago Albano Pilar, "Pacific Commercial Company Building," *CCP Encyclopedia of the Arts*, vol. 3, "Architecture," 259-60.

45 Ibid.

46 1921 is the date proposed by Gerard Lico, *Arkitekturang Filipino: A History of Architecture and Urbanism in the Philippines* (Quezon City: The University of the Philippines Press, 2008), 305; while 1922 is the other date given by the historian Lorelei de Viana in her article "Binondo in the Twentieth Century, 1900-1940," *Manila: Studies in Urban Cultures and Traditions*, edited by José Victor Torres (Quezon City: Manila Studies Association and National Commission for Culture and the Arts, 2007), 47

47 Kwok-Chu, *The Chinese in the Philippine Economy, 1898-1941*, 134.

48 Ibid., 135.

49 Ibid., 136.

50 De Viana, "Binondo in the Twentieth Century," 49.

51 Nellist, *Men of the Philippines*, 104.

52 De Viana, "Binondo in the Twentieth Century," 51.

53 Philippine Education Company, *Manila City Directory 1939-1940*, (Manila: Philippine Education Company Inc., 1940), 1251; Gleeck, *American Business*, 66, 89.

54 Gleeck, Jr., *The Manila Americans*, 223.

55 De Viana, "Binondo in the Twentieth Century," 51.

56 Ibid.

57 Nellist, *Men of the Philippines*, 6.

58 Rene Javellana, "Puente de España," *CCP Encyclopedia of the Arts*, vol. 3, 268.

59 Lico, *Arkitekturang Filipino*, 311.

60 Kwok-Chu, *The Chinese in the Philippine Economy, 1898-1941*, 61-62; Luis R. Sison, "Remembrances and the Streets of Manila," *Philippine Daily Inquirer*, 20 August 2006, A17.

61 De Viana, "Binondo in the Twentieth Century," 64.

62 Ibid.

63 Ibid.

64 Ibid.

65 Ibid.

66 Ibid.

67 Kwok-Chu, *The Chinese in the Philippine Economy, 1898-1941*, 62.

68 Ibid.

69 De Viana, "Binondo in the Twentieth Century," 44-45.

70 Kwok-Chu, *The Chinese in the Philippine Economy, 1898-1941*.

71 Luning B. Ira and Isagani R. Medina, "Binondo," *Streets of Manila* (Quezon City: GCF Books, 1977), 58.

72 Ibid., 57.

73 De Viana, *Three Centuries*, 50.

74 During a tour of Escolta on 21 August 2011, two students reported on the street. They claimed that only Europeans could buy and sell on the Escolta, and that Filipinos and Chinese were confined to Rosario and Dasmariñas. Where did they get such disinformation? From the Internet! This is one more reason why a heavy reliance on the internet without cross-checking with books and journals is risky. In her history of Binondo, De Viana relates that the Escolta shops catered to the rich and famous. But nowhere does she say that *only* Europeans could do business there. And she caps her description by citing Jean Mallat's often-repeated observation that the gathering place for the latest news and gossip about goings-on in the islands in the 1840s was the house of Joaquín, a Chinese merchant whose house stood at the junction of Escolta and the foot of the Puente de España. De Viana, *Three Centuries*, 51.

75 Santiago Albano Pilar, "Perez-Samanillo Building," *CCP Encyclopedia of the Arts*, vol. 3, 265.

76 Miguel R. Cornejo (ed.), *Cornejo's Commonwealth Directory of the Philippines* (Manila: Miguel R. Cornejo, 1939), 1874.

77 Nellist, *Men of the Philippines*, 182.

78 Lico, *Arkitekturang Filipino*, 302.

79 Paulo Rubio, "Regina Building," Arquitectura Manila, 18 March 2014, accessed 15 May 2015, http://arquitecturamanila.blogspot.com/2014/03/regina-building.html.

80 Ditas P. Bermudez, "Enjoying Escolta," *The Daily Tribune*, 21 October 2000, 24.

81 Gleeck, *Manila Americans*, 215.

82 My sources for this information are old photos kept at the Burke-Miailhe Office inside the building.

83 De Viana, "Binondo in the Twentieth Century," 61.

84 Nellist, *Men of the Philippines*, 182.

85 De Viana, "Binondo in the Twentieth Century," 59; Lico, *Arkitekturang Filipino*, 331.

86 Rodrigo D. Perez III, "Luna de San Pedro, Andres," CCP *Encyclopedia of the Arts*, vol. 3, "Architecture," 308–9.

Reimagining Our Former Wall Street

VICTOR S. VENIDA

The preservation of significant, vintage buildings along Escolta and the formulation of design guidelines for both new buildings and for renovating post-1940s buildings will help create a distinctive district that identifies Manila as unique. These will generate a much-needed sense of place. But because these buildings need some form of economic use to survive, we need to identify a range of economic activities that can be accommodated not just in the old buildings but also in the entire district so that heritage preservation becomes integral to an overall strategy of local area development.

The Capitol Theater has largely been demolished recently (2020). Other heritage structures, however, have some current use. There are freight-related firms renting space at the Regina Building. The old Philippine National Bank (PNB) building was occupied by the City College of Manila, emptied after the City College moved over to Mehan Garden by the Manila City Hall, and recently mysteriously burned down. Another is occupied by a Chinese media organization. The new buildings include a massive residential tower that clearly has a substantial population of residents. On a weekday noon, vehicular traffic is remarkably light compared to the nearby Sta. Cruz and Plaza Cervantes/Quintin Paredes areas. The streets are all taken up with parked vehicles.

An unappreciated amenity is the already repaved riverbank promenade along the Muelle del Banco Nacional with stunning vistas of the Post Office Buildings and the Jones and MacArthur Bridges. It has a new, though poorly maintained, ferry terminal (for the Pasig River ferry) and rather classically designed street lamps. The entire block is just a parking area with the buildings turning their backs on it. There used to be abandoned and decaying stalls which began to attract informal settlers but which have since been cleared and removed. The bridges and the Post Office Building are often stunningly well-lit in the evenings but there is no spot to enjoy this vista.

The renewal of the Escolta area might begin at the Muelle del Banco Nacional. It can be developed as a new waterside site that offers inexpensive Chinese and Filipino cuisine in an al fresco setting. It can replicate to a degree the once-successful development of the Ermita-Malate Bay front as a locale for al fresco bars, coffee shops, and restaurants in the previous administration. Unfortunately the latter's success killed the experiment, for it caused traffic jams along Roxas Boulevard—which is one of the city's major traffic arteries.

Happily, neither the Escolta nor Muelle del Banco Nacional are major traffic arteries so that, in fact, either can attract a family crowd to partake of the dining and café experience. If managed properly this can attract business to the area and convert the spaces in the old buildings to rentable office spaces. Examples of proper management include the improvement in the vicinity of San Juan de Letran and the Morato district in Quezon City.

Among the elements that will need to be considered are traffic management and parking. There was a huge parking lot by Calle Pinpin and a rather ugly and unrented one-story structure at the corner of Muelle del Banco and Nueva (now called Yuchengco Street). Here was recently built a huge parking building which generates revenue for the city and also allows the city to control parking along several streets in the district. The restaurants and cafés will also need to have water and sewer connections and regular garbage and sanitation systems. The buildings along the Muelle can then also rent out space for indoor restaurants and cafes and other shopping establishments. These can provide rental income for current and future buildings. To make such a new destination truly attractive to pedestrians and other non-motorized citizens, there will be a need for a well-maintained corridor from MRT1-Station Carriedo straight to Plaza Sta. Cruz and on to Escolta, even on to Intramuros.

BPOs can be attracted to build their businesses in the area to take advantage of the students who can be trained and hired on a part-time basis. However they need to be encouraged by an infrastructure assessment report and an actual infrastructure development program for the long term for the area. Manila and its colleges can arrange for a work-and-study scholarship plan that arranges the students' schedules so that they have time for work, classes, and study. If the city offers courses in hotel and restaurant management (currently and recently in Intramuros) then the students can already get part-time employment in their area of study and obtain practical training. Investors can find this highly-skilled and inexpensive labor (since they are part-time workers) to be an incentive. The city can also develop a building or two as dormitory space and provide lodgings for the poorer but deserving students. Establishments catering to students can then be attracted there like internet cafés, school supplies and bookstores, and the like. The condo residents can benefit from these and also from the presence of neighbourhood grocery and food stores so that they can just walk to shopping places. They can also take advantage of the proposed riverside restaurants and coffee shops. Since the area will also be residential, perhaps the noise level can be regulated; one can imagine not allowing open air band concerts, dance events, and karaoke at least after 10 p.m. even on weekends. Or these night time activities can be encouraged in the nearby areas such as along Plaza Sta. Cruz which is dominantly commercial in the daytime anyway. The building owners can benefit from a livelier night life if these night time events can be allowed or licensed in enclosed areas to minimize noise pollution. This was made possible in the redevelopment of Malate and Ermita. New buildings and renovation of the old buildings can follow design guidelines that enhance the prewar architecture of Escolta.

There is currently a core group of people from the Escolta Business Association coordinating with City Hall which is working out a revitalization plan for Escolta under the lead of Architect Dominic Galicia. The overall plan is to convert Escolta into an IT-outsourcing center. Under this plan, the old Pacific Commercial Building along Muelle de la Industria has recently been renovated by restoration architect Augusto Villalon. Unfortunately, it was badly damaged together with neighbouring buildings in a massive fire in 2017.

Former Mayor Alfredo Lim expressed a desire to develop the Metropolitan Theater as a venue for the performing arts for the masses. He might have had a better chance if he had experimented first with the now demolished Capitol Theater. The structure was extant and not very large so that it could have been be renovated as a venue for inexpensive but popular mass entertainment. It was also more accessible than the Metropolitan which is along a main traffic artery; the noise and pollution will not make the experience there a pleasant one even for a lower-priced admission.

A proposed area redevelopment of this sort will require substantial investment. Eventually the city can realize the revenues from new business and new construction and renovation in the area in the long-term future. But it has to handle the short-term problem of investment funds sourcing and relocation of stalls from Carriedo. The stalls in Carriedo are there precisely because of the proximity to the Quiapo Church crowd. But they do cause vehicular and human traffic in the area. The stall-holders might find the Quinta Market area more preferable than Escolta because Escolta is too far away from the Quiapo crowds. The Quinta Market is not too far away and in fact is quite near the commercial establishments of Palanca and the *Ilalim ng Tulay*. Quinta Market has thus been recently redeveloped and it can attract a larger market as a section of it has also been developed as a parking building for the vehicles in the Quiapo area. Given the distance from Quiapo Church, this will also need an attractively designed and well-maintained corridor to encourage people to walk towards there.

As for investment funding, one source will be the Filipino-Chinese businesses that are already nearby and can be attracted to finance new business in the area. GMA7 can also be enticed to assist in the redevelopment of the Calvo Building and the nearby district as its parent Channel 7 first started in that building. Government will have to provide the financing for the infrastructure redevelopment of the area (ideally part of a city-wide infrastructure redevelopment program). Perhaps one important untapped source is the substantial funds of the city of Makati. Makati has boasted of its revenue capacity and the ability to provide substantial services which the residents hope can be replicated for the whole country (apropos the city's own advertisements). The administration of these two cities can work out a scheme wherein Makati can provide the funds and be credited for the activity and Manila can finance a project that Makati can also benefit from by way of image. A project for the redevelopment of the old commercial and financial center of the country is a way for the new commercial and financial center to pay homage to its origins. Besides, the two cities are connected. Manila is far more famous (or notorious) internationally yet Makati is the actual financial and commercial center of the country. Thus any project that enhances the image and economy of Manila will redound to Makati's benefit as foreign funds will locate in Makati anyway. Though the central business districts of the two cities may be competing, they can also realize substantial complementarities. Their direct connection is via the Pasig River, for they both host ferry terminals. In a sense, if there were an MMDA with taxing powers and greater autonomy then this proposal can be seen as cross-subsidy between two cities within a political entity like Metro Manila.

Makati can start the renewal of its old town which is along the Pasig and finance the renewal of the Binondo and San Nicolas riverfront. In this way the entire National Capital Region benefits from the partnership of its oldest and wealthiest cities.

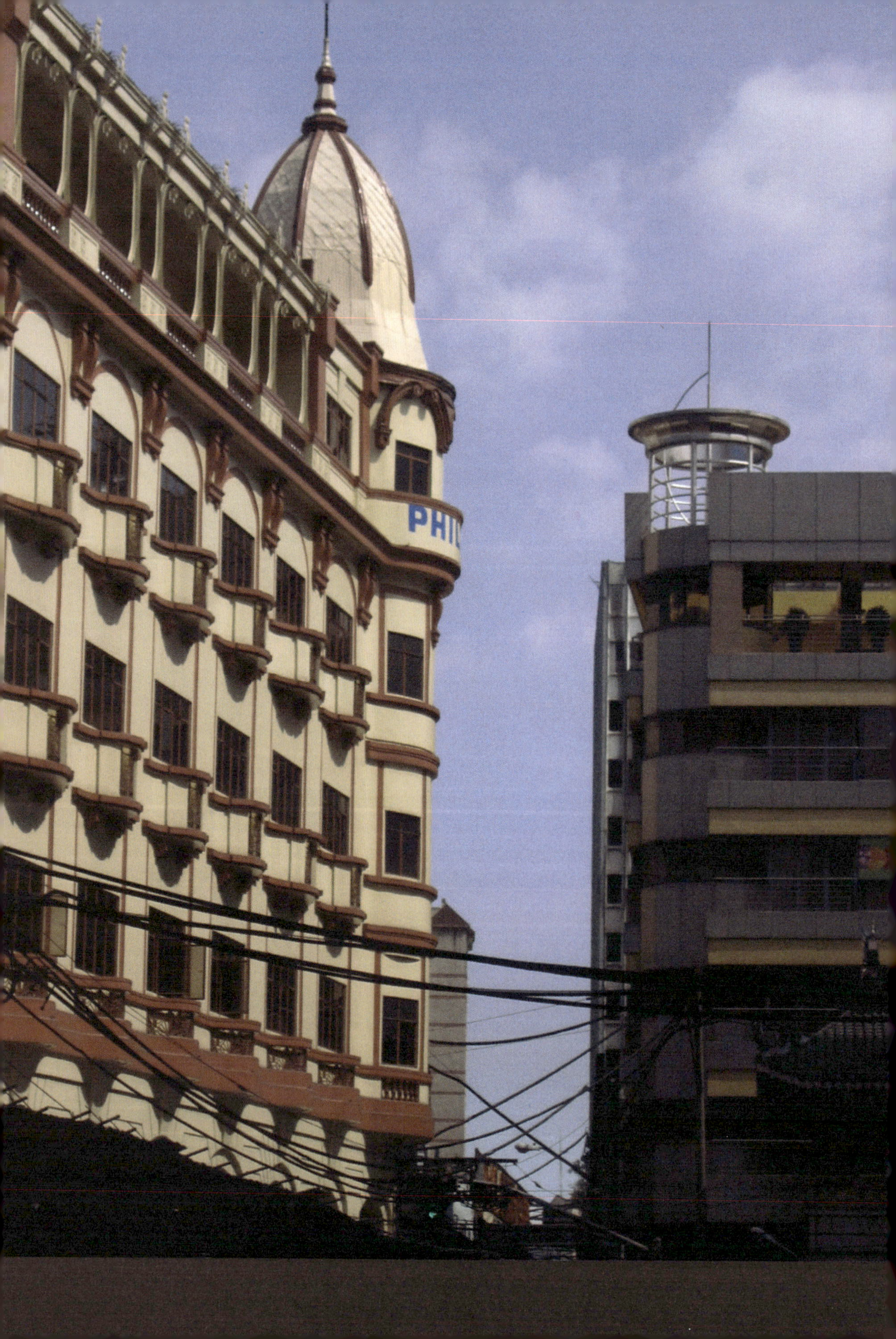
PHIL

New Meets Old—Contemporary Buildings in Historical Context

ERIK AKPEDONU

HISTORIC CITIES, TOWNS, AND DISTRICTS ARE LIVING COMMUNITIES, and as such subject to constant change and evolution. Without contemporary socioeconomic interventions in the use and form of its historic fabric, a community risks stagnation and becoming a mere museum piece. Yet, preservation of historic districts is important not only for tourism but also for our cultural identity as they signify the gradual evolution of the community, helping us understand where we came from, and where the future may take us.

The question then is not so much whether, but how to integrate new developments into historic fabrics. Recent, albeit controversially discussed, trends in heritage management see conservation as "managing change" rather than freezing and "musealizing" a particular style or period.[1] Recognizing the need to reconcile heritage preservation with contemporary needs and forms, the United Nations Educational, Scientific, and Cultural Organization (UNESCO) and the International Council on Monuments and Sites (ICOMOS) organized a series of international conferences; the resulting declarations addressed this issue. The "Vienna Memorandum" of 2005 outlines the basic parameters for the integration of the new into the old. While recognizing that modern architecture plays a significant role in cultural and symbolic place-making even within historic cities and districts, the memorandum, however, demands the contextualization of contemporary architecture in the historic urban landscape by insisting that "proportion and design must fit into the particular type of historic pattern and architecture." Further, that it is "complementary to values of the historic urban landscape and remains within limits in order not to compromise the historic nature of the city"[2] Hence the memorandum discourages "façadism," that is, merely preserving the exterior walls of a historic building and insists that prerequisites for

FIG. 253. Adjacent page: by Chaco Building (left); Charisland Building (right)

successful intervention are a thorough knowledge and understanding of the history, culture, and architecture of the place to enable a careful, culturally and historically sensitive approach. To achieve these objectives, the memorandum calls for thorough scientific inventory, analysis, and assessment of the existing historic urban fabric, such as townscapes, roofscapes, and visual axes. This serves to enable cultural and visual impact assessment studies to examine the relationship between existing old and proposed new buildings.

The preceding 1987 "Washington Charter for the Conservation of Historic Towns and Urban Areas" in Article 2 specifies the elements fundamental to preserving the historic character of a town or urban area, namely urban patterns defined by lot sizes and street layout; green and open spaces; the scale, size, style, construction, materials, color, and decorations of buildings; a town's or district's surrounding setting; and the functions it has acquired over time.

Article 10 states that "when it is necessary to construct new buildings or adapt existing ones, the existing spatial layout should be respected, especially in terms of scale and lot size." And: "The introduction of contemporary elements in harmony with the surroundings should not be discouraged since such features can contribute to the enrichment of an area."[3]

As early as 1976 the "UNESCO Recommendation Concerning the Safeguarding and Contemporary Role of Historic Areas," as declared in Nairobi emphasizes the significance of volume and massing, heights, façades and roofs, forms, and proportions for the character of historic areas (Article 28) and the need to protect them from disfigurement by poles, pylons, and electrical wires or telephone cables (Article 30).[4]

Since then a number of conferences held in Asia have formulated declarations that consider the specific situation of heritage in Asia, such as the "Hoi An Declaration on Conservation of Historic Districts of Asia" in 2003 and the "Xi'an Declaration on the Conservation of the Setting of Heritage Structures, Sites and Areas" from 2005.

The many types of historic districts require that the chosen approach consider the unique characteristics of a given place. Where, as in Vigan, a place is characterized by a uniform and homogeneous historic townscape "frozen in time," it may be important to preserve that homogeneity; whereas in larger metropolises such as Manila, which are defined by many different forms, styles, and historic layers, it may be that very diversity and visible continuum of history that is worthy of protection, rather than concentrating on one particular period of history. In many Asian and African cultures the values and traditions of the community may be expressed in their use of authentic materials in an appropriate, traditional manner for maintaining their vernacular architecture.[5] For example, in the Sahel Region, as in many parts of Africa, traditional adobe (loam) architecture is still commonly used for private and religious buildings such as mosques, using vernacular forms which have been in use for centuries.[6] Once a year, traditional adobe mosques such as the Great Mosque in Djenné, Mali, are collectively replastered by the community in a festive ritual which fosters community spirit and cooperation.

Thus, what matters is not so much the architectural style or the material, but the sensitivity of planners and developers to the local environment and their creativity in approaching it. For, ultimately, their interventions should enhance the historic environment, rather than diminish it. To that end, designers and builders all over the world have used various approaches, such as pastiche, historic forms, historic materials, dialogue between old and new, reconstructions, and extensions and additions.

PASTICHE

In the Philippines, one popular strategy aims to superficially imitate historic buildings by "pasting" onto a modern concrete structure "traditional" trademark architectural elements such as capiz windows, adobe stone facing, and tile roofs, albeit in a somewhat "modern" way. An example of this "citation," popularized by Post-Modernism, is a new Jollibee fast food restaurant in the historic district of Sta. Ana, Manila. The building is visibly modern, with a clever contemporary interpretation of capiz windows. A fake tile roof in front, complete with metal fringes, and faux adobe walls on the ground floor seek to emulate the classic *Bahay-na-Bato* of Spanish times.

FIG. 254. Jollibee in Sta. Ana, Manila

FIG. 255. McDonald's in Vigan

However, the building is surrounded on all sides by rather nondescript modern structures, hence the reason for choosing this "antique style" remains opaque to the casual observer. Still, this type of "pastiche" architecture fits better into the historic streetscape of Sta. Ana than a standard Jollibee design would have.

It is often only a thin line between "adaptation" and "kitsch," especially in sensitive areas where there is an intact ensemble of authentic historic buildings, such as Vigan. Here, too, a recently built McDonald's fast food outlet facing Plaza Salcedo and the cathedral is, although principally problematic in such a sensitive location, less of an intrusion than a typical McDonald's design, complete with giant pylon, would have been. Instead, it tries to emulate a classic Vigan house "*en miniature.*" Unfortunately, the copying is just too literal to be convincing. Particularly problematic is the small

FIG. 256. A 1980s apartment building erected on the main square of the heritage town of Lemgo. Here the challenge was to integrate a visibly contemporary structure into the historically significant, intact ensemble of church, town hall, and merchant houses dating from the thirteenth to the sixteenth century. The solution is a decidedly modern structure of concrete, steel and glass, which however, follows the steep roofs of the neighboring Renaissance structures, and adapts to their overall height, volume and massing. The filigree glass oriels facing the square echo the half timbered house to the right and the Renaissance windows to the left, while the massive plain wall portions harmonize well with the masonry walls of both neighbors.

FIG. 257. Two sixteenth century houses flanking a contemporary structure (middle) with a modern steel-and-glass interpretation of traditional half-timbered façades. The elegant steel-and-glass waiting shed in front gives this centuries-old town a youthful and progressive flair without diminishing its historic ambience.

tower by the side, which visually competes with the bell tower of the adjacent cathedral. The result, as Fernando Zialcita notes, is "a fake house aiming to be a church."

The majority of such superficial and predictable adaptations are commonly denounced as "façadism" more akin to a theme park than to a contemporary progressive metropolis. Many conservationists argue that for a historic streetscape to be authentic, it must be possible to distinguish between old and new, historic and contemporary. This view is also echoed in the Charter of Venice (1964), which states that "any extra [restoration] work which is indispensable must be distinct from the architectural composition and must bear a contemporary stamp" (Article 9).[7]

The same critique is reiterated in the Vienna Memorandum forty years later, that explicitly states that urban planning and contemporary architecture "should avoid all forms of pseudo-historical design, as they constitute a denial of both the historical and the contemporary alike," and that "history must remain readable."[8]

Conservationists' objections are shared by many architects, who insist that each time period has its specific architectural expression, and that superficially reverting to past and outdated styles represents an evolutionary step backward, rather than forward. So, if simulation or outright copying is not the answer, how then can new structures fit into a sensitive historic environment? Various approaches are commonly used:

Historic forms in contemporary materials. The integration of a new structure into any existing ensemble, whether historic or not, is mainly determined by earlier-mentioned key elements, such as volume and massing, height, setback, material, and roof form.

For a modern building to fit into a historic environment, its overall volume must not overpower its neighbors, nor must it diminish next to them. As such, it should be neither exceedingly taller nor lower than immediately adjacent buildings. Finally, its façade should ideally be in one plane with its neighbors, thus have the same setback from the curb.

This is shown in two examples from Lemgo, Germany (FIG. 256–257). In both cases the new structures have the same setback as their neighbors and also follow their floor heights, thus harmonizing with them although being visibly contemporary. The new structures so mediate between two existing historic buildings.

This illustrates the importance of the basic principles laid out in the Vienna Memorandum, which states: "Architecture of quality in historic areas should give proper consideration to the given scales, particularly with reference to building volumes and heights." And: "Townscapes, [historical] roofscapes, main visual axes, [original] building plots and types are integral parts of the identity of the historic urban landscape."[9]

Irrespective of architectural style and materials chosen, if the above parameters are in harmony with existing structures, a building will likely fit in. This also applies to materials, finishes, and detailing. For example, in the historic districts of postwar Manila, it is the heavy concrete parapets and balustrades that do not harmonize with their lighter Bahay-na-Bato neighbors with wooden *voladas* and roof eaves, as can be

FIG. 258.
The Burke-Miailhe Building (top) is one of the few new buildings in San Nicolas that try to blend into the historic streetscape. Although visibly modern (including a flat roof), it takes its design inspirations from the nearby Bahay-na-Bato, such as the stately row of bays, large window openings with louver panels, and faux-ventanilla grills. Most importantly, it is only three stories high and so does not visually overpower its older neighbors.

FIG. 259.
(left) An example from Intramuros, Manila: The headquarters of the Manila Bulletin newspaper from 1976 is an interesting interpretation of a Bahay-na-Bato, executed in Modernist style and contemporary materials, thus fitting into the "Spanish-era" reconstructions without copying them literally.

NEW MEETS OLD—CONTEMPORARY BUILDINGS IN HISTORICAL CONTEXT 229

FIG. 260. The new wing (right) and central staircase (middle) of the municipal building blend well with the old Art Nouveau wing (left) by using the same characteristic red brick. (Nienburg, Germany, 2011)

seen in San Nicolas, Quiapo, and Sta. Cruz. Unequal setbacks and heights in particular can make a streetscape look "butchered," as they lead to massive and unsightly fire walls dominating the vista of a street. In that regard recent plans by the Intramuros Administration to (again) allow unhistorical setbacks and increased building heights must be seen very critically.

Historic materials in contemporary forms. Integration can likewise be achieved by using similar materials as the old building nearby, although executed in a decidedly modern design language. For example, where a new structure is to be built next to a historic one of wood, the new building could employ a similar wooden finish while using contemporary forms (e.g., cubes, cylinders, parables, etc.) for the overall form of the building. An interesting example, albeit not in a historic district, is the new Historic Museum of Ningbo, China, by the Chinese architect Wang Shu, winner of the 2012 Pritzker Prize of Architecture. The museum,

FIG. 261. Ningbo Museum, PR China. Building designed by Wang Shu. By Siyuwj, image licensed under Creative Commons Attribution-Share Alike 3.0 Unported, see p. 394.

FIG. 262-263. Fort San Antonio Abad (left); Metropolitan Museum (right)

albeit decidedly contemporary in form, is laden with symbolic meanings and clad with millions of traditional grey stones, bricks, and tiles, thus linking the building to the local traditional Chinese architecture.

Some interesting examples can also be found in Manila, such as the Metropolitan Museum (part of the National Bank Complex) along Roxas Boulevard in Malate. Here, the brute, modernist form of the museum with its artificial adobe walls is effectually juxtaposed with the ancient adobe walls of the historic eighteenth-century Fort San Antonio Abad behind it, emulating them. However, the main entrance to the museum with its modernist canopy sharply contrasts with the Baroque gate of the old fortress, and clearly anchors it in the present. In fact, the entire Central Bank Complex, built in 1972 by Gabriel Formoso, in its heavy grey monumentality, serene atmosphere, and feel of impenetrability very much harmonizes with and echoes the very same characteristics of the old Fort San Antonio Abad.

FIG. 264. Uy Chaco Building (left), Charisland Building (right)

Dialogue between New and Old. A particularly interesting approach seeks to respond to the form of a neighboring old building and to "communicate" with it, but using decidedly contemporary materials and design. One remarkable such example can be found on Plaza Cervantes in Binondo. Here, the new Charisland Building (212 Quintin Paredes) erected in 2007, stands diagonally opposite the old Uy Chaco

Building from 1914. Importantly, both buildings have comparative massing, height, and setback. Clad in glossy aluminum panels and tinted windows the Charisland Buildings is uncompromisingly modern. It thus looks like the twenty-first century "high-tech" counterpart to its nearly hundred-year older Art Nouveau neighbor across the plaza. A silent dialogue seems to be ongoing between the corner towers of both buildings which together form an imposing entree into Manila's Chinatown. Unlike the tower of the Uy Chaco Building, which is protruding, the Charisland tower is recessed. Likewise, the protruding wavelike balconies of the older building find their reflection in the recessed loggias of its new counterpart, and where the former's corner turret is crowned by a solid and enclosed dome, the latter one's is open and filigree. Even the open gallery on the top floor of the Uy Chaco has a pendant in the roof terrace of its modern neighbor. In all, the new Charisland Building seems like the concave contemporary twin of the older convex Uy Chaco Building, thus expressing a similar design concept in a very different idiom.

The above example illustrates the importance of acknowledging and respecting the presence of existing older buildings, to be inspired by them, and the need to find an appropriate architectural response, which either harmonizes or dialogues with them. More importantly, a good architectural solution as the Charisland Building can stand on its own artistic merits and does not lose its architectural significance or context once its older partner is no more.

RECONSTRUCTIONS

The term "reconstruction" refers to the complete or partial re-creation of a largely or totally vanished building. The reconstruction of historic buildings remains controversial among conservationists and heritage advocates. The notion here is that a reconstruction, no matter how faithful to the original in form, material, and construction techniques, is never the original itself, but an entirely new building. It thus lacks the authenticity of the original, and is therefore considered a "fake" by many. Says the Charter of Venice from 1964 (Article 15): "All reconstruction work should however be ruled out 'a priori.'" "Only anastylosis, that is to say, the reassembling of existing but dismembered parts can be permitted." The "Operational Guidelines of the World Heritage Convention" accept reconstruction provided that "it is carried out on the basis of complete and detailed documentation on the original and to no extent on conjecture," hence based on thorough and complete scientific research.[10]

Some conservationists point to the role the reconstruction of an important historic building—destroyed by war or natural disaster—can serve for the self-assertion of a local community, and that it can also fully take the place in history of the original.[11] Some faithful reconstructions have proven most successful in the long run and have now themselves become historic in their own right, as exemplified by the historic core of Warsaw, Poland. Here, the old city was considered of such immense significance to national history, culture, and identity as to justify reconstruction. It received worldwide recognition, culminating in its designation as a UNESCO World Heritage site in 1980.[12]

Supporters of reconstruction point out that it can give the observer an accurate idea of how a building once looked like, and that the "idea" of a building, that is, its design concept, is more important than the authenticity of its physical components.

FIG. 265-268. Accurate replica (top left); faithful interpretation (top right); "free" variation of the Spanish-era theme (bottom left); unhistoric adaptation on the original site (bottom right)

For example, in Japan, the Ise shrine has been meticulously and faithfully reconstructed every twenty years for centuries in a religious ceremony (the previous "original" is burned thereafter), and still very much looks like it did more than a thousand years ago. In Kyoto, the famous "Golden Pavillion," although a reconstruction from 1955, is officially designated as a National Special Historic Site.

In contrast, most buildings in Intramuros since 1979 do not attempt to accurately replicate previously existing buildings, hence in a strict sense are not "reconstructions." Instead, they aim to recreate a "late-Spanish-era" ambience, albeit with contemporary uses and using modern construction materials and techniques. These buildings display different versions of authenticity.[13] Some are relatively accurate replicas of previously existing buildings, though in a different location (Authenticity of Style) as seen in the Casa Los Hidalgos, or comparatively faithful interpretations of a typical Bahay-na-Bato (Authenticity of Experience) as exemplified by the El Amanecer Building. Others are rather free and fanciful variations of the Spanish-era theme, including un-historic setbacks and roof terraces (TMI Building along Calle Arzobispo). Finally there also are largely un-historic adaptations on the original site (Authenticity of Context and Location) as exemplified by the Palacio del Gobernador from 1978.

A key problem with reconstruction is how to reconcile the quest for authenticity with conflicting contemporary needs such as use, fire safety, structural necessities, urban environment, costs and economics, etc., and which of the unavoidable compromises to enter into and which not. A solution practiced in the reconstruction of the inner city of Dresden, Germany, is the building of relatively accurate replicas of key monuments (churches, palaces, towers, etc.) while giving more leeway in the recreation of the less significant surrounding urban fabric, which gives meaning to them. Among these, certain buildings called *Leitbauten* (lead buildings), which are situated on exposed locations or are architecturally more significant, are likewise more authentic in execution, and serve to anchor less authentic or even entirely modern buildings in the overall fabric of the historic district.

A very interesting variant of reconstruction is the architectural "quotation," whereby a specific, previously existing building is replicated in contemporary material and style, and its key elements "quoted" in abstracted form. These abstracted quotes can refer to original elements such as windows, doors, towers, or entire silhouettes. They merely hint at the lost original without literally copying it. However, the casual visitor may have to be aware of the history of the specific site in order to fully understand and appreciate these quotes. An interesting example in Leipzig, Germany is the Paulinum, which occupies the site of the former Gothic Pauline Church built in 1240, and demolished for ideological reasons in 1968 by the anti-clerical communist government of the German Democratic Republic, together with the neighboring nineteenth-century Augusteum. After German re-unification both buildings were rebuilt in contemporary idiom, but hinting at the historic structures: the modern steel-and-glass Paulinum references to the original through its steep roof and tall spire reminiscent of the original flèche, and a large Gothic window. The neighboring Augusteum, also in glass and steel, merges with the Paulinum and recreates the main façade along the city square, freely quoting the old central portal, while in the inner courtyard a faithful copy of the magnificent original entrance gate has been integrated into a modern glass façade.

One problem with reconstructions on the original site is that any remaining ruins of the original, authentic building often either have to be built over, or have to be removed, thus sacrificing valuable original material. An elegant way of avoiding this dilemma is to build a new structure inside or outside the ruins of the old one without touching the original portions. Such new buildings can thus

FIG. 269. Paulinum in Leipzig, Germany. By Concord, image licensed under Creative Commons Attribution-Share Alike 3.0 Unported, see p. 394

FIG. 270. Ruins of Vlotho Castle, Germany, a medieval castle re-designed and re-interpreted 1999-2003, after an international architectural competition.

FIG. 271. Interior of Dingras Church, Ilocos Norte. Image courtesy of Joel Aldor.

be of modern design and materials (steel, glass, concrete), without diminishing the historic appeal and authenticity of the original. An added advantage is that the continuum of history becomes visible and can be experienced (such as a previous destruction), instead of "faking" history by pretending that destruction never happened, as a conventional reconstruction would. Thus can emerge an intriguing juxtaposition of old and new, modernity and antiquity, and a dialogue between the past and the present.

EXTENSION AND ADDITIONS

Respect for and adjustment to an old building's historic character should also guide extensions and enlargements, which often are unavoidable to maintain a building's economic viability or to extend its useful life. Such additions should subject themselves to the original building and must neither dominate it in terms of volume or height nor compete with it in terms of design. This also implies that extensions are best made at the back of the existing building, or at its sides, but preferably not in front of it, thus obscuring it. As Akpedonu and Saloma write in *Casa Boholana*: "If an extension is directly added to an older building, a small (or larger) joint should be placed in-between, as to clearly distinguish between old and new, original and addition," and "to be constructed at a certain distance (say two to three meters) and linked to it by a connecting, enclosed corridor. Such a corridor or connecting structure could also be a large usable space by itself, which, for example, could be done in glass or other transparent materials. This not only marks a clear distinction between old and new, but also keeps most of the original exterior walls intact."[14]

Under such conditions an extension can be decidedly modern, even avant-garde, in design and outlook, without diminishing the historic ambience of its parent. It is, in fact, preferable that an extension be built in contemporary idiom and materials, instead of simply copying or imitating the original. Every epoch has its specific architecture, which should be immediately readable to the casual observer. It need not mimic the old, but should harmonize with it. As with new buildings in historic quarters mentioned above, this could mean the use of comparable volumes and

FIG. 272. Historic brick house connected to a recent extension by a glass staircase tract. (Nienburg, Germany, 2011)

shapes with modern materials, or similar materials as the original, but in contemporary design, or both.

Ultimately, much of the outcome depends on the talent, sensitivity, experience, and exposure of the architect or urban planner (and his client), who should be consulted when dealing with valuable historic buildings or sensitive historic areas. Do-It-Yourself solutions rarely yield acceptable results. Some ingenious solutions for modern buildings in highly historic context have since achieved iconic status, such as the new entrance to the Louvre, Paris, by Icoh Ming Pei, built in 1989. His famous glass pyramid subtly relates to the Egyptian obelisk at the Place de la Concorde at the other end of the vista called *la Voie triomphale* (the Triumphal Way), thus pairing contemporary design with a historic setting. The key to successful integration of modern architecture lies in high quality of design and execution. Where outstanding architectural quality is assured and historic relations can be experienced, even ultra-modern and avant-garde interventions such as Pei's pyramid can fit into a sensitive historic context and add high-quality cultural expressions to it. Centuries-old cities such as Paris, Barcelona, and London thus manage to retain their historic ambience while at the same time also maintaining a progressive and youthful flair through interventions which are bold and innovative, yet subtle in design, and at the same time, respectful and in harmony with the cities' historic structures.

Conservation and Managing Change are not necessarily mutually exclusive, but can complement each other. While the former aims to preserve as much historic fabric as possible, the latter allows for the careful introduction of contemporary uses and values to ensure the continuing relevance of a site. Says the International Centre for the Study of the Preservation and Restoration of Cultural Property (ICCROM): "Change may also lead to keeping a heritage place in beneficial use, which is generally the best way of ensuring its future maintenance and upkeep."[15] Critically reflected "progress" and conservation can go hand in hand, provided conscious and careful efforts are exerted to harmonize both to create an exciting and inspiring new experience. Such

FIG. 273. Louvre Pyramid by I.M. Pei, Paris, France. By Dinkum, image licensed under Creative Commons Attribution-Share Alike 3.0 Unported, see p. 394 / © Pyramide du Louvre, Arch. I. M. Pei, Musée du Louvre

efforts would likewise go a long way in preserving the historic ambience of the many old, yet fast-developing towns and city centers all over the Philippines, and retaining and enhancing their "Pride of Place."[16]

NOTES

1. The notion of "managing change" was ushered in by 1970s concerns about sustainable development. For a discussion of the history of conservation and sustainability see chapters 1 and 3 in: Dennis Rodwell, *Conservation and Sustainability in Historic Cities* (Oxford: Blackwell, 2007). The term was used by the Council of Europe as early as 2000 and is also used by national conservation bodies in the United Kingdom, such as English Heritage. Managing change is now also integral to the way international bodies (ICCROM, UNESCO) view world heritage. See ICCROM Manual for Managing Cultural World Heritage (Paris: United Nations Educational, Scientific and Cultural Organization, 2013), 24-28, 60, 125.

   However, the concept of "Managing change" is critically viewed by more conventional preservationists focusing on conservation rather than change, who see it as a problematic concept popular in Anglo-Saxon countries, such as Australia, the US, Canada, and the United Kingdom. See, for example: Michael Petzet, "International Principles of Preservation," *International Council on Monuments and Sites* (Berlin: Hendrik Baessler Verlag, 2009), 9-12, http://www.icomos.de/pdf/principles.pdf.

2. UNESCO, "Vienna Memorandum on World Heritage and Contemporary Architecture—Managing the Historic Urban Landscape," *World Heritage*, 23 September 2005, http://whc.unesco.org/archive/2005/whc05-15ga-inf7e.pdf.

   Although the Vienna Memorandum refers to historic cities already inscribed by UNESCO and larger cities that have World Heritage monuments, its general principles can serve as a useful guide even in cases where there is no such inscription, but where an existing historic district is deemed worthy of preservation by the local community, the municipality, or the nation state.

3. International Council on Monuments and Sites, "Charter for the Conservation of Historic Towns and Urban Areas (Washington Charter 1987)" *ICOMOS*, October 1987, http://www.international.icomos.org/charters/towns_e.pdf.

4. UNESCO, "Recommendation concerning the Safeguarding and Contemporary Role of Historic Areas" *UNESCO Legal Instruments,* 26 November 1976, http://portal.unesco.org/en/ev.php-URL_ID=13133&URL_DO=DO_TOPIC&URL_SECTION=201.html.

5   Michael Petzet, "International Principles of Preservation," International Council on Monuments and Sites (Berlin: Hendrik Baessler Verlag, 2009), 26, http://www.icomos.de/pdf/principles.pdf.

6   From Spanish "adobe" for mud brick. This is not to be confused with the volcanic tuff of the same name in the Philippines.

7   Second International Congress of Architects and Technicians of Historic Monuments, "International Charter for the Conservation and Restoration of Monuments and Sites (The Venice Charter 1964), http://www.icomos.org/charters/venice_e.pdf.

8   UNESCO, "Vienna Memorandum," op. cit.

9   Ibid.

10 UNESCO, "Operational Guidelines for the Implementation of the World Heritage Convention," February 1996, http://whc.unesco.org/archive/opguide96.pdf.

11 Michael Petzet, "International Principles of Preservation," 33-34.

12 The recognition by UNESCO does not refer to the medieval authenticity of the core, but as an "exceptional example of the comprehensive reconstruction of a city that had been deliberately and totally destroyed."

13 Greg Ashworth and Peter Howard, *European Heritage Planning and Management* (Exeter: Intellect, 1999), 45.

    In addition, the "Nara Document on Authenticity" from 1994 states that "information sources may differ from culture to culture, and even within the same culture," and that "it is thus not possible to base judgments of values and authenticity within fixed criteria" (Article 11). Hence, "authenticity judgments may be linked to the worth of a great variety of sources of information," such as "form and design, materials and substance, use and function, traditions and techniques, location and setting, and spirit and feeling, and other internal and external factors" (Article 13). International Council on Monuments and Sites, "The Nara Document on Authenticity (1994)," http://www.icomos.org/charters/nara-e.pdf.

14 Erik Akpedonu and Czarina Saloma, *Casa Boholana: Vintage Houses of Bohol* (Quezon City: Ateneo de Manila University Press, 2011), 109.

15 UNESCO, ICCROM, ICOMOS, and IUCN, "Manual for Managing Cultural World Heritage" (Paris: UNESCO, 2013), 24-28, http://whc.unesco.org/en/news/1078.

16 Augusto Villalon, *Lugar: Essays on Philippine Heritage and Architecture* (Makati City: Bookmark, 2001), 42.

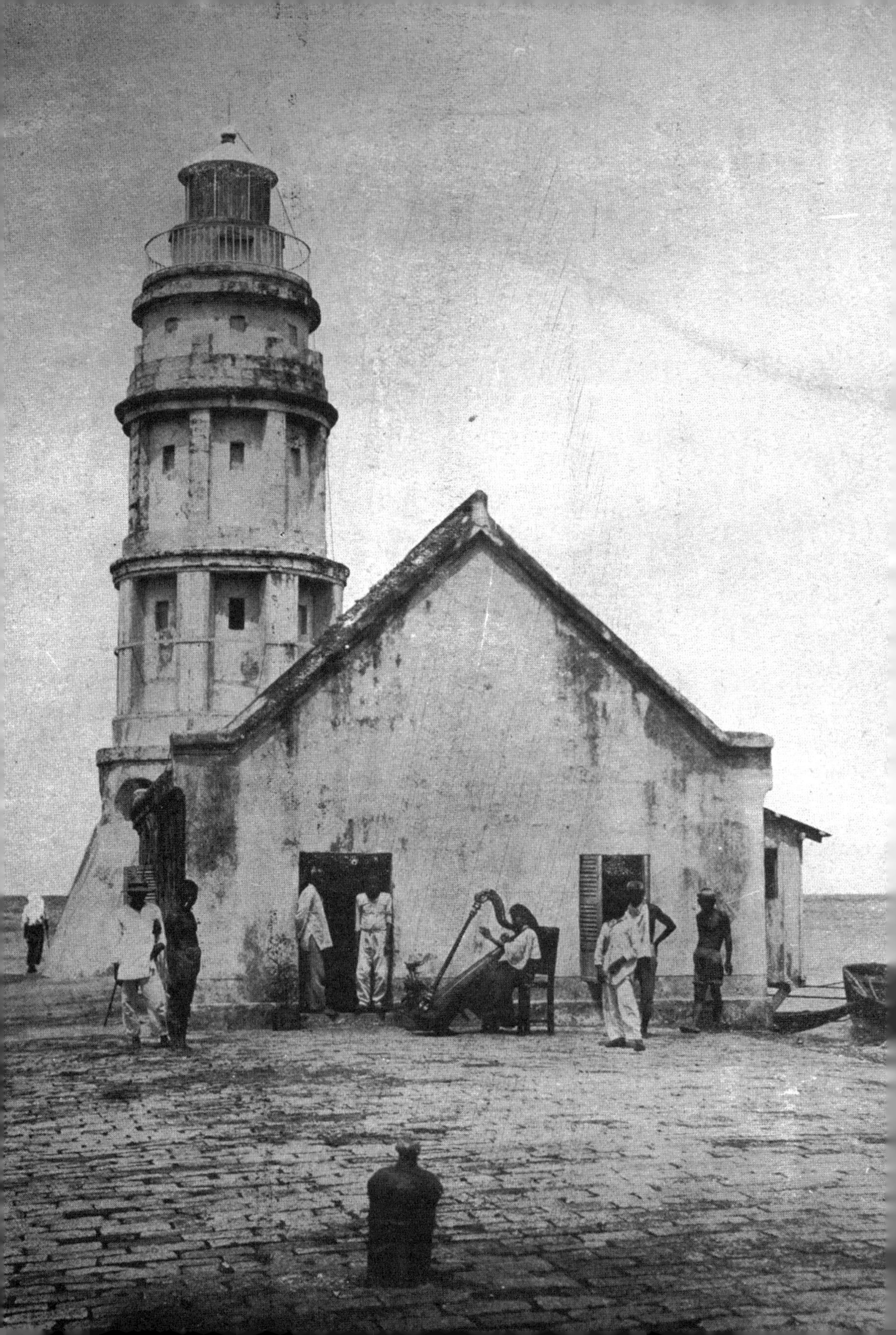

SAN NICOLÁS
Trade and Revolution

FERNANDO N. ZIALCITA

SAN NICOLÁS DE TOLENTINO REPUTEDLY SAVED A CHINESE FROM A hungry crocodile in the Pasig River by turning the reptile into stone,[1] hence the special devotion to him by Manila Chinese during the Spanish period. Before the middle of the nineteenth century, the zone between the Island of Binondo and the sea was known as Murallón, Murallón del Norte, or Baybay. At the dawn of 1820, a *sitio* of the quarter located in the area called Baybay was given the name of San Nicolás. Eventually, at the start of the 1860s the place name was applied to the entire area west of Calle San Fernando.[2] In 1894, San Nicolás finally separated from Binondo. However, as a political unit, it was unusual in that it had no parish church of its own.[3]

San Nicolás plays three important roles in our history: 1) As part of Binondo, it too was the setting for international transactions relating to the Galleon Trade; 2) It marks that moment in the second half of the nineteenth century when restrictions on the Chinese were finally removed, allowing them to live freely anywhere in the archipelago; and 3) It was central in the emergence of the Propaganda Movement of the 1880s and the Revolution of 1896.

This locality's history is interwoven with Binondo's, particularly its international commercial transactions. Thus the Real Alcaicería de San Fernando, an octagonal

FIG. 274. Farola (lighthouse) de San Nicolas, c. 1900

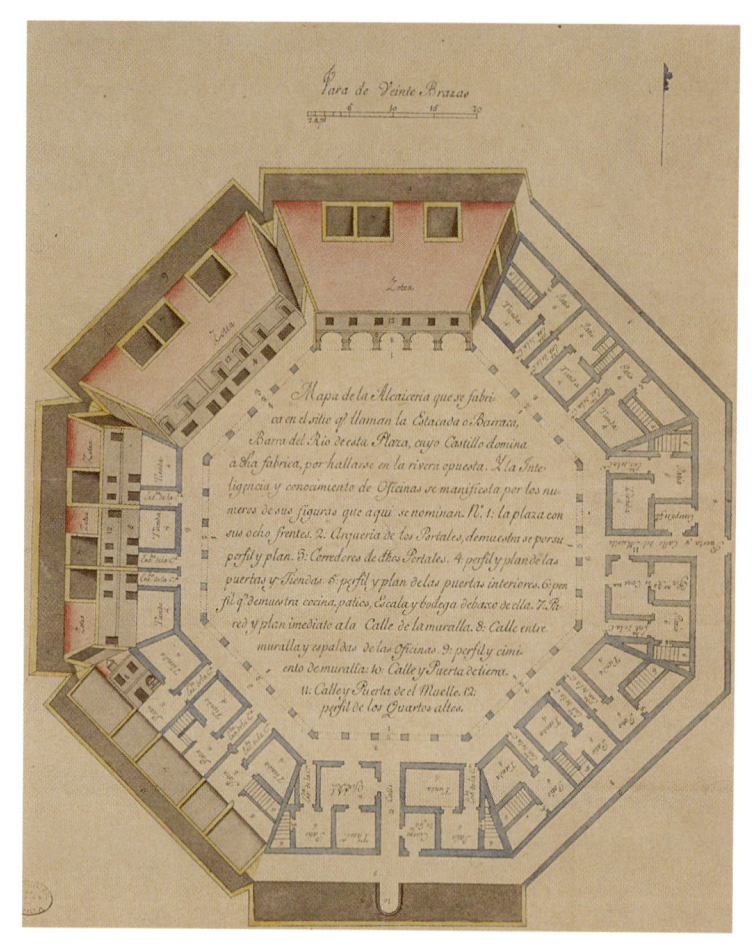

FIG. 275. Floor Plan, Alcaicería de San Fernando (Archivo General de Indias, Seville)

building, was erected in 1758 in what is now San Nicolás to serve as the first local customs house. It was also a bazaar and a place where newly arrived Chinese merchants could stay.[4] Here Asian merchants brought in their goods on which duties were laid by the government. Many of these goods were transshipped via the galleons to Mexico, the rest of the Americas and on to Europe. The Alcaicería burned down in 1810, but an angle of its octagonal plan remains today and is occupied by a fire-station and a school. Two streets nearby are still called San Fernando and Alcaicería.

There is a second major role played by San Nicolás in our history. According to the historian Edgar Wickberg, the years 1850–1898 introduced a new threshold for the Chinese in the Philippines. A more relaxed government policy allowed thousands of them to settle in Manila and from there migrate all over the islands. Their superior business methods enabled them to benefit from the economic boom that followed after the opening of Philippine ports to world trade. They played a crucial role in the importation of goods and the exportation of raw materials.[5] Because of a more lenient policy of assimilation, once baptized they intermarried with the locals, entered Manila schools and became pillars of Philippine social life. Wickberg notes that Chinese in the Philippines are better integrated into the local society than their counterparts in some other Southeast Asian countries, such as Indonesia.[6] For one thing, they and their descendants continued to use their Chinese family names although sometimes, after baptism, they would take the name of their Christian (often Spanish) sponsor.

What are the souvenirs of this transformation in 1850–1898 of Chinese migrants into Filipino entrepreneurs of Chinese descent? None other than the houses of San Nicolás. These were built in the immediate decades after 1863. According to the French historian Xavier Huetz de Lemps, before January of that year, San Nicolás was a helter-skelter of thatch and bamboo houses that were among the first things visitors coming from the sea would see.⁷ The Alcaicería, which was of solid construction, lasted till 1810 when a fire destroyed it, leaving only its ruins. North of it on the opposite side of Calle San Fernando was a terrain dotted with houses of light materials (*materiales ligeros*). However, a fire broke out in January, 1863, and wiped those out too. This gave the authorities an opportunity to forbid the return of houses of thatch and bamboo, and to press instead for houses of stone, tile, and timber (*materiales fuertes*). Unfortunately, those without the means ended up selling their rights to those who could afford to build in stone. Thatch and bamboo houses would remain permissible only in Tondo, north of the wide street acting as a fire breaker, and hence aptly called *Divisoria* (Spanish for "boundary"). From this street the name of Manila's famous central wholesale and retail district is derived. The policy of allowing construction only in hard materials succeeded and resulted in an unusually harmonious and uniform streetscape. Thus, all vintage houses surviving here today date from after 1863 until the 1950s. Because of the danger of carriage collisions at crossroads, Manuel de Azcarraga, Civil Governor of Manila, mandated in 1869 that houses at crossroads should be chamfered so that oncoming carriages could be seen.⁸ This is similar to the Baixa District in Barcelona and created gracious little plazas at crossings. Hence, all houses with such chamfered corners, of which there are many, were likely constructed between 1869 and the early American period, when legislation on the matter relaxed under a new master. Further government ordinances after the major earthquake of 1880 mandated the use of brick set in a timber frame for ground floor walls, while discouraging the use of adobe and tile roofs.⁹ From 1870 onwards, "San Nicolás was, together with Intramuros, the only quarter that was wholly built in stone."¹⁰

Excellent examples of the Filipino urban house style of the nineteenth and early twentieth centuries (often wrongly termed "Spanish") can be found in this district. Many of them remain elegant and splendid, though in a ruinous state. Most of the remaining antique houses in San Nicolás were raised in the watershed years of 1863–1910s, and are thus the oldest in Manila. Some of them are also unique for another reason. Despite their use of a wooden frame with bricks, a few have three, rather than the usual two, stories because land was at a premium in this densely built-up commercial district. However, in 2000, there were only three such houses left, one of which has since been demolished, and another one transferred to Bagac, Bataan.

Finally, it was San Nicolás that cradled the Revolution. On the night of 7 July 1892, after Rizal was arrested and sentenced to exile, Andrés Bonifacio, Ladislao Diwa, and Teodoro Plata organized a secret society called the Katipunan that would fight for the independence of the entire archipelago through armed revolution.¹¹ This event took place in a house, not in Tondo, but in San Nicolás, at the corner of Elcano and Azcarraga (now Recto). In another house in the district, the society's organ, *Ang Kalayaan*, was published and came out in January 1896. While Antonio Luna denied any connection with the Katipunan during the turmoil of 1896, he played an active role in the war against the Americans as the commander of the Philippine army. To build up nationalism, he edited the newspaper, *La Independencia*.

The Battle of Manila in 1945 luckily spared the houses of San Nicolás despite their close proximity to Intramuros, the Japanese last stand. Since then, commercial pressures and the need for residential space have been relentlessly destroying these houses

FIG. 276. Prewar aerial view of the Pasig River. San Nicolas is to the left, Intramuros and South Harbor are to the right.

one by one for decades. The tragedy is that most of Manila's oldest remaining houses from the nineteenth century are located in this district.

There is yet another dimension to San Nicolás. It was (and to a lesser degree still is) an important industrial center. Despite the dense construction and the many semi-wooden houses, many foundries were established here in the second half of the nineteenth century, some of which continue to operate until today. Thus, many a church bell of the country was cast here (e.g., in the famous Súnico foundry). It was also a center of the scent-making industry. Thus the street names: *Aceiteros* (Oil-pressers), Ilang-Ilang (native perfume tree), *Clavel* (Carnation), *Jaboneros* (Soap-makers). As a result this area was more cosmopolitan than we can imagine today. Aside from the Chinese, native Filipinos, and Spaniards, Germans, and other Europeans worked in the area. For example, chemist and history buff Pio Andrade Jr. says that the booming ilang-ilang extraction industry then was dominated by German pharmaceuticals.

STREETS

The streets are laid out on a grid that runs from north to south, connecting two broad streets from the nineteenth century—Azcarraga (now Recto) and San Fernando. The fire of 1863 thus gave the authorities the opportunity to develop a more compact and efficient street plan. Because of the north-south axis, fine views of the Walled City and its cathedral tower across the river greet the stroller in some streets, notably Barcelona. Unfortunately the perspective is now blocked. The advantage of enjoying such vistas has yet to be appreciated by decision-makers and the general populace.

San Fernando. Fernando is the name of several Spanish kings. The street was named after the medieval king Fernando III, who united Castile and Leon, extended Castilian authority over much of Andalucia, except Granada. He was canonized a saint.

This broad street gives an often-painted and often-photographed panorama of Binondo Church, as it crosses an estero that separates San Nicolás from Binondo. A ghost that lingers is the **Real Alcaiceria de San Fernando** mentioned above. An angle of its octagonal footprint remains. The structure was designed by an architect who came from a family of artists and builders in Spain and was himself professionally trained. This was Lucas de Villanova y Laborda, who took on the name of Fray Lucas de Santa María upon joining the Recollects.[12] The two-story building erected in 1756–1758 had a "porticoed gallery inside, and a corridor outside."[13] The polygonal space recalls plazas like Tarazona in Zaragoza, Aragon—the province from which Villanova came.[14] The winner of the building contract was Antonio Mazo, a Chinese. Most likely, like many Chinese migrants, he hailed from Fujian. Among the Hakka of Fujian there developed a building type called the *tulóu* (a communal clan residence) that differed from the Chinese building in not being of wood but rather of brick and stone, and forming an arcaded, well-like circle around a central plaza.[15] The similarities between the tulóu and the alcaceria are indeed remarkable: significantly, documents concerning the alcaicería explicitly use Chinese terms: 1) *pantin*, a house in the upper story; and 2) *lancape*, a story in the ground story.[16] Pedro Luengo, a Spanish scholar, concludes this analysis by saying that the new octagonal structure represented a solution that was in between "the peninsular tradition brought in by Jesús María (Lucas de Santa Maria) and the Hakka type."[17]

Some old adobe walls along Mulier Street may have once been part of the Alcaiceria, which burned down in 1810 and was never rebuilt. Could the building be

FIG. 277. Model of the Alcaiceria, Museo de Alcaiceria, Pedro Guevara Elementary School, San Nicolas. (Courtesy of Wilven Infante)

FIG. 278. San Nicolas Fire Station, the Cradle of Philippine Boxing (Nick Joaquin). The station had an excellent gym where the neighborhood youth was allowed to practice boxing.

reconstructed someday to affirm the presence of the Chinese in Manila's commercial history and to symbolize Manila's status as the original global city? Luengo says that the surviving plans are so detailed that the building can be easily recreated.[18]

In the meantime, an immediate threat looms. Two nearby streets are still called San Fernando and Alcaicería. But for how long? The names of streets continue to be replaced with those of politicians and businessmen whom the next generation will soon forget.

A remarkable site along this street is the former **Leyba-Lichauco House (476–478 San Fernando)**, where the house of Jose Rizal's mother, Teodora Alonzo (born 1827, died in 1911), used to stand. The house (not the original one), however, burned down in the late twentieth century. An NHI plate marks the site.

At the far end of San Fernando street, the **San Nicolás Fire Station** marks the entry into Madrid Street. This simple, wood, and concrete building was established 1901, and was one of the first fire stations built by the then newly established Manila Fire department under the American regime. The building, ironically, burned down in 1941 and was rebuilt in modernized form in 1953.[19] Close by on **Muelle de la Industria**, along the Pasig River and facing Intramuros, is an office building formerly owned by the Ynchaustis, a family of Basque origin. According to Niklas Skalomenos y Ynchausti of Ynchausti Foundation,[20] Jose Antonio (father) and Jose Joaquin de Ynchausti (son) opened the first Ynchausti y Cia in Manila in 1816. Their expertise was in trade and shipping. They then diversified into other noteworthy business endeavors such as the founding of *Destileria Tanduay*, the construction of the *Puente Colgante* over the Pasig River, the *Banco de las Islas Filipinas* (together with the Ayalas), Ynchausti Shipping Company, YCO Paints and Floor Wax, Rizal Cement, Ynchausti Rope, and La Carlota Sugar Central. Their holding company was one of the first, if

FIG. 279-280. Ynchausti-Elizalde Building (left); 500-508 Sto. Cristo (right)

not the first, Philippine-owned and operated multinational, with offices in Hong Kong, Shanghai, San Francisco, Manila, Iloilo, and New York. Manuel de Ynchausti and later his son Antonio voluntarily turned over thousands of hectares of land to tillers and farmers in 1927, established a medical outreach clinic in Manila in the 1920s, and opened various non-profit projects and advocacies throughout the twentieth century. Though rooted in the islands, the family has a history of helping Basques locally and in the peninsula. Stylistically, the **Ynchausti-Elizalde Building** resembles the four buildings erected in 1923 for Judge Alison Gibbs in Binondo by William Odum. It may thus date from the same period and be by the same builder. Rising two-by-five bays to a full five stories along the river quay, the building relies for its effect upon slanting canopies over the street windows, divided from each other by simple pilasters. The effect is a structure that looks sculpted yet has grace because of the parasol-like slanting canopies.

Sto. Cristo. This is the Spanish for crucifix—that is a cross with the figure of Christ. A mere cross would be "*cruz*."

Perpendicular to San Fernando is this street that ends in Divisoria. A wayside shrine affixed to a wall near the corner of Sto. Cristo and San Nicolás streets has a replica of a crucifix. A marker installed by the Hermandad del Sto. Cristo de Longos, Anacleto Lao and Monsignor Josefino Ramirez says that before the church of Binondo was constructed, a poor Chinese man found a crucifix in a well situated under the adjoining building that has since been covered. However, the crucifix on display is only a replica. For safety reasons, the original cross was brought to Binondo Church and replaced with a plain metal one.

FIG. 281-282. Uy Lian Yek Commercial Building (left); 564-568 Sto. Cristo (right)

As though to create a grand entrance to this shrine, several vintage structures cluster in an almost continuous row at the corner of Sto. Cristo and San Nicolás streets.

Formerly a large shopping complex from the 1930s or 40s owned by the **Burke-Miailhes** stood at **474 Sto. Cristo corner San Fernando** and was of two stories in Wood-and-Stone. Thankfully, the new structure that replaced it in 2006 (Burke Plaza) is well-designed and retains some of the outstanding features of the former structure, such as wooden jalousies and ventanilla grills in stylized form.

The house at **500–508 Sto. Cristo corner Jaboneros** belongs to **Cham Sanco and Sons Inc**. The ground story is of adobe stones suggesting a construction date in between the fire of 1863 and the ordinance on chamfering in 1869. Though the Sto. Cristo exterior has vertical bandejas in between the windows, the exterior facing the side street has battens common in pre-1880 houses. The sliding windows, no doubt originally of capiz, are now of glass. The sober mid-nineteenth century look is manifest in the simple wooden balusters of the ventanillas. There is no espejo. Instead, the transom consists of wooden boards. The building measures five bays by four, and seems to have been a shop house, as suggested by the several doors. At the back, along Muelle de Binondo is an interesting small house **500–508 Muelle de Binondo** of two stories in the bandeja style: Strangely, it has a chamfered corner, although it is not a corner building. Was there a street here before?

562 Sto. Cristo is a dignified Wood-and-Brick house in bandeja style. It has three stories, which was rare. This serves as the Office of **Uy Lian Yek Commercial**, distributor of all kinds of plastic products. Most likely this is from the 1900s–1920s.

FIG. 283-284. Chua-Chuan-Huat Glassware (left); 604-608 Sto. Cristo (right)

564–568 Sto. Cristo is a Wood-and-Adobe house with battened boards in the upper story. Though very plain, the continuous row of capiz windows creates a soothing rhythm complemented by the battens on the wall beneath. The combination of battens and adobe suggests a construction of pre-1880. It is now a shop house.

576–578 Sto. Cristo, otherwise known as the **Chua-Chuan-Huat Glassware** is made of Wood-and-Brick in the bandeja style probably from the 1890s to 1910s. The ventanillas have turned wood balusters (*barandillas*). There is an interesting interplay between the vertical bandejas above the window sill and the short bandejas below it. Ornate brackets enliven the roof eaves.

600–602 Sto. Cristo, though much altered, is a corner building with two-by-five bays, that still manages to retain its former features. It now houses a Metrobank office. The whole house used to be a conventional adobe and wood building but was dismantled between 1995 and 1996 and the ground floor rebuilt in concrete, with the wooden upper floor reconstructed atop cantilevered concrete beams. The continuous row of capiz windows with no panels in between together with the plain wooden balusters and the unchamfered corner suggest the "grid" style of the 1850s–1860s.

The shophouse of Wood-and-Brick at **604–608 Sto. Cristo** has three bays and two floors. Underneath the roof eave is a plain canopy over the windows. The brackets under the volada have a profile consisting of two volutes that meet at a short finial at the center. The brackets' body has floral tracery. The style suggests a 1900s origin, whereas the adobe ground floor walls imply pre-1880 construction. The metal grill over the ventanilla has an unusual design—a row of parallelograms with small medallions at the joints. On both vertical borders of the grill are modified fleur-de-lys.

FIG. 285-286. Tan Guiamco Building (left); 513 Fundidor (right)

610–614 Sto. Cristo or the **Concepcion Tan Guiamco Building** is composed of three stories of poured concrete with a transitional style between nineteenth century forms and Early Modernism, dating from 1936 as per the inscription on the cornice. It has a decorative frieze on the top floor and brackets flanking the column.

633–639 Sto. Cristo is a simple, two-story shophouse with four bays from the turn-of-the-century. Albeit partially altered and dilapidated, its roof eaves brackets still hint at its former beauty. At the back of Sto. Cristo at **513 Fundidor** is a noteworthy 1930s concrete building of three stories marked by elaborate Art Deco window grills. Its rusticated façade emulating horizontal wooden boards give it a simple yet stately feel. Given its thick ground floor walls of adobe, the origins of the houses may even date back as far as the 1860s or 1870s.

Jaboneros. The name is Spanish for "Soap-makers." (The Tagalog *sabon* comes from *jabon*). This street is perpendicular to Sto. Cristo. Formerly, it led to the open sea.

San Nicolás used to be a sweet-smelling place. Here scents were distilled. Thus another street is called "Ilang-Ilang," the Tagalog word for this native flower with an intense scent that has entered into English and other languages because it is a vital component of perfumes made in France. (Again, will this information matter or will the names of these streets be changed to honor some easily forgotten politicians?) A nearby street is "Clavel," meaning "carnation." Originally "M. de los Santos" was "Aceiteros" (oil-pressers).[21]

House **406–416 Jaboneros** has five bays. Simple pilasters march across the upper story framing each set of windows and ventanillias, resulting in spaces where the grids of the shell windows, the rectangular shapes of the windows and ventanillas constitute well-quadrants. These quadrants form the chief design element of the exterior in contrast to the flowery decorations that appear towards the 1890s. Pre-1890s houses like this have a refreshing simplicity.

The **313–319 Jaboneros** building and the following used to form one single building. This serves as the headquarters of former congressman Harry Angping and of congresswoman Nayda Angping of the Third District. Adobe is used in both stories, hence no cantilever, and originally no ventanillas either. The structure is very long and had as many as ten bays. (It recalls 331 Jaboneros.) But the eighth and the ninth bays were demolished and replaced by a four-story building. There is one door per bay. It is very low, being two-thirds the height of the usual nineteenth to early twentieth-century two-story house. Was this a storehouse (*camarín*) or a foundry (*fundición*)? De Viana who conducted extensive research in the area says that Jaboneros in the 1870s was the enclave of foundry smiths (*fundidores*).[22] **House 331 Jaboneros** was originally part of the neighboring long building (Jaboneros 313–319) used as a storehouse during the nineteenth century.

FIG. 287-288. 406-416 Jaboneros (top); 313-319 Jaboneros (bottom)

FIG. 289. Hilario Súnico Foundry. Although a declared Category III Cultural Property since 2013, it was demolished in November 2020.

Opposite from here stands an unusual example of an **Iglesia ni Kristo**: This must be an early sample from the 1950s or 1960s, as unlike today's chapels, it is built entirely of wood. But the lines follow the classic INC design, a modernist version of the Gothic.

Possibly from the 1890s to 1900s, the house at **285 Jaboneros** was a beautiful example of the bandeja style. The second story windows were separated from each other by two sets of bandejas. Within each square-shaped bandeja was an incised circle with a floral motif at its core. Four circles were located at the corners. The tall bandejas themselves had cartouches. Before its demolition a few years ago it served as a storehouse.

Truly outstanding is **276 Jaboneros corner Barcelona**. This is the site of the famous **Súnico Foundry**, established here in 1872 and owned by the family of Hilario Súnico, renowned bell-makers from the nineteenth century until 1937, whose bells can still be found in many historic churches all over the archipelago. The foundry was located in a large shed behind the mansion, from where rails ran through the zaguan to Jaboneros Street so as to transport the bells easily to Tutuban Railroad Station.

Beyond argument, this chamfered building is one of the most exquisitely decorated houses in Manila: window grills with floral shapes and medallions, wooden front doors with intricate lace-like grills at the upper part to let in air, floral incisions on the boards, pilasters with ornate capitals, and ornate cast iron columns on the ground floor interior. Its interior grand staircase is remarkable for its exquisite railing, appropriately made not of wood, a common material, but metal. While the upper floor has unfortunately lost all its interior furnishings and former decorations, the ground floor still shows ornate carvings, while parts of the floor are laid out with *piedra china*. It is a classic example of the Wood-and-Brick in the flowers-in-a-trellis style of the 1890s to 1900s, and was an office for many years. According to family tradition,

SAN NICOLÁS: TRADE AND REVOLUTION   251

FIG. 290-292. Hilario Súnico Foundry: main entrance door (top left). The exquisite grand staircase (top right) leads from the zaguan (ground floor) to the first floor, which formed one vast office space without any dividing walls. The Súnico Foundry is one of the few Spanish-era houses for which original plans still exist. The plan (bottom) was submitted by Mario Sunico in 1891. (Courtesy of the National Archives of the Philippines)

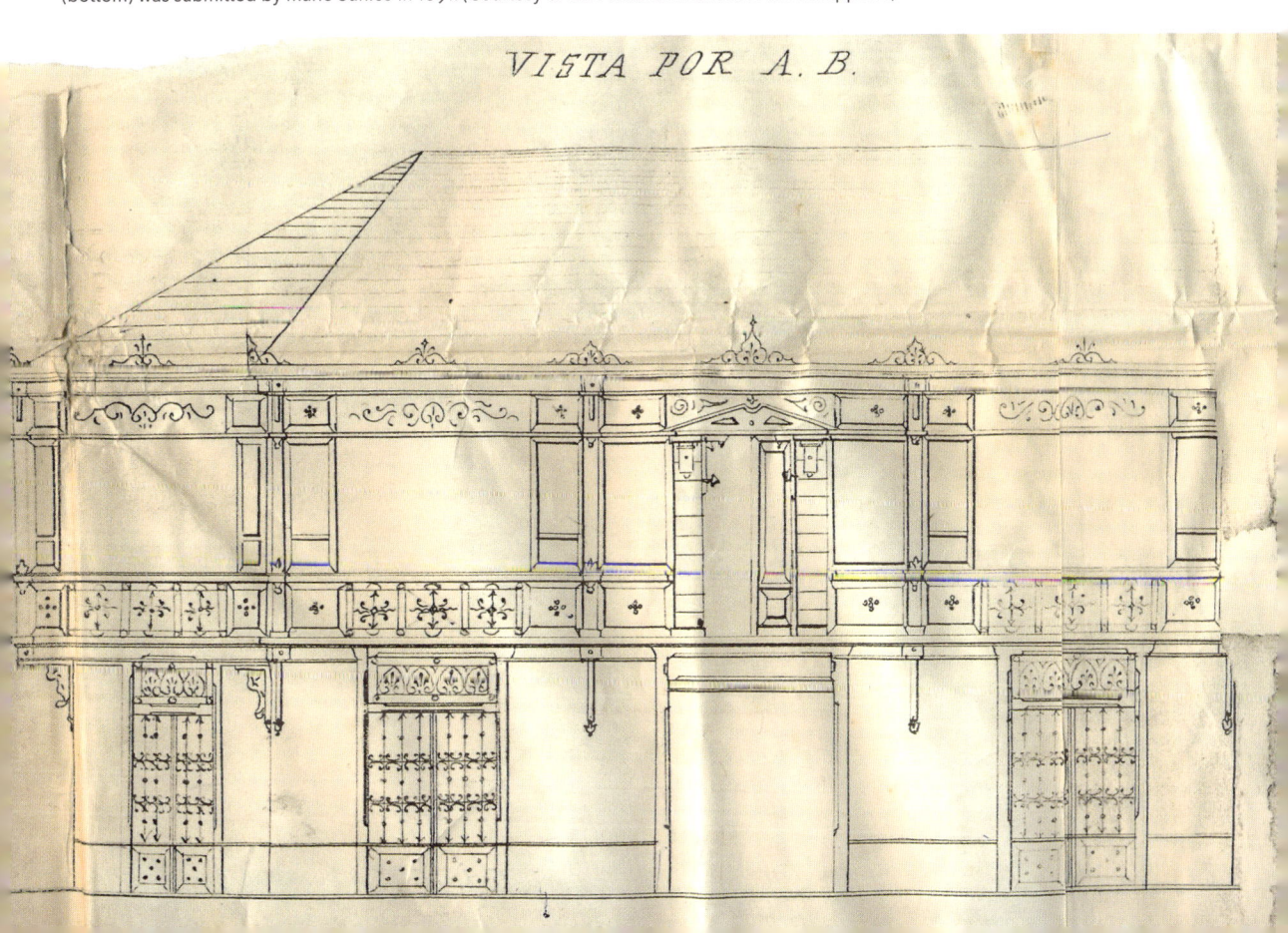

the house was built in the 1870s, although this may refer either to the establishment of the foundry or to an older structure on the site that was subsequently demolished and replaced around 1891 with this building which displays a turn-of-the-century style. As noted above, all over the metropolitan region, the extensive use of brick for the lower story became widespread after the 1880 earthquake. During the same period, house styles became very ornate. After the closure of the foundry, the house was sold to the **Heras**, a renowned Manila family since the nineteenth century, who sold the house after the war.

The **Padilla Accesoria, 501 Barcelona corner Jaboneros** was a very long accesoria measuring about 45 meters in length. The doors faced Barcelona. The second floor had heavy timber posts resting on 60 by 60 centimeters thick first floor adobe columns. Its many bays, its low height (though of two stories) and its use of stone in both floors suggest that it may have originally been a storehouse—or one of those foundries for bell-casting. This was just a few meters south from the foundry of Hilario Súnico on the same Barcelona street. Unfortunately it became a huge slum and caught fire in early 2008 because of faulty wiring. It has since been demolished.

The **Ong-Chan House, 243 Jaboneros corner Sevilla** fronting the Pasig, was an important office (trading, fabrics, and tobacco), as suggested by its size. Its second story had narrow horizontal wood boards from the late 1940s below a very ornate Neo-Gothic transom frieze with acanthus-shaped brackets and a media agua. The second story had graceful rounded corners reminiscent of the vanished houses in Intramuros. In contrast, the unusually tall ground floor with its unique coral stone blocks and lime plaster finish was well conserved. It had lancet windows and unusual oculi. The magnificent yet simple interior stairs had balusters that were thin vertical metal rods topped with rods shaped into quasi-kidney beans. The second floor inner patio had cut-out wooden patterns on transoms. The ample use of coral stone and lack of chamfering suggests it was constructed in the 1860s. Sadly, this then largest surviving historic house in San Nicolas was demolished in 2017.

The house on **360–362 Jaboneros corner 496 Mestizo** (demolished 2017), was a Wood-and-Adobe house with

FIG. 293. 360-362 Jaboneros cor. 496 Mestizo

FIG. 294-297. Ong-Chan House (top), with its unique white coral stone walls. The upper floor burned during WWII and was rebuilt in 1946/1947 in simplified form. Piedre China (granite slabs) paving (middle left); grand staircase (right); Art-Nouveau furniture (bottom left)

FIG. 298. 273 Lavezares cor. Barcelona

Board-and-Batten walls in the upper story, and a continuous row of capiz windows. The combination of battens and adobe hints at a 1860s construction.

Barcelona. Three parallel streets running north to south commemorate Spanish cities. Barcelona is named after Spain's second city which is now regarded as one of Europe's most dynamic cities.

273 Lavezares corner Barcelona, formerly the **Chua House** is a corner house, without chamfering. Made of Wood-and-Adobe, this house may thus date from the 1860s. One of the very few remaining places in San Nicolás with the street names still written on elaborate ceramic tiles on the ground floor walls, as it once used to be all over Manila. This is said to have been a maternity ward before World War II.

Another chamfered house was the **Troncales House, 262 Lavezares corner Barcelona,** built in Wood-and-Brick in the bandeja style, and possibly dating back to the 1890s or 1900s. The original structure had an unsightly one-story annex in front and a room over one part of the roof. This formerly belonged to the Padillas, one of the major landowners in Binondo-San Nicolás, Quiapo, and San Miguel. The house was demolished in 2014.

At **276 Lavezares corner Barcelona,** the former **Mañalac House** is one of the few well-preserved examples of a late nineteenth-century Wood-and-Stone house in San Nicolás.[23] Chamfered, it is of Wood-and-Brick in bandeja style from the 1890s. The bandejas are a light lemon yellow with outlines painted brown, which is truly picturesque. An added source of charm is the ground shop full of different types of brooms!

FIG. 299-300. Mañalac House (top); Troncales House (bottom)

263–265 Barcelona corner Lara is another house formerly owned by the prominent Súnico family until 1972. According to Cecile Sunico, this house once belonged to Dionisio Sunico, a nephew of the famous bell caster, and was at one time also the home of Rogelio de la Rosa, famous movie actor from the 1930s to 1950s. Despite the present condition of the neighborhood,

FIG. 301. Súnico House

this house is well-maintained. It is relatively small, for it measures only three bays by two. The ground story walls are of adobe, the upper story of wood. The capiz windows are protected by a continuous canopy and a generous roof eave. The bandejas are painted a light apple green against an off-white. In the nineteenth century almost all houses in San Nicolás used to be painted in bright, tasteful colors. That the corner wall is not chamfered indicates that the house was built between 1863 and 1870, making this one of the oldest remaining houses in the area and in Manila as well.

FIG. 302-303. 531 Barcelona (left), 613 Barcelona (right)

FIG. 304. Orofeo House

    Calle Barcelona has a relatively high number of surviving late nineteenth and early twentieth-century houses. House **254 Barcelona** is a very long accesoria with six bays in the quadrant style. Further up the street at **531 Barcelona** until 2017 stood one of the most beautiful and well-preserved nineteenth-century houses in San Nicolás. Built in the bandeja style, it had ornate roof eaves, volada brackets, and ventanilla grills. Its bandejas were painted in a tasteful combination of white and mint green. **583 Barcelona corner San Nicolás**: a small and charming, chamfered corner house remarkable for its diamond-shaped patterns on the transom. Sadly, it is now overcrowded and heavily overbuilt. The nearby **Orofeo House, 613 Barcelona** is a four-bay accesoria in the quadrant style. Its simplicity and square glass espejos indicate a late 1930s construction date.

    Halfway between Lavezares and Peñarubia streets is a surprise: Although at first glance, it looks like an ordinary postwar rowhouse, the former **Martinez Accesoria at 675–687 Barcelona** actually dates back to 1896, when it was built by Francisco Martinez as a commercial property. Renato Martinez, owner of the well-known Cacao Filipina, says that the Martinezes, who hail from Balayan, Batangas, used to own more than a dozen properties in Manila before the war. Many of these were subsequently sold to the Padillas, another very prominent family engaged in real estate since the late Spanish era, and who continue to own many properties, including many vintage houses, in San Nicolas up to today. The façade of the former Martinez Accesoria was "modernized" in the 1950s or 1960s, but otherwise the compound with its internal courtyard has remained unchanged since the nineteenth century. Remarkably, this is

FIG. 305-306. 512 Madrid (above, left); 508 Madrid (above, right); 624 Barcelona (bottom left)

one of only a handful of still existing vintage houses for which the original floor plans can still be found in the National Archives.

Finally, **624 Barcelona** is another Brick-and-Wood quadrant-style house, remarkable for its semi-circular espejos, carved pilasters and colonnettes, and ornate grill works. The building used to be twice as long, but half of it was demolished a few years ago, leaving only two bays.

Madrid. This third street is one of the busiest in San Nicolás. It is named, of course, after Spain's capital city.

508 Madrid is an interesting combination of Gothic wooden frieze on the second floor below Greek-style roof eaves. Unfortunately, only the façade remains half-way intact, while the interior has been entirely gutted out. The neighboring house to the left, **512 Madrid** is characterized by its board-and-batten façade and continuous band of capiz windows above. The thick ground floor adobe walls indicate

FIG. 307-308. 500 Madrid cor. 305 Jaboneros (top); 531 Madrid (bottom)

FIG. 309. 614 Madrid

pre-1880s construction. The house to the right, **500 Madrid corner 305 Jaboneros** is a tall, albeit dilapidated corner building in the quadrant style with ornamental wooden brackets for the roof eaves, and metal ones for the volada. Not chamfered, hence probably pre-1869.

The house **531 Madrid corner Lara** has a very strong visual presence, thanks to the broad, generous bandejas between windows. The tall bandejas have Gothic arch inserts, while the short bandejas have oval patterns. The house corner is not chamfered and the stones in the ground floor are of adobe: It must have been built between 1863 and 1869, as it formerly used to have an old-style tile roof. Though there are capiz espejos over the windows, the sliding capiz window panels are gone. Unfortunately, extra doors have been pierced into the ground floor to permit more vehicles into the storeroom there, now used as a garage. Still, the building remains imposing.

More typical of Vigan than of Manila is **614 Madrid**, for it is of stone (in this case adobe) in both stories and has no volada. It has the normal height of nineteenth-century houses and has ventanillas with grills in butterfly-like patterns. It has six bays, each separated from the other by a pilaster with simple mouldings. There are no espejos. Pilasters on the ground floor have been chiseled off, unfortunately. The present color is delightful: light pink pilasters on pale lemon walls. At present it is a row of apartments with many families.

Rosario House, 704 Madrid corner Peñarubia is a classic example of the Flowers-in-a-trellis style. One of the most exuberantly decorated houses in the area, it was nicknamed **"Casa Bizantina"** (Byzantine house). This building, measuring four bays by three, has three stories—one of the few such houses in San Nicolás—peacock-like cutwork over the main entrance door on the chamfered ground floor; cutwork on the entresuelo balconies and on the roof eaves, pairs of wooden pilasters framing each window in the third story, pilaster capitals of either Neo-Romanesque or Neo-Byzantine inspiration; carvings on arches of third floor windows, and floral grillwork over the ventanilla. The interior has a grand staircase and elaborately carved door frames. Built by Lorenzo del Rosario in 1890, it incorporates an older building on the site, still visible on the right side—unique in Manila. Twenty-four years later this became the site of the Instituto de Manila founded at the turn of the nineteenth century, which later became the University of Manila.[24] This was one of the schools started by Filipinos to meet the demand for more education. The house was recently bought by a real estate developer, dismantled, and transferred to Bagac in Bataan.

FIG. 310-312. Rosario House (top); corbel (bottom left); Espejo (bottom right).
Before its translocation to Bagac it is said to have housed as many as fifty families.

The Wood-and-Brick shophouse at **721 Madrid St. corner Clavel** is unusually long with seven bays facing Madrid, though only two bays on Clavel. The espejo's glass windows consist of four trapezoids radiating from a square framed pane—an unusual design, probably dating from the 1930s. The wooden media aguas have triangular trims. The grills have a long, crescent-shaped, boat-like bar over a series of vertical bars. Wooden boards on the upper story are vertical. This house today shelters many poor families.

Despite many losses in past decades Madrid Street still contains more vintage houses than any other street in San Nicolás. The **Ty House**, **675 Madrid** was remarkable for its triangular pediments above its three upper-floor windows, with a star in its center, a unique design feature in San Nicolás. Unfortunately it was recently demolished.

FIG. 313-314. Rosario House (Casa Vizantina): Fan light (top); grand staircase (bottom)

FIG. 315-316. 721 Madrid cor. Clavel (top); 559 Madrid (bottom)

House 665 Madrid is the remnant of a once-much-larger house, with beautiful oval and oblong bandejas. Remarkable are the adobe ground floor walls with neatly inserted rows of red brick, a simple yet very decorative feature. The corner house **631 Madrid corner Lavezares** is chamfered, suggesting a post-1869 origin. While the heavy adobe ground floor walls point to the 1870s, the upper floor with its 1950s-look seems to have been remodeled. Nearby, **Pascual House, 616 Madrid** is remarkable for its finely carved bandejas and tooth-like frieze above the espejos, which however are only visible upon close look. This 1860s to 1870s house is likewise noteworthy for its elaborate cornice and segmented main entry arch on its adobe ground floor. Its builder is said to have been a good friend to Jose

FIG. 317-318. 616 Madrid (top); window detail (bottom)

Rizal's sister in the 1880 or 1890s. Sadly, its three-story wooden neighbor, **618 Madrid**, perhaps once the narrowest house in all of San Nicolás (barely 2.5 meters wide), was recently demolished. **Cruz House, 562 Madrid**, a modest two-bay wooden house is the remnant of a once-much-larger building, most of which has been demolished long ago. Its Art Deco ventanilla grills and trapezoidal glass espejos are typical of the 1930s. Better preserved is the nearby **Enriquez House, 559 Madrid**, once the site of Farmacia Ricafort with elaborate traceried metal roof eaves and beautifully carved pilasters and brackets, and sliding glass windows with ornate ventanilla grills.

FIG. 319. 600 Madrid

Finally, we come to the junction with San Nicolás Street which once was bound by two huge "twin" accesorias. They not only shared chamfered corners, materials, and design, but also a tragic end—fire and subsequent demolition. No. **575 Madrid** was one of the largest accesorias in San Nicolás, with canopies and beautifully carved roof eave brackets. Probably dating from the 1910s to 1920s, it was consumed by a large conflagration in January 2009 probably caused by faulty electric wiring, and was subsequently demolished. Diagonally opposite, no. **600 Madrid** befell the same fate shortly thereafter, and was likewise demolished.

Asunción. Spanish for "Assumption." According to Roman Catholic and Greek Orthodox belief, Mary was assumed into heaven, body and soul.

This runs parallel to Madrid on a north-south axis like the other San Nicolás streets that end north in Recto and the Divisoria Market. Because of this, it is hard to walk about in the street's upper ends which are full of delivery trucks and cargo men pushing crates. Many of the houses in this area, including vintage ones described below, are now warehouses. However, the rest of the street is quiet, spacious, and flanked by high-rises.

Originally the **Tribunal de los Naturales**, the law court of native Filipinos, was located at **558 Asuncion**. The building of Wood-and-Adobe antedates the 1880 earthquake that struck it and caused extensive damage. Plans for repairing the building were drawn up in 1886 by the Municipal Architect Juan Hervas. In the ground story were "storage rooms, *calabozos* or detention cells, a yard.... The main story had an archives room, an office, a court room, and a storage room for weapons."[25] The embellishments that accompanied the reconstruction of the upper story, as proposed by Hervas,[26]

FIG. 320. Tribunal de los Naturales

displays the floral forms that accompanied the West's optimistic Belle Epoque of 1880–1914. The sturdy-looking chalice-like forms of the wooden ventanilla balusters act as a counterpoint to the traceried, ornamental brackets that decorate the top corners of each of the three windows. For dignity, a triangular pediment crowns the middle bay and has Greek-inspired acroteria at the peak and at the bottom slopes. The plan displays the royal seal of the City of Manila in the center of the pediment. Long rectangular bandejas separate the bays from each other and the windows from the eaves.

De Viana says that formerly there existed as well a Tribunal de Mestizos and a Tribunal de Sangleyes (pure Chinese) on San Fernando near the site of the Alcaicería.[27] To repeat Wickberg's note: like the Roman empire, the Spanish empire recognized the diversity of ethnic groups within its domain and the right of each to follow its own traditions, including laws. Other states, too, like China or the Ottoman Empire, also had diverse legal traditions within their borders before the advent of modernizing Western models. Legal divisions in the Philippines soon disappeared with the introduction of the modern Spanish Civil Code in 1889, which recognized only one legal system.

FIG. 321-328. Grills and balusters of San Nicolas (adjacent page)

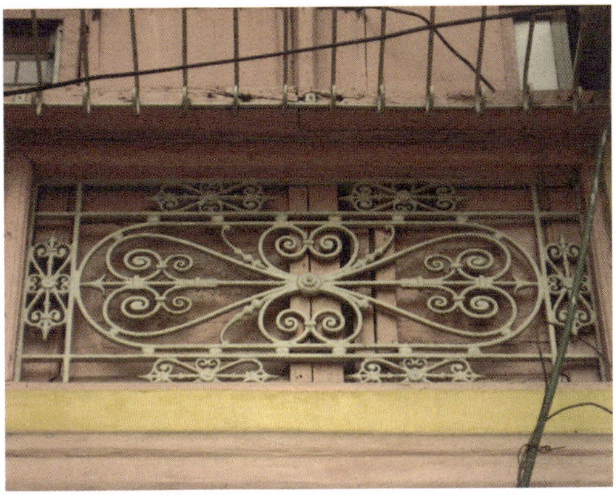
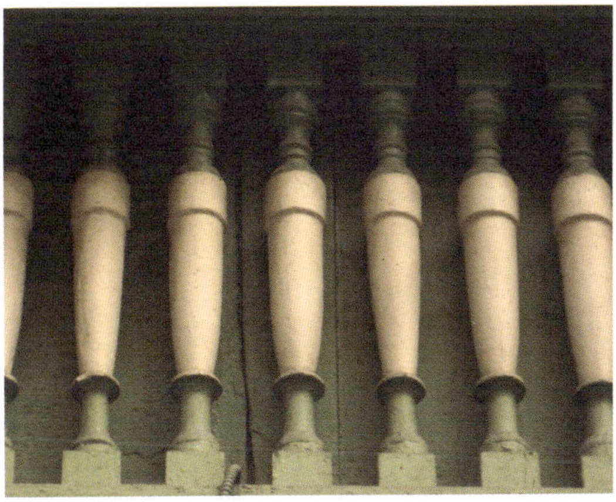
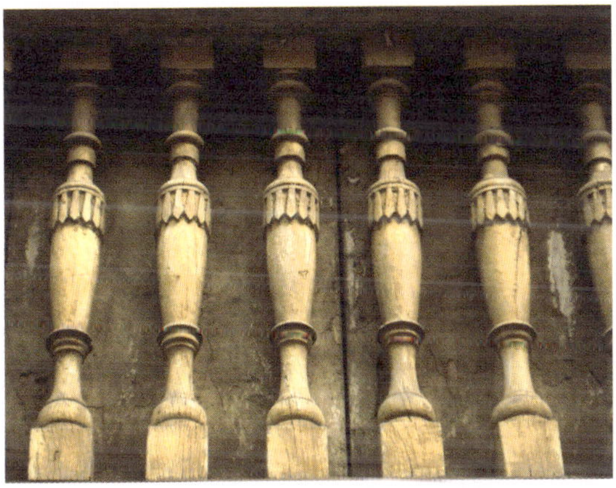
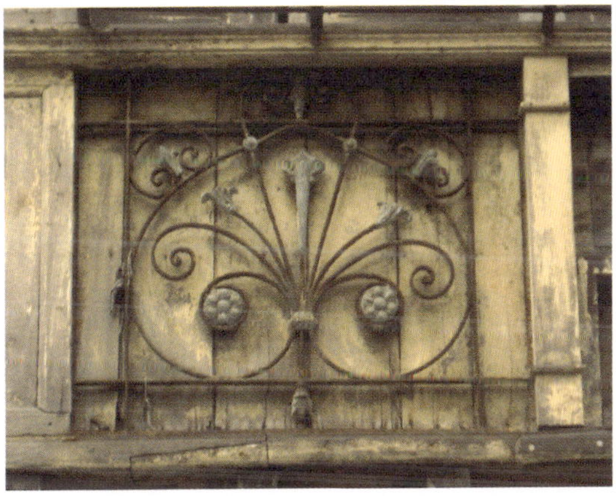
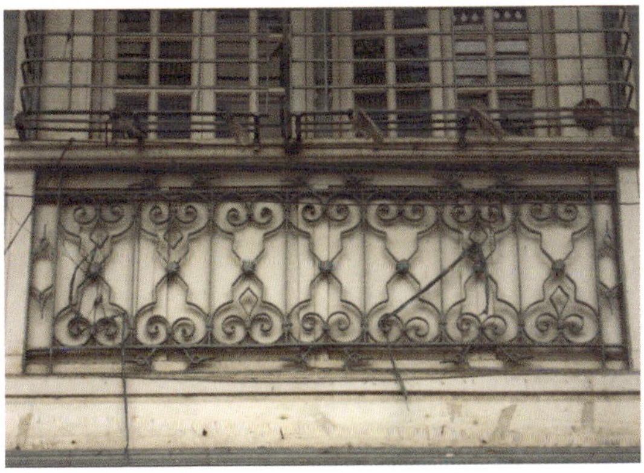
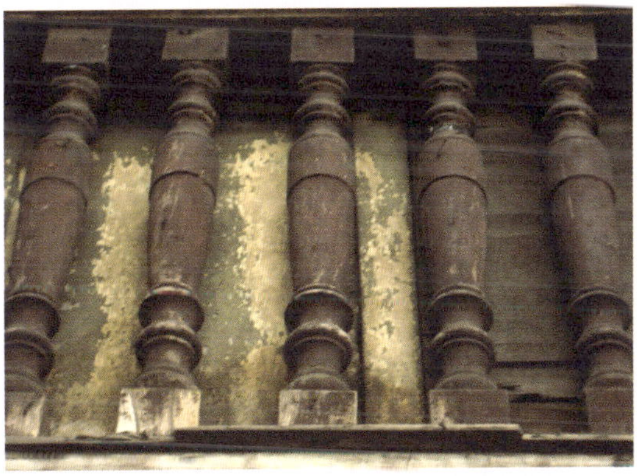
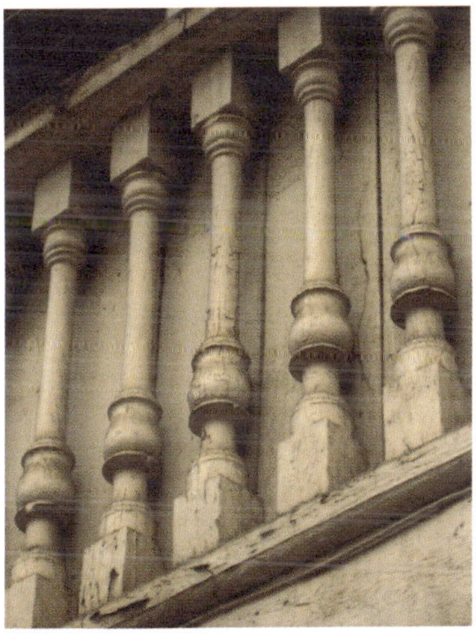
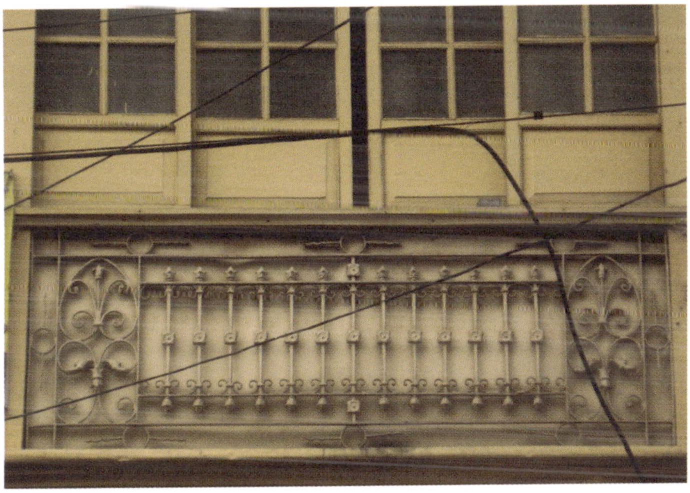

FIG. 329-336.
Ornaments of San Nicolas

FIG. 337. Montenegro Building

On **723–729 Asuncion** is a modest row house of wood above and adobe below, with three bays. Capiz appears both in the windows and in the espejos. In the latter it has a diamond formation. There are two oblong-shaped bandejas between windows. The house appears to date from before 1880.

The small, modest, chamfered corner house on **770 Asuncion corner Clavel**, measuring two by two bays, is of Wood-and-Brick. The wooden boards are mixed in style: tongue-and-groove between windows, and bandejas between ventanillas. Wooden balusters protect the ventanillas. This suggests a probable date of around 1900. This was formerly a factory for tin pails (*timba*) and laundry tub (*batya*).

A most unusual chamfered structure, the **Montenegro Building** at **789–795 Asuncion corner M. de los Santos** recalls 614 Madrid: all massive and no wood in the exterior wall. The difference is that this is of concrete in both stories and has no cornice that divides the lower from the upper story. Its pilasters thus run uninterruptedly from ground to eave, ending in simplified capitals. The house has a sculptural feel. Five of the seven bays along M. de los Santos are covered by canopies. There are glass espejos in simple rectangular rows over each of the glass windows of the seven bays on de los Santos and four on Asunción. The ventanilla grills, which the owner has just lovingly restored, have a French Rococo air. On both sides of the central

FIG. 338-340. 802 Asuncion (top); 777-783 Asuncion (middle left); detail (bottom left). (Source of fig. 339: Mia Quimpo/Dewey Sergio/NCCA)

medallion, the volutes curl out continuously from angles in the upper corners. The year of construction, 1926, is inscribed high on the façade.

The chamfered building of Wood-and-Brick on **802 Asuncion corner M. de los Santos**, possibly from the 1920s, has three bays on Asuncion and one on de los Santos. Two bandejas separate the windows which are now of plain glass. Below the wide roof eaves extends a continuous canopy. Thankfully the original colors of the walls are evident: a deep Nazareno-like maroon marks the borders of the off-white bandejas. The grills feature horizontally laid out rectangle with volutes.

Right beside the long corner house above is a much older and much lower house of Wood-and-Adobe and of two bays at **405–407 M. de los Santos.** The windows are of capiz, the balusters of wood. The upper story wooden walls are unadorned. The charm of the tiny house lies in its proximity to its bigger and taller neighbor.

A few other houses along Asuncion deserve mention, especially **777–783 Asuncion:** a highly ornate, two-story row house of Wood-and-Adobe with four bays. Noteworthy were the highly decorated upper wooden floor with its carved pilasters, bandejas with fleur-de-lis, and espejos with Baroque details. Above the sliding capiz windows were beautifully carved roof eave brackets. Probably dating from the 1870s to 1890s, this gem of a house was demolished a few years ago, as was **Bi House, 842 Asuncion** towards the northern end of the street: a very elegant, yet somewhat dilapidated two-story Wood-and-Brick house with very beautiful, vaguely Gothic-like floral ventanilla grills probably built around the 1890s to 1910s.

Elcano. After Magellan was killed in Cebu, Sebastian Elcano took over the sole remaining ship Victoria and sailed back to Spain. He is internationally recognized as the first man to complete a voyage around the globe. Unfortunately the recent street sign misspells his name as "El Kano"—meaning "The American."

At the corner of Elcano and Recto, a plaque marks the site where the Katipunan was founded on July 7, 1892. As is well-known, the Katipunan was a highly structured secret society whose vision was encompassing—free the entire archipelago from Spanish domination and let the sovereign people (*haring bayan*) govern themselves. Its objective was thus not merely the ouster of colonial rule—other revolts in Asia sought that too—but also the introduction of modern democracy.

Though **549 Elcano** has been demolished, it deserves mention. The rare three-story Wood-and-Adobe structure that stood here had a a second story whose two

FIG. 341-342. 549 Elcano (left), 552-554 Elcano (right). (Source of fig. 341: Mia Quimpo/Dewey Sergio/NCCA)

FIG. 343-344. 562-564 Elcano (left); 556 Elcano (right)

cantilevered balconies with iron balustrades had very Baroque S-shapes. This was the site of an important neighborhood school, **Ban Siong Elementary**, but it was badly damaged by fire in the 1980s and a freak whirlwind in 2008, and was subsequently demolished the same year.

The following three neighboring houses form a unified ensemble. Most likely they were all built between 1863 and 1880:

The Wood-and-Adobe house on **552–554 Elcano** has unusual but elegant pilasters dividing bays from each other. These have acanthus leaves. Unique too are the urn-shaped wooden balusters over ventanillas. Four carved masks decorate the floor sills of the exterior. Inside the well-maintained house is an intimate patio beside the living and dining rooms. The exterior has a refreshing jade green color. Down to the 1960s, most houses in San Nicolás were painted in similar joyful colors.

The Wood-and-Adobe house in the bandeja style on **556 Elcano** has balusters on the second floor ventanilla which differ from the usual design with its ball-shapes.

Again a house in the quadrant style is **562–564 Elcano**. This elaborate Wood-and-Adobe house has refined acanthus-shaped brackets under window sills while the

FIG. 345. 532–542 Elcano cor. Lavezares

wooden balusters have intricately carved trims over their graceful bowling pin shapes. The bandejas between ventanillas have shield-like shapes. Particularly noteworthy is the elegant transom: Greek-style triglyphs with capiz metopes underneath a dentil frieze. Beautiful!

On **532–542 Elcano corner Lavezares** is a most unusual house: not only is it the only house with an adobe ground floor in combination with a brick (in timber frame) upper floor; it retains its tile roof on which patches of grass now grow. It is thus one of only two houses in San Nicolás that managed to retain their original clay-tile roof, and one of only three such houses in all of Metro Manila. It has pilasters with plain capitals reaching up to roof eaves that barely project beyond the exterior wall. Because a tile roof is heavier than the metal roof that became common after the 1880 earthquake, it would have been impossible to extend the eaves forward. At the same time, a tile roof is cooler. The house has six bays on Elcano and two on Lavezares. The capiz has been replaced by glass, but the balusters continue to be of wood. Likely built in the 1860s and with several doors, it must have been a shophouse. Like 614 Madrid, its preference for having both stories in stone recalls Vigan houses that were rising in a similar style at the same period.

On **772 Elcano corner Clavel and corner M. de los Santos** is a giant accesoria, the largest one in San Nicolás. It covers the western side of an entire street block, with eight bays along Elcano Street, and two facing Clavel and De los Santos streets. It probably dates back from the 1890s to 1910s. Designed in the bandeja style, this Wood–

FIG. 346. 772 Elcano cor. Clavel

and-Brick house has subtly carved brackets supporting roof eaves. Between capiz espejos are Xs on wall boards. Chamfered on both corners and a typical shophouse, it is now a warehouse with a series of apartments.

Before its demolition in 2012, **523–529 Elcano's** heavily cantilevered Wood-and-Stone row house from circa 1880s to 1890s exuded a strong sculptural feel, due to its pronounced ornamentation: pilasters and ornate roof eave brackets separated the four bays from each other. Unusual were the series of semicircles on the espejos, and the very slender barandillas in front of the ventanillas. Nearby, **677–679 Elcano** is unusual in that that its upper floor does not cantilever beyond the adobe ground floor, hence it has no volada. It has elegant metal roof eave brackets. Finally, at the southern tip of the street **441 Elcano** is a small, yet charming house with board-and-batten transom above a continuous band of capiz windows. Given the type of construction both latter two houses are probably pre-1880.

Camba. Andrés Garcia Camba was a governor-general (1836–1838). Before that he was the director of the Sociedad Económica de Amigos del País.[28]

On **494–496 Camba** is a Wood-and-Adobe house in the bandeja style, with wave-like trim below the second floor of the façade. Oval medallion-shaped bandejas ornament the walls. This is a residence probably built before the 1880 earthquake. Similarly, **535 Camba corner Lara** is a Wood-and-Adobe house in bandeja style, with

FIG. 347-348. 523-529 Elcano (top); 494-496 Camba (right)

a square footprint and chamfered corner. Likely a residence before, it is now a metal workshop.

Again in the quadrant style is **529 Camba** which is a standard Wood-and-Brick house but handsome nonetheless. Thin pilasters divide the bays from each other. Bandejas below the window sills (*pasamano*) and between windows break up the surface. A subtle contrast between the geometricism of the whole and the floral patterns of the ventanillas is at play. This is the site of Kim Yek Engineering and Foundry, founded 1870.

One of the most beautiful houses in Manila is at **533 Camba corner Lara**. This was once the private home of **Hilario Súnico Chanuangco**, the famous bell maker.[29] His father had a foundry called Chanuangco e Hijos which was located

FIG. 349-351. Hilario Súnico House (top); window pane (bottom left); window grills (bottom right)

at Jaboneros—a street that had several foundry smiths (*fundidores*). He continued his father's business in 1870. So popular was he, according to de Viana, that his bells were imported into almost every province.³⁰ The bells of Binondo Church were cast by Sunico.³¹

FIG. 352. Hilario Súnico House: Ventanilla grills

The elegant combination of apple-green and light yellow bandejas can still be appreciated in this chamfered house, though now faded. The south window has lavishly worked cut-iron grills with a unique shape—a letter "P." Florals grill unfold on the ventanillas. The bandejas feature an oval below the pasamano, and a rectangle above it. Acanthus-shaped brackets curl below and above windows. The entire house is a unique construction: even the ground story is of wood though resting on a continuous stone pedestal (*zócalo*). The quality of the metalwork and the carvings indicate that this was indeed executed by a master of ironworks. Built in 1891 according to family history, this highly floral mansion from the Belle Epoque is now a warehouse. It was declared a Category III Cultural Property by the National Historical Commission of the Philippines in 2013.

On **323–329 Lara** is a conventional Wood-and-Brick shop house with many doors, but grand nonetheless. Thin brick panels are encased within a wooden frame with many joints. Extensive metal media agua protect windows with carvings on the window post. Bandejas appear on the wooden upper story.

Demolished a few years ago, the **Sy House, 552–554 Camba** was in the "grid" style, with capiz windows and espejos over a board-and-batten façade, and with an adobe ground floor.

Probably dating from the 1930s is **561–563 Camba** with its sober tongue-and-groove upper wooden floor, and simple yet elegant ventanilla grills. Painted in tasteful light and mint green, it is both dignified and well-preserved.

568–570 Camba corner San Nicolás is a Wood-and-Adobe house in bandeja style with a distinct old-time flair. Because this is a corner house but with no chamfering, it must have been built between 1863 and 1869. Brackets supporting the projecting second floor are outstanding. They leap gracefully like abstract gazelles. Originally a shop house, it is now primarily a residence. On its adobe ground floor walls the street name is still written on Spanish-era ceramic tiles.

FIG. 353-354. 529 Camba (top); 323-329 Lara (bottom)

FIG. 355-356. 568-570 San Nicolas cor. Camba (top); Volada brackets (bottom)

722 Camba is a long two-story building with an exposed fire wall of adobe stone on its northern end. **751 Camba** is a pre-1880 Wood-and-Adobe house in the bandeja style. Metal grills over ventanillas, metal brackets for roof eaves, generous media agua, calado woodwork above interior door, intricate metalwork on a grand staircase: truly a memorable house. It retains its postern door. Unfortunately, like many old houses in the district, the front façade looks much better than the rear, which is largely in ruins.

Further up north, **327 San Nicolás corner Camba** is another nineteenth-century corner house in the "grid" style, with a long continuous band

FIG. 357-358. 751 Camba (top); 327 San Nicolas cor. Camba (bottom)

FIG. 359-360. 789-793 Camba (top), 325 Camba cor. Velasquez (left). (Source of fig. 360: Mia Quimpo/Dewey Sergio/NCCA)

of capiz windows over a solid ground floor of adobe walls. Its chamfered corner indicates 1870s construction. Sadly, the building is in a poor state of preservation and overcrowded.

The northern end of Camba Street is generally poor and densely populated. An ensemble of two interesting "twin" houses can be found at the corner with M. de Santos Street: **789–793 Camba** is a long accesoria probably from the 1930s of four-by-one bays, with a chamfered corner and a ground floor of half-timbered framework with brick infill. Directly opposite, **801 Camba corner 321 M. de Santos** is of similar design and construction. Sadly, both houses are badly dilapidated and falling apart.

Finally, another chamfered corner house near Recto deserves mention: **House 325 Camba corner Velasquez** used to be a beautiful large Wood-and-Brick house in the bandeja style. Probably late nineteenth-century origin, it is characterized by its maroon and white colored bandejas. Sadly, their original beauty is barely visible anymore underneath all the makeshift additions on all sides.

FIG. 361-362. 318 Clavel (top); 208 Clavel (bottom)

Clavel. Once again a street that hints at the fragrant history of the district. The carnation (*clavel* in Spanish) is a lovely flower from which perfume is extracted. It is widely grown in Spain. Were fragrances also extracted from the carnation in San Nicolás?

House 318 Clavel was one of the first tinsmith factories in the area, made of Wood-and-Brick in bandeja style, probably from the 1890s. The eaves and media aguas have cutwork; it made use of rectangular bandejas as simple decorative elements. There is a pleasant contrast with curving grillwork and elaborate roof eave and volada brackets.

House 314 Clavel is a Wood-and-Brick house in bandeja style. That it has only one bay left is unusual and adds to its charm. It apparently used to be part of 318 Clavel, as can be deduced from their identical designs, but the intervening bay has since been demolished—a common occurrence in San Nicolás. **House 208 Clavel:** This very charming and well-preserved green and white house in the bandeja style is characterized by its fanciful ventanilla grills. They consist of intertwined metal circles, which are repeated in the semi-round glass espejos, probably a later addition.

Caballeros. This was the favorite race track of Spanish cavalrymen (*caballeros*) who would gallop from Jaboneros to Clavel.[32]

Caballeros Street is marked by a series of large two-story accesorias with wooden upper floors and ground floors of brick or adobe. They all likely date from the late nineteenth century.

On **522–526 Caballeros** was an elegant bandeja-style house with capiz windows and slender barandillas. Remarkable were the emphasized X-crossbeams on the ground floor that served to stiffen the wooden framework with brick infill, typical of post-1880 design. However, it was demolished a few years ago. Next to it is house no. **516–520 Caballeros** of similar design and construction, with interesting roof eaves made of crossed wooden slats.

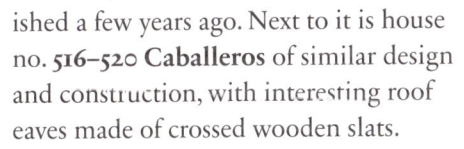

Opposite is **551–559 Caballeros**, a long accesoria of six bays with a ground floor made of adobe blocks, typical of pre-1880 design. Its standard board-and-batten design is simple, but gracious. Further down the road on **714 Caballeros** stood a two-bay Bahay-na-Bato in the bandeja style with ground floor walls made of bricks set in a timber frame. Its deeply recessed carved bandejas together with the slender barandillas gave it a strong sculptural feel. Sadly, it burned down in 2013.

Two more houses here deserve mention: **House 726–732 Caballeros** has elegant metal grills in front of its ventanillas. Note the thick adobe *zocalo* on which the ground floor walls of brick are resting. Typical of the Bahay-na-Bato, its wooden upper floor is cantilevered, like the nearby **756 Caballeros**, which has the same ornamental ventanilla grills, bandeja style, well-preserved and

FIG. 363. 551-559 Caballeros

FIG. 364. 522-526 Caballeros

FIG, 365-366. 714 Caballeros (top); 756 Caballeros (bottom left)

with only few alterations. Its volada extends above a popular *carinderia*.

Ilang-Ilang. This fragrant flower's essence was a major export of nineteenth-century Philippines. It continues to be a key ingredient in world-class perfumes today, for instance Chanel No. 5.

On **570 Ilang-Ilang**, right beside 495 San Nicolás, is this house of Wood-and-Adobe, and three bays. Often the adobe is encased in cement. The upper story walls have battens. The ventanilla's wooden balusters have curving plant-like motifs. Capiz panels still shut the windows. The most interesting feature of the house is the street door which has a flat stone arch with corbel over a rounded arch with a keystone. Flat arches used to be more common in San Nicolás doors down to the 1960s. Many have since disappeared.

A surprising find in this side street was the **Lim House, 613–619 Ilang-Ilang**, a Wood-and-Adobe house in the quadrant style. A former tenant stressed that the molave framework remained tough as ever.

FIG. 367-372.
Doors of San Nicolas

286 ENDANGERED SPLENDOR

FIG. 373-378. Windows of San Nicolas

FIG. 579. 242 San Nicolas cor. Sevilla

Nonetheless, the house was declared unsafe and subsequently demolished some years back, together with the neighboring house at **621 Ilang-Ilang**. Almost identical in style and materials to no. 617, but unlike the latter which had capiz windows, it had such made of glass panes.

San Nicolás. This street is named after the district's patron saint who is believed to have rescued a Chinese fellow from being devoured by a crocodile in the Pasig River during the early Spanish period. It runs on an east-west axis and is perpendicular to Sto. Cristo.

On **242 San Nicolás corner Sevilla** is a conventional chamfered Wood-and-Brick house in the bandeja style probably from the 1900s to 1910s. This houses around seven families of varied occupations.

Four bays are all that now remains of a once huge accesoria, which once covered the entire block between Ilang-Ilang and Asuncion streets with probably ten bays. The house at **466–480 San Nicolás** has since been demolished salami-style: The western three bays were demolished before 2000, three more bays on the eastern end in 2010, leaving only the middle portion. Over the ground story of adobe rises an upper story of wood whose narrow boards are protected by affixing battens on the joints. The roof eave projects over a continuous window canopy that runs across all bays on the second story. When shut, the capiz windows form a continuous screen as in a grid. The ventanillas have wooden balusters. The presence of four doors suggests that it was a shop house. Most likely this was built in between 1863 and 1869.

On **475–479 San Nicolás** is a Wood-and-Brick house (directly opposite 468) with three bays which forms part of a row. The ventanillas have grills consisting of a vertical row of bars with volutes, at both ends, that are paired and evoke hearts. In the middle of the bars are pairs of fleur-de-lis as mirror images of each other. The sliding windows are of glass. The espejos consist of frosted glass in between trapezoidal arches, indicating the Art Deco influence of the 1920s to 1930s. On the roof eaves are traceries with rhomboid motifs.

FIG. 380-381. 466-480 San Nicolas (top); 475-479 San Nicolas (bottom)

FIG. 382. 576 San Nicolas cor. Ilang Ilang

The corner house on **576 San Nicolás corner Ilang-Ilang** is made of Wood-and-Adobe, and is not chamfered, suggesting construction in the 1860s. The many doors of this four-by-two-bay house indicate a shop house which today houses a grocery. Ventanillas are balustered, rather than grilled; windows are of capiz and sliding glass panes. Between each window is a pair of rectangular bandejas. Between the ventanillas are two types of bandejas. The middle bandeja has a lobate end; the two flanking it look like trays—straight sides but with curving corners. The espejo over each bay, now boarded up, may be a later addition. It consists of horizontal rectangles. The eaves of the hipped roof are supported by brackets.

At the western edge of San Nicolás Street—**215–255 San Nicolás**—is a tall five-bay wooden house which is insignificant design-wise, but is one of the few in the district with an *entresuelo*, making it a 2.5-story structure. Being of comparatively simple style, it likely dates from (or was renovated in) the late 1930s to the early 1950s. Today it is inhabited by many poor families. Nearby, the former **Arboleda House, 281 San Nicolás** has been heavily altered, but is still recognizable as a prewar house with barandillas and bandejas.

Lavezares. In 1572 Guido de Lavezares succeeded Miguel Lopez de Legazpi as governor. This street runs from the east (Sto. Cristo) to the west (formerly the bay).

On **254 Lavezares** is a Wood-and-Brick house in bandeja style with fine balusters over the ventanillas. Partly a store room, partly a residence, it was demolished in 2013. Beside it is a concrete building that was raised over the ruins of a historically significant building that was destroyed during the Battle of Manila, 1945. Its wall carries a

FIG. 383-384. 254 Lavezares (top); 215-255 San Nicolas (bottom)

SAN NICOLÁS: TRADE AND REVOLUTION 291

FIG. 385-386. 292 Lavezares (left); 275 Peñarubia (right)

National Historical Institute plaque commemorating the revolutionary newspaper *Ang Kalayaan* which came out on 18 January 1896. This newspaper increased the membership of the Katipunan overnight. The soul of the newspaper was Emilio Jacinto whose essays emphasized the natural dignity of every individual and the principle of equal opportunity for all. Though the marker was affixed to 254 Lavezares, it refers to the now-disappeared neighboring house.

292 Lavezares is a charming little one-bay house from the late nineteenth century, which was probably once much larger. Due to ever-raising street levels one now needs to descend three steps down into the adobe ground floor, which was once above street level.

Peñarubia. Esteban Peñarubia authored regulations mandating a grid plan for San Nicolás after the great fire that swept its shanties in 1863.[33] Peñarubia runs on an east-west axis, and contains two remarkable structures: **213 Peñarubia** and **275 Peñarubia**. 213 Peñarubia is noteworthy for its tall ground floor which contains an entresuelo, making it one of the few remaining 2.5-story buildings in the district. The exterior is rather plain and simple, suggesting a 1930s or early 1940s date. Today it is inhabited by many poor families.

The house on **275 Peñarubia** is a hidden treasure. This dignified and highly ornate house built in 1910 is surprisingly well-maintained, and its intricate ventanilla grills

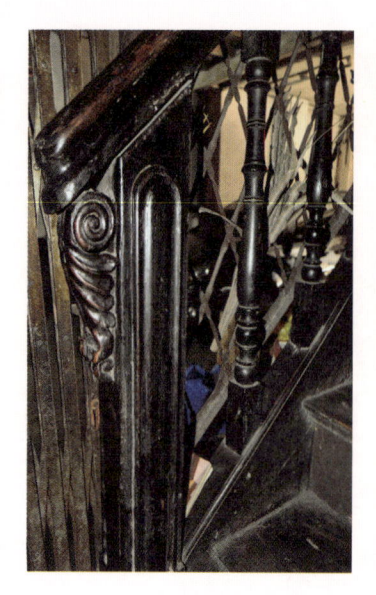

FIG. 387-388. 275 Peñarubia: Staircase detail (left); door (right)

are among the most elaborate in the district. Its joyful bandejas are carved in ovals of various forms and shapes, and painted in a tasteful pastel yellow on off-white ground. Most unusual, however, are the espejos, which consist of appliqued floral designs on wooden boards, unique in San Nicolás. Similar designs can be found on the elaborately carved interior doors, staircase, and archways. The sidewalk in front has been fenced off, presumably to keep away squatters that proliferate in the area.

Carreon. This really should be spelled "Carrión." It commemorates Pablo Carrión who arrived in the Philippines in 1575 and founded Nueva Segovia (present-day Lal-lo) in Cagayan, Northern Luzon.[34]

House 345 **Carreon** is a Wood-and-Brick house in the quadrant style. The decorated media aguas and roof eaves are of metal with elaborate cutwork. **325 Carreon** is another small and simple sky-blue house nearby, whose carved bandejas with pointed arches are reminiscent of Neo-Gothic.

Velasquez. Alonso Velasquez, a Spanish captain, helped defend Manila against the siege by Limahong.[35] Velasquez connects to Carreon in a narrow loop, which contains a few tiny but charming vintage houses of wood. In Velasquez, one of them is **331–333 Velasquez** with its board-and-batten design. The windows of the wooden upper floor are a long continuous row of sliding glass panels in 1950s-look, which may originally have been made of capiz.

Not far away, **361 Velasquez** is another wooden house which has remained largely unaltered since it was built more than a hundred years ago, supposedly by the Zialcita family. Its deployment of capiz windows and persianas, wooden jalousies, barandillas and colonettes in quadrants suggest the quadrant style of the 1860s-1870s. Opposite the house, a large fire in 2007 consumed an entire street block, including the "Old Matadero," a former slaughterhouse.

M. de Santos (formerly Aceiteros). Marcelino de Santos was a respected Filipino philanthropist. The former name of "Aceiteros" honored artisans who pressed oil from the ilang-ilang for export to Parisian perfumeries.[36]

M. de Santos runs perpendicular to Camba in an east-west direction. Notable here is **307–313 M. de Santos**, an all-concrete structure of two stories, thus probably post-1900. Its four bays are separated by flat pilasters, which are topped by elaborate roof eave brackets. Note also the gracious Art Nouveau grillwork in front of the ventanillas.

Further to the east, near the border with Binondo, stands the most unusual **Ides O'Racca Building (543–545 M. de Santos)**. Dr. Isidro de Santos raised the building in 1935 intending it for cold storage. The construction was directed by his German son-in-law, a civil engineer. Unfortunately, the following year, the business failed. Hence the structure was later sold to a Japanese confectionery company located at Urbiztondo Street in the same district. After 1945 it was taken over by the government as "alien enemy property."[37] The topmost floor burned out long ago, a damage that is said to have been inflicted during World War II. This chamfered, four-story corner building of reinforced concrete is climaxed by a five-story tower abutting the next building. The building is highly vertical in movement because of its very narrow windows and its articulated pilasters that extend beyond the roofline to end as finials. The skyline looks jagged because of the protusions over the narrow, upper windows that look like gargoyles (but are not). At the same time bas-relief panels of plants in vases are located over windows. For accent, trapezoid patterns in bas-relief interlock over topmost windows. The building communicates a strong 1930s Expressionistic style that is strange but compelling. Unfortunately, most of the building is abandoned save for a space rented out to a bank and a small store. However, in 2014 it was declared an important Cultural Property by the NHCP.

Let us cross over from the streets north of San Fernando to those on the south.

FIG. 389. Ides O'Racca Building

FIG. 390-393. Street signs of San Nicholas

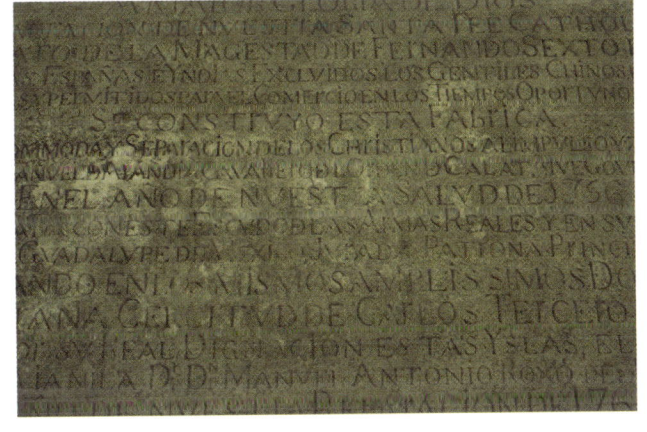

FIG. 394-397. Facets of San Nicolas: Spanish-era clay tile roof (top); roadside Shrine of Sto. Cristo de Longos (left); ruins of the Alcaiceria de San Fernando (middle right); inscription above the main entrance to the Alcaiceria (bottom right), Museo de la Alcaiceria, Pedro Guevara Elementary School

FIG. 398. Antonio Luna House

Urbiztondo. Govenor-General Antonio Urbiztondo personally led an expedition in 1848 to stamp out piracy in Sulu. This feat was later on celebrated in a poem by the young Rizal.

De Viana points out some of the activities that took place in San Nicolás[38] in relation to the birth of the nation. Following his execution, Rizal's remains were kept for a while at a house in Estraude that his family rented while his mother seemed to have stayed at a house on Calle Leyba till her death in 1911. The house of Faustino Villaruel on 8 Asuncion was a meeting place for Masons; his daughter became the first woman Mason in the country. In an accesoria on 28-D Asuncion, Gregoria de Jesus was kept a prisoner by her parents who disapproved of her attraction to the widower Andres Bonifacio. Fortunately, they were eventually married at Binondo Church.

Born here at **Luna House, 457 Urbiztondo**, in 1866 was the versatile Antonio Luna: poet, musician, scientist, and commander of the army of the ill-fated Malolos Republic in the war against the American invaders in 1898–1899. Luna did what he could to organize the Philippine army into a fighting force. Unfortunately, he was assassinated in Cabanatuan.[39] On a lighter note, he reputedly wrote the lyrics of "La Flor de Manila" that was set to music by Dolores Paterno. Now known as "Sampaguita," it remains popular to this day. In itself his birth-house is an attractive example of a Wood-and-Adobe house in what we call the grid style. Typically, the continuous row of capiz windows that form a grid contrasts with the plainness of the lime-covered ground story. It has now been turned it into a bodega. A marker by the National Historical Institute marks the site.

The book *Streets of Manila* (1977), which I have cited throughout, is well-researched. However, it makes a claim that, seen within the context of all that we have said about the families that lived in Binondo and San Nicolás, is odd and unfortunate. It says that these houses were "built for Spaniards in Spanish times."[40] But Hilario Súnico was a Chinese mestizo, the Lunas Indio Ilocano, and the Rizals Indio Tagalog. And what was the Tribunal de Naturales doing in this area if the Indios were so few? As we have seen above, and as we can still see today when promenading its streets, San Nicolás primarily was and still is the enclave of Chinese, Chinoys, Chinese Mestizos, and Tagalogs, with only few Spaniards around. It was these natives, mestizos and Chinese who had the houses built for themselves.

FIG. 399. 441 Urbiztondo

To the left of the Luna House are a series of old, modified prewar houses. Although very small, unpretentious, and fairly dilapidated, **441 Urbiztondo** is outstanding among them, because it is one of only two houses in San Nicolás (and one of only a handful in all of Metro Manila) that still carries a Spanish-era clay tile roof. The house thus probably stems from before 1880, when such clay tile roofs were commonly used before the advent of metal roofs.

Also on Urbiztondo at corner 421 Barraca stands the old **La Tondeña Distillery**. Originally founded in 1902 by famous Chinese businessman Carlos Palanca Sr. in Tondo and incorporated in 1929, the company introduced the production of alcohol from molasses, and is today known as Ginebra San Miguel. Built in the 1930s, the building later became the **O'Racca Confectionary Factory** owned by the same Japanese businessman connected to the Ides O'Racca Building. After the war it was likewise expropriated as "alien enemy property" and was transferred to the government. Today it houses a branch of NAMRIA, the national mapping agency. It is a rather unpretentious and functional 4-storey building, all concrete, with a chamfered corner and a strong presence in the street.

Today few people know that San Nicolas contains the site of the oldest **lighthouse** in the country on the far end of **Muelle de la Industria** towards Manila Bay. The first light house was placed here as early as 1642, while the first modern lighthouse was founded in 1846[42] and rebuilt several times, the last time in 1893.[41] However, the concrete tower that stands at the site today only dates from the 1960s. It tries to emulate a prewar design, and is not accessible. Before the massive expansion of the North and South harbors in the twentieth century and subsequent land reclamation, the lighthouse used to stand at the far end of a long jetty protruding far into Manila Bay. Today, the tower watches over a large informal settlement and is surrounded by reclaimed land on all sides.

LIVING IN SAN NICOLÁS

Yvette, a San Nicolas resident, graciously answered my questions. "There are disadvantages to living in this district. First, the threat of fire is ever-present; second, the pollution. However, there are advantages too." She mentioned the proximity to hospitals such as Chinese General Hospital in Sta. Cruz, Metropolitan Hospital at Masangkay in Binondo; to Chinese schools such as Chiang Kai-shek; to markets such as Divisoria, One Six Eight, and Arranque. Then there are many places of worship: Buddhist, Protestant, Born-Again Christian, and Catholic. Yvette attends mass said in Chinese at a chapel in Binondo Church.

The vintage house where Yvette continues to live measures 180 square meters and is narrow and long. "I like this type of house because it is cool (*malamig*). The ceiling is high. It's just like the house I grew up in at Dagupan in Pangasinan. Also wood is used in the floor and in the walls. This has a comfortable, natural feel that I find lacking in ultra-modern houses. All that cement makes me uncomfortable. Plus it's hot." Unlike concrete, wood does not accumulate heat, but rather isolates from it. Why therefore should we level down houses that work well in a tropical climate and replace them with all-concrete buildings that do not? Of course, the problem is that, as Dr. Venida reminds us, wooden walls are fire hazards in densely populated areas. Perhaps one solution would be to have wood paneling on the walls as insulators?

In addition to the functionality of San Nicolás' Wood-and-Stone houses, there are other reasons why people love them and their setting. In February 2011, I organized a guided tour around San Nicolás for the Heritage Conservation Society. We were fortunate to have with us Alain Burke-Miailhe who owns the Burke Building on the Escolta. His love for history came out when discussing the various landmarks of Binondo and San Nicolás. He recounts that sometime in the 1960s, the parish priest of Binondo started to build a new and higher church within the ruined church and had begun the demolition of the storied walls. Fortunately, Alain and other concerned citizens, notably the architectural critic Rodrigo Perez III (later Dom Bernardo OSB), alerted the public and had the demolition stopped. Now and then Alain would point out the beauty of a particular house, ruinous though it was. He remarked that down to the 1960s, San Nicolás was still a beautiful quarter because of its vintage houses.

FIG. 400. La Tondeña Distillery / NAMRIA Building

Our tour was not an easy walk because of the pollution and the danger posed by passing cargo trucks. I asked why he and his family continued to hold on to their properties in the run-down districts of Binondo and San Nicolás. The answer was a straightforward, "Our roots are here."

As this indicates, Manila still enjoys a stock of what sociologists call "cultural capital" (prestige, pride in ancestry, loyalty to a place) which can be turned to economic capital via investments. If San Nicolás was located in London, Paris, or Madrid, it would long have been turned into a top-tourist destination for locals and foreigners alike, holding a tremendous heritage, entertainment, and tourism potential. Alas, what is lacking is imagination, vision, and above all, political will. If only the City of Manila would capitalize on this love and pride in ancestral roots, by attracting its former residents to return or at least to invest in their ancestral city. Unfortunately, the shabby upkeep of the city is alienating. It drives away badly needed investments that can benefit rich and poor alike. Without a concerted effort to cultivate its prestige for economic gain, Manila may eventually become a vast slum with limited revenues.

NOTES

1   Lorelei D.C. De Viana, *Three Centuries of Binondo Architecture 1594-1898: A Socio-Historical Perspective* (Manila: University of Sto. Tomás Press, 2001), 36.

2   Xavier Huetz de Lemps, "L'aménagement du quartier de San Nicolás (Manille), au XIXe siècle," in *Imperios y naciones en el Pacífico*, edited by María Dolores Elizalde, Josep Maria Fradera and Luís Alonso (Madrid, CSIC: Biblioteca de Historia, 2001), 2, 279-92.

3   Ibid., 290.

4   Sociedad Estatal para la Acción Cultural Exterior, "Mapa de la Alcaicería que se fabrica en el sitio," in *Filipinas: Puerta de Oriente: De Legazpi a Malaspina* (n.p.:,Sociedad Estatal para la Acción Cultural Exterior, 2003), 218.

5   Edgar Wickberg, *The Chinese in Philippine life 1850-1898* (Quezon City: Ateneo de Manila University Press, 2000), 18.

6   Ibid. Dr. Evelyn Hu-Dart of Brown University concurs in this. A specialist in the history of Chinese migration to Southeast Asia and Latin America, she pointed out in lectures in Manila that descendants of Chinese migrants in the Philippines have produced a President (Corazon Aquino) and a very influential Cardinal (Jaime Sin). This is unthinkable in other Southeast Asian societies where the Chinese, though economically powerful, do not exert political power as overtly. She credits this to the Spanish policy of *mestizaje*—interracial and inter-ethnic unions were accepted and even encouraged as long as these were legitimized with an official ceremony before the State and the Church.

7   Huetz de Lemps, "L'aménagement du quartier de San Nicolás (Manille), au XIXe siècle," 285.

8   De Viana, *Three Centuries of Binondo Architecture 1594-1898,* 187. The full text of Azcarraga's decree is provided in English translation on p. 241.

9   Guidelines laid down by the Junta Consultiva de Obras Públicas (Consultative Board for Public Works), following the earthquake of 1880, cited in Luis Merino OSA, *Arquitectura y urbanismo en el Siglo XIX: Introducción general y monografía* (Manila: Centro Cultural de España with the collaboration of the Intramuros Administration, 1987), 67, 163-78.

10 Ibid., 290.

11 Teodoro Agoncillo, *The Revolt of the Masses: The Story of Bonifacio and the Katipunan* (Quezon City: University of the Philippines, 1956).

12 Pedro Luengo Gutierrez, "Intramuros, Arquitectura en Manila: 1739-1788," Sevilla, Departamento de Historia del Arte, Universidad de Sevilla, Unpublished thesis for the Ph. D. in Art History, 2010, 364.

13 Ibid., 378.

14 Ibid.

15 Ibid., 381.

16 Ibid., 382.

17 Ibid.

18 Ibid., 377.

19 Miguel Deala Parungao, *The Saga of Manila's Fire Fighters* (Manila, 1979), 107.

20 Nick personally obliged me by writing a summary of his family company's history.

21 Luning B. Ira and Isagani R. Medina, "San Nicolás," *Streets of Manila* (Quezon City: GCF Books, 1977), 73.

22 De Viana, *Three Centuries of Binondo Architecture 1594-1898*, 124.

23 Ibid., 159-183 gives an architectural overview.

24 Ibid., 160.

25 Ibid., 150-51.

26 Ibid., 150.

27 Ibid., 150-51.

28 Ira and Medina, *Streets of Manila*, 38.

29 *Philippine Daily Inquirer*, 15 March 1998.

30 De Viana, *Three Centuries of Binondo Architecture 1594-1898*, 124.

31 Ibid. De Viana cites the inscription in the bells to this effect.

32 Ira and Medina, "San Nicholas," 75.

33 Ibid., 75.

34 Ibid.

35 Ibid., 71.

36 Ibid., 73.

37 James Ong and Anson Yu, "15 heritage buildings in Metro Manila that should be turned into hotels or something," *Coconuts Manila*, 10 February 2014, http://manila.coconuts.co/2014/02/07/12-heritage-buildings-metro-manila-should-be-turned-hotels.

38 De Viana, *Three Centuries of Binondo Architecture 1594-1898*, 181.

39 Vivencio José, *The Rise and Fall of Antonio Luna* (Metro Manila: Solar Publishing Corporation, 1991).

40 Ira and Medina, *Streets of Manila*, 64.

41 Russ Rowlett, "The 27 Major Lighthouse (in the order listed by *Faros Españoles do Ultramar,*" *Spanish Lighthouses of the Philippines*, 13 September 2014, accessed 1 November 2014. http://www.unc.edu/~rowlett/lighthouse/phl-esp.html.

42 De Viana, *Three Centuries of Binondo Architecture 1594-1898*.

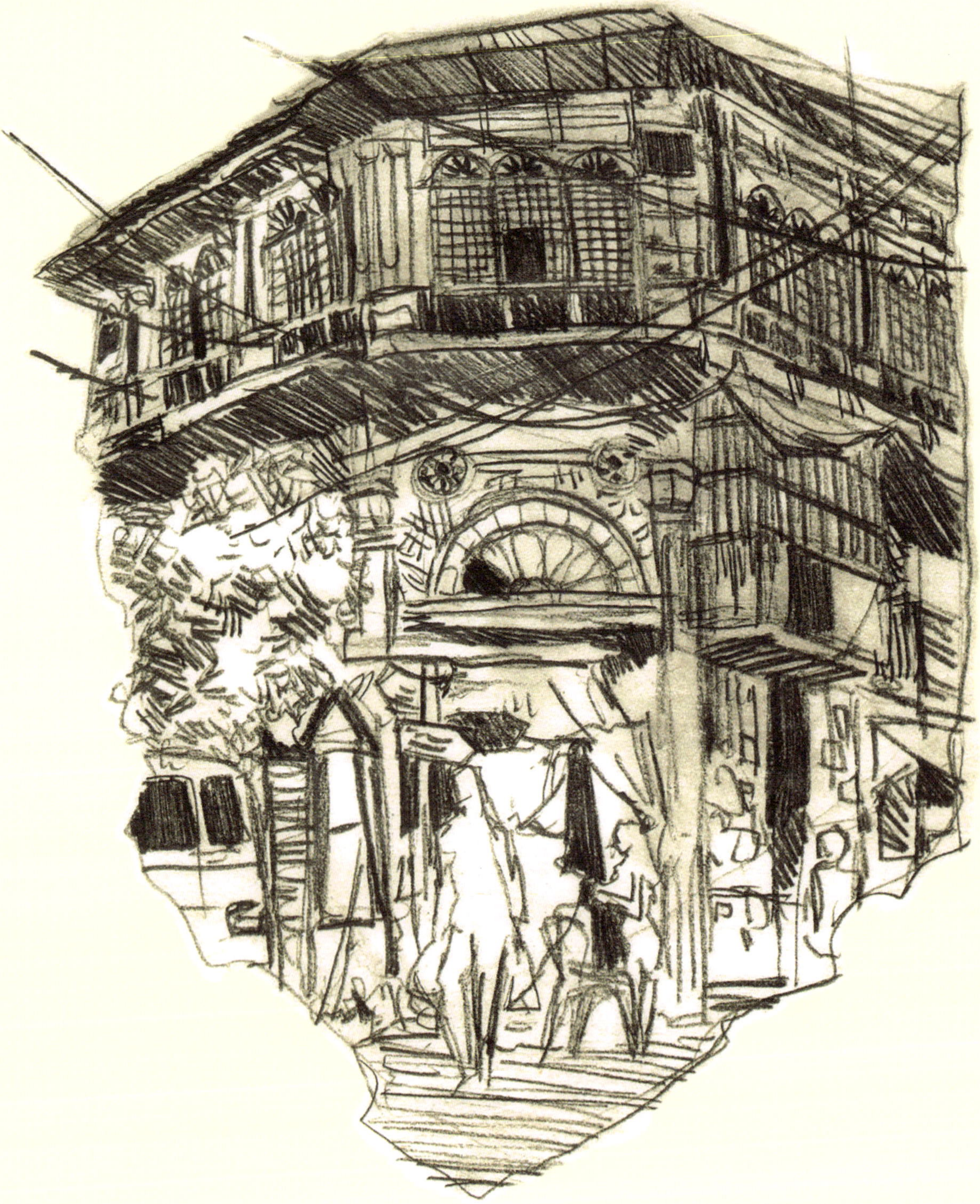

More Economic Uses for the Two Sister Districts

VICTOR S. VENIDA

MUCH OF THE SAN NICOLAS DISTRICT IS LOCATED AWAY FROM major transport flows, unlike the residential part of Quiapo around the basilica of San Sebastian. Calle Hidalgo, from San Sebastian to Quezon Boulevard in Quiapo, attracts several jeepney terminals and is thus a tangle at its western end. Because of its location, the entire district of San Nicolas can be developed as a mixed-use but dominantly residential district. The existing commercial uses can be retained, including the storage and warehousing facilities for as long as the commodities involved are consistent with those specified in the Comprehensive Land-Use Plan and Zoning Ordinance (CLUPZO) of the City of Manila. Moreover this will be consistent with the original nature of these townhouses, with the ground floor (*zaguan*) as an open space for storage and warehousing, the upper floor as residential, with mezzanine (*entresuelo*) if present as office space or additional residential area.[1]

As for the available vacant lots, the buildings to be constructed would need to follow the density and design themes of the nearby antique buildings to approximate the creation of an architecturally and stylistically distinctive street wall. There are substantial clusters of antique buildings along Jaboneros, Sevilla, Madrid, Barcelona, Camba, Elcano, and San Fernando that can provide the design themes that can guide the architecture of new buildings (e.g., design of window grilles or ventanilla, of roof vents, of frosted glass panes, pilasters, capitals, etc). The lamp posts would ideally be adapted from the design of the older street lamps. De Viana and the NHCP have quite a collection of old photos and building plans that can be used as resource material.[2] In addition, one can possibly reconstruct the demolished old buildings (where the empty lot has not yet been redeveloped) to approximate as much as possible the vision and experience of old San Nicolas.

However, although San Nicolas remains the prime candidate for declaration as a heritage district, the question remains: Is it not too late to require that new constructions in the entire district be guided by the style of the remaining nineteenth-century buildings which are dwindling rapidly? It may, however, be a good solution for certain defined areas or streets. A very good example of a "modern" version would be the new Burke Plaza Building on San Fernando corner Sto. Cristo—visibly modern, but visually at ease with its surrounding older neighbours. However, height restrictions will certainly meet stiff opposition. Indeed, numerous high-rise constructions—without any design nor density harmony with the old structures—have already emerged in the last few years.

Some specific areas might need a more distinctive theme in terms of the commercial activities to be encouraged. It is suggested that Calle Barcelona be an area for restaurants, art galleries, and tourist souvenir shops mainly to take advantage of the unique vista of Manila Cathedral and the northern wall of Intramuros. A block or two can even be pedestrianized to maximize this special feature. Calle San Fernando can accommodate office space on the upper floors, apart from residential uses. Since it is the main traffic artery, residential use may not be attractive to middle and upper-middle-income families. Given the generally quiet and residential nature of the entire district (at its central portion, not the fringes), it can also be developed as an artists' and designers' village since most of the old houses have high ceilings and wide inner spaces that can also be replicated in the newer construction if the proposal for a uniform density and ceiling height would be adopted. These potential residents are the very same creative professionals who can develop the restaurants and shops that can create the district's new image.

In the long run, there could even be an exciting pedestrian bridge connecting Intramuros (an existing tourism hub) with San Nicolas (a proposed tourism hub), as was done in London, connecting St. Paul's and Tate Modern. It would be an easy walk, with a panoramic view of the Pasig River, and just a few steps to Barcelona Street with its proposed restaurants, etc.

Beside San Nicolas is its sister district Binondo with which its history has been closely intertwined over the centuries. Binondo's commercial and office activities are still quite vibrant although there seems to be a lot of vacant office spaces. This suggests that the rental market will be attractive for many small and medium-scale enterprises. For the renewal of Binondo—analogous to the proposals in San Nicolas—the overall massing and height of buildings will need to be uniform to create a distinctive street wall, especially in areas with a significant number of old buildings (Escolta and Dasmariñas) that is available for commercial/office use.

One can also encourage the reconstruction of the old façades, specially of the commercial buildings and even the realization of the unbuilt architectural plans of Juan Arellano, Juan Nakpil, and others. Such plans are available in the National Archives. However, reconstructions are generally controversial and problematic in many ways, and ideally should be restricted to few, very significant vanished structures, if at all. Many of these plans were for buildings to be located in these districts. In a sense, San Nicolas can be a showpiece of nineteenth-century architecture, and Binondo, of the 1920s and 1930s styles. It would seem that in Binondo, almost all of its nineteenth-century buildings have been lost. But this is less true of its early twentieth-century architecture. Much of what was lost was replaced with newer construction of likewise high artistic value. The Calvo Building has hosted a museum which displays architectural models of proposed new and renovated old buildings for Escolta and these are excellent suggestions for design and construction along this fabled street.

The Q. Paredes (formerly Rosario) and Escolta areas have antique buildings with less than ten stories. Their façades and external walls can be retained vis-à-vis the higher buildings that would be constructed behind them, such as was done to the Hearst Building in New York. This may be suggested for 433, 483, and 497 Q. Paredes, for 101, 381-387, and 401 Dasmariñas, for Calle David corner Dasmariñas, and Calle Dasmariñas corner Muelle de Binondo, as these streets command substantial real estate value. This approach is currently (2021) applied to the former American Chamber of Commerce (Dasmariñas), the Capitol Theater (Escolta), and the Arellano-designed Hospicio de San Jose (Paredes). But this design suggestion has to be done delicately since the Hearst Building is a rather unusual example and experiences in these types of design have not been encouraging. The buildings on the eastern end of Escolta (specially the Regina and Perez-Samanillo buildings) can retain their densities as they harmonize with the density and style of the buildings across the bridge to Plaza Sta. Cruz, including the Prudential Bank building and Plaza Lacson/Goiti. Residential units in the area ought to be increased among both 1) old buildings for purposes of restoration/adaptive reuse, and 2) new construction to increase economic activity and the residential population. This would also mean encouraging the expansion and improvement of existing public and private elementary, secondary, and pre-elementary schools in the entire area including those across in Intramuros and the schools in the Recto Mendiola area.

A still to-be-updated study of the City's CPDO (1999 survey) has identified the economies of agglomeration in a number of streets/blocks and these can serve as guides in encouraging the location of business activities in the district:

ONGPIN	*Goldcraft, jewelry*
CHINATOWN (whether in Binondo or San Nicolas)	*Novelty items*
BINONDO (as a whole)	*Office and school supplies*
PORT AREA	*Transport and forwarding*
RECTO	*Booking and art works*
S. PADILLA (FORMERLY GANDARA), J. LUNA	*Canvas and upholstery*
S. PADILLA (FORMERLY GANDARA)	*Heavy equipment and industrial products*

A larger resident population will increase demand for food stores, grocery items, and household and home furnishing and services. This will be the case in the immediate and near future as several high-density residential buildings are already being constructed or are nearing completion, mainly to accomodate newly arrived immigrants from China. For the business activities listed in the table, the allied industries will need to be encouraged to locate in the area. There might be a need to review the presence of businesses in heavy equipment and industrial products in S. Padilla (formerly Gandara) to verify if these are consistent with the CLUPZO.

But since the area will also prove to be attractive to the tourist industry once the proposals for heritage renewal are implemented, there will be a need to identify a strategic location for a tourist information office and for tourist accommodations. It is suggested that this can be located on the ground floor of the Prudential Bank building, or in any of the old buildings along Q. Paredes. These are along the main thoroughfares for both vehicular and pedestrian traffic but the Prudential Bank building is at least closer to the LRT station. It is also suggested that parking buildings be constructed in strategic areas throughout the district. This will reduce the need for parking on street level, improve vehicular traffic flow, encourage pedestrian activity, and create a market among the street-level commercial establishments for pedestrians. But this will also depend on the implementation of the proposal to develop the sidewalks and curbs (which will need to be widened with minimal street vending/hawking activity). There will then be the need to create a pedestrianized street to consolidate all the street hawking and vending activities in the area, similar to the activities along Calle Carriedo in nearby Sta. Cruz and Quiapo. This can be integrated in the overall plan for traffic flow improvement. The streets of T. Pinpin and Banquero can be suggested for this.

The above proposal can be summarized as a program of functional diversification which has its own unique possibilities and limitations.[3] For financing purposes, some of the existing large corporations whose original headquarters were in Binondo can be solicited to finance the installation of markers or even the restoration of the old buildings themselves. These include GMA Network (for the Calvo Building), Bank of the Philippine Islands (BPI), and Citibank. Their expenditure can be granted some measure of tax deduction for their property taxes, or be channelled through their corporate foundations. The city government can also consider the San Nicolas district as a location for an experimental social housing program in the old houses for renewal and/or in new construction.

Social housing—at least in the old, wooden houses—has its risks. Without effective supervision, these may quickly become overcrowded slums, with increased danger of fire. Hence, new structures may be the more effective solution. A varied mix of residents from diverse income classes keeps a district vibrant. Social housing can evolve into middle-income housing on the assumption that with economic development, residents eventually become middle-income and at some point can either move to other neighbourhoods or be given the option to buy units in the social housing establishments as happened in the council-houses of the United Kingdom.

NOTES

1 Fernando Nakpil-Zialcita and Martin I. Tinio, *Philippine Ancestral Houses, 1810–1930* (Quezon City: GCF Books, 1980).

2 Lorelei De Viana, *Three Centuries of Binondo Architecture, 1594–1898: A Socio-Historical Perspective* (Manila: UST Publishing House, 2001).

3 Victor S. Venida, "Economic Uses for Quiapo's Antique Mansions," in *Quiapo: The Heart of Manila*, edited by Fernando Nakpil-Zialcita (Manila: Metropolitan Museum and Ateneo de Manila University, 2006), 404–24.

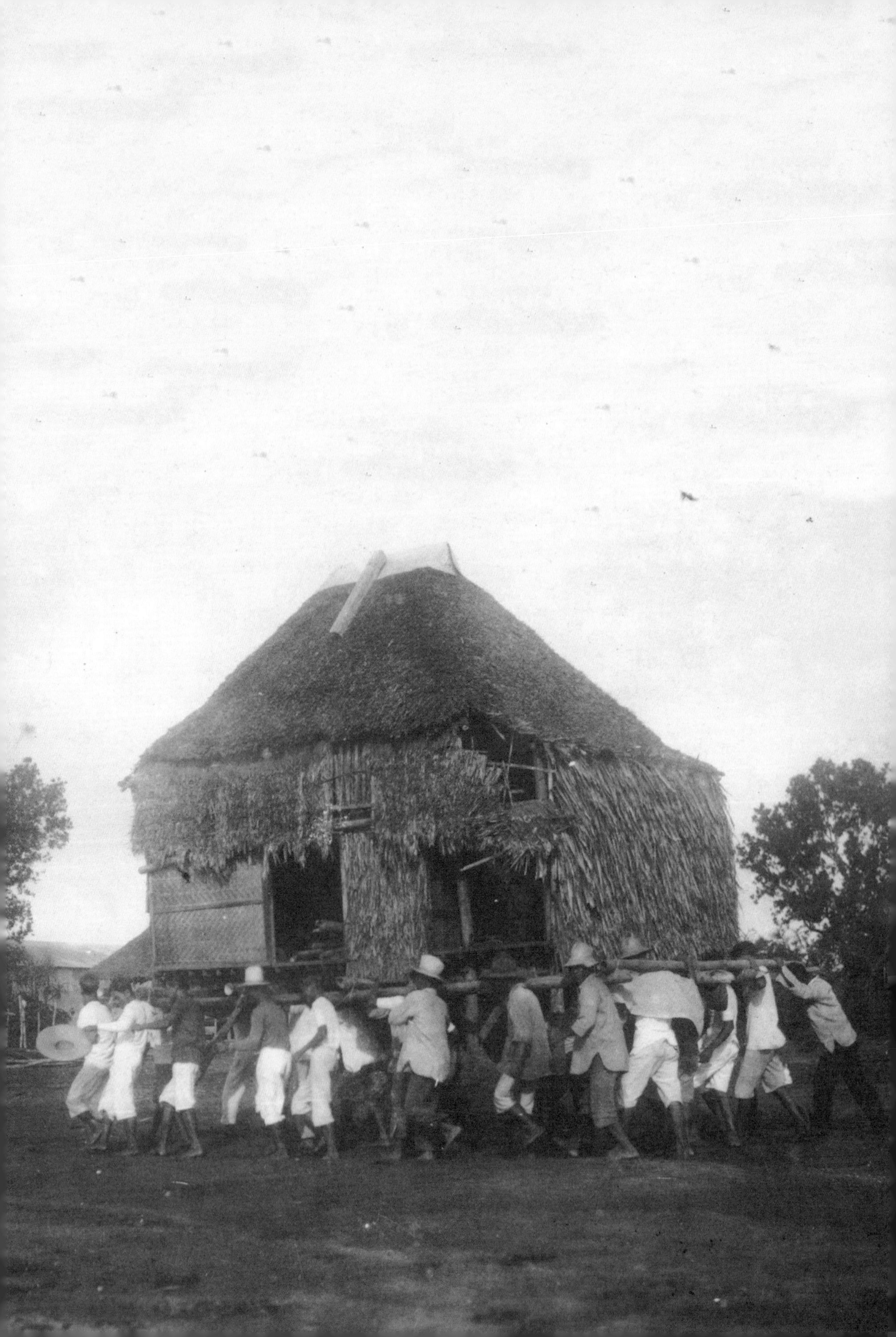

Curse or Blessing?—
Moving Immovable Heritage

ERIK AKPEDONU

THE RECENT CONTROVERSY OVER THE ALBERTO HOUSE IN BIÑAN, Laguna, has once again drawn attention to a debate that started fifteen years ago when a prominent real estate developer started his 400-hectare heritage resort "Las Casas Filipinas" in Bagac, Bataan.[1]

Since its conception around 2005, Jerry Acuzar has bought, dismantled, and rebuilt twenty-seven antique houses (as of 2014) mostly from Luzon in his resort, which is located about three hours from Manila.[2] Yet, many of his recent acquisitions have not gone un-opposed by heritage advocates and local heritage groups, who argue that transplanting a structure out of its original cultural and historical context diminishes its heritage value, and worse, deprives the local community of its tangible heritage, identification marks, and "pride of place." However, Las Casas Filipinas is only the largest and best-known such heritage resort in the Philippines; there are a number of smaller ones in Luzon, such as Sitio Remedios in Ilocos Norte, and Sulyap Cafe and Museum in San Pablo, Laguna.[3] There is even a small, largely unknown such ensemble in Pasay City. While the latter sites merely recreate old houses from recycled materials, in Bagac houses are rebuilt relatively authentic to their original appearance. Even in the Cordillera of Luzon, traditional Ifugao houses have of late been moved to form part of heritage inns and bed-and-breakfasts, as happened in Banaue and Batad.

Translocation is fiercely debated, often with high emotions. The basic question is: Is the relocation and concentration of historic buildings into a "heritage resort" a saving grace or another disaster for the nation's fast dwindling built heritage?

FIG. 401. Bayanihan or "Move Home," undated

NATIONAL AND INTERNATIONAL CONVENTIONS ON TRANSLOCATION

Though not explicitly prohibiting it, international conservation charters discourage the translocation of historic structures. For example, Article 7 of the Venice Charter (1964) says: "A monument is inseparable from the history to which it bears witness and from the setting in which it occurs. The moving of all or part of a monument cannot be allowed except where the safeguarding of that monument demands it or where it is justified by national or international interests of paramount importance."[4] Here the transfer of an existing historic building is acceptable only if the building cannot be preserved in any other way in situ and would otherwise be lost. The problem is that translocation could be used as an "easy way out" instead of the potentially much more difficult and expensive preservation on site. Because the historical and cultural context in which a building is located is of such importance to its actual heritage value, conservationists demand that a translocated building "at least [be] re-erected in a comparable topographical situation. In general relocation to a site that is as close as possible to the original location and as similar as possible to the original landscape situation is to be preferred." And: "Scientific documentation and recording of the original condition of a building are essential requirements for correct dismantling and rebuilding."[5]

In the same vein, the new National Cultural Heritage Act of 2009 (Republic Act 10066) states in Section 23 that declared structures "shall not be relocated, rebuilt, defaced or otherwise changed in a manner, which would destroy the property's dignity and authenticity, except to save such property from destruction due to natural causes."[6]

Since the days of the Venice Charter the range of conservation objects and their value operators has broadened significantly, accompanied by a shift of emphasis in cultural heritage conservation and management on not only preserving material artifacts, but also and in particular, their meaning, value, and significance. As the importance of material is de-emphasized and relativized, it brought with it an increased acceptance of flexibility towards practical procedures.[7] However, on-site conservation still takes priority over relocation. The Australian Burra Charter (drafted in 1979 and last revised in 1999) states in Article 9 that "the physical location of a place is part of its cultural significance. A building, work, or other element of a place should remain in its historical location. Relocation is generally unacceptable unless this is the sole practical means of ensuring its survival." There is one situation where relocation is more readily acceptable, namely in the case of movable buildings: "Some buildings, works or other elements of places were designed to be readily removable or already have a history of relocation. Provided such buildings, works or other elements do not have significant links with their present location, removal may be appropriate." And: "If any building, work or other element is moved, it should be moved to an appropriate location and given an appropriate use. Such action should not be to the detriment of any place of cultural significance."[8]

FIG. 402. LWL Open-Air Museum, Detmold, Germany. By Michael Pereckas, image licensed under Creative Commons Attribution 2.0 Generic, see p. 394

INTERNATIONAL PRACTICE AND LOCAL TRADITIONS

International Practice. The relocation of historic buildings for museum purposes is common practice in Europe, North America, and parts of Asia. The oldest open-air museums date back to the late nineteenth century, when the Skansen in Stockholm, Sweden's oldest open-air museum opened in 1891. It is still the largest museum of its kind in the world.[9] In Oslo (Norway), the Norsk Folkemuseum opened three years later and today displays over 150 historic buildings collected from all over Norway, with some dating back as far as 1200 AD[10] Unlike the former museums, the Gamle By in Denmark does not depict rural but urban culture and history right in the city center of Arhus. Founded in 1909, it now houses 75 translocated historic buildings from the seventeenth to the nineteenth century.[11] The largest such ensemble in Germany, the LWL-Freilichtmuseum (LWL open-air museum) in Detmold, has since its establishment in 1971 relocated more than a hundred centuries-old structures from all over Westphalia to its 90-hectare museum ground, and attracts about 250,000 visitors each year.[12] Similar museums can be found in the USA (e.g., Heritage Village Museum, Ohio).[13] In Asia, the Korean Folk Village in Seoul-Yongin, founded in 1974, displays 270 traditional Korean houses translocated and reconstructed here from all parts of South Korea.[14] In Japan, the Meiji-mura (Meiji Village Museum) near Nagoya aims to preserve historic buildings from the Meiji and Shōwa Period, which are threatened by the immense development pressure in Japan's inner cities. To date over 60 buildings from all over Japan have been moved here and were faithfully restored.[15] In Tokyo,

FIG. 403. Inside Meiji-Mura Museum, Japan (Image courtesy of Ryan Indon)

the mission of the Edo-Tokyo Open-air Architectural Museum with its 30 buildings, opened in 1993, is "to relocate, reconstruct, preserve and exhibit historical buildings of great cultural value that are impossible to preserve at their actual places."[16] However, all the above museums are managed to high scientific standards and primarily for educational purposes, less for leisure, let alone as a private resort. Closer to Las Casas Filipinas perhaps is the Jiming Mountain Resort in Longyou County, Zhejiang Province of China, where forty-one heritage houses were relocated to starting in 1985 with the support of the local government.[17] The Longyou resort was recognized on the national level as an important heritage site in 2013 (likewise, in Japan reconstructed buildings can retain heritage status). In contrast in Germany, for example, translocated buildings automatically lose their listed status, as the original environment is a significant factor for their initial listing. Because of their translocation to a protected environment dedicated to their preservation, such as an open-air museum, listing as an additional legal protection is not necessary in the first place.[18]

Local traditions. The relocation of existing houses is actually not unusual in Philippine culture, and was (and sometimes still is) frequently practiced in Manila and especially in the provinces, there helped by the spirit of *Bayanihan* (mutual community help). This is facilitated by the wooden construction of most ancestral houses,

FIG. 404. Santos-Andres House, moved from Navotas to Antipolo

which makes it rather easy to dismantle and reassemble them. For example, when lands are divided among heirs, it is not uncommon for the one inheriting the ancestral house, but not (all of) its lot, to totally or partly move it to a new site (or just a few meters to the side, as happened, for example, in one site in Sampaloc). Quite a number of vintage houses have been translocated from Manila to the province and vice versa, or within the Metro itself, such as the Tuason House in Sampaloc, now the centerpiece of a new housing development in Taguig. Other houses (e.g., in San Juan and Malabon) have even been relocated from one province to another, either completely, or partially. One remarkable example is the relocation of the Santos-Andres House from Navotas to Antipolo, immortalized in the book *Tahanan—A House Reborn*.[19] An important difference here is that the house was not sold before its transfer. Saved from urban decay, the house was moved and is still inhabited by the same family who originally owned it. Hence the "soul" of the house was retained, that is, all the memorabilia, stories, events, and episodes, small and big, trivial or significant, which make the house come alive. It thus makes a difference whether a house is translocated by family members who have a personal connection to it, or by an unrelated third party more interested in the material artifact as such. Says architect Richard Bautista: "Translocation is okay, as long as it remains within the family and is done by family members." Hence, there are varying degrees of connectivity, with Bagac and Antipolo at opposing ends on the scale. Taking Las Casas Filipinas as a case study, what are the negative and positive aspects of translocation?

NEGATIVE CONSEQUENCES OF TRANSLOCATION

Conventions on translocation are stringent, because there are important negative consequences that have to be weighed against any potential advantages:

Loss of local heritage. Most importantly, the local community loses part of its unique history and identity. Old buildings, such as churches, cemeteries, and ancestral houses are the visible and tangible symbols of a community's history and its past cultural achievements and prosperity. With their removal, the local community loses its roots and connection to its past. After all, heritage is defined by space (location) and time.

Loss of context. As for the structures themselves, their transplantation far from their original location puts them out of their original urban, historical, and cultural context. As such, they lose a substantial part of their original narrative, like an antique artifact that is not labeled and put in a museum where it is placed in context, but in a private home where it remains mute. It is indeed striking that most houses in Bagac feel strangely out-of-place, empty (in both a literal and figurative sense), and silent. Although the staff guiding visitors around the houses know the basic facts about their history, what is missing are the memorabilia and little personal stories that would make these houses come alive.

At the same time, old houses are placed in a context in which they have never existed, be it in terms of style (houses from different provinces and thus built in various regional styles next to each other) or location (urban houses in a rural configuration and landscape.) Thus, translocation leads to a loss of socio-historic authenticity of not only the original site, but also of the new site.

Privatization of history and culture. Where old houses in their original location face a public street, even if privately owned they form part of the public sphere (if visible from the street): everybody, rich or poor, locals or tourists, can look at them and enjoy their beauty and read whatever message they may carry, free of charge. By relocating them to a remote and fenced-off private property, these houses disappear into someone's private sphere, and whoever wants to see them may have to pay, be it an entrance fee, accommodation, or consumables, let alone considerable travel costs. That is, if the owner decides to open the site to visitors at all, and does not keep it to himself and his relatives or friends. Given the relatively high costs of access to Bagac (time-consuming and cumbersome without a private car) and entry fees, the "enjoyment" of the nation's heritage becomes the privilege of a wealthy few.

Loss of Original Substance. Although even entire stone buildings can be translocated (as, for example, sometimes in the USA) this is rarely done due to the significant technical challenges and high costs. Thus, foundations and masonry walls are usually not transferred and are thus lost, as are historic alterations to the building over time if it is reconstructed in its supposed "original state."

Loss of Authenticity. Many heritage advocates claim that a relocated building is basically a new structure, even if it was reassembled from its original parts. Moreover, structures in Bagac are not always restored faithfully. In particular, masonry brick or adobe ground floor walls, which cannot be translocated (or only at considerable expense), are replaced with somewhat "fake-looking" surrogate materials, such as narrow tile strips on slender cement walls to imitate the original thick, all-brick walls; or slender cement imitations of original massive adobe walls. In addition, the chosen "adobe look" only perpetuates the romantic but misinformed notion that adobe stone should be visible instead of lime-plastered. In addition, it gives the houses a somewhat gloomy look unlike in their original condition, which was usually bright-colored and cheerful, as can be seen in many restored houses in Vigan today. Walls are likewise subject to aesthetic and functional amendments, and are frequently "improved" with un-historic decorations. Sometimes, the original *haliguis* would not be transferred, and instead be replaced with wood-clad concrete columns. Often interiors are not faithfully reproduced true to the original, but overdecorated with fancy paintings, ornaments, and designs that never existed. Some row houses, which originally only had windowless fire walls on their gable sides have, for practical reasons, been given capiz windows on all sides, thus turning a row house into a single-detached structure.

FIG. 405. Saving the Alberto House in Biñan, Laguna, an LGU-declared cultural heritage landmark. (2011)

Endangerment. The site in Bagac is facing the sea, where the relocated structures (especially their metal components) are at risk from highly corrosive salt water and salt-spray winds, apart from the risk of rising sea levels and floods during storms, especially at high tide.

Encouragement of demolitions. Importantly, translocations may encourage owners of vintage houses to sell them even in cases when they are not actually endangered. Says Ivan Henares, former president of the Heritage Conservation Society: "We pointed out that while the project may be saving houses from demolition or the lumber yards, it is encouraging agents to convince more old-house owners to sell because they keep on buying them at a premium in many cases."[20] The same problem is mentioned by Akpedonu and Saloma in connection with the recycling of architectural elements of vintage houses in Bohol: "It could eventually create a thriving demand for materials from old houses, thereby resulting in the unbridled demolition of old houses that currently continue to exist simply because society does not attach any monetary value to them."[21]

ADVANTAGES OF TRANSLOCATION

While thus generally problematic, translocation can have certain advantages:

Saving grace. Defenders of translocation say that such initiatives are actually saving houses from neglect or demolition, a claim not without merit: the first house to rise in Bagac, the "Mexico House," is said to have been bought from an antiques dealer, who had already dismantled the structure. Had it not been for its purchase, its parts would likely have ended up as mere accessories in, say, Makati condominiums and Alabang mansions to "give your modern home a special touch," as the website of one salvager/recycler aptly put it. The Candaba House, said to date back to 1780, had to make way for a filling-station in its original location.[22] The largest structure on site, the Casa Bizantina from San Nicolas, Manila, had been in a state of gross neglect and decay for decades, when it was bought and transferred in 2009. So deteriorated was the structure that the Office of the City Engineer, fearing for its structural integrity and the safety of the fifty or more families inhabiting the building, had already issued an evacuation and demolition order.

Costs. Translocation often seems the only way to save vintage houses, as the land on which they are situated (often prime inner-city locations) is usually much more expensive that the building itself, and thus too expensive to buy for either heritage groups or local government units. In Biñan, the value of the 2,000-square-meter property of the Alberto House was estimated at PHP 50 million, whereas the historic 600-square-meter house itself was estimated to be worth only around PHP 200,000.[23] Thus, in order to save the house in its original location, a potential buyer would have to pay 250 times more for the land than for the building itself, which is often beyond the capacity of even very wealthy individuals. Private or government entities tasked with preserving built heritage, the latter being accountable to the taxpayer, simply do not have the same purchasing power as real estate developers with their deep pockets, who are tasked with profit maximizing for their owners or shareholders. It was the same cost considerations which prompted the Quezon City government in 2013 to translocate and partially reconstruct the historic Quezon House from its original site in New Manila to Quezon Memorial Circle. Purchasing the original lot and preserving the house in situ would have cost at least PHP 110 million.[24] Instead, the house was donated by the owners and relocated at a cost of about PHP 10 million.[25]

Restoration. Houses are meticulously, though not always accurately, rebuilt. The upper floors, in particular, are usually faithfully restored close to the original. Both the Casa Bizantina and the Enriquez Mansion which had deteriorated dramatically on their original sites, have since been painstakingly put back to their former glory at considerable expense. In fact, the concentration of restoration works in Bagac has since made it an important training ground and source of livelihood for artisans from Paete and Betis as well as local women, and has led to the sustenance or even resurrection of many traditional crafts (brick-making, carving, ironworks) and even the invention of new ones, such as handicrafts and locally made silk wallpaper.

Accessibility. Where translocated buildings are opened for public viewing, formerly private houses become accessible to a wider (usually paying) audience, especially the hitherto inaccessible interior.

Heritage cluster. Individual houses widely scattered over a region or province rarely entice tourists to visit on their own. And in Manila, where old houses are concentrated in decaying historic districts such as San Nicolas, Quiapo, and Sta. Cruz, even many Manileños are unwilling or afraid to visit these areas due to the deteriorating urban environment. By concentrating historic houses in one site, they form an attractive cluster, which, as in Vigan or Taal, is far more appealing to a large-enough number of local and foreign visitors, and can thus be put to substantial income-generating use for touristic purposes, such as restaurants, boutiques, souvenir and antiques shops, hotels, museums, etc. Thus, the Filipino "theme park" in Bagac could actually spark a wider interest in the nation's largely ignored built heritage and history. Many houses were largely unknown to the general public prior to their transfer to Bagac, but in their new location are now being noticed and appreciated.

In addition, the concentration of houses from different regions and historical eras, and their different styles give the visitor a good impression of the wide variety of Philippine styles and their evolution, and of the achievements of Filipino artistry. It creates a similar ambience to an open-air museum, as in the popular Nayong Pilipino, an open-air theme park in the Clark Freeport Zone, Pampanga.

Providing a vision. Although the NHCP and the National Museum place historic markers to educate the public about history, such markers (which unfortunately do not usually contain much historical information or context) follow the site, not the historic artifact. Hence historic markers are often found on modern structures completely unrelated to the historic event, institution, or personality they are referring to. History thus remains abstract and academic, rather than visible and alive. Jerry Acuzar himself laments that what he learned about Philippine history in school remained abstract and incomprehensible, because unlike countries such as Italy, in the Philippines there is comparatively little physical evidence of the past left to make history visible and thus come alive: "To be able to remember history, you need to see it." And: "If we do

FIG. 406. Ordoveza House from 1744, Majayjay, Laguna, before translocation

not have this, history would just stay in the books.... You need to be able to see it and touch it."²⁶ As such, the Casas Filipinas provide a rare glimpse of what many old town centers and historic quarters in the Philippines and especially Manila, like San Nicolas and Quiapo, could look like today if politicians (and those who voted them in) had more vision, foresight, and political will in the past and present.

The above-mentioned Quezon House provides a remarkable example of "responsible" relocation by an LGU, which avoids most of the negative consequences associated with private translocation, as discussed earlier:

Re. Loss of heritage: Although the house is no longer situated in the New Manila subdivision, it is at least still within Quezon City and can still be visited by its citizens.

Re. Loss of context: While the house has been removed from its original urban context, the museum it now contains is well-appointed, including informative brochures, and well-informed tour guides, which somewhat mitigates the lack of personal memorabilia and historic ambience.

Re. History and culture privatized: Admission is free, and poorer citizens are explicitly enticed to visit, hence the site is open to all social classes. The house is thus much more accessible today than when it was still privately owned. Because the house is still within Quezon City and centrally located, it is easily accessible without much travel expense.

Re. National and international conventions: While discouraging translocation, conservationists demand at least the relocation site to approximate the original site. Here, the park-like setting in Quezon Memorial Circle is reminiscent of the original lush garden surrounding the house in New Manila.

Re. Lack of authenticity: Because the original house was mainly built of concrete, only wooden and metal elements could be translocated. Thus, the house suffered a very substantial loss of material authenticity. On the other hand, however, the reconstructed parts are very accurate replicas of the original.

Re. Encouragement of demolitions: For the Quezon City government, this likely remains a unique project, hence encouragement of further demolitions or translocations is unlikely.

CONCLUSION

It is a sad fact that the preservation of the nation's built heritage ranks very low, if at all, on the priority list of most politicians and government officials, be it on national, provincial, or city/municipal level, and irrespective of the historic or cultural significance of a place. For example, the oldest domestic house of the Philippines, the Ordoveza House from 1744 in Majayjay, Laguna, remained undeclared by any government agency and in a state of almost complete ruin until it was translocated to Bagac in 2015. The ongoing loss of historic structures in Manila mirrors that in countless towns and villages all over the country. This lack of political will, in turn, is a reflection of the generally low awareness of many local communities with regard to their cultural heritage. Even in communities where commitment to heritage is verbally pro-

FIG. 407-408. Quezon House, translocated to Quezon Memorial Circle, Quezon City

fessed both the public and the private sector frequently fail to take substantial action and to make significant financial contributions in time. Meanwhile, expropriation of private property by the state as done in Biñan is a risky endeavor and rarely resorted to for the sake of heritage conservation.[27] Not surprisingly, politicians, eager to be reelected, do not act on heritage preservation when they feel that it is not high on their constituents' agenda. Meanwhile, limited funds and other pressing social issues remain perennial—and thus, priority—problems, although heritage preservation and cultural vitalization can actually be effective tools in poverty eradication, as Zialcita, Venida, and other authors argue.[28]

Subsequently, laws protecting cultural heritage in the country are relatively weak, largely unknown among the general public, and rarely enforced.

Thus, given low societal awareness and subsequent indifference, lack of political will, and lack of meaningful financial contributions towards their upkeep from both the public and the private sector, in many cases the relocation of old buildings from their original location currently seems to be the lesser of two evils. The alternative for most owners would be to sell their vintage house and its lot to the highest bidder, who would have little scruples about demolishing the old house. Instead of being resurrected elsewhere, it parts would likely end up in a landfill, as fire wood, or as material for the local furniture industry.[29] While restoration on site would be the ideal, it would probably be too much to ask for from private "collectors," who, after all, are primarily interested in the (cheap) historic structure, not the (expensive) ground underneath, and who may not want to see their collection scattered over many locations all over the archipelago with the accompanying expenses and comparatively little financial return to be expected, if at all. In the same vein it is unrealistic to expect a private citizen to fund the restoration of an old building in situ if he or she does not own it. On the other hand, merely building replicas of these historic houses inside the resort, as suggested by some heritage advocates, would not save the much more valuable original.

Finally, it is also somewhat unrealistic to expect owners of heritage buildings to alone bear the immense costs of preserving the national built patrimony. The benefits of the sale of an old house to a developer, especially in high-priced inner city areas, are obvious. Gains are high, immediate, certain, easy to divide, independent of external

FIG. 409. "Casa Bizantina" in its original location along Madrid Street in San Nicolás

factors, and do not require any partners or financial outlays. In contrast, keeping a house and adaptively reusing it is a financial gamble: Gains are lower, delayed, uncertain, harder to share, require investments and/or work or a partner, and depend on external factors beyond one's control, such as urban environment, competition, legal frameworks, LGU policies, etc. Thus, heritage protection may be good and profitable for the community (at least in the long term), but not necessarily for the individual property owner, especially where development pressure is high. Adaptive re-use is thus not as attractive as a sale, unless the legal framework changes the "rules of the game" with height and use restrictions for new constructions, tax holidays, restoration grants, etc. Such changing of the rules is however impossible without some "cruelties" toward vintage house owners and developers alike and unlikely to get broad societal and political support anytime soon. Under these circumstances heritage preservation remains a labor of love.

Society and its representatives have failed for decades to sufficiently protect and maintain many of these buildings on their original sites, hence a private investor may understandably feel irritated if these same groups suddenly show an interest and want to have a say in what is being done with these buildings only after he bought them. As one blogger argued, a community that allows its heritage to fall apart may simply not deserve it.[30] This is echoed by Acuzar himself, who, when heritage advocates expressed anger over the dismantling of the Enriquez Mansion, replied "You did not take care of it."[31] Because private, not public, capital is involved, it would likewise be unrealistic (albeit ideal) to expect a collector to faithfully rebuild purchased structures. After all, he is risking his own private money, and can hence be rightfully expected to seek some degree of financial return. It would be different if the project were partially or

FIG. 410. "Casa Bizantina" translocated and rebuilt in Bagac, Bataan

completely funded with public tax money, in which case the public could duly expect all structures to be rebuilt and restored to the highest international and scientific standards, provided the taxpayer is willing to shoulder the resulting bill. Ultimately, Las Casas Filipinas is still primarily a resort with all the accompanying necessities, and only secondarily a museum. Acuzar himself claims not to compute the expenses and says he primarily does it for fun, and to leave a legacy for future generations.[32]

One should not, however, entertain the hope, as some heritage advocates do, that one day these houses could return to their original location, thus being merely "parked" in Bagac until public awareness for heritage has sufficiently increased. Once a heritage building has been transferred, it can never be returned for the simple reason that its original site will most likely have new structures by then, as this is the very reason why these houses were sold and moved in the first place.

The assessment of the merits and demerits of translocation can thus only be made on a case-to-case basis. Obviously, when houses are transferred which would otherwise surely be lost to collapse or demolition, translocation seems a laudable deed. Where, on the other hand, well-maintained houses whose continued existence on their original site is in no way endangered are bought up, relocation indeed becomes highly questionable.

The former, of course, is closely connected to the question of how much interest and effort the local community, above all its LGU, is exerting to protect its cultural heritage, and whether they are able and willing to muster the political will and financial means to that end. Many heritage advocates say that they would rather see an old building rot in situ rather than see it transferred. They argue that instead of (irreversible) relocation, the local community should be taught about the value and importance of its heritage, and they are right: support of the local community is an indispensable condition for long-term sustainable heritage conservation.[33] The problem with this "buying of time" is that not only is there currently no systematic and comprehensive-enough program to do so; it would take many years, if not decades, to reach a general level of consciousness which would be sufficient enough to effectively preserve most local heritage. By the time this is achieved (and money for restoration is available), there are likely hardly any heritage buildings left to save.

In summary, the translocation of vintage houses is not a good, let alone ideal, solution. Yet, given the large-scale failure of state and society to protect the bulk of the national built patrimony, it may currently still be the best option in those cases where a building will otherwise be completely lost. In fact, if current trends continue, those translocated houses in Bataan and elsewhere may one day be the only remaining houses of Old Manila. The most important thing to do, then, is to see to it that heritage finally gets the attention and financial means for its upkeep that will ultimately make places like Las Casas Filipinas unnecessary. A place like Bagac is the logical result of the current dismal societal, legal, political, and financial situation of heritage preservation in the country. This is not likely to dramatically improve anytime soon, as hundreds of vintage buildings continue to be lost every year. Amidst the steady work of the tireless demolition crews, the debate continues.

NOTES

1. The nineteenth-century Alberto House in Biñan is one of the oldest houses in the Philippines, and said to have been at some time the home of Teodora Alonzo, the mother of national hero Jose Rizal. It was bought in June 2010 by Jerry Acuzar, to be transferred to his resort town in Bagac, a move vigorously opposed by heritage advocates.

2. Las Casas Filipinas de Acuzar, "The Property," Las Casas Filipinas de Acuzar, accessed 24 May 2014, http://lascasasfilipinas.com/index.php/perfect-experience/22-the-property.html.

3. Christine S. Dayrit, "Sitio Remedios: Newest crown jewel of the North," *Philippine Star*, 5 March 2007, http://www.philstar.com/travel-and-tourism/387761/sitio-remedios-newest-crown-jewel-north; Sulyap Gallery Café and Restaurant, "History of Sulyap Museum," Sulyap, accessed 24 May 2014, http://www.sulyap.net/museum.php.

4. International Council on Monuments and Sites (ICOMOS), "International Charter for the Conservation and Restoration of Monuments and Sites (The Venice Charter 1964)," ICOMOS, accessed 12 December 2013, http://www.international.icomos.org/charters/venice.pdf.

5. Michael Petzet, "International Principles of Preservation," International Council on Monuments and Sites (Berlin: Hendrik Baessler Verlag, 2009), 34, http://www.icomos.de/pdf/principles.pdf.

6. National Commission for Culture and the Arts, "Implementing Rules and Regulations of Republic Act No. 10066," NCCA, 3 April 2012, http://www.ncca.gov.ph/downloads/IRR-heritage.pdf.

7. Honorio N. Pereira, "Contemporary Trends in Conservation: Culturalization, Significance and Sustainability," *City & Time* 3, no. 2 (2007): 2, http://www.ct.ceci-br.org.

8. Australia ICOMOS Inc., "The Burra Charter: The Australia ICOMOS Charter for Places of Cultural Significance, 2013," accessed 6 November 2014, http://australia.icomos.org/wp-content/uploads/The-Burra-Charter-2013-Adopted-31.10.2013.pdf.

9. Skansen, "About Skansen," Skansen, accessed 25 September 2012, http://www.skansen.se/en.

10. Norsk Folkemuseum, "About the Museum," Norsk Folkemuseum, accessed 25 September 2012, http://www.norskfolkemuseum.no/en.

11. Den Gamle By, "Facts about Den Gamle By (The Old Town)," Den Gamle By, accessed 25 September 2012, http://www.dengamleby.dk/the-old-tow.

12. LWL-Freilichtmuseum Detmold, "Eine zugkräftige Idee: Das LWL-Freilichtmuseum Detmold," LWL, accessed 25 September 2012, http://www.lwl.org/LWL/Kultu.

13. Historic Southwest Ohio, "Heritage Village Museum," Heritage Village Cincinnati, accessed 25 September 2012, http://www.heritagevillagecincinnati.org/village.asp.

14. Korean Folk Village, "Establishment Background," Korean Folk Village, accessed 25 September 2012, http://www.koreanfolk.co.kr/folk/english/index.ht.

15. Museum Meiji-Mura, "About the Museum Meiji-Mura," The Museum Meiji-Mura, accessed 23 May 2014, http://www.meijimura.com/english/about/index.htm.

16 Edo-Tokyo Open-air Architectural Museum, "Purpose," Edo-Tokyo Open-air Architectural Museum, accessed 23 May 2014, http://www.tatemonoen.jp/english/index.html.

17 Li Li, "Relocating heritage sites: Rebuilding architectural treasures at new locations sparks debate" *Beijing Review*, 31 October 2013, http://www.bjreview.com.cn/nation/txt/2013-10/29/content_574726_2.htm.

18 Correspondence with Dr. Hubertus Michels, Landschaftsverband Westfalen-Lippe (LWL), LWL-Open-Air Museum Detmold, 2 June 2014.

19 Reynaldo Alejandro and Vicente Roman Santos, *Tahanan: A House Reborn* (Malabon: Duende Publishing, 2003).

20 Ivan Henares, "Discussions on the Bagac Project," Heritage Conservation Society, 17 August 2008, http://heritageconservation.multiply.com/journal/item/28?&show_interstitial=1&u=%2Fjournal%2Fitem.

21 Akpedonu and Saloma, *Casa Boholana: Vintage Houses of Bohol* (Quezon City: Ateneo de Manila University Press, 2011), 91

22 As narrated by tour guide of Las Casas Filipinas to author on site, 26 May 2010.

23 Maricar Cinco, "In Biñan, Money Matters in Fight to Keep House of Rizal Mom," *Inquirer Southern Luzon*, 24 March 2011, http://newsinfo.inquirer.net/inquirerheadlines/regions/view/20110324-327417/In-Bian-money-matters-in-fight-to-keep-house-of-Rizal-mom#.

The case of the Alberto House also demonstrates the necessity to commit substantial financial funds if one is serious about preserving a place's cultural assets. In March 2011 the municipal government pledged up to PHP 80 million to keep the house in its original location along the plaza. It also illustrates the need for serious, sustained political will. Since June 2010 the municipal government of Biñan had refused to issue a demolition permit, and instead considered expropriation procedures, which were finally granted by the courts in June 2017. However, already in October 2012 the house largely collapsed on site. It has since been restored and reconstructed by the city government of Biñan.

24 Julie M. Aurelio, "QC Gov't Acts to Save House of Founding Father," *Philippine Daily Inquirer*, 14 August 2011, http://newsinfo.inquirer.net/41185/qc-gov%E2%80%99t-acts-to-save-house-of-founding-father.

25 As narrated to author by tour guide on site on 8 November 2013.

26 panikfreakxx, "Interview with Jerry Acuzar," *Youtube*, uploaded 9 November 2010, www.youtube.com/watch?v=xjuuHQsgY_w&NR=1.

27 Jaime C. Laya, "Biñan's Once-Grand José Alberto Heritage Home, Risen Like A Phoenix," *Manila Bulletin*, 16 September 2012, http://www.mb.com.ph/articles/373745/bi-s-oncegrand-jos-alberto-heritage-home-risen-like-a-phoenix.

Expropriation requires a potentially expensive and drawn-out legal case before a court of law, with uncertain results. Bonds have to be deposited by the expropriating party, which may be partially forfeited if the case is lost. And even if it is won, fair market value compensation would still have to be paid to the owner.

28 Anthony M. Tung, *Preserving the World's Great Cities: The Destruction and Renewal of the Historic Metropolis* (New York: Clarkson Potter Publisher, 2001). Tung discusses this in his chapters on Vienna, Amsterdam, and Warsaw. Other sources: Fernando N. Zialcita (ed.), *Balangkas: A Resource Book on the Care of Built Heritage in the Philippines* (Manila: National Commission for Culture and the Arts, Committee on Monuments and Sites, 2007), 2, 4; Fernando N. Zialcita (ed.), *Quiapo: Heart of Manila* (Manila: Metropolitan Museum and Ateneo de Manila University, 2006), 404-24; and Victor S. Venida, "Conflicts over Heritage: The Case of Quiapo," *Kritika Kultura* 2 (December 2002), https://journals.ateneo.edu/ojs/index.php/kk/article/view/1580.

29 Akpedonu and Saloma, *Casa Boholana,* 89–90.

30 Pinoyshooter, "Point of View on Heritage Conservation (& Las Casas Filipinas de Acuzar)," The Philippines and then some, accessed 25 September 2012, http://pinoyshooter.org/bogs/category/philippine-house/page/2.

31 panikfreakxx, "Interview with Jerry Acuzar." While the translocation of the Enriquez Mansion may indeed have saved it from complete decay, the outsized 15-story high rise that was put in its place by San Jose Builders, has drastically altered the historic streetscape of Hidalgo Street. Although somewhat mitigated by the protruding two-story podium, a rather crude imitation of the old mansion, the massing, height and volume of the tower overpowers the low-rise buildings of Hidalgo Street, both new and vintage structures. That high rise's podium, however, very well demonstrates the need for the volume of new buildings to fit into older historic streetscapes.

32 panikfreakxx, "Interview with Jerry Acuzar."

33 Antil Kumar, "Aihole set to relocate for monuments' sake," *The Times of India*, 25 May 2012, http://timesofindia.indiatimes.com/city/bangalore/Aihole-set-to-relocate-for-monuments-sake/articleshow/13466505.cms.

Instead of relocating historic structures, in Bangalore, India, an entire village agreed to move out of their current site in order to protect the Aihole temples and monuments from being destroyed by villagers' use of "resting, storing material and housing cattle, carts and tractors," thus voluntarily relocating themselves in order to preserve their heritage.

STO. NIÑO DE TONDO

TONDO
Warrior Haven

FERNANDO N. ZIALCITA

A RECURRING THEME IN SOME PHILIPPINE EPICS IS THE WARRIOR-Child. Newly born and still holding his placenta, the Miraculous Child speaks and promises his mother that he will avenge the humiliation suffered by his father. Thus the Ilocano Lam-ang sets off to look for the Highlanders who beheaded his father. Finding them, he singlehandedly battles an entire troop, and inevitably vanquishes them. On the other hand, in Panay, Aso Mangga and Abyang Baranugon, the newborn sons of Labaw Donggon, fight and defeat a giant who has imprisoned their father. The theme was popular because of the frequent wars between even neighboring settlements in the indigenous past.

It may well be that this popular theme[1] paved the way for the devotion to the Santo Niño. Fond of children to begin with, the island-dwellers accepted an icon that represented God Almighty as an Infant with a crown, an orb, and a scepter of authority. The Child would defend them from their enemies. In Luzon, the undisputed center of the devotion is Tondo's ancient parish church. It houses a statue of the Child in royal regalia, and attracts many pilgrims, especially on His feast during the third Sunday of January.

Fittingly, this Christian avatar of a pre-Christian devotion is enshrined in Tondo, one of the oldest recorded settlements in the islands. The Pila copperplate dating back to circa 900 AD states that the Great Lord of "Tundun" pardoned a debt incurred by Lady Angkatan and her brother Bukah, children of Lord Namwaran.[2] Unfortunately,

FIG. 411. Sto. Niño de Tondo

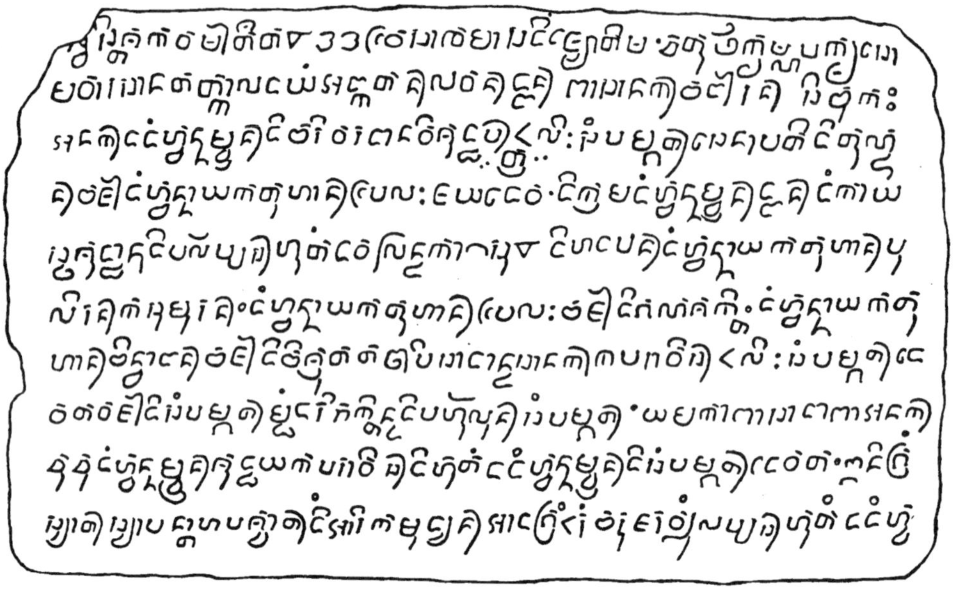

FIG. 412. Laguna Copper-Plate Inscription. Image taken from the article by Antoon Postma, "The Laguna Copper-Plate Inscription: Text and Commentary," originally published in 1992 in *Philippine Studies*, vol. 40, issue no. 2, pp. 183-203.

the copperplate is but a fragment of a larger (and now lost) document. However, it establishes Tondo's importance even then, for it indicates that Tondo was the seat of a Great Lord who commanded the allegiance of other subordinate lords. But what happened between the tenth and the sixteenth centuries? The well-known historian Luciano Santiago suggested, in a conversation with this author, that an earlier eruption by Pinatubo Volcano in the fourteenth century may have caused a major disruption both in Pampanga and in the coastal settlements along Manila Bay, including Tondo. Hence the absence of any records. This needs to be studied further, of course.

Another major, but not fully analyzed, development is the entry of the Sultan of Brunei in the early sixteenth century. According to Bruneian chronicles, Bolkiah (Nakhoda Ragam) not only conquered Sulu but also made a "dependency" of "Selurong." The latter is said to be Manila.[3] Was it really Manila, or was it not rather Tondo which was far older and already wealthy? By subduing Tondo, the Bruneians were able to found a rival entrepot on that tongue of land that better controlled the entry from Manila Bay to the Pasig River. That entrepot called Manila would be ruled by Bolkiah's grandson, Rajah Ache, later on called Rajah Matanda (The Old Ruler).

When the Spaniards first sailed up the Pasig, on the south bank was Manila, ruled by Rajah Soliman and his uncle Rajah Matanda. Opposite it was Tondo ruled by Lakandula.[4] At that time Tondo extended down to the Pasig. As is well-known, the Spaniards defeated Soliman and took over Manila. North of the Pasig, the Spaniards contracted an agreement with Lakandula permitting them to incorporate Tondo into their realm. Tondo lost its riverine extension when a new settlement was carved out from it and was called Binondo. In exchange, however, Tondo became the capital of a

FIG. 413. Bonifacio Monument, Tutuban, Tondo

province bearing the same name that in the 1800s extended "as far north as Polo, Bulacan; south to Cavite, west to Manila Bay, and whose eastern limits extended to both sides of the Pasig up to the mountains of San Mateo."[5] Eventually Tondo's realm shrank. Indeed, at the turn of the nineteenth century, it became a district of an expanded Manila, albeit its largest. As a major pueblo, Tondo had a large stone church, part of which survives to this day and, as late nineteenth-century photos indicate, a core of houses of stone and wood. However, much of it, unlike neighboring Binondo, was a settlement of wood and thatch. Hence, during the later decades of Spanish rule, a fifty meter–wide firebreak was opened between Binondo, which was of solid materials, and Tondo, which had plenty of thatched and bamboo houses.[6] Fire from settlements with light, combustible materials (*materiales ligeros*) had to be kept from spreading to those with sturdier materials (*materiales fuertes*). "Boundary" in Spanish is *divisoria*. Thus the name of the huge market complex today, Divisoria, which is Manila's major wholesale complex.

The Warrior Child is the appropriate patron of Tondo for another reason. True, the Infant Jesus was brought in by the colonialists, but once upon a time He may have signified liberation from oppression. The settlement has a long history of resistance against oppression, whether foreign or local. After Soliman was dislodged by Legazpi from Manila, he rallied his allies and fought the invaders at Bangkusay Channel in Tondo but was defeated.[7] By 1574, the friendship between the Spaniards and Lakandula had soured. The latter led an attack on the former but stopped when assured that he and his descendants would be exempt from taxation.[8] However, in 1587–1588, Tondo chiefs and their allies in Manila, Pandacan, and Pulo, led by Magat Salamat (son of Lakandula), Agustín de Legazpi (nephew of Lakandula), and Martin Panga, led a revolt against the Spaniards. The revolt was crushed. The leaders were beheaded, and their allies exiled to New Spain.[9] Centuries later, on 3 July 1892, José Rizal, upon his definitive return to the islands, organized La Liga Filipina so that Filipinos would have a vehicle with which to press for meaningful reforms.[10] Present were Andrés Bonifacio and Apolinario Mabini. The authorities reacted by exiling Rizal to Dapitan. In anger, Bonifacio, a son of Tondo, organized the Katipunan four days later at 72 Calle Azcarraga (now Recto) in nearby San Nicolás to wage an armed

FIG. 414. Throughout the Spanish and American eras, proletarian Tondo was also known as the "Nipa District" as most of its houses were made of wood, bamboo, and thatch.

struggle against Spain. His ideologue was the brilliant Emilio Jacinto, born in Paco but raised in Tondo.[11] Baby-faced and just seventeen years old when he joined the Katipunan he can be regarded as an avatar of the Warrior-Child. During the early twentieth century, Plaza Moriones was the favorite venue for huge rallies by labor unions seeking social justice. The first Communist Party of the Philippines was thus born in 1930 in this working class district.[12] Amado V. Hernandez, poet and novelist, who wrote on the struggles of the workingman, came from Tondo.

Some still existing sites and structures form an urban landscape, a context within which this activism unfolded. Andrés Bonifacio (1863–1897) was born in a house in the Tutuban area close to where the railroad station would be built in 1887 when he was then a young man of twenty-four years.[13] Almost daily he would have seen Tutuban Station. A monument honouring him stands before the station. Being from Tondo, Bonifacio and other Katipuneros would have been baptized at the still-existing parish church. The Katipunan was uncovered by the authorities when Teodoro Patiño told Fr. Mariano Gil, Tondo's parish priest, about its activities.[14] Plaza Moriones, once a dignified park-like venue for conscience-raising rallies, survives but has been ruined by monstrous cement structures now running inexplicably through its middle.

Tondo cradled many literary greats between the middle of the nineteenth century and the first half of the twentieth: José de la Cruz, popularly called Huseng Sisiw, Bienvenido V. Santos, Manuel Principe Bautista, Francisco Arcellana, Andrés Cristobal Cruz, Virginia Moreno, Buenaventura Medina, Rolando Tinio, and Amado V. Hernandez.[15]

FIG. 415. Divisoria Market in the 1920s

It has also been a patron to the visual arts. It was here that in the 1820s, Damian Domingo opened the first academy to train Filipino painters.[16] One of the most original painters in Southeast Asia during the twentieth century, Hernando Ocampo, came from Tondo. When Emmanuel Torres and I visited him at his house in 1962, he told us that he drew inspiration from the sights in his neighborhood to create abstractions that pulsated and glowed from within.

Tondo has not always been strictly proletarian. While large swaths of the area may have been working-class areas before 1945, areas like Gagalangin (literally "Honorable" or "Respectable"), where the famous couturier José Moreno and his poetess-sister Virginia grew up, used to have a very bourgeois ambience. As in other pre-1950s neighborhoods, rich, middle class, and poor once lived side by side in Tondo. This changed after World War II when Manila became the nerve center of the country's industrialization. Thousands of migrants came by ship, escaping poverty in the countryside, only to find that in the city, jobs were not always available, wages were insufficient, and housing was scarce. Makeshift dwellings sprouted in large parts of Tondo and nearby San Nicolas, both located near the harbor. The well-off began to flee. Post-1950s Tondo was soon associated with another type of warrior: gangs of young men, mired in poverty, fighting each other to death over a turf. But it is unfair to imagine the entire district as an unsafe slum, once epitomized by its most notorious landmark, the "Smokey Mountain" of Tondo. As in other parts of Manila, there remain neighborhoods where the stranger can walk around freely and safely. Indeed Tondeños themselves distinguish between Tondo 1 (just behind Divisoria) and Tondo 2 (roughly

FIG. 416. Tondo Church c. 1900

north of Pritil and which includes the Gagalangin area). The latter is supposedly orderly in comparison to the first.

Let us also note that for all the upper class snootiness about Tondo, the wealthy do go shopping in Divisoria's vast market to look for that rare but cheap item, like lace or suiting material, found nowhere else in the city. Class prejudice is no match vis-à-vis the profit motive.

Dedicated to the Sto. Niño, the **Tondo Church** houses one of the oldest parishes in the country. The Augustinian Martín de Rada baptized Lakandula. Around 1611, a convent was built. The church and its convent were completed circa 1625. However, in 1661, Governor Manrique de Lara ordered it demolished for fear that the Chinese warrior Koxinga might use its stone walls as a fortification during an attack. Another church was built but was destroyed by a 1740 earthquake. Though rebuilt shortly after, the new church fell apart in the 1863 earthquake.[17] The existing structure was built in 1863 by Luciano Oliver, who also designed Taal Basilica, San Sebastian Basilica, and Malabon Church. The approach to the church is magnificent, for the church rises on a high stone platform with a wide series of steps in front and on the north side.

As in Taal and Malabon, the style chosen by Oliver was Neoclassicism. The façade's triangular pediment rises between two perfectly symmetrical towers. Both towers have decorative pediments near their crown that repeat the façade's triangular pediment. Six wide Ionic-inspired pilasters rise uninterrupted from the pedestal to the base of the towers and the pediment, imparting a sense of gravitas. The severity is softened somewhat by the round arches of the three entry doors, two niches and

FIG. 417-418. Tondo Church: Side aisle (left), retablo de Sto. Niño (right)

the window over the middle door. A round dome rises over the church's crossing. Unfortunately, the interior has been heavily altered by insensitive eyes and hands. The usual problems of post-1970s Philippine churches are repeated here. Parts of the interior walls have been stripped of lime plaster and substituted with faux adobe facings. Inexplicably, two windows overlooking the high altar have been framed by this faux adobe facing. The result is visually heavy.

It was in this church that key figures of Philippine history, like Andrés Bonifacio and other Katipuneros, were baptized, for Tondo was their parish and many of the Katipuneros came from this area.

CLARO RECTO AVENUE (FORMERLY AZCARRAGA)

This is one of the longest avenues in Manila. It connects five districts and honors the indomitable statesman who roused his countrymen to the dangers of allowing US Bases to remain in the islands.

In the middle of the the nineteenth century, the Spanish government launched projects to make the interior of Luzon easily accessible to commerce and thus spur development. Heretofore the rivers had been the favorite transport channels, but they did not penetrate wide swaths of plains and forests. The newest transport technology—the steam locomotive—promised to connect Manila and Dagupan in Pangasinan to open up the still-forested interior of the Central Plain of Luzon. British expertise was brought in. Eventually the Manila Railway Company Ltd., a

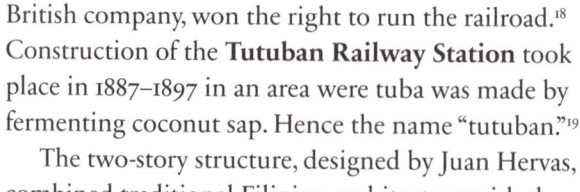

FIG. 419-421. Tutuban Railway Station (top); British steam locomotive Kerr-Stuart 777 from 1905 in front of new PNR terminal (middle left); cast-iron column of the former train shed (bottom left)

British company, won the right to run the railroad.[18] Construction of the **Tutuban Railway Station** took place in 1887–1897 in an area were tuba was made by fermenting coconut sap. Hence the name "tutuban."[19]

The two-story structure, designed by Juan Hervas, combined traditional Filipino architecture with the latest technology. It was larger, of course, than the usual house. Its front has many bays and has three projecting pavilions. As in the usual Filipino house, the ground story has brick walls while the upper story was of wood with generous media aguas over the windows. But the Industrial Age is clearly present in the "extensive use of clear glass for the windows, metal brackets to support the skirt roofs which surround the building, cast-iron columns with stylized Corinthian capitals to support the huge area for waiting passengers."[20]

The railway played a vital role during the struggle for independence. Revolutionaries attacked it for transporting Spanish colonial troops. During the war with the Americans, Filipino troops themselves used the trains to ferry troops and supplies.[21] Under US rule,

FIG. 422-425. Tutuban train sheds (top); details of windows and canopy brackets (middle left and right); new terminal building proposed in the 1930s, but never realized (bottom)

FIG. 426-430. Facets of Tondo: Plaza Moriones with bust of Domingo Franco Tuason (top left), one of the "13 Martyrs of Bagumbayan," who were executed in 1897 for their role in the Philippine Revolution; NHI marker for Domingo Tuason (top right); window canopies (center left); Baldoza ("Machuca") floor tiles (bottom left); Sala of an elegant prewar house in Tondo (bottom right)

the line was extended north and south, making it easier to transport rice, sugar and other goods. With independence, the Manila Railroad Company was converted into the Philippine National Railways (PNR).

When the PNR transferred its offices to its Caloocan and Paco compounds, it allowed the Tutuban Properties, Inc. (TPI) to redevelop the station.[22] The latter converted the interior into a shopping center, strategically located near Divisoria, while preserving its tall cast-iron columns, its large, generously curving iron brackets, and its wooden floors. It is an excellent example of adaptive reuse.

FIG. 431. El Porvenir (ELPO) Building

Tondo, too, has its share of early twentieth-century Filipino-style houses. However, these are much fewer than in other districts, probably because the district was always more proletarian in nature than its southern neighbors, and beginning in the 1950s many homeowners left. The houses are not particularly concentrated and are dispersed throughout. To avoid repetitiveness, let us explore the district by quadrants.

On **907 Recto corner Planas** is the magnificent **El Porvenir Building** (meaning "The Future") from 1933. Measuring four bays by three and rising to a height of three stories with a superstructure above, the building exhibits a trait common in some local examples of Art Deco: plain pilasters that rise to the full height of the building and that divide the bays neatly from each other. But because the pilasters are rusticated in treatment, that is, they occur in blocks, the result is an interesting edgy rhythm.

FIG. 432. 1317-1321 Balintawak

BALINTAWAK—A. RIVERA—BENAVIDES—LA TORRE—FERNANDO GUERRERO-MASANGKAY

Balintawak was where the Revolution against Spain was launched on 24 August 1896. It is not clear who Rivera was that is honoured. On the other hand it was on this street that Honorio López, a young lieutenant-colonel of the Revolutionary Army, subdued the Spanish stronghold in 1896.[23] Miguel de Benavidez OP was the founder of the University of Sto. Tomás. Guillermo Masangkay, a Tondeño, was a general in the Revolution.[24] Fernando Guerrero was a nationalistic poet who joined in the war against the Americans. He is remembered for his beautiful poem in Spanish praising the Philippines. This cluster of streets lies in the southeast section of the district. Close to Tutuban and Divisoria, it presents a striking contrast in its relative stillness and order.

On **1317-1321 Balintawak** is a Wood-and-Brick rowhouse with three bays and three front windows, probably from the 1920s. A metal canopy protects each window and has perforated fringes. Between the windows and the edges are tall vertical bandejas. Ornate ventanilla grills feature pairs of taro leaves which most likely are really very pointed interpretations of the lotus leaf. Espejos were originally all of glass but some now have plexiglass. The roof eaves have cut-out vents in floral patterns.

FIG. 433. 1318–1322 Rivera

On **1387 Balintawak** is a house from circa mid-1930s. This is an all-wood house with thin strips of wood laid horizontally: a media agua hangs over each of the two front windows, turned wooden balusters frame the ventanillas, frosted colored glass window enliven the triangular-peaked espejos. The media agua has cut-out figures that resemble watermelon slices with seeds. An exterior staircase invites us into the house and suggests that Tondo in the 1920s and 1930s was a tranquil and safe place.

The Wood-and-Brick house on **1318–1320 A. Rivera** from circa the late 1930s in bandeja style has three bays in front and the usual media aguas and grilled ventanillas. Each panel of the grill features a fleur-de-lis, shooting from abstract acanthus leaves. A daisy opens above the fleur and a rosette below it. Each bay is defined by a pilaster with floral capitals. Instead of a wide stretch of glass to create an espejo, it has unusual four-pointed star openings.

The three-story Wood-and-Stone house with mezzanine appeared in nineteenth-century Binondo, as we saw, in response to land scarcity. It also appeared in some streets outside it, as in the house at **1448 Rivera corner Mayhaligue**, a simple, but huge accessoria from the 1920s or 1930s.

The house on **1128 La Torre corner Fernando Guerrero** is tall, chamfered, and made of wood above and cement bricks below. It has three bays (including the corner one) on each side. This house is just a few minutes' walk from busy Tutuban Shopping Center. It was originally intended to be a row house as suggested by several

FIG. 434-435. 1128 La Torre cor. Guerrero (top); 1216 Masangkay (bottom)

FIG. 436. Railroad Signal Tower, J. Abad Santos. Signal towers ensure that passing trains run on schedule and on the correct track, by means of mechanical signals by the operator in the tower to the train driver. Today, electronic communication and computerization have rendered most signal towers obsolete.

street doors on both sides. It continues to have capiz windows. Walls in between have bandejas. The ventanilla grills feature sunbursts. These, plus the cement bricks, suggest a construction date of the late 1920s to early 1930s. The series of cut-out concentric circles in the fringes of the window canopies evoke the tabletop radios that became commonplace in the 1930s: rounded silhouettes with rounded screens.

Another noteworthy chamfered building in the area is a house at the **corner of Balintawak and La Torre.** This circa 1930s house is sprawling with two-by-four bays. A media agua wraps around the entire façade.

Juana Lopez had the house on **1216 Masangkay** built in the 1930s. This two-story rowhouse in Wood-and-Brick has three bays, the middle of which has a triangular pediment for dignity. The result nonetheless is still homey thanks to the wide windows with sliding glass panels and the Art Deco ventanilla grills with their typical sunburst patterns. At one point the house served as storage for tobacco. Today it is still a beautiful residence, though needing some repairs.

Mina House on **2421 Reyes** is a conventional two-story detached Wood-and-Stone house in the bandeja style. An interesting contrast is at play between the row of plain verticals in the two espejos and the curving tendrils of the ventanilla grills.

FIG. 437-438. Tondo Intermediate School today (top); in the 1920s (bottom)

JOSE ABAD SANTOS

José Abad Santos was the Chief Justice who was executed for refusing to cooperate with the Japanese invaders.

This busy main road has a landmark on the west side. **1347–1351 J. Abad Santos corner La Torre,** a corner Wood-and-Cement house from the 1920s or 1930s, is unusual in having a third story, although its trademark top floor may be a later addition. It has three bays on both sides. The style is horizontal-and-vertical: a large canopy or media agua running continuously over the windows, large sliding shell panels at the windows, grills over the ventanillas.

A two-story **Railroad Signal Tower,** presumably from 1905, stands alongside the rails at J. Abad Santos, and is described as "one of the few remaining structures of the Manila Railroad Company Antipolo Extension (from Tutuban to Pasig) ... [which] was opened on 22 December 1905 making this segment from Abad Santos Signal Tower to Pandacan the oldest railroad segment still in use here in the Philippines."[25] The wooden upper story does not cantilever but recedes vis-à-vis the brick ground

FIG. 439. 1401 Zamora cor. Pavia

story, thus highlighting the latter's stockiness; the metal hip roof sits squarely on this short tower-like structure. All these plus a square footprint convey the image of a solid and reassuring sentinel. Sliding glass windows on all four sides allow the guard to look out at the trains. Inside, British-made signal levers and locking mechanisms made by Saxby & Farmer, London, England, are still intact (most of the technical equipment of railroads all over the world was then supplied by England, in those days the leading industrial nation of the world). The signal tower was recently restored by the Railways and Industrial Heritage Society of the Philippines, a local NGO devoted to the country's industrial heritage.[26]

NICOLAS ZAMORA

Eager to organize a church that would spread the Word of God, and yet be run by Filipinos themselves, Nicolas Zamora, descendant of the martyred Padre Jacinto Zamora, founded a Methodist Evangelical Church in 1909.[27]

William Parsons's works are all over Manila, sometimes in the most unexpected places. An example is the **Tondo Intermediate School**, built in 1909 between **N. Zamora and Juan Luna**. Located behind the Tondo Catholic church, it is an unassuming two-story building of concrete, marked by three tall pediment gables rising high above Zamora street. Typical of Parsons, the school is largely devoid of any ornamentation save of decorative urns on said gables. Parsons's trademark round arches can still be found on the ground floor. Largely originally preserved the building today houses the Isabelo delos Reyes Elementary School.

At **1765 N. Zamora corner Calle Dandan** is a wonderful example of the "mother-and-child" roof silhouette. Painted in off-white, the front pavilion juts forward into an

FIG. 440-441. St. Paul United Methodist Church (top); Stained glass window (bottom)

enclosed garden. Behind it is the rest of the house with a slightly higher gable roof. There is a subtle interplay between the sharp triangular gables and the horizontals of both the narrow wall boards of the second story and the tile canopies generously protruding over the windows. As is often the case, lace grills over the ventanillas enliven the texture of the entire ensemble, which likely dates back to the 1920s or 1930s.

Nearby, the house at **1401 Zamora corner Pavia** is an elaborate example of the Neo-Spanish style that emerged in the late 1920s and 1930s, and remained popular with the elite until the 1950s. The building was supposedly owned by a Chinese immigrant from Macau, who ran a bakery on the ground floor (many bakeries flourished after the war when flour was sold at very low prices). Typical of the style, pre-cast floral reliefs adorn the façade, while the rounded corner sports a pair of solomonic columns underneath a curved gable which in turn sports a medallion with initials, presumably those of the original owner. The protruding central risalit facing Zamora and the stepped attic are reminiscent of the Art Deco style that was popular then.

STA. MARIA—MORGA—RAJAH SOLIMAN

Antonio Morga's *Sucesos de las Islas Filipinas* was eagerly studied and annotated by Rizal because of the balanced view it gave of Filipinos at Spanish contact. Rajah Soliman was the last ruler of prehispanic Manila. Gallantly, but unsuccessfully, he defied Spanish attempts at colonizing his domain.

Protestant churches in the islands propagated a Neo-Gothic look that was inspired by those of New England and Britain. An example is the **St. Paul United Methodist Church**, built in 1930. Founded in 1900, this is the first Protestant church in Tondo, established solely by Filipinos. The first

FIG. 442. St. Paul United Methodist Church, interior

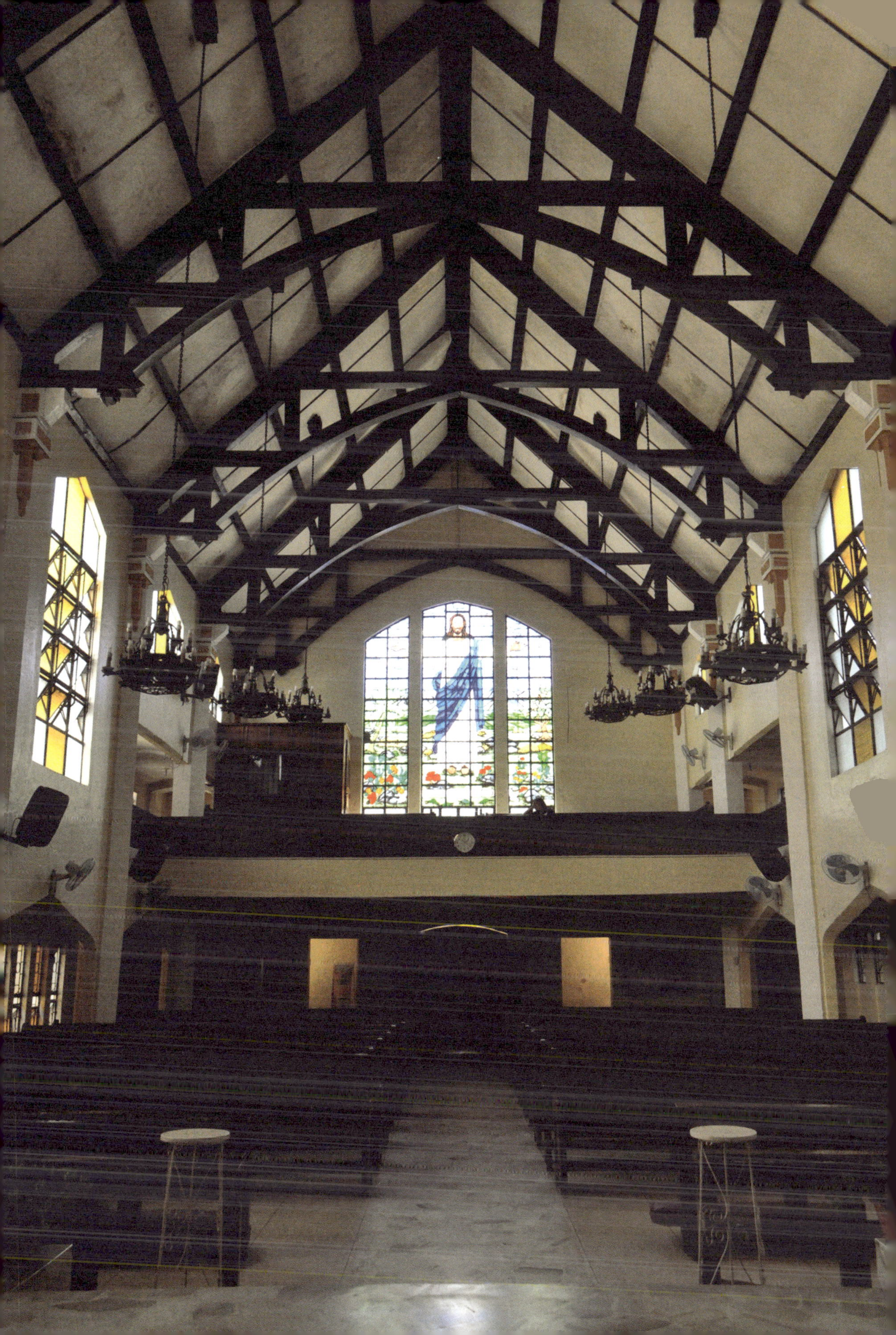

FIG. 443-444. Cathedral of the Evangelical Methodist Church (Bartolome House) (top); balcony (bottom)

building of thatch and bamboo, sponsored by a local fisherman was called Bangkusay Methodist Episcopal Church (MEC).[28] The affinity between this and the United Methodist Church, built in Ermita in 1932, is obvious. St. Paul has its own distinct appeal. Reflecting the Art Deco spirit, the arch of the central grand window over the portal is almost triangular in shape and is flanked by two monumental pylons.

Another place of worship at **Calle Sta. Maria Street corner Morga** is the Cathedral of the Evangelical Methodist Church in the Philippine Islands also known as the **Bartolome House** from 1938 to 1939. Following the separation of Church and State under the Americans, devout Filipinos began their own churches that focused on the Word of God. An example is the *Iglesia Metodista Evangélica en las Islas Filipinas*, founded in 1909 by Nicolas Zamora.[29] The aim was to have a Methodist Church that was run not by American missionaries but by Filipinos themselves. As it was originally built as a residential mansion of the Bartolome family, and only occasionally used for church services,

FIG. 445-448. Bartolome House: Sala (top left); balcony doors (top right); elaborate grill work (bottom left); staircase (bottom right)

the structure does not fit the usual stereotype of a church building. Occupying a corner, the two-story concrete building has three bays on one side and five on another and looks more like a combination of mansion and office building. There is an entry at the building's rounded corner under a half-moon balcony protected by a half-moon canopy surmounted by a short round turret. Quite original! Interesting also is the combination of Art Deco massing, exemplified by the turret, with classic Neo-Spanish design elements such as solomonic columns, medallions, and pre-cast reliefs and ornamentation.

An early example of the Gabaldon type of school is the **Magat Salamat Elementary School**, established 1907. A colonnade of round arches that form a protective loggia before the main entrance welcomes the students as they enter. Round medallions decorate the spandrels. The school is located at the confluence of three streets: Sta. Maria, Sande, and Pavia.

FIG. 449. Magat Salamat Elementary School

For completeness, we included some examples of the International Style in the Philippines, despite their sometimes-doubtful artistic merits. But the presumably 1950s villa at **Morga corner Soliman** is definitely visually arresting. The articulated stairwell lit up with one long vertical window was a favorite of the 1940s–1950s. It is used here to integrate all three stories into one unity. Two of these stories have open porches that cantilever to the right of the stairwell. Since the third-story porch is much shorter than the second underneath it, the effect is like seeing a monumental staircase.

TAYUMAN

Tayum is an indigenous term for "Indigo," an important source of blue dyes. There must have been an extensive garden here of indigo plants. Dominating this busy main street, running north-south, is another Gabaldon-type schoolhouse: the **Rizal Elementary School** from 1917 with the typical colonnade of round arches at the entry, similar to the Magat Salamat Elementary School.

FIG. 450-451. Rizal Elementary School (top); hallway (bottom)

VELASQUEZ–NEPOMUCENO

As in neighboring San Nicolás, this street probably honors Antonio Velasquez, one of the defenders of Manila against Limahong.[30] Julián Nepomuceno headed the Katipunan.[31]

The house on **380 Nepomuceno** was constructed for **Mariano Mangalonzo** probably in the 1910s or 1920s. This is a single-detached house with two bays and two windows in front over which a continuous media agua runs. The ground story must have been constructed of brick sometime in the 1900s but now has a decorative adobe facing. Its windows have been altered and reduced to one-third their original size. Fortunately, the upper story with its tall and narrow bandejas framing each window and the discreetly distributed curled grills over the ventanillas have been preserved.

FIG. 452-453. Emilio Jacinto Elementary School

The **Emilio Jacinto Elementary School** on **Velasquez** is a refreshing new take on the Gabaldon mode. Built in 1931, it has the Art Deco features of its time. Accentuating a two-story pavilion that juts out slightly from a long façade is a finely made portal with a trapezoidal arch. Above it is a glass window with square medallions on both sides. There is, however, a dark side to this bright building: during World War II the school was taken over by the Imperial Japanese army as a garrison, and became the site of much torture and rape. Heavily damaged during the Liberation of Manila, it was rebuilt in 1947.

JUAN LUNA

Once again, as in Binondo, we meet the great nineteenth-century painter, for this very long street spans two districts.

An unusually elegant corner house, number **2325 Juan Luna,** with three bays by two and with two stories, shows off fine lace grills. Thin pilasters dividing the walls between windows suggest the 1910s as the probable period of origin.

The all-wood accessoria on **2514–2518 Juan Luna** with six bays and two stories was built in 1935 by Dr. Carriedo. Pilasters define each bay. On both sides of each pilaster are appliqués of long and thin floral stems ending in abstract, square-shaped flowers redolent of the Viennese Secession. The windows now have sliding glass panels. Below are ventanilla grills in two types of designs: one vaguely evokes a bee with its stretched wings—two volutes at the center from which straight lines radiate to curl at the corners of the ventanilla. The other design is simpler, consisting of a series of bars with volutes at the center of the entire grill. Each window has a protective canopy above it.

The **Moreno House on 2457 (formerly 1999) Juan Luna** was the birthplace of two famous artists. José Moreno, popularly called Pitoy, was a couturier with superb taste who clothed celebrities both in the islands and abroad in the 1960s to

TONDO: WARRIOR HAVEN 349

FIG. 454-457. Houses of Tondo: Moreno House (top left and right); 2728 Juan Luna (middle right); 2514-2518 Juan Luna (bottom)

FIG. 458-460. Windows of Tondo

the 1990s. His sister Virginia is a renowned poetess. Her poems ("Batik Weavers") and drama ("The Onyx Wolf"), both literary landmarks, were conceived in the house. The structure has three bays on the street front. The upper story is of wood and features sliding windows of glass. Protecting them is a continuous media agua. The ventanilla grills represent clusters of honeysuckles, a favorite motif of the 1930s, fanning outwards and downwards. The cement ground story has three street doors that suggest possible use as shops. A very large yard opens to the south and to the rear of the house. According to Virginia Moreno, the house was transferred from Quiapo to its present site sometime in the first or second decade of the American era, hence its origins may date back as far as the nineteenth century.

FIG. 461-462. 2325 Juan Luna (bottom); window detail (top)

FIG. 463-464. 2116 Juan Luna cor. Trinidad (top and bottom)

Dominating the street is the imposing house at **2728 Juan Luna** with three bays abutting the street, a fourth one at the rear; large wall boards between sliding capiz windows; rich ornamentation on the boards and on the iron ventanilla grills; a continuous canopy casting a cool shadow over the windows; and a large hipped roof. The house conveys a fullness of form. It was likely built around the 1910s.

Albeit dilapidated and much modified, traces of the former grandeur of the mansion on **2116 Juna Luna corner Trinidad** are still visible. Likely dating from the 1920s or 1930s, this Concrete-and-Wood villa is set in the middle of a vast compound, which must once have been a lush garden. The building is characterized by its elegant protruding two-story verandah (now walled up) facing Juan Luna, complete with metal balustrades depicting birds and deer. Particularly elegant are the metal canopies on the wooden upper floor, carried by very ornate curving metal brackets in Art Nouveau style. Today, the building houses an Ang Dating Daan ("The Former Path") community center, a religious broadcasting program of the Members Church of God International.

FIG. 465. 1029 Solis cor. Molave

BULACAN–SOLIS–MOLAVE

Bulacan honors the Tagalog province just north of Tondo and a cradle of great Filipino leaders. The Marquis of Obando, after whom a town in Bulacan was named, was José Francisco de Obando y Solis.[32] The Molave tree, famed for its toughness, has become a symbol of the Filipino. This part of Tondo is locally called Gagalangin, where many elite families used to live. Many of them have since moved out. Nonetheless some quiet streets remain where houses form picturesque postcard-like ensembles.

The former **Almeda House** on **520 Bulacan** was built in 1937 by a former director of the National Bureau of Investigation. The house is of wood in the upper story and cement bricks in the lower. It is compact: one large bay with a narrow bay on the west side. Light pink-colored bandejas frame the windows. The sliding windows are of white, green, and yellow frosted glass in tartan patterns—large rectangles framed by smaller ones. The espejo above repeats the rectangles in the same colors. A continuous canopy extends over the large front window underneath a large Swiss-style jerkin roof above. Hence the coolness that the present owner loves about her house.

Constructed probably in the late 1920s or early 1930s this two-story detached house on **622 Bulacan** is largely of wood consisting of long strips laid horizontally. Unlike most of the old houses in Tondo, its roof is gabled. The house front thus has a triangular pediment—which unfortunately has been covered with a metal sheet for protection. The formal air of the pediment is reinforced by the presence of pilasters at the corners. The front has two bays with sliding window panels and grilled ventanillas.

FIG. 466. 2712 Molave. (Source: Mia Quimpo/Dewey Sergio/NCCA)

The latter has fan patterns while the glass espejos are arched. The ground-story wall is of cement with geometric designs typical of Art Deco.

Originally owned by Catalino Mendoza, a dermatologist, **1013 Bulacan corner Paterno** is a chamfered-corner, two-story wood-and-masonry residential house probably from the 1930s. It was designed in the horizontal-and-vertical style typical of its time: capiz windows, ventanilla grills, and wooden slats over the eaves.

The house on **1029 Solis corner Molave** is another chamfered corner. It has four bays on Solis and two on Molave. This is a two-story Wood-and-Stone house in the horizontal-and-vertical style. It has sliding glass windows and wooden jalousies, glass espejos and ventanilla grills. Judging by its design and details the house was built sometime in the 1930s: One bay facing Solis street has an unexpected trapezoidal, Swiss-style roof. Directly underneath, a wooden sunburst is appliquéd to the walls. The sunburst is repeated on the ventanilla grills, though framed by Art Deco honeysuckles. Do these display the patriotic fervor that burned brightly when the Commonwealth was inaugurated in 1935? Semi-circular cuts evoking 1930s radio sets appear in the cut-out fringes of the canopies over second-floor windows.

The house on **2712 Molave** is a quiet haven within busy Tondo. It was built probably in the 1930s for the **Castaño** family whose patriarch was an official in the Department of Education. This two-story villa with wooden bandejas has a beautiful garden with palm trees to one side. The front has three bays with sliding windows, ventanillla grills, and a wide, continuous media agua that runs around the house.

Impressive is the wide frontage of **2729 Molave**—two large bays—framed at both ends by transitional spaces: on the southside by a porch overlooking a garden, on the north a small balcony. The two front gables group together in a mother-and-child fashion. The upper story is of wood, the lower story of cement that has been covered with brick tiles from the 1990s. Capiz windows line the upper story framed by the wall's bandeja panels. With good intentions the wooden story has been given a "natural" finish. Unfortunately, the result is a dark, gloomy look. At the same time its brown finish does not go with the brick tiles of the story below. An outstanding feature of this 1920s or 1930s house are the ventanilla grills where fleurs-de-lis spike upwards from within taro leaf designs. Together with the fleur-de-lis spring metal tendrils.

Another **Railroad Signal Tower** guards the rails at Solis. Unlike that at Jose Abad Santos, this one is dilapidated. However, it is fairly intact, and presumably dates from the same period as its twin on Abad Santos (1905).

FIG. 467. Railroad Signal Tower, Solis

The International Style, called "Modern" by Filipinos, became popular as a house style after World War II. However, its clean, sharp lines were married to an older aesthetic, as in the **former Cecilio House** on **2517 Tindalo**, from 1949. With its three-story tower, at first glance this building, erected by Engineer Edilberto Cecilio, looks like a Neo-Spanish house. But, in place of surface décor, it has instead a play of shapes: three two-story vertical windows on one side of the street front; an equally plain horizontal window on the other side; in between the two, a tall, narrow but arched window for the stairwell.

PAMPANGA

Close allies of the rulers of prehispanic Tondo and Manila were the Pampangos. It is fitting that a Tondo street honors that people.

Houses with "mother-and-child" profiles are common all over the Tagalog Region. The **Centeno House,** built in 1932 by civil engineer Jesus Centeno at **1424 Pampanga corner Pamana** is unusual in having one "mother" gable and two more "children" gables under its roof. Hence a profile with strong diagonal rhythms. As counterpoints, sharp vertical finials shoot up from the corner ridge of each gable while the jutting metallic window canopies create strong horizontals, resulting in an emphatic rhythm. This was one of the first houses in the area and later served as a school for some time.

FIG. 468. 2450 S. Reyes. (Source: Mia Quimpo/Dewey Sergio/NCCA)

FERDINAND BLUMENTRITT–TOMÁS MAPUA–SEVERINO REYES

Two long streets, Mapua and S. Reyes, cross Blumentritt in Tondo and in Sta. Cruz's northernmost part. Ferdinand Blumentritt, an Austrian scholar specializing in Philippine studies, became the good friend of José Rizal. He translated the Noli into German and expressed his support for reforms in the islands.

Down to the 1950s when cars finally became more common, neighborhoods close to a railroad station were regarded as prime location because trains—like streetcars—encouraged mobility. Hence it comes as no surprise that, in the now decayed, polluted, and congested area of Blumentritt and Avenida Rizal, there are some magnificent houses. One of them in fact, the Evangelista house, is arguably one of the best-designed houses of prewar Manila.

Though not in mint condition, the house at **2450 S. Reyes** has decorative details that are outstanding. Below the wooden upper story is a ground story that may have been of brick, but now seems cemented. On the street side, the house has three bays and a wide projecting porch with turned wooden balusters. Metal canopies protect the windows in both stories. They are more finely cut than in most other houses. For instance, the fringe of the ground-story window is so intricately cut out that it seems to hang from the rest of the canopy by just a thin support. The fleur-de-lis point downwards in between triangles arranged in a series. Cutwork four-leafed clovers connect the fringe to the canopy's slope. Above each triangle and in between fleur-de-lis and clover is a cutwork representation of perhaps an incense censer. As a whole the hanging fringe recalls one of those lace doilies popular in the living rooms of 1920s

FIG. 469. 2510 Mapua cor. Cavite

to 1930s houses. Below the lintel of the porch hangs an ornamental piece of traceried wood. It is not a flat cut-out, but rather a carefully carved and therefore more intricate design. A simple inscription below the porch states that the house was built in 1930.

Though rotting, the magnificent house at **2510 Mapua corner Cavite** has a commanding presence. It has a T-shaped footprint and stands at the corner, thus allowing itself to be seen from several angles, as well as allowing more light to enter its interior. The upper story is of wooden boards laid out horizontally. The lower story is of concrete stucco finish. It has two bays on the Mapua side and six on Cavite. The use of formal looking pilasters to mark the boundary between each suggests either a 1890s or 1900s date of construction. Wooden arches with colonnettes unfold over each window, and are supported by angular capitals that flare upwards in a somewhat Neo-Romanesque manner. The windows have sliding glass panels with jalousies behind. They have no canopies—perhaps because the jalousies protect the interiors from the sun. Ventanillas have grillwork with volutes. In this ensemble, the espejos call attention, being flower-like circles with short petals. Noteworthy too are the wide eaves with traceries that recall rectangular pastilles whose festive paper wrappers sport elaborate tails at both ends.

Located at **2231 Earnshaw corner Antipolo** is a small, but very charming affair thanks to its glass espejos made of a series of trefoil arches atop each capiz window. Solomonic colonettes and filigree canopy fringes add to the feel of lightness and playfulness.

Built in an unusual composite but picturesque style is circa 1930s–1950s **Fernando House** at **1577 T. Mapua corner Antipolo**. Though Neo-Spanish elements are visible

FIG. 470. Evangelista House

(a chamfered corner tower, a balcony with a trio of arches), it has the feel of a Filipino Wood-and-Stone house thanks to elements such as a projecting upper story, espejos, and decorative vertical trims on the walls between windows. Shops occupy the ground story of this well-situated building.

Enclosed by protective walls, the **Evangelista House**, an unexpected gem at **2459 Avenida Rizal**, was designed in 1929 by renowned Filipino architect Andres Luna de San Pedro for Eugenio and Petrona Evangelista. The traditional contrast between a buoyant upper story of wood and a massive ground story of stone is reprised in this ochre-colored house, though in an original manner, given that it is entirely of reinforced concrete. To create a buoyant upper story, the architect opened its walls with balconies and French doors. On the walls between balconies, he embedded panels of red-orange bricks that create an expansive feel. In contrast to these balconies, in between each window in the ground story are panels of stucco that create a feeling of mass. At the entry, a two-story pavilion advances forward. On the ground story, a portico with a subtle series of receding round arches welcomes the visitor to the main door. Above the portico is a porch over which a trapezoidal gable roof gloriously opens like a parasol. Its expansive mood is highlighted by the false crossbeams that jut out in series over the porch. For accent, as well as ventilation, a wide oculus consisting of a pair of joined trapezoids marks the space between the trapezoidal gable and the crossbeams. In contrast to the trapezoid, an undulating gable, possibly inspired by Japanese models, curves over the portico.

Luna de San Pedro's designing prowess shows in the grills as well. Very Art Deco in feeling, the leitmotifs are shafts of diagonal lines that overlap and form sharply edged Greek frets. Diamond grills enclosing two angular and initialed letters, E-E, appear at the core of the overlaps. For contrast, another favorite Art Deco motif, the flaming line, snakes through the ventanillas and, over the stairwell, a two-story-high stained glass window by the famous glass-maker Kraut.

TONDO: WARRIOR HAVEN 359

FIG. 471-474. Windows of Tondo

FIG. 475-477.
Doors of Tondo

FIG. 478-480. Houses of Tondo: Fernando House (top); 506 Herboso (bottom left); Almeda House (bottom right)

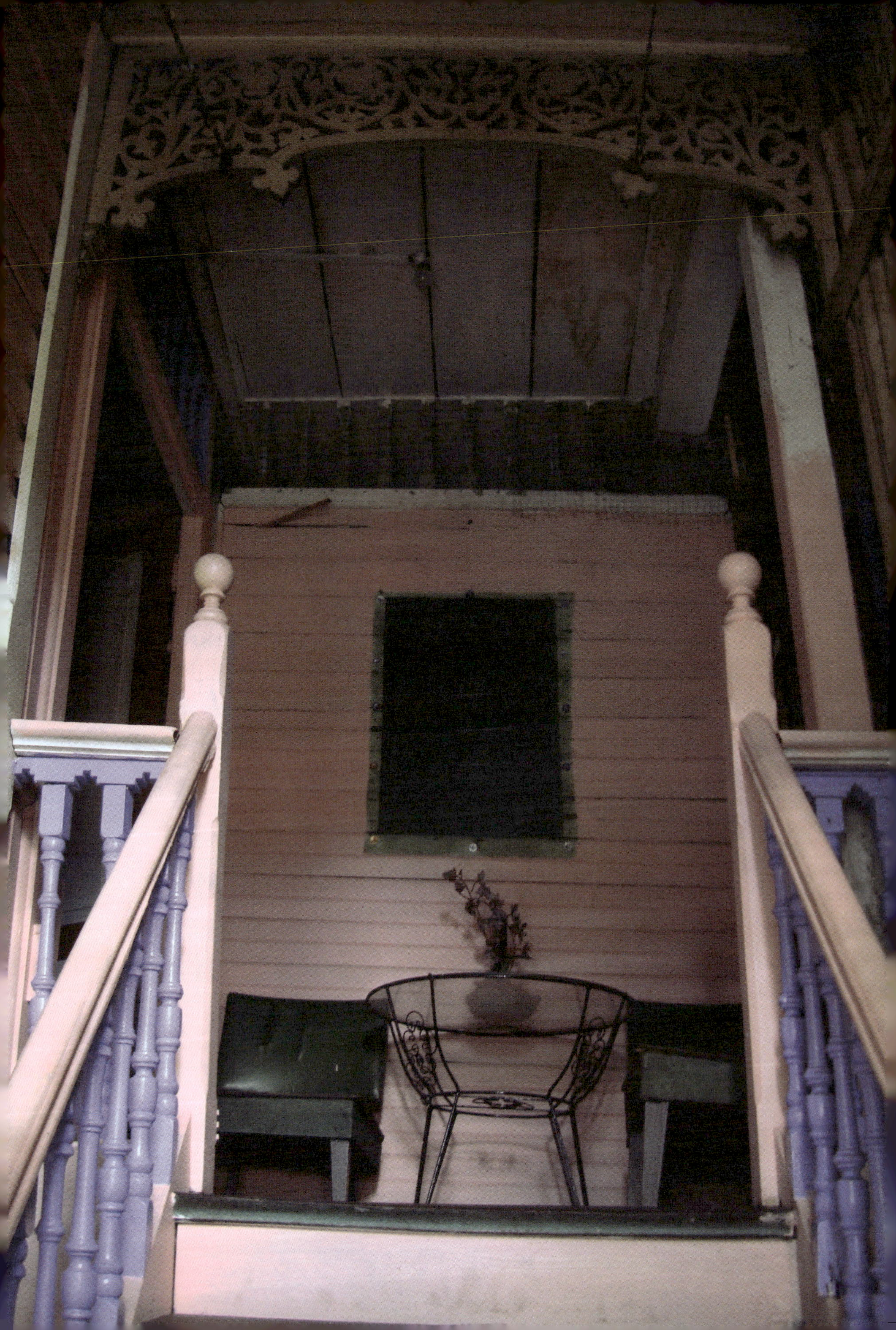

FIG. 481. Rosales House. (Source: Mia Quimpo/Dewey Sergio/NCCA)

OTHER INTERESTING HOUSES

Tondo has several other interesting two-story houses from the 1900s to 1940s. Many are in the classic Filipino Wood-and-Stone style, others in wood in both stories. Many have lace grill ventanillas.

The former **Gonzales House, 630 Gerona** is single-bayed and with a simple gable roof; this circa 1920s house has a compact feel to it. Resembling it is the house at **809 Fullon,** most likely from the same period.

The recently demolished house at **476 Cavite corner Alcalde**, sported fluted pilasters on its wooden upper floor, reminiscent of Art Nouveau. This, and the triangular glass espejos, suggest the 1910s to 1920s. Together they gave the house an ornate feel despite its relative simplicity.

The nine-bay shop house on **637–653 Moriones,** was built in the late 1930s or early 1940s by businessman Antonio Rivera. It continues to have an arcade over the sidewalk with wooden columns. This feature, plus the ventanillas and wide window canopies, expresses a gracious concern for the pedestrian, painfully absent nowadays.

On Moriones Extension along the estero facing Tutuban stood the **Destileria La Fortuna,** a prewar industrial site consisting of a series of green sheds covered in GI sheets. Here was produced the "Crema de Menta" (crème de menthe, a mint-flavored alcoholic liquor) and other alcoholic beverages popular during the American and postwar era.

A refined version of the above from circa 1935 is the former **Rosales House** at **290 Guidote** built by Bedastro Rosales, a lumber dealer with business in Mindoro and Masbate. Rectangular bandejas appear all over the walls but are painted an off-

FIG. 482. Constantino House

white. The house has three bays facing the street. The middle one projects slightly beyond the two other bays, resulting in a very elegant profile.

506 Herbosa, from circa the 1930s, is well-preserved. The middle bay (among three) is formed as a risalit with a short gable over it rising from the rest of the hip roof. Underneath sliding glass windows are richly conceived geometric ventanilla grills. Similar to it are the **Bernal House** (1913) at **782 Endaya** and the **Constantino House** at **1149 Narra.** The latter, together with its neighbour, is one of the most beautiful houses in Tondo. Classic Art Deco sunburst grills, which still bear the initials of the owner, and colored glass espejos indicate that it was built in the 1930s. Its protruding central risalit crowned by a pediment gable and resting on elaborate corbels, give this relatively small house in the bandeja style a feel of both stateliness and playful elegance. The no less elegant house to its right side at **1153–1157** probably also dates from the 1930s or 1920s. Three equal bays are marked by protruding metal canopies with perforated fringes, above which rise arched glass espejos. The roof space is ventilated by ornamental roof eave vents of perforated metal sheets, giving the house a light and airy feel.

Aside from the above, Calle **Narra** has other beautiful row houses, such as the equally elaborate house **at 1409 Narra** from the 1930s. Beautifully carved brackets carry a media agua which wraps around the upper floor, and is bordered by pierced fringes. Today the house, built in the bandeja style, is squeezed in by tall modern concrete buildings on all sides. Also with wide bandejas are a 1935 house at **J. Abad**

Santos, the house at **2427 Baldwin**, and **2429 Tirso Cruz corner Callejon T**, all of which likely date from the 1920s to the 1930s.

Calle Perfecto has three well-preserved houses from the 1910s to 1920s, all of them with cantilevering upper stories, ventanillas, and canopies. These are the 1930s **Abad House** at **1763 Perfecto**, which was transferred to its present location from Dagupan. It is particularly noteworthy for its elaborate carved brackets which frame its front windows, and the ornamental fringes of its canopies.

Another is the **Tionloc House** at **1809 Perfecto**, built in 1922 by Ildefonso Tionloc, a trader, and the former **Panenta House**, at **1731 Perfecto**, well-preserved and charming.

Sadly, the house standing tall at **1349 Mayhaligue corner Callejon dela Cruz**, said to have been built in 1924, is in an advanced stage of decay, but once must have been an imposing sight. Typical of the time, ventanilla grills and colonettes below glass espejos adorn the façade.

FIG. 483-484. 1153–1157 Narra (top); 1409 Narra (bottom)

FIG. 485-486. 1417 Sanchez cor. Mayhaligue (top); 1443-1445 Sanchez (bottom)

At **1417 Sanchez corner Mayhaligue** is the **Tanganan House** which, though somewhat faded, remains very attractive because of its ornate Art Deco grills and upper-story wooden walls. This house is said to have been erected in 1939 and shows all the architectural trademarks typical of the era: long bandejas stretching from floor to ceiling, sliding glass windows, and arched glass espejos above metal canopies with decorative fringes. Above, ornamental metal roof eaves complete the picture of an imposing prewar residence.

FIG. 487. 1216 Batangas (Aquino House)

Also on **Sanchez (1443–1445)**, the **Pilande House** is a simple but dignified affair, built in 1936 by the couple Severino and Sabina Pilande. Well maintained, it sports metal roof eaves panels in floral design, which match the delicate fringes of the media agua protecting the front façade from the elements. The sunburst motif of the ventanilla grills is typical of 1930s Art Deco.

2506 Bato corner Callejon M is a well-preserved and very charming 1920s or 1930s house with a jerkin-head roof, which became popular all over the archipelago at that time.

Of similar style is the **Toledo House** at **3504 Del Rosario**, built in 1927 by Ines and Agapito Toledo who was a chef in the US Navy. Although the house was remodeled in 1945–1948, its classic prewar features are still evident: traceried media agua, metal ventanilla grills, and wooden tongue-and-groove walling.

Very different from the rest of these houses is the **Aquino House** at **1216 Batangas**, built by businessman Felipe Aquino in the early 1930s. Its two middle bays are framed by two corner bays topped by a gable each, for emphasis. Most vintage buildings in this area date from the 1920s and 1930s, when Manila experienced a major construction boom.

At Buendia is a small but very picturesque 1920s to 1930s corner house: **2339/266 Buendia corner Younger.**

On Lico Street, two neighboring houses deserve mention: The **Latorre House**, built in 1926 by government employee Catalino Latorre and his wife Angela Barinque on **2739 Lico**, is an unpretentious but charming Wood-and-Stone house marked by its exterior staircase leading to an open entrance porch on the upper floor, and served as set for movies. Nearby, the **Navarro House** at **2741 Lico** was commissioned by businesswoman Encarnacion Navarra in the mid-1930s and once housed the Mariano

FIG. 488-489. 619 Cavite cor. Tirso Cruz (top); 2506 Bato cor. Callejon M (bottom)

Ponce Elementary School on its ground floor. Like its neighbor, it sports an exterior staircase and porch, giving it an inviting air.

Tondo has houses that do not fit the Wood-and-Stone style. An example is the beautiful mansion overlooking the corner of **619 Cavite and Tirso Cruz.** The 1930s house, built probably in the early 1930s by Victorino Tanlayco, a physician, has an irregular footprint. Pavilions abut, some with their own roof. One has a triangular gable, another a jerkin head. The whole is unified by a three-story mirador tower designed by Rufino Antonio on one side of the house with a large hipped roof.

TONDO: WARRIOR HAVEN 369

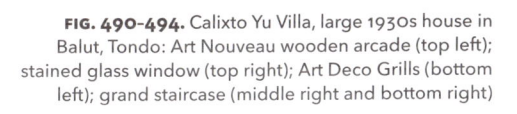

FIG. 490-494. Calixto Yu Villa, large 1930s house in Balut, Tondo: Art Nouveau wooden arcade (top left); stained glass window (top right); Art Deco Grills (bottom left); grand staircase (middle right and bottom right)

370 ENDANGERED SPLENDOR

FIG. 495-498. Tondo Evangelical Church (top left and bottom); Westminster High School (top right); IEMELIF Church (middle right, by Hannachiever07, image licensed under Creative Commons Attribution-Share Alike 3.0 Unported, see p. 394)

FIG. 499 Iglesia de Jesucristo Templo de Caridad Jerusalem

TONDO NEO-GOTHIC

In addition to the Methodist St. Paul Church, described above are two other medieval-inspired structures: the **Tondo Evangelical Church** from 1950, the oldest Presbyterian congregation in the Philippines (founded 1903), whose steep turret and pointed Neo-Gothic window rises above **Antipolo Street corner Fernandez,** and the **Westminster High School**, founded 1933, on **Honorio Lopez Boulevard.** The latter is a close cousin of both the Tondo Methodist Church and the more visible one in Ermita. Another noteworthy sample of Tondo Neo-Gothic is the twin-towered church of the Iglesia Evangelica Metodisa en las Islas Filipinas (IEMELIF), founded in 1909 by Nicolas Zamora as the first Filipino Protestant congregation, recognized by an NHI marker installed in 1984. The current church along Zamora street with spires and stained-glass lanced windows was completed in 1959 after its precessor burned down in 1941. Also inspired by the Gothic but executed in a very local manner is the **Iglesia de Jesucristo Templo de Caridad Jerusalem,** probably from the 1910s to 1920s, at Dagupan Extension between Bulacan and Solis Streets. Like those Wood-and-Stone Neo-Gothic mansions then emerging in other districts of Manila, it too has a gable topped by a triangular pediment. Unlike them, it was a place of worship for ordinary people who believe in combining worship with healing. Neither Catholic nor Protestant, this is an original island congregation. Also take note of the antiquated wooden entrance gate to the compound, complete with a *postigo* (small door), typical of Spanish-era houses—was this formerly the site of an old Bahay-na-Bato?

FIG. 500. Sovereign Grand Lodge of the Philippine Archipelago

MASONIC LODGE

As befits a district that gave many sons to the Masonic-inspired Katipunan, the Masonic **Sovereign Grand Lodge of the Philippine Archipelago,** built in the 1950s, stands in Tondo on **Cavite corner Kusang Loob Street (between Ipil and Tindalo Streets).** The two-story all-concrete temple has a Roman mien: a carved triangular pediment capping an entablature carried by four pilasters. Although the current façade was only erected in 1972, according to the marker on site, it provides a striking contrast to current attempts to look "Neo-Classical." Its proportions are conceived vis-à-vis the human body, while the details are executed academically correct. This Lodge reminds us of the important role lodges played during the Philippine Revolution, as illustrated by an important event that played out in Tondo: In 1912, after Rizal's remains were exhumed from Paco cemetery, his family decided that these should be kept temporarily among his brother Masons. Accordingly, the brethren, led by Timoteo Paez, carried Rizal's remains to his lodge in Tondo for proper funeral rites, before handing them over to the government the following day. After the Rizal Monument was completed at the Luneta, the remains were transferred there.[33]

LIVING IN TONDO

"What is nice about living in Tondo is that it is peaceful (*tahimik*)." This assertion by several Tondo residents will surprise outsiders who imagine it to be a den of crime. Particularly intriguing is its reiteration by Tina, a sari-sari store owner, whose 1930s-era house is in a quiet neighborhood just a couple of blocks northeast of rowdy Divisoria. She actually used to live on P. Guevarra in nearby Sta. Cruz but chose to leave it because of the drug addicts. As the casual visitor wanders northward in Tondo, for instance into the Juan Luna-Solis-Molave area, he soon realizes that other neighborhoods in the notorious district are actually quite peaceful. Moreover, they are light-years away from Divisoria's garbage and traffic mess. Indeed says Robert, a graduate of UST, who lives in northern Tondo in a beautiful 1930s house, "I dislike going to some areas in Quezon City because of the traffic."

Accessibility is another attraction. Camilla, a retired pharmacist, agrees with other residents that many key destinations can be quickly reached. Such would be Tutuban Shopping Center, the famous bargain place 168 Mall in Binondo, or SM San Lazaro. Any rented motorized side-car easily brings her to those places. "Our place is close to everything (*malapit sa lahat*)" adds Robert. "When the train service is finally restored, it will be easy for us to go to Guiguinto in Bulacan where we have properties—indeed to other provinces, too." Their house is just a block away from the train station at Solis.

While Tondo is associated with the Sto. Niño Church, there are other churches like St. Joseph that form the core of many people's lives. Camilla goes to the Sto. Niño Church during the January fiesta, but otherwise goes to nearby St. Joseph.

Their houses are cool inside, say the Tondeños. "When the wind strikes (*paghampas ng hangin*), it enters the inside of the house," says Tina. Camilla recalls how, after lunch, she and her family would sleep on mats on the wooden floor of the sala by the open ventanilla. "So cool!" For this and other reasons, Robert feels attached to the house. "Our grandparents invested in this house. We should respect that. And this is where we all grew up."

Outsiders to Tondo glibly swallow negative generalizations about the district. They forget that similar generalizations are also made about where they live, like Manila as a whole, or about the Philippines as well. Much harm is done by uncritically believing and spreading them.

NOTES

1. Laura Lee Junker, *Raiding, Trading and Feasting: The Political Economy of Philippine Chiefdoms* (Quezon City: Ateneo de Manila University Press, 2000), 336, 339-40, 343-45, 347-48.

2. Antoon Postma, "The Laguna Copper Plate Inscription: Text and Commentary," *Philippine Studies* 40, no. 2 (1992), 183-203.

3. Cesar Adib Majul, *Muslims in the Philippines* (Quezon City: University of the Philippines Press, 1973), 78-79.

4. Luciano P. R. Santiago, "The Houses of Lakandula, Matanda and Soliman (1571-1898): Genealogy and Group Identity," *Philippine Quarterly of Culture and Society* 18 (1990), 42-43.

5. Luning B. Ira and Isagani R. Medina, "Tondo," *Streets of Manila* (Quezon City: GCF Books, 1977), 33.

6. Xavier Huetz de Lemps, "Territorio y urbanismo en las Islas Filipinas en el entorno de 1898," *Ciudad y Territorio Estudios Territoriales* 30, no. 116 (1998), 411-13.

7. Carlos Quirino, "The Native Quarter of Tondo," *Filipino Heritage: The Making of a Nation*, vol. 7, edited by Alfred Roces (Manila: Lahing Pilipino Publishing, Inc., 1978), 1952-56.

8. Ira and Medina, *Streets of Manila*, 27.

9. Quirino, "The Native Quarter of Tondo," 1953.

10 Ira and Medina, *Streets of Manila*, 29.

11 José Buhain, "The Steel Magnet," *Filipino Heritage: The Making of a Nation*, vol. 7, edited by Alfred Roces (Manila, Lahing Pilipino Publishing, Inc., 1978), 1957-60.

12 Ira and Medina, *Streets of Manila*.

13 Teodoro Agoncillo, *The Revolt of the Masses: The Story of Bonifacio and the Katipunan* (Quezon City, University of the Philippines, 1956); Carlos Quirino, "The Proletarian Hero," *Filipino Heritage: The Making of a Nation*, vol. 7, edited by Alfred Roces (Manila: Lahing Pilipino Publishing, Inc., 1978), 1948-51.

14 Agoncillo, *The Revolt of the Masses*.

15 According to Dr. Michael Coroza of the Kagawaran ng Pilipino of the Ateneo de Manila University.

16 Ira and Medina, *Streets of Manila*, 33.

17 Monica Felicia Consing, "Tondo Church," *CCP Encyclopedia of the Arts*, vol. 3, "Architecture," 289-90.

18 Milagros C. Guerrero, Emmanuel C. Guerrero and Ramon N. Villegas, *Tutuban: Progress and Transformation* (Manila: Tutuban Properties, Inc.), 27; Serafín D. Quiason, "The Philippine Iron Horse," *Filipino Heritage: The Making of a Nation*, vol. 7, edited by Alfred Roces (Manila: Lahing Pilipino Publishing, 1978), 1827-33.

19 Ira and Medina, *Streets of Manila*, 33.

20 Guerrero et al., *Tutuban*, 27.

21 Ibid., 29.

22 Ibid., 39.

23 Ira and Medina, *Streets of Manila,* 37.

24 Carlos Quirino, *Who's Who in Philippine History* (Manila, Tahanan Books, 1995).

25 "Abad Santos Signal Tower Project," Railways and Industrial Heritage Society of the Philippines, Inc., http://www.rihspi.org/projects.

26 Ibid.

27 Floyd Cunningham, "Diversities within Post-War Philippine Protestantism," Asia-Pacific Nazarene Theological Seminary, 17-18, accessed 28 December 2012, http://resourcecenter.apnts.org/mediator/Cunningham_Diversities.

28 "St. Paul United Methodist Church (Manila)," Wikimapia, accessed 27 September 2012, http://wikimapia.org/5742839/St-Paul-United-Methodist-Church.

29 "Evangelical Methodist Church in the Philippines," World Council of Churches, accessed 27 December 2012, http://www.oikoumene.org/en/member-churches/regions/asia/philippines/evangelical-methodist-church-in-the-philippines.html; Cunningham, "Diversities within Post-War Philippine Protestantism," 17-18.

30 Ira and Medina, *Streets of Manila,* 71.

31 Ibid., 40.

32 Ibid., 38.

33 Ayala Foundation, "Rizal the Mason," Filipinas Heritage Library, accessed 9 January 2013, http://www.filipinaslibrary.org.ph/filipiniana-library/filipiniana/70-features/160-rizal-the-mason.

Toward a Worker-Friendly District

VICTOR S. VENIDA

HERITAGE STRUCTURES IN TONDO CLUSTER IN ABOUT THREE identifiable areas, two of which are adjacent to the Sta. Cruz district, the third in the vicinity of the old church. What makes this district distinctive is that it has been the setting of important events and the cradle of outstanding individuals in Philippine political, cultural, and literary history. In contrast to the lordly histories of Quiapo, Sta. Ana, and Ermita, Tondo's history has both bourgeois and proletarian dimensions that should be emphasized.

Vibrant city centers always provide a spatial diversity of social classes, traditions, and cultures that create not only social tension and anxiety but also dynamism and creativity. These need to be emphasized in developing an image of Tondo as part of its long-term development. For starters, as with the rest of the city, plaques would need to be installed in the places associated with Andrés Bonifacio, Lakan Dula, Amado Hernandez, José "Pitoy" Moreno, Jose de la Cruz, etc. Walking tours for students, specially majors in history, Philippine literature, design, art history, and sociology can be encouraged as they will be the future patrons of heritage districts and historic locations.

The Tondo church and the Plaza area will need to be restored and renovated. The overall structure appears to be in relatively good shape, at least superficially. Ideally this vicinity will need to be a "special design area" where the buildings would have ornamental grills, wall reliefs, cut-out transoms, and the like following the motifs of antique houses in existing neighborhoods in Tondo itself. The area should, however, be cleared of visual clutter and urban decay (wires, peeling-off paint, plants sprouting in walls, etc.). Uniform heights and setbacks for modern structures could be proposed.

Tondo church—like the churches of Quiapo, Pandacan, Malate, and to a certain degree of Sampaloc and San Sebastian—is a popular center of devotion with a famous religious festival. All these churches attract devotees on a regular basis. This generates commerce for the surrounding blocks of streets. Tondo church can attract cultural tourism as well, especially during its several festivals. But cultural tourism would require a museum to explain the history, background, and traditions of the devotion. The festivals (including the annual Lenten celebrations) would need special seasonal guidebooks detailing the routes of the processions and explanations of the rites, rituals, popular practices, images of the event, and souvenir items. Such festivals would draw educated cultural tourists who can develop an intelligent appreciation of these elements of Philippine popular culture. Hence, in addition to religious devotees, there would be a larger and more regular patronage exercised by tourists. This creates a new market for Tondo; it also encourages the rehabilitation and adaptive reuse of heritage structures and the application of a more unified design scheme for all the buildings in the respective vicinities. The proposed museums for these devotionals can be housed in any of the old houses or buildings nearby. An antique structure can thus also be a museum of the district's unique architectural history.

The old structures of Tondo are largely residential and cluster in two main districts. The A. Rivera–Balintawak area is adjacent to the proposed design area of Avenida Rizal to Masangkay of Sta. Cruz. This area can thus be a unified design area. The other proposed design areas are one bounded by Caloocan in the west, Corregidor in the north, Abad Santos in the east, and Solis in the south; and from Nepomuceno and Simoun along Velasquez. The old houses can provide the design motifs and ornamentation that can be proposed to all the nearby buildings and structures, like a modern version of the Bahay-na-Bato.

But in addition, Tondo is along the North harbor which provides substantial employment and small-scale commercial activities. Large areas to the north all the way to Navotas and the Dagat-dagatan area are filled with informal settlements and government low-income housing projects. The probability is that in the foreseeable future, the working class and low-income nature of these large areas will remain. And they will also attract proposals for expanded government housing for the residents. It is thus proposed that these mass housing projects follow the experience of the mass housing programs of Vienna and Amsterdam (see General Issues). The housing projects should be integrated into a holistic community development project where open spaces, defined commercial areas, public schools and social service centers with the necessary infrastructure are provided. This has already been attempted by the Gawad Kalinga project which might need some evaluation. But since structures tend to be permanent and durable, it is suggested that, although an added cost factor or an investment, these buildings and housing schemes adopt some decorative and ornamental features that will add beauty and identity to the district and not make it look truly "plebeian"—in the negative sense of the term. The buildings can be equipped with the traditional windows with ventanillas, awnings, sliding panes and frosted transoms with patterns based on the old houses of the district. Each floor will allow for high ceilings and open transoms in the wall partitions. These features will make the housing units more environment-friendly.

The experience of Amsterdam and Vienna was that the residents of the low-income housing projects regarded their new units as permanent, rather than merely transitional, residences because of their beauty and solidity and their location in attractively redone neighborhoods. Thus they tended to maintain their units well, and developed a sense of community and of pride in their own communities.[1] In contrast, the plain and anonymous housing projects in Paris and London were regarded by the recipients as transitional to more attractive residential possibilities once their economic circumstances improved. In time these housing projects not only became unsightly, they became crime-ridden.

Thus to create a more permanent and productive residential population it is suggested that the government and community housing projects (like Gawad Kalinga) attempt a similar design and community development element. This would mean greater expenditure, of course, but one can see this as a form of social investment. It is an investment that ought to keep, within the city, a young, vibrant, and productive population of tax-paying residents. Widespread decay will compel them to migrate to the suburbs—as indeed has been happening in Manila since the 1970s.

Finally, one has to note a successful model of adaptive reuse, the conversion of the old Tutuban train station into a reasonably viable shopping mall. It no longer is used as a train station but one can still see the beautiful cast iron columns and other ornamental features. Perhaps, a section of the mall can be devoted to a mini-museum of the history and design features of the station for a greater general understanding of the value of adaptive reuse of heritage structures.

NOTE

1. Anthony M. Tung, *Preserving the World's Great Cities: The Destruction and Renewal of the Historic Metropolis* (New York: Clarkson Potter Publisher, 2001), 206–11.

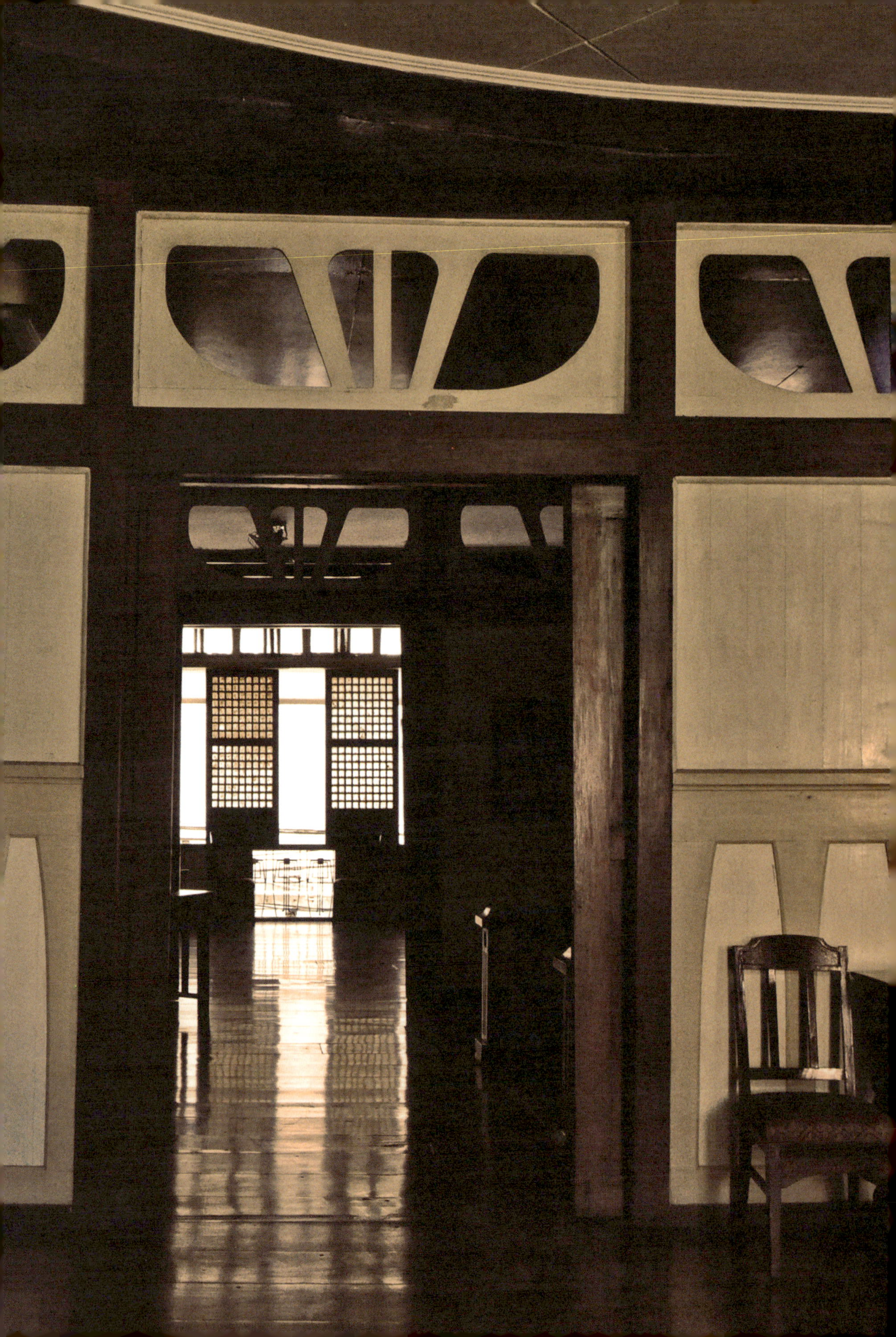

Cool Design—
Building for a Tropical Climate

ERIK AKPEDONU

"A style well-suited to the tropics"
—ARCH. WALTER GROPIUS, *co-founder of the Bauhaus*,
during a visit to Manila houses in the early 1950s[1]

IN A TIME OF UNDENIABLE CLIMATE CHANGE IT MAKES GOOD SENSE to preserve vintage buildings for many reasons. For one, the construction of a new building requires tremendous natural resources for building materials such as steel, glass, timber, concrete, etc. Many of these resources are becoming increasingly scarce, such as wood, whereas others emit dangerous or harmful chemicals during extraction, production, and processing, such as paints, sealants, and glues.

Many construction materials require vast quantities of energy to extract, process, and produce (e.g., aluminum and steel, as well as cement, which is also a major source of CO_2 emissions[2]), plus transport, let alone actual construction on site. Meanwhile, the demolition of old buildings creates large volumes of debris, most of which cannot or are not recycled and are dumped in landfills, again requiring precious energy and land.

But there are more good reasons to preserve old houses: being the product of many centuries of evolution, in the Philippines most prewar buildings are almost perfectly adapted to their tropical environment, having evolved before the era of omnipresent air-conditioning, electric fans, and electric lighting. Today, buildings account for about 32 percent of total energy consumption worldwide, and for about 40 percent of primary energy consumption in most industrialized countries (e.g., 41 percent in the USA in 2011).[3] When one considers the enormous amount of energy necessary to first erect, and then mechanically operate a building and especially to ventilate or air-condition it, the preservation of vintage houses makes good sense even for ordinary homeowners: the installation of one small air-con unit in just one room of an average-sized row house can easily double that household's monthly electricity consumption, and subsequent electricity bill.[4] According to a 2011 study by

FIG. 501. Inside the Bahay Nakpil-Bautista, Quiapo

Marlyn Sahakian, a Research Associate at the University of Lausanna (Switzerland) who conducted studies on consumption practices and energy use in Southeast Asia, 15 percent of households in Metro Manila use air-conditioning (8 percent nationwide), which is widely seen as a status symbol, especially among lower-income groups. Not least because of aggressive marketing of air-conditioning which in turn enabled the adoption of unsuitable Western building designs, electricity consumption in the Philippines has grown five times as fast as Gross Domestic Product (GDP) since the 1970s. Private households in Metro Manila now have the highest electricity rates in Asia,[5] mainly because unlike in other countries, electricity in Metro Manila is not subsidized.[6] Sustainable alternatives must be found in light of dwindling precious fossil resources such as oil, coal, and gas needed to produce this energy, along with the disastrous, negative, long-term effects of fossil fuel-based energy generation—such as air pollution, carbon dioxide emissions, and subsequent Global Warming and rising sea levels, which will disproportionately affect the Philippines.[7]

Both vernacular building traditions and postwar developments as espoused by Tropical Modernism provide useful insights into energy-efficient and climatically-adapted design principles.

BAHAY KUBO AND BAHAY-NA-BATO

Vintage houses can serve as functioning examples of time-tested and efficient low technology with near-zero emissions, thus inspiring contemporary designers, architects, builders, and real-estate developers alike to consider clean and sustainable alternatives to expensive, polluting, and ultimately non-sustainable air-conditioning and artificial lightning.

The aim should thus be the adaptive re-use of historic structures that display environmentally sustainable principles, and to promote energy-efficient design for new buildings and retrofitting of existing ones. Vintage houses in the Philippines, especially the traditional Filipino Bahay-na-Bato (House of stone) and Bahay Kubo (Nipa hut) display most of the key elements of energy-passive, climatically-adapted architecture in the tropics: natural cross ventilation, thermal insulation, air space, and shading.

CROSS VENTILATION

Residential upper floor. Unlike modern townhouses and suburban houses, which are either single-storey or where the ground floor is used for residential purposes, vintage houses traditionally have their residential quarters on the upper floor, thus taking advantage of the higher wind velocities several meters above ground level. At the same time their wooden floors accumulate less heat than contemporary cement floors.

Windows. For cost reasons, many modern buildings have only one small window per room, resulting in poor ventilation. In contrast, traditional Filipino houses are characterized by their large, wide-open windows, which are ideal for maximum cross ventilation. They have the additional advantage of admitting much natural daylight, unlike many modern buildings that tend to be very dark without artificial lights.

COOL DESIGN—BUILDING FOR A TROPICAL CLIMATE

FIG. 502. Ventilation

Ventanillas. Unlike modern developments since the 1950s, almost all prewar houses have *ventanillas* (small, operable windows below the main windows) which enable a breeze to cool the entire body, not just the part above the waist.

Layout. Most modern dwellings (especially apartments and townhouses, but also single-detached homes) consist of individual and separate rooms isolated from each other, resulting in poor air flow, thus necessitating the heavy use of fans and air-conditioning. In contrast, the internal layout of traditional houses is usually arranged in a "free-flow" configuration to enable and maximize cross-ventilation from one side of the house to the other. This is achieved by minimizing the number of internal walls, and having permanently kept open doors (which are only closed on certain occasions, with curtains providing privacy the rest of the time). Where walls and doors are indispensable (such as bedrooms) air movement from room to room is still made possible through *calados*, decorative wall perforations in the upper portion of the wall, below the ceiling.

THERMAL INSULATION

Wooden walls and floors. Unlike modern constructions, whose relatively thin (unshaded and un-insulated) concrete walls quickly absorb heat and re-radiate it into the interior (especially at night), most vintage houses consist of organic materials, such as wood, thatch, and bamboo, with low thermal storage capacity. Thus, they hardly

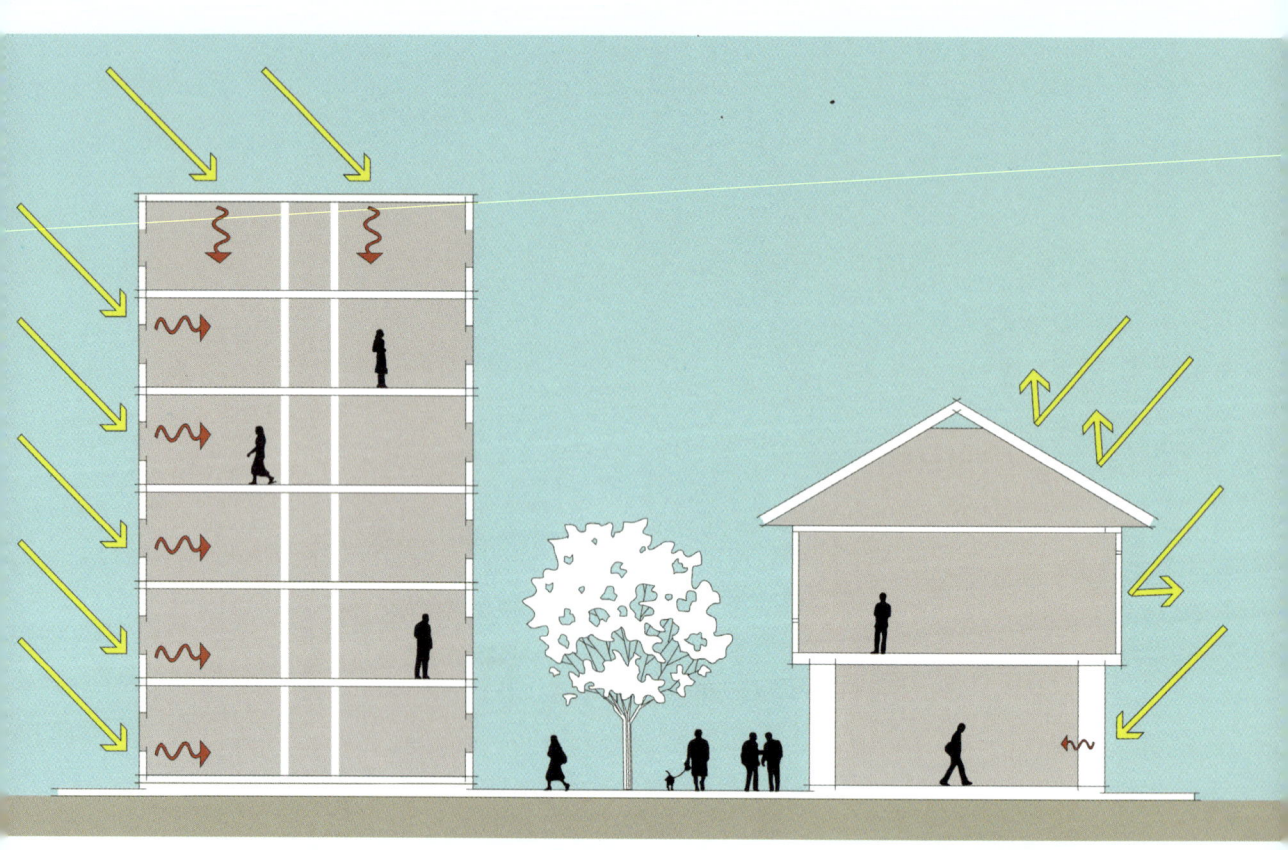

FIG. 503. Thermal Gain

accumulate heat and keep the interior relatively cool day and night (in cold countries, cellulose-based insulation materials are now commonly used to keep buildings warm in winter and cool in summer.) In fact, the upper floor of most vintage houses in Manila and the Philippines consist of wooden panels or boards.

Thick walls. Where ground floor walls of vintage houses consist of stone (typically adobe, brick, or coral stone), they are often so thick (over half a meter), that, although accumulating heat during the day, it takes a long time for it to penetrate to the interior, thus likewise keeping it cool.

Roofs. Although nowadays unacceptable and thus banned in a (typically densely-packed) urban environment due to their high fire risk, thatch roofs are particularly effective in keeping a house cool, as many residents who live in a thatched house attest to. Where thatch roofs are unacceptable, light-colored roofs (so-called "cool roofs") and light-colored walls of any material reflect a greater portion of sunlight and thus reduce absorption and conduct of heat, thus aiding in keeping the building cool.

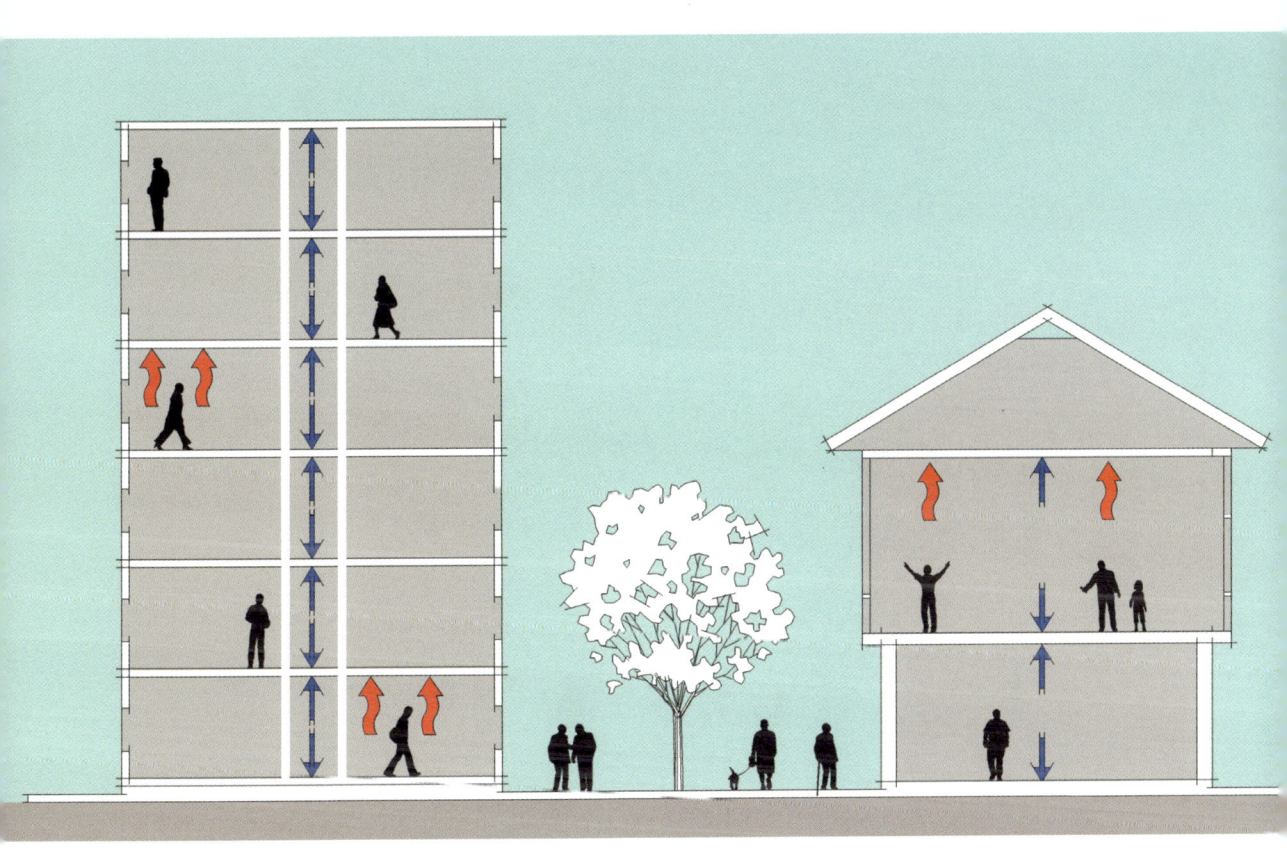

COOL DESIGN—BUILDING FOR A TROPICAL CLIMATE   383

FIG. 504. Air Space

AIR SPACE

High ceilings. Unlike modern apartment buildings which for cost reasons (and because they are designed for air-conditioning) have relatively low ceilings, rooms in vintage houses are typically much higher and airy. As warm air rises up, tall rooms are thus noticeably cooler than low ones, as warm air largely rises above body level.

Roof design. Unlike many modern developments that have flat concrete roofs (which accumulate heat and tend to leak) vintage houses have steep rooflines, which not only minimize leaks, but also keep the airspace below the roof relatively cool by allowing hot air in the attic to rise up all the way below the ridge, thus keeping it away from the residential rooms below. Meanwhile, these rooms are insulated from the attic airspace above by a suspended ceiling, thus introducing a "double roof." Finally, the airspace between these two roofs is ventilated through—often elaborately carved or traceried—eave and gable vents, reducing the accumulation of hot air. The same effect is achieved by various types of roof vents, such as dormer windows and rooftop exhaust fans (e.g., turbine vents), which a number of vintage houses still sport today.

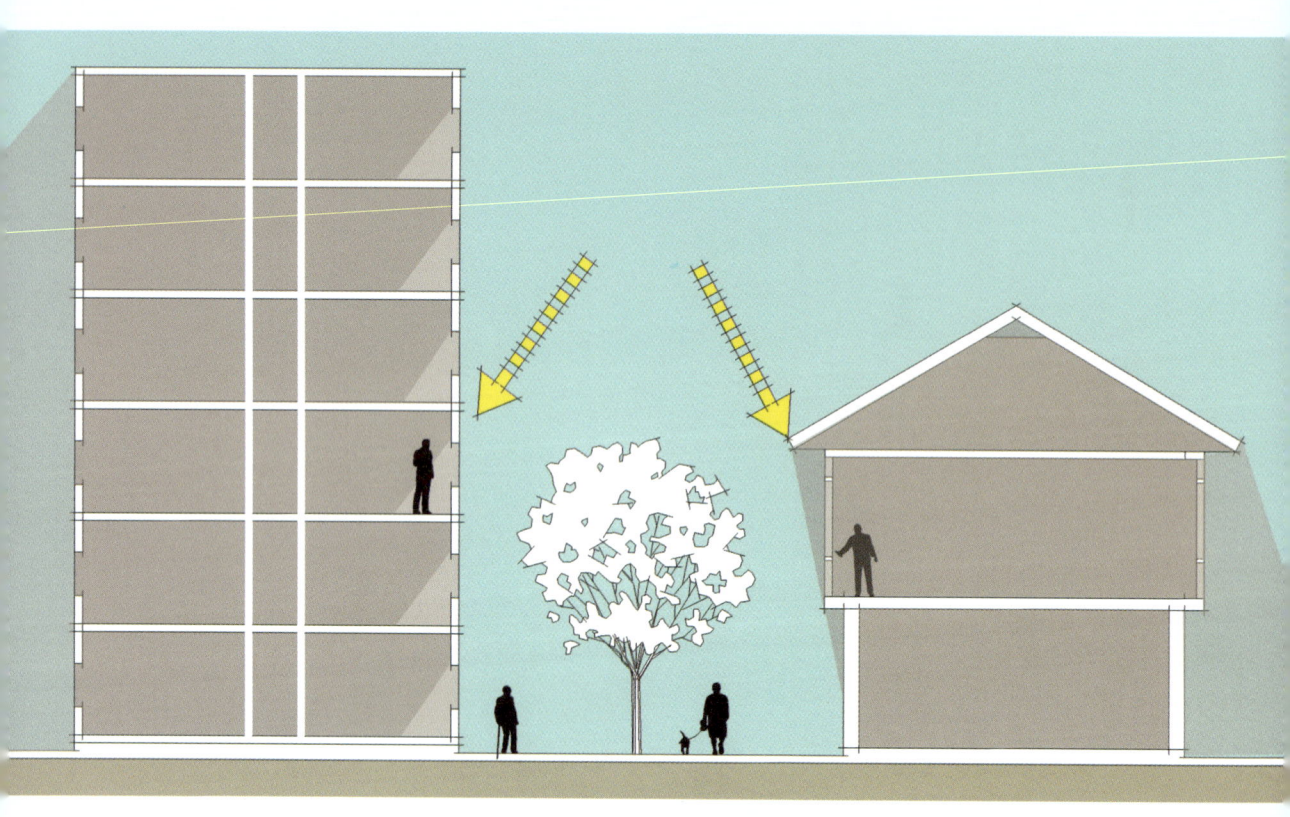

FIG. 505. Shading

SHADING

Walls and windows. Unlike the straight, un-molded facades of many modern buildings, which are fully exposed to heat accumulation (especially tall ones), the walls of old houses are shaded from the sun by overhangs, such as wide roof eaves and the *volada* (that portion of the wooden upper floor that projects beyond the ground floor beneath it). Also, while the (often un-insulated) windows of most modern apartment houses are fully exposed to sunlight, windows of old houses are often protected from glare and thus thermal gain by a *media agua* (a continuous smaller roof below the eaves, running the entire length of the façade) or by individual canopies. They also protect the windows from driving rain and enable them to be kept open permanently for maximum cross-ventilation.

TROPICAL MODERNISM

Modernism, which came to dominate global architecture after World War II, did not do away, at least initially, with the sensitivity towards the tropical climate as displayed by traditional Filipino architecture. Instead, Modernism in the tropics initially adapted to the local climate and developed into an offspring aptly termed *Tropical Modernism*, until the advent of omnipresent air-conditioning superseded all sensibility to local conditions. While introducing its own Modernist design language, Tropical Modernism carried on concepts known from the Bahay-na-Bato, such as high ceilings, shading by

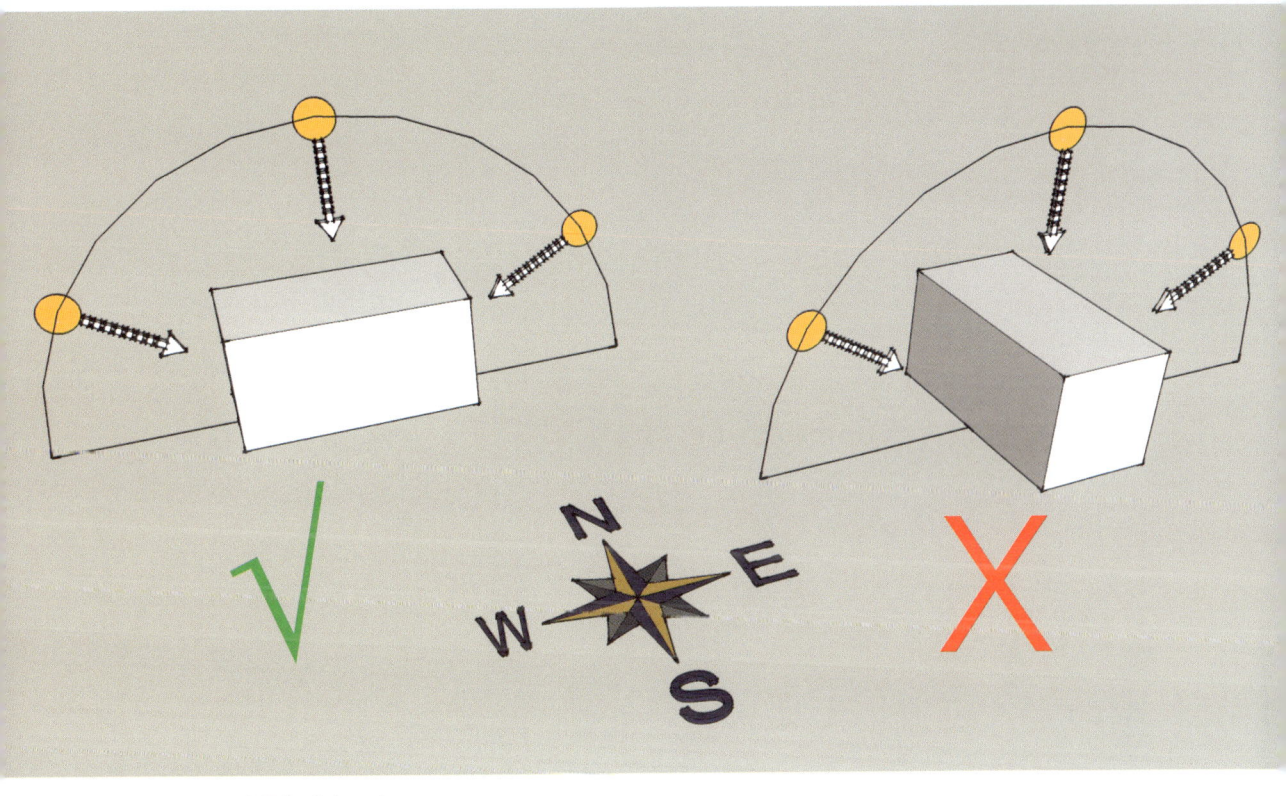

FIG. 506. Solar Orientation

brise-soleils (sun-breakers), and emphasis on cross-ventilation. To enable the latter, many buildings from the 1950s and 1960s are only one room deep, and, as an added advantage, less than the critical eight meters beyond which artificial lighting becomes necessary. In addition, Tropical Modernism introduced new design principles, which in the tightly packed urban setting of central Manila would previously have been impossible, but which the abundance of vacant land, as in Quezon City, made possible; such as orientation with regard to sun and wind direction, and urban layout.

EAST-WEST ORIENTATION

An important aspect of modern tropical design is to minimize the exposure of the walls to sunlight by orienting a building in East-West direction, thus exposing only the narrow ends to the low-angled rising and setting sun. Thus one long façade would be facing south (facing north, if the building is located in the southern hemisphere), only exposed to the high sun in its zenith, where it can easily be protected by sun-shading devices such as roof eaves and horizontal *brise-soleil*. Meanwhile, the other long façade would face north and receive almost no sunlight at all most of the day. While the majority of prewar urban buildings do not follow this orientation due to constraints imposed by the historic inner-city street layout, it can be well-observed in many 1950s developments, where there were no such constraints, such as the new campuses of the University of the Philippines in Diliman, Ateneo de Manila University, and Miriam College in Quezon City.

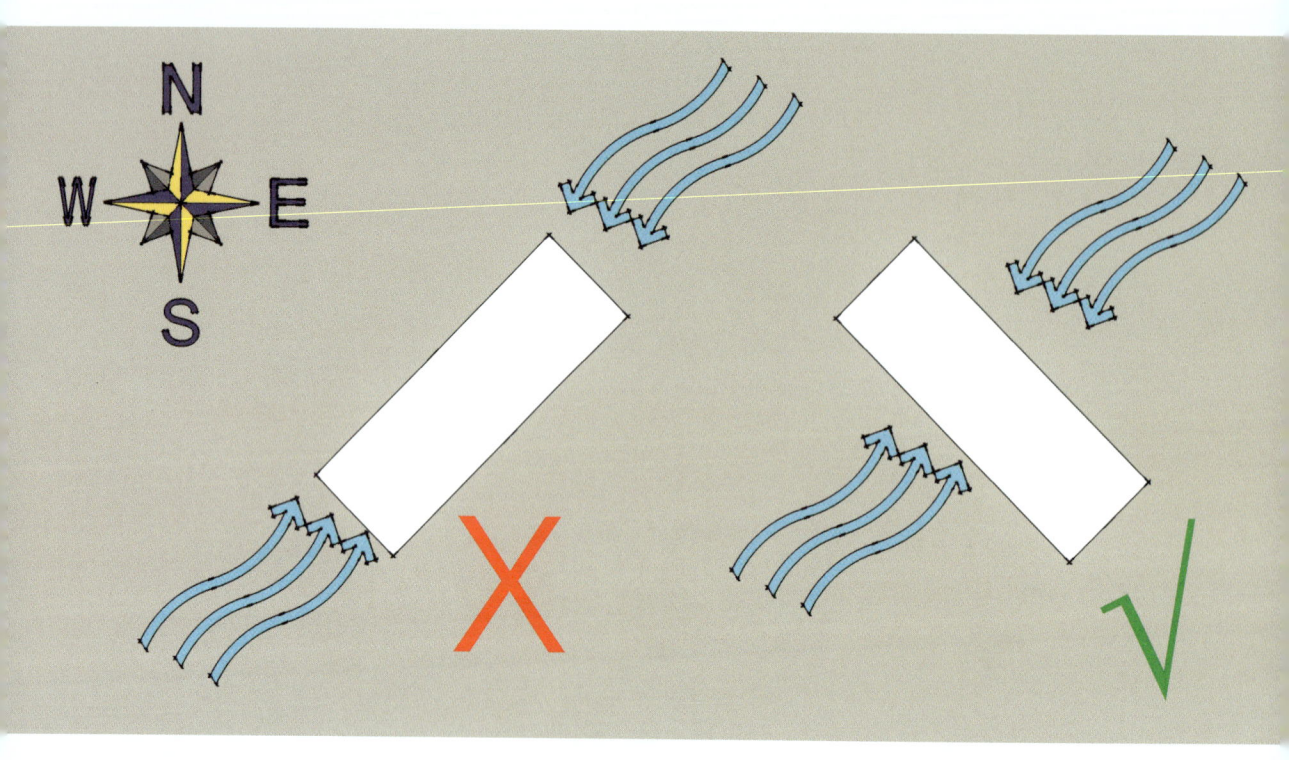

FIG. 507. Wind Direction

ORIENTATION TOWARDS DOMINANT WIND DIRECTION

Similar to above, the predominant wind direction can be taken into account for the orientation of a building to maximize natural cross-ventilation. This will depend on the local wind conditions, and may coincide with or stand contrary to the optimal solar orientation. Thus, sometimes a compromise between the two may be necessary. As with solar orientation, the impositions of the urban grid and relatively small lots often make it difficult or impossible to optimize the prevailing winds. In the Philippines, the *habagat* monsoon winds blow from southwest to northeast from late May to October, and in the opposite direction during the *amihan* monsoon from November to early May.

URBAN LAYOUT

Spacing. The general layout is often wide-spaced, with buildings being single detached and at a good distance from their next neighbor, thus not impeding air flow as blocks of modern row houses do, nor, at the other extreme, creating wind tunnels associated with densely packed high-rise towers.

Gardens. Traditional houses as well as new 1950s university campuses are often set amidst large compounds or gardens, which help cool the building as plants not only cool their surroundings by evaporation, but also accumulate much less heat as do, for example, asphalt or concrete. These can heat up to a considerable degree, thus causing the well-known "Urban heat-island-effect," the phenomenon that in vast, densely built

FIG. 508. Vegetation

up and sealed areas such as large cities, temperatures tend to be several degrees Celsius higher than in the surrounding rural areas. Contributing to this effect are emissions from heating or cooling buildings, and by industry and vehicular traffic, among others. Finally, large, old-growth trees help in additionally cooling the buildings by shading them and the ground surrounding them, without impeding the free flow of air.

As shown above, traditional houses are perfectly adapted to their tropical environment. Their already high ecological efficiency can be further increased by modernizing them with contemporary ecological fixtures, such as energy-efficient lighting (energy-saving bulbs, LEDs, etc.) and water use (e.g., water-saving flush toilets), use of solar collectors for water heating, and of photovoltaic technology for local electricity generation.

If maintained and restored, vintage houses not only in Manila, but all over the Philippines can significantly contribute to a healthier, and ecologically sustainable environment, and to the fight against global warming.

May the buildings of the past inspire the designers of today to build the architecture of the future.

NOTES

1   Fernando N. Zialcita and Martin I. Tinio Jr., *Philippine Ancestral Houses* (Quezon City: GCF Books, 1980), 85.

2   U.S. Energy Information Administration, "Emissions of Greenhouse Gases Report," EIA: Environment, last revised on 8 December 2009, http://www.eia.gov/oiaf/1605/ggrpt/carbon.html.

3   U.S. Energy Information Administration, "How much energy is used in buildings in the United States?" EIA: FAQs, accessed 2 February 2013, http://www.eia.gov/tools/faqs/faq.cfm?id=86&t=; International Energy Agency, "How much of the world's energy is consumed by buildings?" IEA: FAQs, accessed 2 February 2013, http://www.iea.org/aboutus/faqs/energyefficiency.

4   Personal experience of author.

5   "Beating the Power Rates," *Philippine Daily Inquirer*, 25 February 2013, http://opinion.inquirer.net/47659/beating-the-power-rates.

6   Marlyne Sahakian and Julia Steinberger, "Staying cool in Metro Manila: Energy Reduction Through a Deeper Understanding of Household Consumption," *Journal of Industrial Ecology* 15, no. 1 (2011); Marlyne Sahakian, "Keeping Cool: Air-Conditioning Consumption in Metro Manila," (lecture, VRA Lecture Series, Institute of Philippine Culture, Ateneo de Manila University, Quezon City, 14 August 2013).

7   Alexis Romero, "Phl Among World's Top 10 Most Vulnerable to Climate Change," *Philippine Star*, 30 October 2013, http://www.philstar.com/headlines/2013/10/30/1251165/phl-among-worlds-top-10-most-vulnerable-climate-change.

Acknowledgments

We extend our gratitude to the following:

Ms. Narzalina Z. Lim, Ms. Regina Sy Co Seteng and Ms. Phyllis Zaballero for their unwavering support for our field research, the writing of this book and its publication;

Current and former directors of the Institute of Philippine Culture: Dr. Czarina Saloma, Dr. Marita Concepcion Guevarra, Dr. Maria Elissa Jayme Lao and Dr. Enrique Niño Leviste for patiently supporting this important project;

The Institute of Philippine Culture of the Ateneo de Manila University for generously providing funds toward the publication of this book;

Atty. Sedfrey Candelaria and Atty. Ferdinand Negre of the Ateneo Law School for providing valuable legal advice;

Ms. Roshni Balani, Ms. Maria Cynthia Barriga, Ms. Ma. Criselda Dana Buñag, Ms. Aesha Cruz, Mr. Reamur David, Ms. Patricia Gonzalez, Ms. Maan Javier, Ms. Katrina Kwan, and Ms. Cassandra Teodosio for their work on haligui.net;

Mr. James Alcantara, Mr. John Arcilla, Mr. Bernardo Arellano, Ms. Maria Cynthia Barriga, Mr. Conrado Bugayong, Ms. Amaris Cabason, Mr. Paolo Camacho, Mr. Jan-Michael Cayme, Mr. Jeffrey Flores, Mr. Romeo Galang Jr., Mr. Jose Guerrero, Mr. James Kagahastian, Ms. Katrina Kwan, Ms. Maya Lyn Manocsoc, Ms. Teresa Marfil, Mr. Carlo Montano, Ms. Diana Moraleda, Mr. Stephen Pamorada, Mr. Michael Pante, Mr. Joven Ramirez, Ms. Vanessa Sorongon, Ms. Cecile Sunico, and Mr. Jeffrey Yap of the IPC 297's architectural survey team;

Arch. Janeil Arlegui, Arch. Justin Basco, Arch. Richard Tuason Bautista, Arch. Michael Bulosan, Arch. Peter Bontuyan, Arch. Minerva Laudico, Arch. Ramil Tibayan, Arch. Mar Ticao, Arch. Michelle Ting, Arch. Charles Tobias, Arch. Aileen Tobias, and Arch. Adrian Tumang of the IPC 297's architectural survey team. Some had just finished their studies while others were experienced practitioners when they joined us;

The students of the Ateneo Cultural Laboratory at San Juan del Monte in 2011, Ms. Dana Davide, Mr. Jan Ong, Mr. Francis Panuncialman, Mr. Harold See; Ms. Ana Tamula, and Ms. Mona Yap;

Arch. Mia Quimpo who had done a rapid inventory of heritage buildings for the National Commission of Culture and the Arts, and who then generously shared her inventory and experience with us. We hereby acknowledge the photographs of Dakilang Pamana, "An Inventory of Heritage Structures in the City of Manila," headed by Arch./EnP Maria Theresa Quimpo and Photography Team Leader, Mr. Dewey Sergio, for the National Commission for Culture and the Arts;

The Department of Sociology and Anthropology of the Ateneo de Manila University and its Cultural Heritage Studies Program for fostering the conditions that made this research possible;

Ms. Ana Marie Harper, former Administrator of Intramuros Administration, for allowing us to make use of their research facilities;

Atty. Guiller Asido, current Administrator of Intramuros Administration, for facilitating further research on Intramuros;

Mr. John Arcilla, Archives Chief of the Intramuros Administration, for his artistic inputs and for indicating valuable historical documents and images in their collection;

Mr. John Tewell for his expert advice on historic photographs to include and their sources;

Mr. Mario Fer and Mr. Steve Feldman for assisting our search for historical images;

The Library of the Colegio de San Juan de Letrán;

The University of St. Tomás for facilitating research in its archives and library;

Mr. Jeremy Barns, Director IV and Agency Head, and Dr. Ana Maria Theresa Labrador, Director III of the National Museum of the Philippines;

The National Historical Commission of the Philippines;

The National Archives which yielded valuable archival data on Manila;

The Library of Filipinas Heritage Foundation;

The staff of the Filipiniana Section of the Ateneo de Manila University's Rizal Library;

The staff of the American Historical Collection of the Ateneo de Manila University's Rizal Library;

The late Rev. Fidel Villarroel OP for giving us an overview of the history of education in UST even before his book was published;

The late Mr. Pio Andrade Jr., a history aficionado, who shared ideas on archival sources to examine at the American Historical Collection and Filipiniana Section of the Rizal Library;

Dr. Xavier Huetz de Lemps of the Université de Nice for sharing his own research on aspects of Manila's history

Dr. Pedro Luengo of the Universidad de Sevilla for sharing his articles on varied aspects of Philippine architectural heritage;

Ms. Sylvia Lichauco whose work in saving the heritage of Sta. Ana has been an inspiration;

Mr. Jose J. Panlileo for a tour of selected mansions in San Miguel with commentary;

Arch. Paulo Alcazaren, Arch. Manolo Noche, Greg Dorris, and Rence Chan for touring us around various historic sites in Metro Manila;

The late Dom Bernardo Perez (Rodrigo Perez III) for giving us an in-depth tour of San Beda Chapel and Our Lady of Montserrat Abbey;

Ms. Gigi Tuason for opening the doors of their superbly preserved mansion during festive occasions;

Ms. Luisa Fermin for her account of the Paco and neighborhood of her youth;

Mr. Edmond Burke–Miailhe and Mr. Alain Burke–Miailhe for information on Franco-Filipino heritage and on Binondo-San Nicolas;

The Calvo Museum on Escolta for sharing knowledge on Escolta's history;

Mr. Ivan Man Dy for sharing his extensive knowledge of Art Deco and of Chinatown;

Mr. Manolo Quezon who gave us an extensive introduction to the Malacañang Museum when it was under his care;

The late Dr. Benito Legarda y Fernandez for his stories about Manila;

The late Dr. Hilario Zialcita and Mrs. Mercedes Zialcita for sharing their recollections of the different districts of Manila;

The Philippine Institute of Volcanology and Seismology for assisting us in our research;

Engr. Carlos Villaraza for generously sharing his expertise in seismic construction design;

Urban planner Dinky von Einsiedel for his valuable advice on urban rehabilitation;

Ms. Patricia Gonzalez and Atty. Michael Dizon for their valuable advice, comments and suggestions;

Tutuban Center Mall for facilitating our research on site;

Ms. Dodit Reyes for facilitating our research in New Manila;

Substation Commander Geronimo Juico and Substation Deputy Commander Ruben Malacas for sharing their expertise in fire prevention;

Arch. Dominic Galicia and Tina Paterno for sharing their expertise in restoration and adaptive re-use;

Arch. Lorelei de Viana for welcoming us to the Far Eastern University;

Arch. Reynaldo Lita of the NHCP for assisting us in finding rare archival images;

Mr. Ryan Indon for securing copyright permission in Japan;

Dr. Paulina Machuca of the Colegio de Michoacán for helping us secure copyright permission in Mexico;

Dr. Jorge Mojarro of the UST for advising us on the protocols of the Biblioteca Nacional de España.

Mr. Wilven Infante who toured us around the ruins and museum of the old Alcaícería;

The members of the Sta. Ana Heritage Tourism Association who welcomed us into their midst;

The members and organizers of the FB Group Advocates for Heritage Preservation who organized various eye-opening heritage tours in Metro Manila;

All those many helping hands and minds who contributed to making this book finally see the light of day; and

All those who generously welcomed us into their houses, offices, and institutions, and freely shared with us the history of their wonderful Filipino heritage, an endangered splendor.

Illustration Sources

INSTITUTE OF PHILIPPINE CULTURE (IPC),
FIELD RESEARCH PHOTOGRAPHS

Erik Akpedonu, FIGS. 1, 12–15, 17–20, 22–24, 26–29, 33, 55–57, 59–64, 66, 68–70, 75, 77, 79-80, 82, 86, 93–94, 96–97, 109–112, 124, 134, 136, 138–143, 145, 172, 175, 178–184, 187, 189–190, 192–194, 200, 202–203, 207, 209, 211–212, 215–217, 219–226, 228, 240, 249, 253–254, 258–259, 264–268, 279, 281–282, 284, 286, 288, 290, 295–297, 310, 319, 329, 333, 336, 340, 342–344, 348, 350, 356–357, 364, 366–367, 369–371, 380–381, 384–385, 389, 393, 409, 420, 421, 423–424, 435, 437, 440, 444, 449

Joseph James Alcantara, 191, 199

Justin Joseph Basco, 35, 230, 418–419, 429, 431

Richard Tuason-Sanchez Bautista, 436, 452, 465, 499

Conrado Abjelina Bugayong II, 11, 36, 78, 170, 174, 185, 214, 218, 374, 378, 387–388, 390, 394, 411, 413, 417, 426, 427, 441–442, 454

Jan-Michael Cayme, 490

James Long Kagahastian, 430, 456–460, 463–464, 467, 469, 470–472, 474–478, 488, 491–494, 500

Diana Jean Moraleda, 432–434, 439, 443, 479, 482–487

Ramil Belleza Tibayan, 196–198, 205, 227, 231, 236–239, 242–244, 246–247, 301, 321–328, 330, 332, 334–335, 351–352, 368, 372, 376–377, 391, 395

Mar Lorence Ticao, 428, 455, 461–462, 473, 480, 489, 495–496

Michelle Bracero Ting, 362

Adrian Plastina Tumang/Maria Cynthia Barriga, 445–448, 450, 451, 453, 498

Jeffrey Pascual Yap, 21

DONATED PHOTOGRAPHS

Erik Akpedonu, 1, 5, 38, 50–52, 65, 67, 72, 74, 85, 95, 101, 125–133, 135, 137, 146–147, 155–156, 159, 161, 186, 201, 208, 210, 229, 232–233, 241, 251, 255–257, 260, 262–263, 270, 272, 277, 311–314, 396–397, 404, 406–408, 410

Paulo Alcazaren, 3, 47

Joel Aldor, 271

John Paul Arcilla, 32, 58

Justin Joseph Basco, 84, 88–92, 113, 188, 248, 250, 375

Conrado Abjelina Bugayong II, 37, 48, 53–54, 71, 144, 171, 173, 302, 331, 373, 392, 405, 501

Michael Dizon and Patricia Gonzalez, 34

Ryan Indon, 158, 403

Andrew Chester Ong, 49, 169, 278, 280, 283, 285, 287, 289, 293–294, 298–300, 303–309, 315–318, 320, 337–338, 345–347, 349, 353–355, 358–359, 361, 363, 365, 379, 382–383, 386, 398–400

Ramil Belleza Tibayan, 83, 195, 213, 234–235, 245

Michelle Bracero Ting, 291

ILLUSTRATIONS

John Paul Arcilla, pages 22-27
Justin Joseph Basco, 502–508
Mel Patrick Kasingsing, pages 140, 217, 302, 307, 377

ARCHIVAL IMAGES

Rizal Library, Ateneo de Manila University:
American Historical Collection, 4, 6, 45, 100, 102, 115–116, 120–121, 123, 164–166, 176–177, 204, 206, 274, 276, 401, 414–415, 425, 438
Pardo de Tavera Library and Special Collections, 105, 108

Philippine Studies (journal), 412

Archivo General de Indias, 275

Ayala Foundation, Inc./Filipinas Heritage Library, 41–44

Biblioteca National de España, 40

Museo de America, 162

Intramuros Administration Archives, 46, 73, 76, 81, 98–99, 103–104, 114, 117–119
National Archives of the Philippines, 292
Lopez Memorial Museum and Library, 8, 9, 168
Mario Feir Filipiniana Library, 87, 122, 163, 416, 422
Museo José Luís Bello y González, 38
National Commission for Culture and the Arts (NCCA)/Mia Quimpo, 16, 339, 341, 360, 466, 468, 481
Ortigas Foundation Library, 39 (original with British Museum)
Gerard Lico Collection, 30
University of Wisconsin-Milwaukee, 167
Conrado Bugayong Collection, 148
John Oren Tewell Collection, 252
Wikimedia Commons (see full attributions below), 2, 7, 10, 31, 149, 150, 151, 152, 153, 154, 157, 158, 160, 261, 269, 273, 402, 403, 497

WIKIMEDIA COMMONS ATTRIBUTIONS LIST

2. Johannes Vingboons, "Bird's eye view of Manila," c. 1665. This is an image from the Atlas of Mutual Heritage and the Nationaal Archief, the Dutch National Archives. The metadata of this file is public domain under a Creative Commons Public Domain Dedication (CC-ZERO). This permission has been archived as ticket #2014051410008887, Public Domain, https://commons.wikimedia.org/w/index.php?curid=33328427.
7. Andrew Ellicott, revised from Pierre Charles L'Enfant, "Plan of the City of Washington," March 1792. Thackara & Vallance sc., Philadelphia 1792 - Library of Congress, Public Domain, https://commons.wikimedia.org/w/index.php?curid=12171178.
10. National Capital Planning Commission, Washington, D. C., "The McMillan Plan of 1901," https://web.archive.org/web/20100527181647/https://www.ncpc.gov/Images/Maps/McMillanPlan,%20 1901.jpg, Public Domain, https://commons.wikimedia.org/w/index.php?curid=11983112.
31. Judgefloro, "Plaza Miranda Quiapo Church, Quiapo, Manila, Legislative districts of Manila, City of Manila," 2016. Own work, Public Domain, https://commons.wikimedia.org/w/index.php?curid=49290523
149. M.Świerczyński, "Warsaw, the capital of Poland, destroyed by German Nazis," January 1945. By M.Świerczyński - Stanisław Jankowski, Adolf Ciborowski "Warszawa 1945 i dziś"; Wydawnictwo Interpress, Warszawa, 1971, page 6, Wiesław Głębocki; Karol Mórawski (1985), Kultura Walcząca 1939-1945, Warsaw: Wydawnictwo Interpress, p. 64, ISBN 83-02-00773-0 Antoni Przygoński, (1980) Powstanie Warszawskie w sierpniu 1944 r.; Tom 1, Warsaw: Polskie Wydawnictwo Naukowe ISBN 83-01-00293-X, Public Domain, https://commons.wikimedia.org/w/index.php?curid=2255273
150. Shalom Alechem, "Royal Castle Square," 2005. Own work (originally at en.wikipedia), Public Domain, https://commons.wikimedia.org/w/index.php?curid=2586152.
151. "Luftaufnahme von Königsberg," 1925. By Unknown author - G. v. Glinski, P. Wörster: Königsberg. Die ostpreußische Hauptstadt in Geschichte und Gegenwart. Berlin/Bonn 1992, Public Domain, https://commons.wikimedia.org/w/index.php?curid=10293250.
152. Georgy Dolgopsky, "Trams on Moskovsky Prospekt in Kaliningrad," 2007. By Георгий Долгопский at Russian Wikipedia, CC BY-SA 3.0, https://commons.wikimedia.org/w/index.php?curid=18337147.
153. Rüdiger Wölk, "Münster, Prinzipalmarkt," 2005. Photo taken by Rüdiger Wölk, CC BY-SA 2.0 de, https://commons.wikimedia.org/w/index.php?curid=237620
154. Rijksdienst voor het Cultureel Erfgoed, "Nederlands Hervormde Kerk (Grote- of Sint Laurenskerk): Exterieur Overzicht na Bombardement (Oorlogsschade), 1940. CC BY-SA 4.0, https://commons.wikimedia.org/w/index.php?curid=23878384.
157. 門田房太郎, "Former Japanese colonial Korean Government-General Office, at Gyeongbokgung," 1929. By 門田房太郎 - 朝鮮博覽會記念寫眞帖, Public Domain, https://commons.wikimedia.org/w/index.php?curid=29177258.
160. Adiput (talk), "Malacca Sultanate Palace," 2009. I (Adiput (talk)) created this work entirely by myself using my Olympus. Transferred from en.wikipedia, Public Domain, https://commons.wikimedia.org/w/index.php?curid=17969421.
261. Siyuwj, "Window setting of Ningbo Museum," 2014. Building designed by Wang Shu - Own work, CC BY-SA 3.0, https://commons.wikimedia.org/w/index.php?curid=30929597.
269. Concord, "The Paulinum – Aula und Universitätskirche St. Pauli during construction," 2012. Own work, CC BY-SA 3.0, https://commons.wikimedia.org/w/index.php?curid=20210757.
273. Dinkum, "Vue du Louvre sur la cour Napoléon, le jardin des Tuileries et Paris au loin," 2014. Own work, CC BY-SA 3.0, https://commons.wikimedia.org/w/index.php?curid=46528986.
402. Michael Pereckas, "Westfälisches Freilichtmuseum Detmold," 2017. By "Beige Alert" – Michael Pereckas, Milwaukee, WI, USA - flickr.com, CC BY 2.0, https://commons.wikimedia.org/w/index.php?curid=3303298.
498. Hannachievero7, "Iglesia Evangelica Metodista en las Islas Filipinas," 2014. Own work, CC BY-SA 3.0, https://commons.wikimedia.org/w/index.php?curid=36072230.

Index

A

Abad House, 365
accesoria, 3, 5, 6, 49, 141
Aceiteros (street), 242, 248, 292. *See also* M. de Santos (street)
Acuzar, Jerry, 309, 317, 320–321, 322
Aduana Building, 114, 139
Aduana (street), 99, 114
aesthetic, 2
Aguinaldo Department Store, 185, 186
air space, 383
Alberto House, 49, 55, 309, 315, 316, 322, 323
Alhambra Cigars, 172
alienation, 1, 7
Almacenes Reales, 82, 122
Almeda House, 353, 361
Anloague (street), 165, 179. *See* Juan Luna (street)
Aquino House, 367
Araullo Building, 113, 114, 143
Arboleda House, 289
Archdiocese of Manila, 96, 110
architectural quotation, 233
A. Rivera (street), 336, 337, 376
Army and Navy YMCA, 99, 101
arquitectura mestiza, 3
Artillery Barracks, 84, 85, 86
Arzobispo (street), 108–114, 127, 232
Asunción (street), 265–271
Ateneo de Manila, 67, 78, 108, 109, 119, 127, 131, 142
Augustinian Casa Provincial, 129
authenticity, 231–234, 237, 314–315
Avenida Rizal, 34, 55, 356, 358, 376
Ayuntamiento, 47, 87, 91, 92–93, 94, 99, 120, 142, 156
Azcarraga, 241, 242, 327, 331. *See also* Recto Avenue

B

Bahay Kubo, 380
Bahay-na-Bato, 225, 227, 228, 232, 283, 372, 376, 380, 384
Bahay Nakpil-Bautista, 379
Balintawak (street), 186, 336, 337, 339, 376
Baluarte de San Diego, 73, 75, 80, 87
Baluarte de Sta. Barbara, 86
Baluarte San Diego, 78
Baluartillo de San Francisco Javier, 82
Banco Filipino Condominium, 99
Ban Siong Elementary, 272
Barcelona (street), 242, 250, 252, 254–258, 303, 304
Barrio San Luis Complex, 122–127, 141
Bartolome House, 344–345
Basilica of the Nazarene, 134
Battle of Manila (1945), 69, 79, 82, 99, 114, 163, 241, 289
Bayanihan, 309, 312
Beaterio de la Compañía, 47, 119, 129, 132, 142
Beaterio de Sta. Catalina, 119, 120
Benavides, 336
Benjamin Orofco House, 257
Bernal House, 364
Bilibid Prison, ix, 82
Binondo, 11, 33, 39, 46, 53, 57, 61, 67, 122, 154, 159–217, 221, 230, 239, 243, 245, 254, 297, 298, 300, 304, 305, 326, 327, 337
Binondo Church, 9, 53, 148, 164, 165–169, 176, 186, 194, 243, 245, 277, 296, 298
Binondo Riverfront, 159
Blue Horizon, 208
Bonifacio, Andrés, 72, 186, 241, 296, 327, 328, 331, 375
Bonifacio Drive, 80, 88, 89
Bonifacio Monument, 327
Bulacan (street), 353, 354, 372
Burgos Drive, 80
Burke Building, 206, 208, 298, 304
Burnham, Daniel, ix, 10, 11, 28, 30, 35, 77
Burnham Plan, 32, 34

C

Caballeros (street), 282–284
Calixto Yu Villa, 369
Calvo Building, 39, 207, 210, 220, 305, 306
Camba (street), 274–281, 292, 303
Canal de la Reina, 161

Candaba House, 316
Capitol Theater, 210–211, 218, 220
Carreon (street), 292
Carriedo (street), 41, 220, 306
Carvajal (street), 164, 194, 196
Casa Bizantina, 260
Casa Blanca, 125, 128
Casa El Hogar, 127
Casa Los Hidalgos, 125, 232
Casa Manila, 122–124, 126
Casa Ruiz, 126, 128
Casa Urdaneta, 125, 128
Casa Vyzantina, 55, 316, 320, 321
Centennial Hall of Justice, 9
Centeno House, 355
Central Bank Complex, 230
Chamber of Commerce Building, 132, 133, 192
Charisland Building, 223, 230–231
Charter of Venice (1964), 227, 231, 310
China Banking Corporation, 183, 194
Chinatown, 173, 194, 231, 305
Chua-Chuan-Huat Glassware, 247
Chua House, 254
Citibank Building, 175
city, 1–3, 5–8, 29, 59–61, 135, 160
City Chain Trading Building, 176
Clavel (street), 242, 248, 262, 263, 269, 273, 274, 282
Claveria, 197–199
Co Ban Kiat Building, 176
Colegio de San José, 119, 120
Colegio de San Juan de Letrán, 116, 119
Colegio de Sta. Isabel, 119, 120, 127
Colegio de Sta. Potenciana, 121
Colegio de Sta. Rosa, 117, 119, 129, 131
Comprehensive Land-Use Plan and Zoning Ordinance (CLUPZO), 303, 306
Concepcion Tan Guiamco Building, 248
Constantino House, 364
Cortes-Ochoa Building, 194
Cruz House, 264
Crystal Arcade, 214
Cuartel de Caballería de Meisic, 173
Cuartél de Santa Lucía, 79
Cuarto Escuela, 85, 86. *See also* Dulaang Raha Sulayman
cultural inventory, 15–19

D

Dasmariñas (street), 163, 174, 183, 190–194, 194, 199, 305
demolition, 13, 46, 47, 48, 49, 51, 55, 86, 149, 150, 151, 172, 192, 218, 250, 265, 274, 298, 315, 316, 318, 321, 322, 379
design: building, 36–37; energy-efficient, 379–389
Destileria La Fortuna, 363
dilapidation, 48
Divisoria, 90, 241, 245, 298, 336
Divisoria Market, 185, 265, 327, 329, 330
Dulaang Raha Sulayman, 85, 86. *See also* Cuarto Escuela

E

earthquake, 1, 3–5, 14, 91, 92, 95, 96, 101, 108, 109, 115, 116, 119, 120, 125, 142, 148, 154, 166, 186, 206, 241, 252, 265, 273, 274, 330
Eduardo Cojuangco Building, 121, 127, 129
El Amanecer Building, 127, 130, 232
Elcano (street), 45, 241, 271–274, 275, 303
El Hogar Building, 57, 179–181
El Porvenir Building, 335
Emilio Jacinto Elementary School, 348
Enriquez House, 264
Enriquez Mansion, 55, 56, 316, 320, 323
Ermita, 11, 14, 32, 46, 49, 55, 68, 73, 74, 90, 113, 125, 134, 154, 219, 220, 344, 371, 375
Escolta, 13, 161, 162, 163, 164, 181, 185, 190, 194, 200–214, 216, 218–221, 298, 305
Estraude (street), 162, 296
Evangelista House, 358
extension, 234–236
extramuros, 67

F

Fabella Memorial Hospital, 57
façadism, 38, 143, 156, 223, 227
Feast of La Naval, 169
FEMII Building, 99
Ferdinand Blumentritt (street), 356
Fernandez Hermanos Building, 183, 184
Fernando Guerrero (street), 336, 337
Fernando House, 357, 361
finance, 39–41

fire, 46, 48, 49, 50, 59, 64, 95, 114, 116, 127, 148, 189, 191, 241, 242, 246, 252, 265, 272, 291, 292, 298, 306
First Monastery, 102, 105
First United, 202, 203. *See also* Perez-Samanillo Building
Fort San Antonio Abad, 230
Fort Santiago, 73, 80, 81–86, 134, 141, 143, 148
foundry, 242, 249, 277

G

Gaches Building, 208. *See also* Natividad Building
Galleon Trade, 71, 86, 159–161, 239
General Luna (street), 134
Go Hoc Building, 195
Gonzales House, 363
Guison Building, 194

H

Hap Hong Building, 174, 175
Hearst Building, 305
heritage resort, 309
Hidalgo (street), 6, 8, 55, 303, 323
Hong Kong and Shanghai Banking Corporation (HSBC), 181, 182
Hospicio de San Jose Building, 175
Hospital de San Juan de Dios, 120, 121
Hotel del Oriente, 170
housing, 2, 14, 36–37, 329, 376–377; high-rise, 7, 36, 157; low-cost, 36–37, 41, 141; social, 40, 306

I

identity, 18, 32, 36, 57, 145, 149, 152–153, 154–156, 223, 227, 231, 314
ideology, 150, 153
Ides O'Racca Building, 293, 297
Iglesia de Jesucristo Templo de Caridad Jerusalem, 371, 372
Iglesia Evangelica Metodisa en las Islas Filipinas (IEMELIF) Church, 370
Ilang-Ilang (street), 242, 248, 284–287, 289
Ilustre Mansion, 40, 51, 52
infrastructure, 8, 33–35, 36–37, 141–145, 219–221, 376
Insular Ice Plant, 34, 143
Insular Life Building, 186–187, 189
insulation, 380, 381–382

Intendencia, 94, 142
Intramuros, 10, 11, 12, 33, 38, 40, 45, 46, 47, 55, 59–145, 148, 153, 154, 156, 162, 164, 186, 219, 228, 229, 232, 241, 242, 244, 252, 304, 305
Intramuros Administration, 69, 73, 79, 86, 87, 95, 110, 121, 127, 129, 142, 229
Intramuros de Manila, 64, 67, 72

J

Jaboneros (street), 242, 246, 248–254, 260, 277, 282, 303
Jai-Alai Building, 41, 49
J. Luna, 305
Jones Bridge, 164, 174, 186, 189, 218
Jose Abad Santos, 340–341, 355
Juan Luna (street), 165, 171, 179–186, 194, 341, 348–352, 373. *See also* Anloague (street)

K

Katipunan (group), 241, 271, 291, 327–328, 347, 372
Kodak Building, 193

L

Laguna de Bay, 10, 60, 61, 165
La Insular Cigar and Cigarette Factory, 170–171
Lam Bee Building, 196
Las Casas Filipinas, 309, 312, 313, 317, 321, 322
La Tondeña Distillery, 297, 299
Latorre House, 367
La Torre (street), 336, 337, 338, 339, 340
Lavezares (street), 254, 257, 263, 273, 289–291
Laws of the Indies, 90
Legazpi, Miguel Lopez de, 62, 81, 94, 99, 105, 289, 327
L'Enfant Plan of 1791, 29
Leyba-Lichauco House, 244
Leyba-Martinez Corporation, 191
Liwasang Bonifacio, 34, 88, 143
Luna House, 172, 296, 297
Luneta Hotel, 41, 144

M

MacArthur Bridge, 218
Madrid (street), 244, 258–265, 269, 273, 303, 320
Maestranza Wall, 47, 74, 86, 156
Magallanes Drive, 132
Magat Salamat Elementary School, 346
Malacañang Palace, 46, 95
Malate, 7, 38, 46, 55, 62, 68, 90, 154, 219, 220, 230, 375
Malate Church, 8, 42, 88
Mañalac House, 254, 255
Manila Bay, 32, 55, 62, 80, 81, 298, 326, 327
Manila Cathedral, 95–99, 135, 148, 304
Manila Hotel, 11, 78, 144, 190
Manila Veterans Hospital, 57
Martinez Accesoria, 257
Masangkay (street), 197, 298, 336, 338, 339, 376
M. de Santos (street), 281, 292–293. *See also* Aceiteros
Media Naranja, 86
MERALCO Building, 49
Metropolitan Museum, 230
Metropolitan Theater, 143, 220
Miguel Lopez de Legaspi and Andrés Urdaneta Monument, 79, 80
Minor Basilica of San Lorenzo Ruiz, 169
Molave (street), 353, 354
Monasterio de Sta. Clara, 119, 130
Montenegro Building, 269–270
Moreno House, 348, 349
Morga (street), 342, 344, 346
Muelle de la Industria, 161, 165, 179, 220, 244, 298
Muelle del Banco Nacional, 161, 165, 204, 218, 219
Museo Pambata, 11
Museum of Natural History, 143
Museum of the Filipino People, 143

N

National Archives, 116, 125, 126, 142, 172, 251, 258, 305
National Cultural Heritage Act of 2009 (RA 10066), 18, 310
nationalism, 12, 19, 99, 153
National Museum, 47, 142, 144, 317

National Museum for Art, 143
National Press Club of the Philippines, 132, 134
Natividad Building, 207, 208, 209
Navarro House, 367
Nepomuceno (street), 347, 376
Nicolas Zamora (street), 341, 342
Nuestra Señora de Guía, 73
Nuestra Señora de los Angeles, 119
Nuestra Señora de Lourdes, 119
Nuestra Señora del Pronto Socorro, 169
Nuestra Señora del Santísimo Rosario, 169

O

Old Supreme Court, 9
Ong-Chan House, 252, 253
Ongpin (Street), 164, 167, 194, 196, 305
O'Racca Confectionary Factory, 297
Ordoveza House, 317, 318
Oscar Ledesma Building, 108, 148

P

Pacific Commercial Company Building, 179, 181, 182, 183, 214, 220
Palacio Arzobispal, 120
Palacio del Gobernador, 95, 99, 121, 142, 232
Palacio de Sta. Potenciana, 120
Pampanga (street), 355
Pandacan, 35, 46, 327, 340, 375
Panenta House, 365
Parsons, William, 11, 32, 190, 341
Pascual House, 263
Paseo de Azcarraga, 90
Pasig River, 11, 45, 46, 61, 66, 81, 86, 88, 89, 159, 160, 164, 165, 194, 218, 221, 239, 242, 244, 287, 304, 326
pastiche, 225
Peñarubia (street), 260, 291–292
Perez-Samanillo Building, 185, 202, 203, 207, 209, 305
Philippine Assembly, 92, 94
Philippine General Hospital, 11
Philippine National Bank, 163, 183, 204, 214, 218
Philippine National Railways (PNR), 335
Philippine Normal University, 11
Pilande House, 367
Pinpin (street), 192, 219, 306
Plaza Cervantes, 186–189, 218, 230

Plaza de Armas, 64, 86
Plaza de Moriones, 82, 85
Plaza de Sto. Tomás, 117
Plaza Lacson, 305
Plaza Mayor, 91, 117. *See also* Plaza Roma
Plaza Moraga, 174
Plaza Moriones, 328, 334
Plaza Roma, 91, 99, 113, 117, 135. *See also* Plaza Mayor
Plaza San Lorenzo Ruiz, 169–172, 173
Plaza Sta. Cruz, 191, 200, 219, 305
Poblete, 197–199
Postigo del Palacio, 77, 87
Post Office Building, 143, 218
preservation, 13, 19, 29, 32–33, 49, 52, 218, 223, 236, 310, 318–322, 379
privatization, 314
Prudential Bank Building, 305, 306
Puente de Binondo, 171, 172
Puente de Meisic, 173, 174
Puente de San Fernando, 162
Puente General Blanco, 171
Puerta de Almacenes, 86
Puerta de Isabel II, 77, 87
Puerta de la Aduana, 77
Puerta de los Almacenes, 77
Puerta del Parian, 77, 87
Puerta del Postigo, 88, 113
Puerta de Santa Lucía, 76, 77, 79, 87, 88, 89
Puerta de Sto. Domingo, 77
Puerta Isabel II, 76, 134
Puerta Real, 76, 77, 87, 143

Q

Quezon House, 316, 318, 319
Quezon Institute, 57
Quiapo, 3, 6, 8, 10, 13, 38, 40, 42, 46, 49, 50, 51, 52, 53, 55, 71, 129, 133, 134, 154, 165, 220, 229, 254, 303, 306, 317, 318, 351, 375, 379
Quiapo Church, 8, 53, 220
Quinta Market, 220
Quintin Paredes (street), 162, 174–178, 189, 193, 194, 218, 230, 305, 306. *See also* Rosario (street)
Quirino Grandstand, 81

R

Railroad Signal Tower, 339, 340, 355
Rajah Soliman, 62, 73, 81, 326, 327, 342
Rajah Soliman (street), 342, 346
Real Alcaicería de San Fernando, 114, 239–240, 243, 266, 295
Real (street), 99, 105, 107, 126
reconciliation, 147–148
reconstruction, 47, 48, 53, 79–80, 121–131, 147–157, 172, 228, 231–234, 305
Recto Avenue, ix, 90, 173, 185, 241, 242, 265, 271, 305, 327, 331–335. *See also* Azcarraga
Reducto de San Francisco Javier, 82
Regina Building, 204, 205, 207, 209, 214, 218
Reina Regente, 172–173
relocation, 55, 309–322
remodeling, 52–53
renovation, 32, 33, 40, 47, 48, 52–53
restoration, 29, 33, 39–41, 47, 48, 54, 316
Rex Theater, 196
Rizal Elementary School, 346, 347
Rizal, José, 19, 82, 86, 327
Rizal Monument, 55, 372
Rizal Park, 55, 78, 81, 189
Rizal Shrine, 84, 85, 86
Rosales House, 363
Rosario House, 260, 261
Rosario (street), 162, 163, 174, 190, 305. *See* Quintin Paredes (street)
Roxas Boulevard, 10, 114, 120, 214, 219, 230

S

Sampaloc, 4, 6, 46, 49, 51, 55, 72, 197, 313, 375
San Agustin, 69, 122, 134, 144, 148
San Agustin Church, 4, 9, 99–108, 134, 141
San Fernando (street), 171, 172, 173, 239, 240, 241, 242, 243, 244, 245, 246, 266, 303, 304
San Francisco Church, 117–118, 119, 148
San Ignacio Church, 108–112, 119, 120, 142, 156
San Miguel, 13, 20, 46, 48, 57, 90, 175, 206, 254
San Nicolas, 12, 13, 33, 40, 45, 46, 50, 114, 122, 160, 164, 179, 199, 221, 228, 229, 239–307, 327, 329
San Nicolas de Tolentino, 119, 148
San Nicolás Fire Station, 244
Santo Cristo de Longos, 169
Santo Domingo Church, 142

Santos-Andres House, 313
San Vicente (street), 192, 199–200
Second Monastery, 105, 107, 148
Severino Reyes (street), 356
Sevilla (street), 303
shading, 384
Shipping Center Building, 99, 100
Shrine of Sto. Cristo de Longos, 295
Solis (street), 353, 354, 355, 373, 376
South Harbor, 35, 89, 242, 298
Sovereign Grand Lodge of the Philippine Archipelago, 372
S. Padilla (street), 195, 305, 306
Sta. Ana, 11, 45, 46, 49, 55, 61, 107, 225, 375
Sta. Ana Church, 54
Sta. Cruz, 6, 7, 12, 13, 46, 49, 50, 53, 55, 57, 67, 82, 134, 164, 165, 218, 229, 298, 317, 356, 373, 375, 376
Sta. Cruz Church, 186, 204
Sta. Maria (street), 342, 344, 346
Sta. Mesa, 46
Sto. Cristo (street), 245–248, 304
Sto. Domingo Church, 65, 68, 117–118, 119, 129, 147, 148, 169
Sto. Niño Church, 373
St. Paul United Methodist Church, 342–343
Streamline Corporation Building, 192
Su Kuang Institute, 197
Súnico foundry, 242, 250–252
Súnico House, 256, 275–277
Sunny Commercial Building, 196, 198
Sy House, 277
Sylianteng Building, 202, 203. *See also* Perez-Samanillo Building

T

Taft Avenue, 10, 34, 38, 55
Tanganan House, 366
Tayuman (street), 346
technology, 4
Tiong Building, 197
Tionloc House, 365
Toledo House, 367
Tomás Mapua (street), 356, 357
Tomas Pinpin Monument, 170
Tomas Pinpin (street), 196–197
Tondo, 6, 46, 59, 61, 81, 161, 241, 298, 325–378
Tondo Church, 330–331, 375–376
Tondo Evangelical Church, 370, 371
Tondo Intermediate School, 341

tourism, 13, 15, 38, 141–145, 156, 223, 300, 376
Traders Building, 185
training, 38–39
translocation, 47, 48, 55, 56, 172, 261, 309–322
Tribunal de los Naturales, 265, 266
Troncales House, 254, 255
tropical environment, 379, 387
Tropical Modernism, 384
Tutuban, 161, 327, 328, 336
Tutuban Railway Station, 250, 332–333
Tutuban Shopping Center, 337
Ty House, 262

U

United States Armed Forces of the Far East (USAFFE), 82
Universidad de Sto. Tomás, 99, 117–118, 119. *See also* University of Sto. Tomás
University of Sto. Tomás, 4, 17, 67, 72, 184, 206, 336. *See also* Universidad de Sto. Tomás
urban center, 17, 40, 59–61
urbanism, 59–60, 70, 135–136, 136, 150–151, 154
urban layout, 55, 150, 386–387
Urbiztondo (street), 162, 179, 293, 296–298
Urdaneta (street), 90, 125
Uy Chaco Building, 186–189, 223, 230–231
Uy Lian Yek Commercial, 246
Uy Su Bin Building, 176, 177

V

Velasquez (street), 281, 292, 347–348, 376
Venerable Orden Tercera, 117–118, 119
ventilation, 5, 33, 36, 358, 380–387
Vienna Memorandum, 223, 227, 236
Vigan, 4, 20, 39, 224, 225, 315, 317
Vigan Conservation Complex, 39

W

Westminster High School, 370, 371
Wilson Building, 184
wind direction, 385, 386
World War II, ix, 5, 38, 45, 46, 53, 67–70, 91, 108, 142, 143, 148, 149, 150, 154, 155, 157, 171, 208, 254, 293, 329, 348, 355, 384

Y

Ynchausti Building, 195. *See* Go Hoc Building
Ynchausti-Elizalde Building, 245
Yuchengco (street), 192, 194–195, 196, 219
Yu-Tan Building, 195
Yutivo Building, 192, 193
Yutivo Warehouse, 199

Z

Zuellig Building, 193, 194